College Geometry Using GeoGebra®

College Geometry Using GeoGebra®

Barbara E. Reynolds, SDS
Cardinal Stritch University

William E. Fenton
Bellarmine University

WILEY

SENIOR VP	SmitaBakshi
SENIOR DIRECTOR	Don Fowley
SENIOR EDITOR	Jennifer Brady
SENIOR MANAGING EDITOR	Judy Howarth
DIRECTOR OF CONTENT OPERATIONS	Martin Tribe
SENIOR MANAGER OF CONTENT OPERATIONS	Mary Corder
PRODUCTION EDITOR	Loganathan Kandan
COVER PHOTO CREDIT	© WhiteHaven / Shutterstock

This book was set in 10.5/13 pt Minion Pro by SPi Global.

Founded in 1807, John Wiley & Sons, Inc. has been a valued source of knowledge and understanding for more than 200 years, helping people around the world meet their needs and fulfill their aspirations. Our company is built on a foundation of principles that include responsibility to the communities we serve and where we live and work. In 2008, we launched a Corporate Citizenship Initiative, a global effort to address the environmental, social, economic, and ethical challenges we face in our business. Among the issues we are addressing are carbon impact, paper specifications and procurement, ethical conduct within our business and among our vendors, and community and charitable support. For more information, please visit our website: www.wiley.com/go/citizenship.

ISBN: 978-1-119-71811-6 (PBK)
ISBN: 978-1-119-71812-3 (EVALC)

Library of Congress Cataloging-in-Publication Data

Names: Reynolds, Barbara E., author. | Fenton, William E., author.
Title: College geometry using geogebra / Barbara E. Reynolds, SDS, Cardinal
  Stritch University, William E. Fenton, Bellarmine University.
Description: First edition. | Hoboken, NJ : Wiley, [2021] | Includes
  bibliographical references and index.
Identifiers: LCCN 2020038281 (print) | LCCN 2020038282 (ebook) | ISBN
  9781119718116 (paperback) | ISBN 9781119718147 (adobe pdf) | ISBN
  9781119718086 (epub)
Subjects: LCSH: Geometry—Study and teaching (Higher) | Mathematics.
Classification: LCC QA462.2.C65 R48 2021 (print) | LCC QA462.2.C65
  (ebook) | DDC 516—dc23
LC record available at https://lccn.loc.gov/2020038281
LC ebook record available at https://lccn.loc.gov/2020038282

The inside back cover will contain printing identification and country of origin if omitted from this page. In addition, if the ISBN on the back cover differs from the ISBN on this page, the one on the back cover is correct.

BRIEF CONTENTS

CONTENTS

Several years ago, we co-authored the book *College Geometry Using The Geometer's Sketchpad®*. In the time since then, friends and colleagues have expressed substantial interest in using our course materials with an alternative software package, GeoGebra®. Indeed, some reported to us that they have used the Sketchpad book with GeoGebra and have experienced good success. Spurred on by those reports, we began experimenting ourselves with this other option for geometry software.

This new book is the result of our course experiences with GeoGebra. Of course, there are differences in commands and tools between the two software packages. Those differences imposed frequent rewording and revising of the computer investigations. Further, the algebraic presentation used by GeoGebra required us to rethink many of the investigations to encourage students to grapple with the geometric content. The activities have been rewritten to match GeoGebra, as have the portions of the text that discuss the specific software. However, the geometric content remains the same as our earlier text.

We hope this new version of *College Geometry* will support students and instructors who desire a pedagogy that incorporates technology in an active, exploratory classroom.

ESPECIALLY FOR STUDENTS

We invite you on a journey—a journey with your mind! The course for which this textbook is designed will lead you to explore geometric worlds, visually at first, and then using both inductive and deductive reasoning processes. We invite you to explore geometry through computer-based investigations, to make observations and conjectures about what you see, and then to develop proofs or disproofs to support or refute your conjectures.

Playing can be a gateway to new ideas. In this course, we ask you to play with geometric figures, to explore their properties, and to observe relationships and interactions among those figures. As you play, you will be asked to make conjectures about what you see happening. Although you may have heard it said that "seeing is believing," mathematicians tend to be a bit skeptical in this regard. Once mathematicians think they see something, they often ask, "Is this really true, or does it just appear to be so?"

GeoGebra is a tool that supports this kind of investigative learning. Throughout this course, you will be asked to use GeoGebra to construct various geometric figures—and to play with them, observing what is happening. One of the nice features of GeoGebra is that you can *construct* figures that have certain properties. Constructed figures retain their properties as they are manipulated. If you merely draw figures, geometric properties will not hold.

Your instructor might ask you to work in a cooperative learning group throughout this course. If so, it will be important for you to develop a good working relationship with the members of your group. For a cooperative learning group to be effective for every member, each member of the group must be regularly engaged in the group work. Each must be committed to keeping up with her or his own individual study of the course materials. Your group will need to meet regularly to share ideas about the problems you are working on, and each of you must keep up with your own study.

We have worked closely with our students as we developed this book. When we asked these students what suggestions they would give to others who use this textbook, they asked us to share the following strategies, which they feel contributed to their success as students:

- The activities that open each chapter are an introduction to the concepts that are covered in the chapter. Take time to do these activities, and to reflect with each other on your observations. Try to decide what the crucial idea is in each activity. You might not get the answers right at first, but keep trying to understand the ideas. When you work on the activities, ask yourselves, "Why are they asking us that question here?" The purpose of the activities is to prepare you to understand the concepts when you read the discussion in the text, and this does work! If your group has done a good job on the activities, the discussion in the text will be much easier to read.

- Play with the figures and make observations. Construct robust figures. Move the objects around, and observe what is happening. Take notes while you are working. Type your notes directly into your GeoGebra worksheets. That way, you can articulate your ideas while you are working together. At the end of your working sessions, you can save a copy of your GeoGebra worksheets so that each member of your group has notes from your working session.

- Talk with your colleagues. Trying to tell someone else what you observe helps to solidify the ideas in your own mind. Formulate conjectures about what you see happening. Test your conjectures. Try to find the extremes at which they hold. Talk with each other about why you think your conjectures hold.

- Listen to each other. Sometimes the person who seems to be working a bit slowly is seeing something that others have overlooked. Answering one another's questions promotes learning for everyone.

- Prepare ahead of time for each working session with your group. Read over the activities before coming to the computer lab. Think about what you will have to do to solve a particular problem, and perhaps even read ahead into the chapter to see what topics are discussed there. Your work with your small group will be much more rewarding if everyone comes prepared.

- Save your work on the explorations you do while working on the activities and exercises. Frequently, later work refers back to earlier work. Develop a system of naming your files so that you can easily retrieve your work to review the way that you solved earlier problems and articulated concepts that challenged you to think.

- Don't rush through the activities just to get them done. The objective of the activities that open each chapter is to help you learn geometry. If you get stuck on one activity, go ahead to the next one—and return later to the one that stumped you at first. Sometimes working ahead will give you some additional ideas to use on a previous activity.

The authors of this book hope you enjoy your study of geometry. Remember that learning mathematics is not a spectator sport. We hope that the GeoGebra activities help you to participate actively in learning geometry. Keep in mind that for your learning to be effective, your participation in these activities needs to be reflective. Pay attention to what you see, ask lots of questions, and think about the meaning of the answers your find. Bring a playful spirit to your geometric investigations, and have some fun!

NOTES FOR INSTRUCTORS

Our Motivation, Philosophy, and Pedagogy

College geometry serves many purposes. Some students taking the course will be introduced to mathematical proofs for the first time, while others may have taken a prior course that required writing proofs. Many will be preparing to teach geometry at the high school or middle school level. The level of mathematics background of the students will differ from institution to institution. Due to the varied audience for this course, we chose to write a book that makes use of the power of GeoGebra to help students visualize difficult geometric concepts. We introduce the need for developing mathematical proofs in the context of hands-on explorations that help students develop insight into these ideas before they attempt to write rigorous mathematical proofs. A course based on this text can be taught with high school geometry and college algebra as the minimal prerequisites. If calculus and linear algebra are additional prerequisites (as is the case in some institutions), students will be able to cover more of the text and explore ideas in greater depth.

Many of our students are in teacher preparation programs. This text includes content recommended by the National Council of Teachers of Mathematics

(NCTM) and the Common Core State Standards Initiative. To address the needs of future teachers, we have included several exercises in each chapter that invite the students to explore these professional standards, and to reflect on how they will integrate what they are learning in this course in their own future classrooms.

When we started this project, we surveyed many existing college geometry texts before deciding on the content of our text. Unlike the standard calculus curriculum, an undergraduate course in geometry does not have a standard table of contents. We found much variation and a few common threads. We talked with colleagues who teach this course at a variety of institutions, and we found that everyone has a personal list of favorite topics. To be honest, each of us had our own list, and, although they intersected, our lists were not identical. We realized very early that we would have to decide which topics to include. Eventually, we noticed that we were using four simple questions to determine whether to include a topic:

1. Does this topic lend itself to exploration and conjecture with geometry software?

2. Does this topic allow us to examine some interesting questions in geometry—and connect the study of geometry to the larger tapestry of mathematics?

3. Does this topic allow explorations that lead students to make and test their own conjectures?

4. Is this topic useful content for future middle school and high school mathematics teachers while leading to important ideas that reach considerably beyond the content of a high school geometry course?

Those topics for which we answered "yes" to all four of these questions were included.

We wanted to develop a coherent text in which topics from each chapter would relate to each other, and larger ideas and themes would emerge that would run through the course. We offer several distinct approaches to the study of geometry: a *synthetic approach* (Chapters 2–4, 6, 7, 11, 12), an *analytic approach* (Chapters 5, 6, 9, Appendix A, and Chapter 12), and a *transformational approach* (Chapters 8–10, and Chapter 12). While we do not follow a strictly *axiomatic* treatment, in this new edition we address the importance of axiom systems throughout the course. *Euclid's Postulates* are introduced in Chapter 2, and discussed in increasing depth over the next several chapters. Chapter 6 (Taxicab Geometry) introduces the axioms for metric geometry, and Chapter 7 (Finite Geometries) presents sets of axioms for affine and projective geometries. In Chapter 11 (Hyperbolic Geometry), we explore in depth the implications of choosing the hyperbolic parallel axiom instead of Euclid's Parallel Postulate. Chapter 12 is a culminating chapter in which we examine the real projective plane axiomatically, analytically, and through projective transformations, thus bringing together these different approaches to the study of geometry.

An important goal of this course is to teach students to write good mathematical proofs. At the core of our pedagogical approach is a belief that students tend to write in a way that reflects their understanding of the underlying concepts and ideas. That is, if the students understand the mathematical concepts, they tend to write correct proofs; and when a student does not quite understand an important concept, the weaknesses or errors in the proof reflect this. Thus, we approach the development of proofs from two directions. First, in the activities that open each chapter, we ask students to spend a lot of time working with GeoGebra diagrams, observing, making conjectures, and talking to each other about their ideas. We give students lots of room to form their own ideas about particular geometric situations, all the while listening to their conversations. Then in the ensuing discussion—both in class and in the text—we talk about their conjectures, affirming what they have seen where it is correct and helping them to reshape their ideas where their reasoning is weak. The discussion in the text illustrates specific proof strategies, giving examples and explaining accepted patterns of logical reasoning for developing proofs.

Throughout this text, we use the dynamic power of GeoGebra to engage students in explorations leading to conjecture. To construct a diagram in a GeoGebra worksheet, the students have to think about certain geometric ideas. Our experience has been that if students understand what is going on in a particular geometric situation—if they see the relationships made visible in their GeoGebra diagram and if they engage in discussions about what they see in the diagram—they will find words to express what they see. Through both small-group and whole-class discussion, we guide students toward accepted mathematical language for expressing these ideas. In the discussion following their explorations with GeoGebra, we engage students in conversation, listen to what they are saying, and shape their language toward generally accepted (mathematically correct) expressions of these ideas.

Keeping in mind future teachers and their needs, we have included questions at the end of each chapter that are particularly designed to be answered by mathematics education majors. These questions are based on the recommendations presented in the NCTM *Principles and Standards for School Mathematics*, the recommendations in the Common Core State Standards Initiative, and the Mathematics Tests in the Praxis Series Subject Assessments that many states use as part of the requirements for teacher licensing. Through class discussion, we emphasize connections between the concepts and highlight issues that are important for future teachers.

As we developed these materials, we envisioned a course taught in a cooperative learning environment. In our own classes, we form groups with two to four students and have these groups work together in a computer lab on the activities that open each chapter. Our pedagogical approach is to guide students toward foundational insight and conceptual understanding through their group work on the activities. In our experience, groups who have diverse backgrounds often have fruitful discussions as they work on the activities. Each person sees things in a different way and brings a different viewpoint to the small-group discussion. We see our role as facilitators, guiding students to formalize their mathematical ideas as they develop correct proofs of conjectures that arise from their work on the activities. While we have found that teaching geometry in this manner is quite effective, each instructor adapts these materials to her/his preferred teaching style.

Prerequisites and Chapter Dependencies

High school geometry and college algebra are the minimal prerequisites for a course taught using this text. In Chapter 1, we introduce the basic tools available in GeoGebra while asking students to experiment with a variety of geometric constructions. We raise a lot of questions, and encourage students to ask their own questions. We review some basic geometry vocabulary, and guide students into explorations where some things are familiar, so that students learn the basics of GeoGebra while reviewing some elementary geometry.

Chapters 2–4 draw on experiences from high school geometry. Some of our students (particularly returning adult students who took high school geometry many years earlier) find that their recollection of high school geometry is rather dim, but by the end of Chapter 4 they have recalled the elements of geometry that they need to draw on throughout the course. Yet there are several theorems in these early chapters that go substantially beyond the high school curriculum and thus encourage everyone to engage in substantive discussions. The elementary geometry presented in the first four chapters goes well beyond a mere review of high school geometry, and it is worth the time taken to review this material. In these chapters, we also introduce Euclid's Postulates, the formulation of conjectures, elements of logical reasoning, and strategies for beginning to develop proofs of their conjectures.

Chapter 5 (Analytic Geometry) and Appendix A (Trigonometry) assume familiarity with college algebra and at least minimal exposure to basic right-triangle trigonometry. Once Chapters 1–5 and Appendix A (if needed) have been covered, students are prepared for Chapter 6 (Taxicab Geometry), Chapter 7 (Finite Geometries), or Chapter 8 (Transformational Geometry). After completing Chapter 8, students are ready to study Symmetry (Chapter 10). Preservice elementary and middle school teachers find Taxicab Geometry and Transformational Geometry appealing, and they enjoy Symmetry as well. The concepts from Chapter 8 (Transformational Geometry) are given an analytic treatment in Chapter 9 (Isometries and Matrices). Chapter 9 requires some familiarity with linear algebra, and can be skipped if students do not have this background.

Chapters 6 (Taxicab Geometry) and 7 (Finite Geometries) provide an introduction to non-Euclidean geometry, and either of these is a good segue into Chapter 11 (Hyperbolic Geometry). Once the students have seen the impact of changing the way that we measure the distance between points as they investigate familiar conic sections in the taxicab plane, or have experimented with axiom systems for a seven-point geometry, they are more comfortable exploring what happens when we exchange the Euclidean Parallel Postulate for the hyperbolic parallel postulate. Some of our students have suggested that an instructor might not wait until the end of the course to cover Chapter 11 (Hyperbolic Geometry). At times each of us has covered Chapter 11 immediately after Chapter 6 or Chapter 7, and then gone back to complete the course with one or two of the earlier chapters (for example, Chapters 8 and/or 10). Explorations in the hyperbolic plane challenge everything the students know about the shape of the world, and it can be difficult to digest these ideas at the end of the course.

Chapter 12 (Projective Geometry) draws together themes that run through nearly every chapter and serves as a capstone to the course.

It is important to note that we do not expect students to have any experience with GeoGebra at the start of the course. Basic GeoGebra skills are presented in Chapter 1, then new skills are introduced gradually as the course progresses. Once Chapters 1–5 are completed, students will be confident users of GeoGebra—though a few additional tools will appear in Chapters 8 and 11.

There is more material in this book that can covered in a typical one-semester course. Each instructor will, of course, have favorite topics. After the first five chapters there is a great deal of flexibility in how the chapters can be selected. Here are two possible paths through the book:

For a second proof course, with prerequisites Calculus and Linear Algebra	*For a first proof course, with prerequisites* College Algebra and some basic Trigonometry
Chapter 1	Chapter 1
Chapter 2	Chapter 2
Chapter 3	Chapter 3
Chapter 4	Chapter 4
Chapter 5	Appendix A
Chapter 6 or 7	Chapter 5
Chapter 8	Chapter 6 or 7
Chapter 9 and/or 10	Chapter 11
Chapter 11	Chapter 8
Chapter 12 (time permitting)	Chapter 10 (time permitting)

Instructor resources are available at the companion website, **www.wiley.com/go/reynolds/collegegeo1e**. These include an overview of the book, sample solutions to all activities and exercises, and lesson plans for each chapter. (These resources were originally developed as Sketchpad files; we are in the process of making these materials available in GeoGebra format.) An instructor can also find suggestions for teaching in collaborative learning groups and tips for teaching with technology.

Acknowledgments

Writing a book is not something that one does alone. Looking back over the many years that this book has been a part of our professional lives, we are grateful for the many people who have accompanied us on this journey. It took us five years to produce the Preliminary Edition. Instructors who have used this book have been generous with both questions and feedback as they've used this book in their classes, as have the reviewers of our many drafts. Some individuals who have been especially generous with their time and expertise include:

Thomas Banchoff—Emeritus, Brown University, Rhode Island

Anne Brown—Emeritus, Indiana University-South Bend, Indiana

Jim Cottrill—Ohio Dominican University, Ohio

Joseph Fiedler—Emeritus, California State University-Bakersfield, California

Patricia Giurgescu—Pace University, New York

Catherine Gorini—Maharishi University of Management, Iowa

Susan Pustejovsky—Alverno College, Wisconsin

Judy Silver—Emeritus, Marshall University, West Virginia

Sr. Pat Sullivan—Emeritus, Mount Saint Mary College, New York

We gratefully acknowledge the contributions of students who worked with us on the editions of this book. Students in our geometry classes at both Cardinal Stritch University (in Milwaukee, Wisconsin) and Bellarmine University (in Louisville, Kentucky) gave us feedback on early drafts of the Preliminary Edition, and continued offering feedback as they took our geometry courses. Their feedback challenged us to refine and clarify what we have written, and we have drawn on that feedback as we have worked on this new edition. A number of student assistants have worked with us over the years, testing the activities and critiquing their effectiveness in introducing the concepts that are discussed in each chapter. Ken Bellinger, Lindsey Blue, Lindsay Bronson, Howard Fahje, Bryna Goeckner, Katherine Kubicek, Stephanie Nass and Vanessa Sowinski worked closely with Sister Barbara Reynolds at Cardinal Stritch University, while Ryan Church and Jon Lamkin worked with Bill Fenton at Bellarmine University. Most of these students have gone on to successful mathematics teaching careers.

In the summers of 2005 and 2006, we were fortunate to present PREP workshops on Geometry, under the sponsorship of the Mathematical Association of America. The faculty who attended our workshops worked computer activities from many chapters. By observing their work and listening to their frank feedback, we learned many things that have influenced this project. Our sincere thanks to all of them!

As we worked on revisions, Jorgen Berglund, one of our adopters who has used the Preliminary Edition several times with his geometry students at California State University, Chico, stepped forward and offered to work with us. Jorgen offered extensive comments on every chapter of the book, and critiqued early drafts of our revisions as we developed the First Edition. He brought the insights of a mathematician with a deep love of geometry, and of a faculty member who had used the book as a text with his own students. Jorgen Berglund's invaluable feedback has helped us to deepen the development of concepts in several chapters of this text.

During our development of the GeoGebra version of this book, three students from Cardinal Stritch University—Angela Fallon, Sam Pointon, and

Paige Ruka—worked closely with Sister Barbara. They did every activity in the draft manuscript using GeoGebra and gave us valuable feedback from the student perspective.

We also would like to thank Jen Brady of Wiley for her support and encouragement as we developed the first edition and this new edition. Among her many tasks, she arranged for feedback from reviewers, which helped us to improve the manuscript. We wish to thank them as well.

Julie Christensen—Kent State University, Ohio

David Gove—California State University-Bakersfield, California

Susan Hagen—Virginia Polytechnic Institute and State University, Virginia

Kevin Hartshorn—Moravian College, Pennsylvania

Tami Martin—Illinois State University, Illinois

John Neuzil—Emeritus, Kent State University, Ohio

Judith Silver—Emeritus, Marshall University, West Virginia

Colin Starr—Willamette University, Oregon

Draga Vidakovic—Georgia State University, Georgia

This project was supported in part by grants from the National Science Foundation (NSF DUE #01-25130 and NSF DUE #03-38301). We would like to thank those who served on our NSF Advisory Board: Thomas Banchoff (Emeritus, Brown University, Rhode Island), Anne Brown (Emeritus, Indiana University South Bend, Indiana), Robert Megginson (University of Michigan), and Draga Vidakovic (Georgia State University). In addition, Jack Bookman (Emeritus, Duke University, North Carolina) and Susan Pustejovsky (Alverno College, Wisconsin), our NSF Evaluation Team, gathered feedback from our class testers and their students, which was very helpful in improving the manuscript.

Finally, Bill would like to thank his family, Ann Jirkovsky and Billy Fenton, and Sister Barbara would like to thank the Sisters of the Divine Savior (Salvatorians) and the Clavius Group for their ongoing personal support over the many years we have spent writing and rewriting this book.

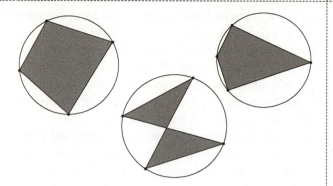

CHAPTER ONE

Using GeoGebra

Mathematics is too often viewed as a static list of facts and procedures. This is unfortunate since this perspective leaves no room for the excitement and satisfaction that can come from exploring mathematical ideas and discovering mathematical relationships. We hope to include this part of "doing mathematics" in your study of geometry. To this end, we hope to enhance your ability to visualize and reason about geometric ideas. GeoGebra®, a powerful geometry software package, will make it easier to see, literally, what happens to various geometric objects—points, lines, segments, circles, and so on—and the relationships among them as they are moved with respect to one another. As you work on the activities in this chapter, think about what it means to create a dynamic construction and how that differs from a static drawing. By the end of this chapter, we expect you will be familiar with some of the basic constructions available in GeoGebra.

As you begin your study of college geometry, you will be invited to look at many examples and explore many ideas using GeoGebra as a tool for your explorations. You will be asked to make a lot of observations and to formulate conjectures based on your observations. In general, a conjecture is a statement expressed in the form

If . . . [hypothesis] . . . **then** . . . [conclusion] . . . .

The *hypothesis* includes the assumptions you are making and the facts or conditions given in the problem. The *conclusion* is what you claim will always happen if the conditions named in your hypothesis hold. As you grow in mathematical maturity, you may be able to express your conjectures without using *If . . .*, *then . . .*, but for now we encourage you to use this format. Because the conclusion must follow from the hypothesis, writing your conjectures in this format makes your hypothesis explicit and clear—and this will help you develop clear and robust proofs. Once you have developed a proof for a conjecture—and tested it by having your colleagues critique it with you—you can call it a theorem.

We hope that engaging in the set of activities that open each chapter will pique your curiosity about some important ideas in geometry. You will get the most out of this course if you put serious effort into these explorations and think about the ideas that are introduced through these activities. Following the activities, we present a discussion about these important ideas. In the discussion, we answer many of the questions raised in the activities, so reading ahead in the text is always a good practice—but we hope that you will really engage in the explorations and activities before reading very far ahead.

The geometric constructions introduced in the activities of this chapter will be used throughout the course. So you should pay attention to the GeoGebra tools as you work on the activities. However, the focus at this point is on exploring certain geometric configurations and then making conjectures about what you observe. You will not be asked to prove anything in this chapter—but you should be asking yourself if you can explain what is going on. Ask yourself questions such as "What is happening here?" . . . "Why is it happening?" . . . "What properties of the figures might lead to the apparent results?" . . . .

Some of the interesting geometric ideas presented in this opening chapter will be investigated in greater depth in later chapters. While in some mathematics textbooks it is essential to thoroughly master every idea in the opening chapters before going on to later chapters, that is not the case for this book! Rather, in this opening chapter we hope to instill in you a bit of geometric curiosity and not to bog you down at the beginning of the course with a myriad of details. Enjoy the questions, and trust that in later chapters we will guide you gently toward the answers.

1.1 ACTIVITIES

GETTING STARTED WITH GEOGEBRA

GeoGebra is an interactive tool for geometry that you can use to create very elaborate figures. Fortunately, even a beginner can do many interesting things right away. As the course progresses, you will become more and more sophisticated with GeoGebra. As with any good software tool, there are multiple ways of doing most tasks. Share the shortcuts you discover with each other. In a short time, you may even find that you can teach some useful tricks to your instructor!

In this opening chapter, you are invited to experiment with some of the capabilities of GeoGebra. Several versions of GeoGebra are available: Classic 5, GeoGebra Geometry online, and now Classic 6. There is even a GeoGebra app for cell phones! The activities presented in this text were developed using GeoGebra Classic 5, but any of these versions can be used. Be aware that the software tools for different versions may be in different locations on the screen from what is described here.

Let's get started. First, launch GeoGebra in a computer. At the top of the screen are the tools that GeoGebra has available. Look through the various options for these tools. If you click on a tool, you will see a menu of options available on that tool. In the first few chapters, we use only some of these tools, saving the more specialized ones for later.

Initially, you will see that the GeoGebra window is divided into two panes, one for Algebra and another for Graphics. Everything done in the Graphics pane will have a corresponding entry in the Algebra pane. This will be particularly useful for Chapter 5 on Analytic Geometry. For the moment, however, the Algebra pane will be used only occasionally. On the Graphics pane, there is a small triangle next to the word Graphics. Click on this to open the **Style Bar**. One of the buttons on the Style Bar will toggle the axes. For the first few chapters, you should use this button to hide the axes, for we will not need them.

At the top of the window are the buttons for various tools, some of which you will use frequently. As you let the mouse move over these tools, you will see that each tool has a name, which is also the first of several options available on that tool. As you click on each tool, you will see a menu of different options available on that tool. It is worth discussing each of these tools individually. Some of the icons can be used to perform several different geometric constructions. Read through this discussion of the icons you see on the GeoGebra worksheet as you experiment with them.

We will start with the **Move**, **Point**, **Line** and **Angle** tools:

Use the **Move** tool (the one with the Arrow) to select and move objects in the sketch. Click on any object—a point, a line, a segment, a circle, an arc—to select it; the object will be highlighted. Click on the object again to deselect it, or click on an open region (i.e., "white space") anywhere on the sketch to deselect all objects. To select more than one object on a PC, hold down the CTRL key and click on additional objects. (The keystroke commands will be different on a Mac computer.) You can drag selected objects across the sketch, or you can delete them. Also, the color and thickness of a selected object can be changed by using commands on the Style Bar. (Note: If you examine the menu attached to the Move tool, you will see some other options. For now, we will use only the basic Move arrow.)

The **Point** tool is next to the Move tool. Click on the Point tool to see a menu of options, including Intersect and Midpoint. Use the Point tool to construct points in the sketch. When you construct a point on another object such as a line, the new point will be restricted to stay on this object. This is useful for putting points on lines or circles. (The option for Point on Object works the same way.) If a point is constructed in an open region, then it is free to move over the entire plane.

The **Line** tool and its various options are used for constructing straight objects—segments, rays, or lines. If you hold down this button, you will see the seven options available. For this chapter, we focus on the Line and Segment options.

The **Angle** tool will allow you to construct angles and has options for measuring the size of an angle as well as the length of a segment and the area of a region. To measure an angle, choose the Angle tool. Then do one of the following things: either select the two rays (or segments) that define the angle or select three points that define the angle. You must be careful of the order in which you make these selections. GeoGebra will measure angles *counterclockwise* (the mathematically positive direction) from the first ray to the second ray. This will be relevant in Activity 1 and later.

Another useful tool is the **Text** tool. You will find this tool among the options on the **Slider** tool. You will be able to insert comments and answers to questions directly into your GeoGebra diagram by using the Text tool. (The Style Bar will allow you to change the size and color of your text if you wish.)

As you do the following activities, pay attention to anything that you observe as you construct each diagram. Use the Text tool to write your observations directly into the GeoGebra window. Try to think of explanations for the things you observe, and express your explanations in complete sentences.

Get into the habit of saving your work for each activity, as later work sometimes builds on earlier work. You will find it helpful to read ahead into the chapter as you work on these activities. Use a different GeoGebra window for each of the following activities.

1. Use the **Line|Segment** tool to construct a quadrilateral. Check to see if your sketch is robust by moving one of the vertices and seeing if the figure remains a quadrilateral.

   a. Use the **Midpoint or Center** option from the Point tool to construct the midpoints of the sides of the quadrilateral. Connect these midpoints in order. What kind of figure is formed? Complete the following sentence: "If the midpoints of an arbitrary quadrilateral are connected in order, the resulting midpoint quadrilateral will be . . . ." Drag the vertices of the original quadrilateral to help you decide whether your conjecture is always correct.

   b. Use the Angle tool to measure the angles of this midpoint quadrilateral. What do you observe about these angles?

   c. To measure the area of a polygon, it is necessary to construct its interior. The **Polygon** tool will do this. Choose the Polygon tool, then select the vertices—in the proper order—for the desired polygon, repeating the first vertex to finish the construction. Measure the areas of the original quadrilateral and its midpoint quadrilateral. Notice that the area of the polygon is reported in the Algebra pane. You can also use the **Angle|Area** tool to measure the area.

What do you observe about these areas? Express your observation as a conjecture by completing the following sentence: "If the midpoints of an arbitrary quadrilateral are connected in clockwise order, the area of the resulting midpoint quadrilateral will be ...." Drag the vertices of the original quadrilateral. Does your conjecture continue to hold?

Use the Text tool to type your observations and conjectures into the worksheet. Select the Text tool and click anywhere in the diagram. This opens a text box. Your text can include mathematical symbols, chosen from a collection of menus. You can also include the value of a measurement by selecting the object from the list of objects in the text box. Once the text is complete, the Style Bar can be used to change its size, color, etc. A text box can be moved around the screen like any object.

GeoGebra automatically labels objects in a sketch. Labels move to stay with their objects. If you right-click on an object (on a PC) or double-click (on a Mac), you will see an option to rename the object. There will also be an option to **Show Label**; this same option will also hide the label.

The default setting for GeoGebra is to label every object, and you may find that all these labels begin to clutter the diagram. Clicking on the **Options** menu at the top of the GeoGebra window, you can select **Labeling|New Points Only**, and then **Save Settings** to control the proliferation of labels that appear in the diagram.

2. In a new window of GeoGebra, construct and label an arbitrary quadrilateral, *WXYZ*. Draw the diagonals *WY* and *XZ*. (The diagram will be easier to analyze if you use an option on the Style Bar to choose different colors for some of the lines.)
   a. Try to manipulate the quadrilateral so that the diagonals don't intersect each other. What do you observe about the shape of the quadrilateral?
   b. Write some conjectures about your observations to summarize what you notice by completing the following sentences:
      i. If the diagonals of a quadrilateral intersect each other, then the quadrilateral ...
      ii. If the diagonals of a quadrilateral don't intersect each other, then ...
   c. What if the diagonals bisect each other? (Two line segments are said to *bisect each other* if they intersect each other at their midpoints.) Can you construct a quadrilateral with this property? Write a conjecture to summarize what you learn in this exploration by completing the statement: "If the diagonals of a quadrilateral bisect each other, then ..."

d. The *converse* of a conjecture is a statement that interchanges the role of the hypothesis (if-part) and the conclusion (then-part) of the statement. Write the converse of one or more of the conjectures you have formulated in this activity. Does the converse mean the same thing as the original statement?

3. Construct an arbitrary triangle, and measure its interior angles. Drag a vertex to check whether these measurements are always interior angles; if necessary, change the range of the angles by using an option on the Style Bar. You can also change the range of the angle measurements by a right-click on the angle, selecting **Object Properties|Basic**, and then choosing the desired range.

   a. Calculate the sum of these angle measures. This is done in the **Input** line at the bottom of the window. There is a button marked with the Greek letter α; pressing this button opens a menu of symbols that can be inserted into the calculation. Look for the Greek letters that represent the angles of your triangle. The sum will appear in the Algebra pane. Complete the following sentence: "The sum of the measures of the interior angles of an arbitrary triangle is . . ." Drag the vertices of the triangle to help you decide whether your conjecture is always correct.

   b. Repeat this experiment for an arbitrary quadrilateral, and write a conjecture about the angle sum of a quadrilateral. (As before, check that the angle being measured is always interior to the quadrilateral.) Drag the vertices to see whether your conjecture always holds.

   c. Are your conjectures about the angle sum of triangles and the angle sum of quadrilaterals related to each other? Why or why not?

 Use the **Circle with Center Through Point** tool to construct circles, just as you would with a mechanical compass. Click to select the center and move out to construct the circle. This will create a circle with a center point and a point on the circle. These two points define the circle; moving either of them will alter the circle.

4. Construct a circle with center point C. Then construct three points P, Q, and R on this circle. Make sure than none of these points are defining points of the circle.

   a. Construct chords PR, PQ, and QR. Measure ∠PQR. The angle PQR is called an *inscribed angle* for the circle. Drag point Q around the circle, or right-click on Q to see the **Animation On** option. (A Mac computer will work differently.) What do you observe about the measure of ∠PQR? What happens when Q moves past point R? What happens if you change the radius of the circle? The angles that you are looking at as Q moves around the circumference of the circle are *angles subtended by the chord PR*. Express your observation in the form of a conjecture: "If PR is a fixed chord of a circle and Q is a point on that circle, then the measure of ∠PQR is . . . ."

   b. Now construct radii CP and CR. Measure ∠PCR, which is called a *central angle* of the circle. There are two choices for this angle; you may wish to measure both. (Using different colors may make your diagram easier to analyze.) What do you observe about the measures of a central angle and the corresponding inscribed angle of a circle? Vary the points P, Q, and R by dragging them around the circle so that you examine many different angles. Does your observation still hold? Express your observation as a conjecture by completing the following sentence: "If $\angle PQR$ is an inscribed angle of a circle centered at C, then the measure of $\angle PQR$ will be ... [compared to] the measure of $\angle PCR$."

5. Construct a circle with diameter PR. Make sure you construct your circle in such a way that PR is certain to be the diameter, not merely a chord, of the circle.

   a. Construct a point Q on the circle, and measure $\angle PQR$. Move the point Q. What do you observe? What happens if Q moves past the point R?

   b. Make a conjecture about this situation. How is this conjecture related to the conjectures you made in Activity 4?

6. Construct an *equilateral triangle* using GeoGebra. (Don't just estimate; use circles and intersection points to guarantee that your triangle is equilateral.) This construction may require you to use objects that are not part of the final diagram. These objects can be hidden by locating the name of each object in the Algebra pane and clicking the button next to that name.

   a. Create a point P in the interior of the triangle. Construct line segments from P that are perpendicular to each side. Then hide the extra objects you used to do this. The lengths of the three segments will appear in the Algebra pane. Have GeoGebra calculate the sum.

   b. Drag P around your picture. Your segments should remain perpendicular to the three sides. What do you observe? Drag P onto one of the vertices of your triangle. What do you observe?

   c. Make a conjecture about this situation by completing the following sentence: "If P is a point interior to an equilateral triangle, then the sum of the lengths of the three perpendicular segments from P to the sides of the triangle is ...."

   d. Draw another triangle that is not equilateral, and repeat this experiment. What do you observe? Does anything different happen when the triangle is acute or obtuse?

7. A *rectangle* can be defined as a quadrilateral with four right angles.

   a. Construct a rectangle in GeoGebra. The **Perpendicular Line** tool will be useful to do this. Did your construction use the definition given here, or did it use some additional properties of a rectangle?

   b. Construct the diagonals of this rectangle, and notice how they intersect. The **Point|Intersect** tool can be helpful here. Express your observation as a conjecture by completing the following statement: "If a quadrilateral is a rectangle, then its diagonals ..."

   c. Write the converse of your conjecture. Explore whether or not the converse appears to be true.

8. A *square* can be defined as a regular quadrilateral. A polygon is said to be *regular* if all of its sides are the same length, and all of its angles have the same measure.
   a. Construct a square in GeoGebra. Did your construction use the definition given here, or did it use some additional properties of a square?
   b. Is every rectangle a square, or is every square a rectangle? Express your answer to this question as a conjecture by completing the following statement: "If a quadrilateral is a . . . , then it is a . . . "
   c. Write the converse of this conjecture. Does the converse mean the same thing as the original statement?

9. A quadrilateral is called *cyclic* if its four vertices lie on a common circle. Construct an example of this, and measure the four angles of your quadrilateral. What do you observe about the opposite angles? Express your observation as a conjecture. Does your conjecture still hold if you move the vertices? Use the observations you made in Activities 4 and 5 to explain why your conjecture is correct.

To complete our discussion of the tools available at the top of the GeoGebra screen, let's look at some additional options. On the Perpendicular Line tool, there are options for **Parallel Line**, **Perpendicular Bisector**, and **Angle Bisector**, among others. These will be useful later in the course. On the Polygon tool, there are options for **Regular Polygon** and **Rigid Polygon**. An equilateral triangle is an example of a regular polygon and so is a square. The Regular Polygon tool offers a shortcut method for the construction you created in Activity 6. On the other hand, the Rigid Polygon tool is used to construct polygons that, once created, do not change. These rigid polygons can be moved or turned, but will retain their original shape.

On the Circle tool, there are many additional options. The **Compass** tool lets you create a circle by selecting a segment or a pair of points to represent the radius, then selecting a location for the center of the desired circle. With the **Circle by Center and Radius**, you can construct a circle with any center and a radius given by a number value.

Under the Slider tool, there is the **Image** option. The Image tool lets you insert images into the GeoGebra window. These images can be manipulated like any other object in the window. Under the Move tool is the **Pen** option. The Pen will let you draw with your mouse. This drawing can be moved, and there are options on the Style Bar for it as well.

Other tools will be discussed as they are needed in later chapters. Feel free to experiment!

One more tip before we conclude these activities: Sometimes you will want to print the work you have done using GeoGebra. Go to the File menu and choose **Print Preview**. Here you can control the size of the printed image by adjusting the numbers in the boxes labeled *units* and *cm*. You can select Portrait or Landscape printing. Also, you can add a title and the author's name; these will appear on the printed copy.

EXPLORING AND CONJECTURING

SOME GEOGEBRA TIPS

A quadrilateral consists of four line segments connected at their endpoints to form a closed figure. For Activity 1, you can use the Line|Segment tool to construct one segment, then another segment connected to it, then a third segment, and finally, a fourth segment connected to both the first and third segments. Or you can use the Polygon tool. Click somewhere in the white space of your GeoGebra diagram to construct each of the four vertices, then click again on the first vertex to complete the polygon. With the Point|Midpoint or Center tool, you can either click on the endpoints of a segment or on the segment itself to construct the midpoint of each edge. The Segment tool then comes into play again as you construct the midpoint quadrilateral.

Using different colors can help focus your attention on certain portions of a figure as you experiment with a construction. For instance, select the four line segments that join the midpoints of the original quadrilateral. (Recall that by holding the CTRL key you can select multiple objects.) On the Style Bar, the **Color** menu gives you many choices. Pick a new color. Look again at the quadrilateral you constructed by connecting the midpoints. Because this midpoint quadrilateral is now in a contrasting color, it may be easier to see why it is interesting. Use the Move tool to drag one of the original vertices around the sketch and watch what happens.

The Text command can be used to type statements into your GeoGebra document. With the Symbols menu, you can insert a great variety of mathematical symbols and other symbols into your text. The Objects menu allows you to insert values from the document into the text. These values are dynamic; that is, as objects are moved around the diagram, the values for the objects in the text will be updated. After the Text box is created, selecting it with the Move arrow produces a selection of options in the Style Bar, such as text color, boldface, italics, and text size.

There are many other ways you might have done Activity 1. For instance, you might visualize a quadrilateral as four vertices connected by line segments. In this case, your construction would begin with four points. Then you would choose Segment and select these points two at a time. As you become familiar with the tools and the menus available, you will think of many approaches to any particular construction.

CONSTRUCTING → EXPLORING → CONJECTURING: INDUCTIVE REASONING

The process of observing and conjecturing is called *inductive reasoning*. By examining many examples, you can begin to see patterns and make educated guesses—conjectures—about what might be true. Looking at specific examples can suggest something that might be a general truth, and if that suggestion holds true for many examples, it is more likely to be true in a general setting. This process of exploring, experimenting, and conjecturing lies at the heart of scientific investigations.

GeoGebra is a wonderful tool for examining examples in geometry. Once a figure is constructed, it is easily varied by dragging objects around the sketch. Doing this makes it possible to explore many examples very quickly. Dragging objects in a GeoGebra construction can also help you see how the components of the construction are related to each other, which may suggest a reason why the conjecture is true.

Formulating a conjecture is an important step in the process of doing mathematics. The next step is justifying the conjecture—finding an explanation for why the conjecture holds. Once you have an explanation, it is important to communicate it to others in a detailed, logical presentation—a proof. The proof process relies on *deductive reasoning*. In the early chapters of this book, we will introduce the rules and methods of logic and deductive reasoning. As the course progresses, you will grow in your skill and confidence with developing valid geometric proofs.

LANGUAGE OF GEOMETRY

In the activities, we assumed that you already know some basic geometric vocabulary. We hope that you recognize most of the geometric terms used so far, even if you don't know their formal definitions. Formal definitions play an important role in mathematics, since the precision necessary in mathematics requires precision in the language. Unlike descriptive definitions often used in language arts, mathematical definitions are prescriptive. A good mathematical definition is complete and concise, using only terms that have been previously defined.

It is important to distinguish between a geometric object's definition and its properties. For instance, if a square is defined as a regular quadrilateral, then a property of a square would be that its interior angles are right angles. Similarly, in this text, we define a rectangle as a quadrilateral with four right angles. All the other features that we associate with a rectangle— opposite sides are equal and parallel, the diagonals bisect each other, and so on—can be proved as a consequence of that definition. In general, we can think of properties as consequences of a definition.

As you continue this course, it will be increasingly important to use geometric language carefully. It is important to have clear, concise definitions of the terms we are using in your own mind. Writing out a careful definition of a term is one way of clarifying its meaning for yourself; thus, you should practice writing careful definitions. Once you have written a definition, try to construct the figure you have defined, using only the properties you have stated in the definition. For example, a kite could be defined as a quadrilateral with two disjoint pairs of adjacent congruent sides. How would you use this definition to construct a kite?

A *polygon* is a closed figure in the plane formed by a set of line segments, each of which shares each endpoint with exactly one other line segment in the set.

Because it has many (*poly-*) angles (*-gons*), it is called a polygon. A *triangle* could be called a 3-gon, because it has three angles. It could also be called a *trilateral* because it has three sides (*laterals*). A *hexagon* has six angles. The corners of a polygon are called its *vertices* (singular, *vertex*). Does a polygon with n vertices always have n sides? Why or why not?

A *regular* polygon is a polygon whose angles all have the same measure, and whose sides are all the same length. So both a square and an equilateral triangle are regular, but a right triangle cannot be regular. (Why not?)

EXPLORATIONS, OBSERVATIONS, QUESTIONS

In several of the activities, you worked with various quadrilaterals. The most general *quadrilateral* is simply a polygon with four sides. The word quadrilateral comes from the Latin *quadrilaterus*, meaning four (*quadri-*) sided (*-laterus*). We could easily use the Greek roots and call a four-sided figure a *tetragon*, which means four (*tetra-*) angled (*-gon*). Within the family of quadrilaterals, there are some that have special names and specific characteristics such as rectangles, squares, parallelograms, and others. As you worked on Activity 1, did you observe that the quadrilateral formed when you connected the midpoints in order is a parallelogram? No matter what shape the original quadrilateral has—even if it is self-intersecting—its midpoint quadrilateral appears to be a parallelogram. In other words, if the midpoints of an arbitrary quadrilateral are connected in clockwise order, the resulting midpoint quadrilateral is a parallelogram.

A *parallelogram* is a quadrilateral whose opposite sides are parallel. Why does the construction you did in Activity 1 lead to a parallelogram? The opposite sides appear to be parallel, but how can you be sure that these segments really are parallel for any midpoint quadrilateral? While in this chapter we are not focused on explaining why, or proving that, our conjectures are true, it is a natural question to ask. In the next chapter, we will investigate these types of questions. If you are interested in trying to answer the question at this point, you might find it helpful to add line segments to create triangles that let you compare opposite sides of the midpoint quadrilateral.

What did you observe about the area of the midpoint quadrilateral compared to the area of the original quadrilateral? Your explorations may have led you to suspect that the area of the parallelogram is half the area of the original quadrilateral, at least in the case of non-self-intersecting quadrilaterals. In fact, Pierre Varignon established this as a theorem in 1731. What would you need to know in order to prove this result?

While working on Activities 1 and 2, you were faced with the question of what sorts of figures qualify as quadrilaterals. Certainly, there must be four sides. Are these sides allowed to cross each other? You can easily cause this to happen in your sketch by dragging a vertex. Should we allow this figure to be called a quadrilateral? Apply the definition of a polygon stated earlier: A quadrilateral is a closed figure in the plane formed by a set of four line segments, each of which shares each endpoint with exactly one other line segment in the set. Thus, the unusual-looking figures you observed while working on Activities 1 and 2 can be called quadrilaterals. Polygons whose sides intersect are called *self-intersecting* figures.

Even if we avoid self-intersecting quadrilaterals, there is still another issue raised in Activity 2. Think again about the figures you constructed while working on this activity. How are the quadrilaterals for which the diagonals don't intersect different from those for which the diagonals do intersect? Notice that the definition of quadrilateral allows us to call all of these figures "quadrilaterals" even though they fall into two distinctly different sets. Those quadrilaterals for which the diagonals intersect are *convex* quadrilaterals. Quadrilaterals and hexagons can be either convex or not convex. However, every triangle is convex. What about pentagons?

What does it mean for a polygon, or even a more general closed figure, to be convex? Try to state a clear definition for a convex figure. Your definition should allow you to decide whether any example of a polygon (or other closed figure in the plane) is convex, no matter what type it is. Experiment again with your sketch for Activity 2, and try to formulate a rule or strategy for determining whether a quadrilateral is convex. Does your rule work only for quadrilaterals, or does it work for other polygons (and other geometric figures) as well?

How did you construct the *equilateral triangle* you worked with in Activity 6? It is not enough to simply draw three line segments that look congruent. If your construction is *robust*, you will be able to select any of the vertices or edges of the triangle and move them around without losing the property that the figure is an equilateral triangle. Is your construction of an equilateral triangle robust? (*Hint*: The radii of any particular circle are all congruent. So if the base of your triangle is a radius, each of the sides can be a radius too, though maybe not for the same circle.) Once you get a robust construction that produces an equilateral triangle, ask yourself why that construction works. In other words, how can you be sure that the three sides are truly congruent? (If your construction is not a robust construction, go back now and redo Activity 6.)

As you worked on Activity 6, something interesting should have happened as you moved P around inside the triangle. What conjecture did you make about the sum of the lengths of the three segments you constructed? Viviani's Theorem states that this sum is always the same and, furthermore, that this sum is equal to an important value for this triangle. Does your conjecture say something similar?

When we talk about a point being *on* a circle, by the definition of circle, we mean that it is one of the points that is an equal distance from the fixed center point. Similarly, when we say that a point is *on* a triangle, we mean that it is on one of the segments that form the triangle, including the endpoints of the segments that are the vertices of the triangle. What does it mean for a point to be *interior* to a particular circle or triangle? This is a bit harder to define or explain. (Just to complicate things a bit, imagine that a large triangle is drawn on the surface of a sphere. Where is the interior now?) What does it mean for a point to be *exterior* to a triangle or circle?

Although in Activity 6 you were directed at first to put the point P interior to the equilateral triangle, GeoGebra might allow you to move P beyond the boundary of the triangle. (This depends on how you constructed the figure.) Does your conjecture still hold when P is on the triangle? Does it hold if P is outside the triangle? If not, it may be possible to modify your conjecture so that it still holds even when P is on or outside the triangle.

Did your conjecture continue to hold when you used an arbitrary triangle instead of an equilateral triangle? It appears that it does not, which may be an indication that the equal-length sides of the equilateral triangle play a key role in explaining why Viviani's Theorem holds true. While the sum of the lengths of the perpendicular segments is not constant for all points on the interior of an arbitrary triangle, it appears to remain fixed for some subset of points in the interior. Did you find such a set of points? The properties of these sets are not known to the authors, making this an intriguing exploration for the interested student.

You can take this activity in many directions. What happens for isosceles triangles? What if the figure is a square instead of an equilateral triangle? What about a pentagon? Perhaps you could investigate segments from P to each of the vertices instead of from P to the sides of the triangle. One of the exercises at the end of this chapter invites you to explore some of these questions. Let your imagination guide you to new discoveries.

The previous few paragraphs raised many questions! You may have answered some of these questions already as you worked on the activities. Many more questions will arise throughout this course. As questions arise in your explorations or in your reading, pause and try to answer them, or at least make sure you understand the questions and why we are asking them. As you work on the activities and read the discussions in this book, learn to ask your own questions: "Is that always true?" ... "Why might it be true?" ... "Will it still be true if I change some part of the problem?" ... "Can I explain why it works?" .... Engaging in explorations and looking for explanations for the phenomena we observe is what "doing mathematics" is about.

THE FAMILY OF QUADRILATERALS

As you worked on Activities 1, 2, 7, 8, and 9, you encountered quite a few different quadrilaterals. Within the family of quadrilaterals, there are some special types—rectangle, square, kite, rhombus, trapezoid, parallelogram, and cyclic, to name a few. Try to write a one-sentence definition for each. If some of these names are not familiar to you, look up distinguishing characteristics to help you write these definitions.

When you write a definition for a geometric figure, try to use the smallest possible list of requirements to describe it. For example, in Activity 8 we defined a *square* as a regular quadrilateral. This means that a square has four sides (it's a quadrilateral), plus all of the sides have the same length and all of the angles are congruent (it's regular). However, it is sufficient to define a *square* as a quadrilateral with four equal angles and one pair of adjacent sides equal in length. From this shorter list of requirements, it is possible to prove the other features as properties of a square. Can you explain why knowing that a quadrilateral has four equal angles makes it possible to prove that the angles must be right angles? Similarly, in this book, we define a *rectangle* as a quadrilateral with four right angles. All the other features that we associate with a rectangle—opposite sides are equal and parallel, the diagonals bisect each other, and so on—can be proved using Euclid's postulates. We will examine these questions in greater depth beginning in the next chapter.

Every square is a rectangle; in other words, if a quadrilateral is a square, then it is a rectangle. The converse of this statement—if a quadrilateral is a rectangle, then it is a square—is not true. It is easy to sketch a figure of a rectangle that is not a square. Thus, we see that the converse of a statement does not mean the same thing as the original statement. This is an idea that we will return to again and again throughout this course.

There are many special types of quadrilaterals. Activity 9 introduces a type of quadrilateral that may be new to you. A quadrilateral is *cyclic* if its vertices lie on a common circle. Another way to say this is that a cyclic quadrilateral can be inscribed in a circle. Some familiar quadrilaterals, such as squares, are cyclic, but others are not necessarily cyclic. What did you observe about opposite angles in a cyclic quadrilateral? Does your observation still hold if the center of the circle is exterior to the quadrilateral—that is, if the quadrilateral lies entirely on one side of a diameter of the circle? You should be able to use your observations from Activity 4 to explain why your conjecture is correct. How is your conjecture different if the cyclic quadrilateral is self-intersecting?

A Venn diagram is a useful tool for picturing the relationships among various sets of figures. Consider some of the sets of figures we have been discussing in this chapter: parallelograms, quadrilaterals, rectangles, and triangles. In this situation, we are talking about sets of geometric figures that can be drawn in the plane, so we say that our *universe of discourse, U*, is all plane geometric figures. Let P denote the set of parallelograms, Q the set of quadrilaterals, R the set of rectangles, and T the set of triangles.

Figure 1.1 illustrates the relationships among these sets of figures. The large rectangle, labeled U, represents our universe of discourse. Within this universe, sketch a loop to represent each set. If two sets have things in common but each set also contains things that are not in the other set, draw the loops so that they overlap. If all of the objects in one set also belong to another set, we say that the smaller set is a *subset* of the larger set; draw the loop for the subset entirely within the loop for the other set. If two sets do not share any objects, we say that these sets are *disjoint*; in this case, draw the loops so that they do not overlap. For example,

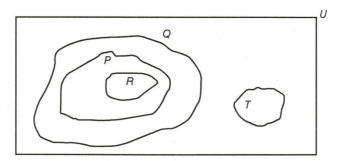

FIGURE 1.1
A Venn Diagram

in Figure 1.1, since every rectangle is a parallelogram, the set of rectangles, *R*, is drawn entirely within the set of parallelograms, *P*. Rectangles and parallelograms are subsets within the set of quadrilaterals, and we can see this in the way that the Venn diagram is drawn. Why is the set *T* off to the side by itself?

More sets can be added to this diagram. Let *S* denote the set of squares, and *K* the set of kites. A *kite* is a quadrilateral with two disjoint pairs of consecutive congruent sides. Since every square is a rectangle, the loop for squares must lie completely within the loop for rectangles. This illustrates the statement: If a quadrilateral is a square, then it is a rectangle. Since there are points in the loop for rectangles that are not in the loop for squares, the diagram also illustrates that the converse of this statement—if a quadrilateral is a rectangle, then it is a square—is not true. How would you add the loop for kites to this Venn diagram? You must decide if a kite could be a square or not. You must also decide whether all kites are parallelograms, or just some of them.

ANGLES INSCRIBED IN CIRCLES

A *circle* can be defined as a set of points that are equidistant from a fixed center point. Notice in this definition that the circle itself is only the set of points at a fixed distance from the center. This fixed distance from the center is the *radius* of the circle. Points that are closer to the center are not on the circle; rather, they are interior to the circle. Points whose distance from the center of the circle is greater than the radius are exterior to the circle.

If *PR* is a fixed chord of a circle and *Q* is any other point on the circle, then ∠*PQR* is *subtended by the chord PR*. This angle is an *inscribed angle* of the circle. The angle *PCR*, where *C* is the center of the circle, is a *central angle* of the circle. As you worked on Activity 4, how did the measure of ∠*PQR* change as you moved *Q* around the circle? What did you observe about the relationship between the central angle and the inscribed angles for a fixed chord *PR*? Your conjecture for this situation might say something like "If *PR* is a fixed chord of a circle with center *C* and *Q* is any point on the circle, then the measure of the central angle, ∠*PCR*, will be twice the measure of the inscribed angle, ∠*PQR*." Your conjecture should still be true if the central angle measures 180° (in which case *PR* will be a diameter of the circle). What happens when the central angle becomes greater than 180°? (You can force GeoGebra to display angles greater than 180° by an option on the Style Bar.) Isosceles triangles can be used to prove this conjecture.

If *PR* is a diameter of the circle, as in Activity 5, the central angle, ∠*PCR*, is formed by two opposite rays, $\overrightarrow{CP}$ and $\overrightarrow{CR}$. In this case, ∠*PCR* is sometimes called a *straight angle*. What is its measure? An angle that subtends a diameter of a circle is said to be an *angle inscribed in a semicircle*. To be consistent with your conjecture from Activity 4—or if you've proved it, your theorem from that activity—the measure of an angle inscribed in a semicircle should be half the measure of the corresponding central angle. Is this what you observed?

These observations about inscribed and central angles will be useful throughout this course as you work on various problems involving circles.

RULES OF LOGIC

A *statement*, mathematical or otherwise, is a declarative sentence that can be evaluated as true or false. Not every sentence is a statement. For instance, a question or a command would not be a statement. On the other hand, every sentence in this paragraph is a statement. A *closed statement* is a sentence that is either true or false. An *open statement* contains a variable; once a value is given for the variable, the statement becomes either true or false. In Chapter 3, we will discuss another way that an open statement can be closed.

Many interesting statements are built up from simpler statements. The simpler statements are combined using the logical connectives *and* and *or*. For example,

- This figure has a right angle *and* two of its sides are congruent.
- Triangles have three vertices *and* every rectangle is a square.
- This figure is a rectangle *or* it is a rhombus.
- The diagonals of a parallelogram bisect each other, *but* the diagonals of a cyclic quadrilateral do not necessarily bisect each other.

To evaluate the truth value of compound statements like these, we first determine the truth value of each component of the statement, then combine these truth values using rules of logic. For example, the first statement has two components: "This figure has a right angle" is the first component and "two of its sides are congruent" is the second component. The word *figure* is a variable for the statement in each of these components. To evaluate this compound statement, we have to know which figure is being discussed. Then we have to decide whether each part of the statement is true or false for that particular figure. *Both* components of the statement must be true to make the compound statement "This figure has a right angle *and* two of its sides are congruent" be true. There are figures that make both parts of this statement true and hence make the entire statement true. Can you draw a few examples? Also draw a few non-examples. You should be able to draw figures that make the first component false, other figures that make the second component false, and finally figures that make both components false.

In the second statement, we know that triangles indeed have three vertices. However, some rectangles are not square. A compound statement of the form *P and Q* is true only if both parts of the statement are true. So the compound statement "Triangles have three vertices *and* every rectangle is a square" is false.

In the third sentence, we again have a statement with two components, but the components are connected by the word *or*. For this statement to be true, it is only necessary for one of the two components to be true. It can happen that both components are true, which also makes the statement true. Try to draw examples of figures that make the first component true but not the second; figures that make the second component true but not the first; and figures that make both components true. All of your examples will make the statement "This figure is a rectangle *or* it is a rhombus" true.

The fourth statement is correct English. How should we interpret it logically? There are two components, namely, "the diagonals of a parallelogram bisect each other" and "the diagonals of a cyclic quadrilateral do not necessarily bisect each other." The difficulty is knowing how to treat the word *but* connecting these components. Typically, *but* is used to connect components that contrast in some way, as in the example statement. At its most basic level, however, *but* means *and*. Thus, we are deciding the truth value of "The diagonals of a parallelogram bisect each other, *and* the diagonals of a cyclic quadrilateral do not necessarily bisect each other." Both components are true, so the statement is true.

There is another important logical operator—*not*. The logical connectives *and* and *or* discussed above are used to connect two statements, but the word *not* is applied to a single statement. This allows statements such as "This figure is *not* a rectangle." The *not* in this statement reverses the truth value, so a rectangle makes the statement false while a trapezoid makes the statement true.

Let us summarize:

AND The compound statement *P and Q* is true only when both components are true. This is called *conjunction* and its mathematical symbol is $P \wedge Q$.

OR The compound statement *P or Q* is true when one or both components are true. This is called *disjunction* and its mathematical symbol is $P \vee Q$.

NOT The statement *not P* is true when *P* is false and it is false when *P* is true, thus *not* reverses the truth value of the statement. This is called *negation* and its mathematical symbol is $\neg P$. (Some authors use $\sim P$ to represent the negation of *P*. We will use the symbol $\sim$ to denote similar figures, and we will use $\neg$ for negation.)

Is it clear to you how to simplify $\neg\neg P$? Can you express the negation "It is not the case that $\triangle ABC$ is not equilateral" more simply in clear English?

Here is another question about expressing a negation clearly and simply: How would you simplify $\neg(P \vee Q)$? Be careful! Try it for a specific statement: *It is not the case that this figure is a rectangle or it is a rhombus.* To make this negated statement true, its components must both be false. How could you say this more naturally?

1.3 EXERCISES

Give clear and complete answers to the following problems and questions. Remember to write in complete sentences and grammatically correct English. Include diagrams whenever appropriate.

1. A *rhombus* is a quadrilateral whose four sides all have the same length. Construct a rhombus. Is your construction based on this definition? List some additional properties of rhombi (or rhombuses).

2. A *parallelogram* is a quadrilateral whose opposite sides are parallel. Construct a parallelogram. Is your construction based on this definition? List some additional properties of parallelograms.

3. What are the relationships among a rhombus, a parallelogram, a rectangle, and a square?

4. Within the family of quadrilaterals, there are some special figures—rectangle, square, kite, rhombus, trapezoid, and parallelogram. Write a one-sentence definition for each of these terms. Try to write each definition using as small a list of defining characteristics as possible.

5. A *kite* is a quadrilateral with two disjoint pairs of consecutive sides congruent. Is it possible for a quadrilateral to be both a square and a kite? Are all squares kites? Add the sets of squares, *S*, and kites, *K*, to the Venn diagram of Figure 1.1, page 14.

6. In mathematics we talk about numerical values being equal if they are quantitatively the same. For example, $2 + 3 = 5$, because the sum $2 + 3$ represents the same quantity as the number 5. When two different geometric figures are the same size and shape, we say that they are *congruent* rather than equal figures. We say that two line segments are congruent if they have the same length. What might it mean for each of the following pairs of figures to be congruent?
    a. Two angles
    b. Two circles
    c. Two triangles (or other polygons)
    d. What is the difference between *congruence* and *equality*?

7. Triangles can be equilateral, isosceles, scalene, acute, right, and/or obtuse. Define each of these terms, and include a sketch of each. Describe how these different kinds of triangles are related.

8. Explain what it means for a point to be *on*, *interior to*, or *exterior to* a circle.

9. Teachers often use a disk to represent a circle. What do they mean by this and what kind of confusion could this create?

10. Some textbooks define a *trapezoid* as a quadrilateral with exactly one pair of parallel sides, while other textbooks say that a trapezoid has at least one pair of parallel sides.
    a. What are the consequences of choosing one of these definitions over the other? Which is correct?
    b. Is a parallelogram a trapezoid? Why or why not?

11. What is the converse of the statement: "If a quadrilateral is a square, then it is a rectangle"? Is this converse a true statement?

12. Rewrite the following statement as an if-then statement: The angles of an equilateral triangle are congruent. What is the converse of the statement you wrote? Is this converse a true statement?

13. A statement can be negated by putting "not" in front of the statement. For example, the negation of "Some cars are blue" is "Not (some cars are blue)." However, this is awkward and unclear. A more useful form of this negation is "No cars are blue." Note that in this case, the original statement is true, and its negation is false.
    a. Negate the following statement, and express the negation clearly in simple English: "All polygons are convex." Which statement is true, the original statement or its negation?
    b. Is it possible for a statement and its negation both to be true? Both to be false?

14. Define the property *convex* for quadrilaterals. Does your definition hold for convex polygons or convex geometric figures in general? If not, rewrite your definition so that it can be applied to any geometric figure in the plane.

15. If the diagonals of a quadrilateral bisect each other, could the quadrilateral be a parallelogram? A rhombus? A rectangle? A square? A cyclic quadrilateral? Construct diagrams in GeoGebra to support your answers.

16. If the diagonals of a quadrilateral are congruent, could the quadrilateral be a parallelogram? A rhombus? A rectangle? A square? A cyclic quadrilateral? Construct diagrams in GeoGebra to support your answers.

17. Does a polygon with *n* vertices always have *n* sides? Why or why not?

18. What are the common names of polygons with 2, 3, 4, . . . sides? What is the minimum number of sides for a polygon? What is the maximum number of sides?

19. Why can't a right triangle be regular?

20. Can a parallelogram be inscribed in a circle? In other words, can a single circle pass through all

four vertices of a given parallelogram? Why or why not?

21. Take another look at your investigation with the midpoint quadrilateral in Activity 1. Repeat that investigation using a triangle and its midpoint triangle.
    a. What is the ratio of the area of the midpoint triangle to the original triangle? Make a conjecture, and vary the vertices of the triangle. Does your conjecture continue to hold?
    b. Can you explain what is going on?

22. In Activity 6, you investigated the sum of the lengths of the perpendicular segments from the point P to the each of the sides of an equilateral triangle.
    a. Use GeoGebra to explore the sum of these lengths for some other polygons such as isosceles triangles, rectangles, and hexagons.
    b. Use GeoGebra to investigate the sum of the lengths of the segments from P to each of the vertices.

23. Identify which of the following sentences is a statement. If the sentence contains a variable, identify the variable. If possible, determine whether the sentence is *true* or *false*.
    a. The angle sum of a triangle is 360°.
    b. Is $\angle A$ in $\triangle ABC$ a right angle?
    c. X is a quadrilateral.
    d. $a^2 + b^2 = c^2$.
    e. All rectangles are equiangular quadrilaterals.
    f. A kite is a quadrilateral.
    g. Triangles have three sides and rectangles have four right angles.
    h. The diagonals of a trapezoid bisect each other.
    i. Some cows are purple.
    j. Wow! That is a beautiful design!
    k. All right triangles are equilateral.
    l. Grizzly bears make affectionate pets.

24. Explain how to evaluate (find the truth value of) a statement of the form $P \vee Q$. Apply your evaluation method to the statement "$\triangle ABC$ has a right angle *or* two of its sides are congruent."

25. Explain how to evaluate a statement of the form $P \wedge Q$. Apply your evaluation method to the statement "$\triangle ABC$ has a right angle *and* two of its sides are congruent."

26. Set up a truth table for a statement of the form $P \vee Q$.

27. Set up a truth table for a statement of the form $P \wedge Q$.

28. For each of the following statements, sketch several figures that make the statement true; then sketch several figures that make the statement false. If some of these sketches are not possible, explain what is happening.
    a. This triangle has a right angle and two of its sides are congruent.
    b. This triangle is equilateral and it has a right angle.
    c. This quadrilateral is a rectangle or it is a rhombus.
    d. This quadrilateral has a right angle and its diagonals bisect each other.
    e. This quadrilateral is a kite and it is not convex.
    f. This figure is a pentagon and it is not convex.

29. How would you express the negation of a statement of the form $\neg(\neg P)$? Express your answer as a rule, and use this rule to negate the statement "It is not the case that $WXYZ$ is not a square."

30. How would you express the negation of a statement of the form $\neg(P \wedge Q)$? Express your answer as a rule, and use this rule to negate the statement "This figure is a rectangle and it is equilateral."

31. How would you express the negation of a statement of the form $\neg(P \vee Q)$? Express your answer as a rule, and use this rule to negate the statement "This figure is a rectangle or it is a rhombus."

Exercises 32–34 are especially for future teachers.

32. The Praxis Series™ Subject Assessments are tests designed by Educational Testing Service (ETS) to assess your knowledge of subject areas you plan to teach, and are used as part of the licensing procedure in many states.
    a. Is the Praxis test of *Mathematics Content Knowledge* required for teacher certification

in your state? Is the *Mathematics: Proofs, Models, and Problems* test required?

b. Questions on the Praxis tests are of two types: *multiple choice* and *constructed response*. How is a constructed-response question different from an essay question? How are constructed-response questions graded?

33. In 2000, the National Council of Teachers of Mathematics (NCTM) published the *Principles and Standards for School Mathematics,* which presents a vision for school mathematics in the twenty-first century. One of the principles identified in this document is the Technology Principle. Find a copy of the Principles and Standards, and study the discussion of the Technology Principle [NCTM, 2000, 24–27].

a. What are the specific recommendations of the NCTM regarding the use and integration of technology in the mathematics classroom?

b. What opportunities does technology make possible in the mathematics classroom? What might be some benefits of learning and teaching in a technology-rich classroom?

c. What cautions does the NCTM raise regarding the use of technology in the classroom?

34. Find the Common Core State Standards for Mathematics online: http://www.corestandards .org.

a. What is the Common Core State Standards Initiative?

b. What are the eight Standards for Mathematical Practice? How are the Standards for Mathematical Practice distinct from the Standards for Mathematical Content?

c. Study the Introduction to the section on High School: Geometry. How can dynamic geometry tools, such as GeoGebra, be used to enhance student learning in the high school (or middle school, or elementary school) classroom?

Reflect on what you have learned in this chapter.

35. Review the main ideas of this chapter. Describe, in your own words, the concepts you have studied and what you have learned about them. What are the important ideas? How do they fit together? Which concepts were easy for you? Which were hard?

36. Reflect on the learning environment for this course. Describe aspects of the learning environment that helped you understand the main ideas in this chapter. Which activities did you like? Which stretched you beyond your personal comfort zone? Why?

1.4 CHAPTER OVERVIEW

One of the goals of this opening chapter was to introduce you to some of the basic constructions in GeoGebra. By now, you should be comfortable launching GeoGebra and beginning a new sketch. You should be familiar with many of the tools available; in particular, you should be comfortable using the Move, Point, Line, Circle, Text, and Angle tools. You should also have experimented with some of the options available on these tools.

There are options on the Style Bar that allow you to change the thickness, color, and style of points and lines. By a right-click on an object, you can open a menu with options to show or hide an object, to show or hide a label, and to animate a point on a line or circle. (Again, note that the commands will be different for a Mac computer.) The Algebra pane offers another method for hiding or showing objects and displays values of lengths, angles, and areas. The Input line lets you enter arithmetic expressions using numbers and/or measured quantities; this makes it possible to calculate such things as the angle sum of a polygon or the sum of the distances from a point to each side of a given triangle.

An important purpose of the activities in this chapter is to introduce you to the practice of engaging in explorations and making observations, which leads to making conjectures. Making conjectures based on your observations will lead you to develop theorems that you will learn to prove (or sometimes disprove) in the coming weeks of this course. In developing a proof, you will be basically answering such questions as "What happens in this sketch?" ... "Can I expect it to happen this way again?" ... "Can I explain why this is happening?" ....

We have introduced some mathematical language in this chapter, and we will build on this in future chapters. This mathematical language includes both the names of geometric objects (square, polygon, line segment, and so on), and language describing different kinds of mathematical statements (conjecture, statement, converse, and so on). We also have introduced the logical operators, *and* (denoted $A \wedge B$), *or* (denoted $P \vee Q$), and *not* (denoted $\neg S$), which can be helpful in reasoning about statements involving these operators.

Finally, we hope that we have piqued your curiosity about geometry. We are inviting you to join us on an intellectual journey. We hope that you will find the experience both fun and rewarding.

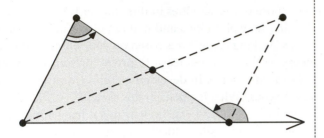

CHAPTER TWO

Constructing → Proving

An important objective of this course is to develop your mathematical reasoning and your ability to read and write mathematical proofs. In this chapter, we use a historical perspective to introduce these ideas. In about 300 BC, Euclid and his colleagues gathered the ideas about geometry known at that time into a book (or series of books) called Euclid's *Elements*. For about 2000 years, this was the most widely circulated book about mathematics, and it served as a textbook for anyone who was considered an educated person. Although it appears to be a geometry text, the *Elements* is essentially a catalog of ideas—postulates (or axioms) and theorems—that apply to all areas of mathematics. It advanced deductive reasoning as a tool for analyzing and understanding mathematics.

For ancient Greek philosophers, the only tools allowed for geometry were the *straightedge*, which, unlike a ruler, has no measurement markings, and the *compass*. In other words, you can draw only lines and circles. You are not allowed to measure things using the calibrations on a ruler, because such measuring is considered imprecise. Furthermore, the compass, when it was lifted from the drawing surface, collapsed so that one could not directly copy the radius of a circle. However, the Greeks were able to show how to use such a compass to compare and even to copy lengths. In fact, this is one of the first propositions that Euclid established. (Because the compass would collapse when it was lifted from the drawing board, it is sometimes called a "floppy compass.")

In this course, you are using a tool that was not available to ancient Greeks: GeoGebra. This program has been designed to include a virtual straightedge and compass, and it captures some of the essence of Euclid's *Elements*. The **Line** and **Circle** tools on the Toolbar are the *straightedge* and *compass* of Euclid's *Elements*. Other tools reflect propositions that Euclid proved from the use of the straightedge and compass. Because of its dynamic capability, GeoGebra is more powerful than the straightedge and compass of Euclid's day. You can construct a diagram in GeoGebra in the same way you would with a straightedge and compass, and then by dragging objects around your diagram, you can explore many different examples very quickly. But an example—even 10,000 examples—does not constitute a proof! In this chapter, we begin to discuss what is needed to prove your conjectures.

As you construct geometric figures using GeoGebra and observe what happens as you move some of the elements of the figure around the diagram, you should formulate *conjectures* based on your observations, stating what you think is happening in a given situation. Then test your conjectures to see if they hold up in different circumstances. In stating a conjecture, certain conditions are given; these form the *hypothesis* of your conjecture. Your conjecture is an assertion (or a claim) that if the conditions required in the hypothesis are met, then the *conclusion* will hold. Only after you have proved that your conjecture always holds (is valid), are you allowed to call it a *theorem*.

2.1 ACTIVITIES

We invite you to do the following activities in the spirit of their historical context. That is, restrict yourself to using only the *straightedge* and *compass* tools (the **Line** and **Circle** tools on the Toolbar) as you work on these activities. This will help you to get into the mind of Euclid and to begin to think like a geometer.

As you do these activities, pay attention to anything that you observe as you construct each diagram. You will be able to answer many of the questions posed here by typing a sentence or two directly into your GeoGebra diagram. Write your observations clearly in complete sentences. Try to think of explanations for the things you observe, and express your explanations in complete sentences.

Not all of these activities require the use of GeoGebra. For those that do, you will not need coordinate axes. Use a button in the Style Bar to hide the axes.

Save your work for each activity, as later work sometimes builds on earlier work. You will find it helpful to read ahead into the chapter as you work on these activities.

1. For two triangles to be congruent, the three sides and three angles of one triangle must be matched with the sides and angles of the other triangle so that corresponding sides are congruent and corresponding angles are congruent. However, it is not necessary to verify all six pairs of correspondences; it is sufficient to check just three carefully chosen pairs. For instance, showing that two sides and the included angle of one triangle

are congruent to the corresponding parts of the second triangle is enough, for then the other side and the other two angles are guaranteed to be congruent as well. This is the Side-Angle-Side (SAS) criterion for congruence of triangles.

  a. List all possible triples of sides and angles (SAS, AAS, etc.).
  b. For each of the triples in your list, construct (or sketch) two noncongruent triangles with the given corresponding parts congruent, or give an informal explanation for why it is impossible to do so.

2. Draw $\angle AOB$ in a GeoGebra window. Using only the **Circle with Center through Point** and **Line** tools, construct the ray OX that bisects this angle. Do not use the angle bisector or midpoint tools to do this construction. (*Hint*: One way to do this construction uses an equilateral triangle.)

3. Draw a line segment RS in a GeoGebra window. Using only the **Circle with Center through Point** and **Line** tools, construct the perpendicular bisector of RS, and label the midpoint of RS as M.

4. Given a line m and a point P, we want to be able to construct a line passing through P that is perpendicular to m, using only the **Circle with Center through Point** and **Line** tools. There are two situations to consider:

  a. Consider the situation where P is not on m. Find the point X on m so that line PX is perpendicular to m. The point X is called the *foot of the perpendicular* from P to m.
  b. Consider the situation where P is on m. Construct a line through P that is perpendicular to m.
     (*Hint*: Euclid found ways to do these constructions that build on the ideas of Activity 3.)

5. The *negation* of a statement is a statement whose truth value is the opposite of the original statement. What is the negation of each of the following statements?

  a. Triangle ABC is *not* equilateral.
  b. $WXYZ$ is a parallelogram *or* it is a cyclic quadrilateral.
  c. Points R, S, and T are collinear *and* T is not a point on the circle centered at R with radius RS.
  d. *All* triangles are equilateral.
  e. Given a line ℓ and a point P that is not on ℓ, there is *exactly one* line through P that is parallel to ℓ.

6. Consider the statement "If $\triangle ABC$ is an equilateral triangle, then $\angle A$ is not a right angle." Which of the following statements means the same thing as this statement? Make sketches to support your answers.

  a. If $\angle A$ (in $\triangle ABC$) is not a right angle, then $\triangle ABC$ is an equilateral triangle.
  b. If $\triangle ABC$ is not an equilateral triangle, then $\angle A$ is a right angle.
  c. If $\angle A$ (in $\triangle ABC$) is a right angle, then $\triangle ABC$ is not an equilateral triangle.

7. Consider the statement "If ℓ is a line and P is a point that is not on ℓ, then every line through P intersects ℓ." Which of the following statements best expresses the *negation* of this statement?

   a. ℓ is a line and P is a point that is not on ℓ, and every line through P is parallel to ℓ.

   b. ℓ is a line and P is a point that is not on ℓ, and no line through P intersects ℓ.

   c. ℓ is a line and P is a point that is not on ℓ, and at least one line through P intersects ℓ.

   d. ℓ is a line and P is a point that is not on ℓ, and at least one line through P is parallel to ℓ.

8. If one side of a triangle is extended at one vertex, the angle it creates with the other side at that vertex is called an *exterior angle* of the triangle. Construct an example of this in GeoGebra. Measure the exterior angle.

   a. Compare this measurement with the measure of one of the interior angles at either of the other two vertices. These two angles are referred to as the *remote interior* angles with respect to that exterior angle. Manipulate the triangle by moving the vertices so that the measure of the remote interior angle you chose comes as close as possible to the measure of the exterior angle. What do you observe? Express your observation as a conjecture by completing this sentence: "If an exterior angle is formed by extending one side of a triangle, then . . ."

   b. Now compare the measure of the exterior angle to the measures of both of the remote interior angles. What do you observe? Express your observation as a conjecture by completing this sentence: "If an exterior angle is formed by extending one side of a triangle, then . . . ." (This statement is intended to be different from the one you made in part (a).)

9. Draw line ℓ and, using the **Parallel Line** tool, construct line m parallel to ℓ. Draw a third line t that intersects both ℓ and m. These three lines will form eight angles. Use GeoGebra to measure the size of each angle. What do you observe? Express your observation as a conjecture, clearly indicating your hypothesis and your conclusion. You might find it helpful to write your observations first, and then write a conjecture using the form "If a pair of parallel lines are crossed by a transversal, then . . . ."

10. The conjecture you wrote in the preceding activity may have discussed interior angles as part of its conclusion. In that situation, the converse of the conjecture might begin "If two lines, ℓ and m, are crossed by a transversal t in such a way that the interior angles on one side of the transversal . . . , then . . . ."

    a. Complete the statement of this converse.

    b. Let line ℓ be crossed by line t. Use this converse to construct line m parallel to ℓ.

EUCLID'S POSTULATES AND CONSTRUCTIONS

EUCLID'S POSTULATES

Let's take a closer look at the way that Euclid's *Elements* has been organized. You can see a complete text of the *Elements* with interactive diagrams online at

https://mathcs.clarku.edu/~djoyce/java/elements/elements.html

Since this is a fairly faithful translation of an ancient Greek text, you might find the style and language archaic. It may take some time to get used to the way these ideas are expressed.

Euclid attempted to develop all of the ideas in geometry from a few *definitions*, five *postulates*, and five *common notions*. Euclid's first four postulates are simple statements, and then there is the fifth postulate! While improvements have been made in the logical structure of the *Elements*, we can learn a great deal about the development of a mathematical system from Euclid's work.

Euclid's postulates shape the way GeoGebra operates. So as we present the statements of Euclid's postulates, we will reflect on how these postulates are implemented within GeoGebra's environment.

1. *Given two distinct points P and Q, there is a line (that is, there is exactly one line) that passes through P and Q.* In GeoGebra, you can construct or draw points. If you select two points, you can construct a single line through these points, or a single line segment with these points as endpoints.

2. *Any line segment can be extended indefinitely.* If you have constructed a line segment, you can select both endpoints, and construct a ray or a line through those points, thus allowing you to extend the line segment to any extent you wish.

3. *Given two distinct points P and Q, a circle centered at P with radius PQ can be drawn.* Using the **Circle with Center through Point** tool, you can construct a circle by selecting a center and then selecting a point you want the circle to pass through.

4. *Any two right angles are congruent.* GeoGebra allows you to move figures around so that you can see whether one figure can be superimposed on another. Any right angle can be moved until it coincides with any other right angle. (We will discuss this idea of moving figures around the plane in Chapter 8, *Transformational Geometry*.)

5. *Euclid's Fifth Postulate.*
   a. Euclid's statement: *If two lines are intersected by a transversal in such a way that the sum of the degree measures of the two interior angles on one side of the transversal is less than the sum of two right angles, then the two lines meet on that side of the transversal.* In GeoGebra, if you draw ℓ, m, and t as arbitrary lines with the property that the two interior angles

formed by ℓ and m with t on the same side of t sum to less than two right angles, GeoGebra will allow you to construct the point of intersection of ℓ and m by selecting these two lines and the **Intersect** tool. This intersection point may not appear on the screen, but you can manipulate the diagram using the scroll bars to bring the intersection point into view. However, if you construct ℓ and m as parallel lines, GeoGebra will not let you construct their point of intersection. In other words, GeoGebra is making the same assumption that Euclid made about parallel lines—they do not intersect.

b. Over the years, other mathematicians formulated different ways of expressing Euclid's Fifth Postulate. John Playfair, a mathematician working in the late eighteenth century, developed perhaps the best-known alternative to Euclid's Fifth Postulate.

Playfair's statement: *Given a line ℓ and any point P not on ℓ, there is exactly one line through P that is parallel to ℓ.* If, in GeoGebra, you select line ℓ and a point P not on ℓ, you can construct a line through P that is parallel to ℓ. However, if you do this multiple times, GeoGebra simply constructs the same line over and over again. You can see this by examining the items listed in the Algebra pane. The repeated lines through P parallel to ℓ will have the same algebraic description, because they are just one line. In other words, GeoGebra implements Playfair's Postulate by constructing only one line through P parallel to ℓ.

CONGRUENCE AND SIMILARITY

In ordinary English, we sometimes use the words *congruous* or *congruent* to say that two things agree in nature or quality. For example, your instructor's use of GeoGebra as a teaching and learning tool might be congruent with the way she teaches other courses. In mathematics, *congruent* has a more exact or specialized meaning. Two geometric figures are said to be congruent if they are exactly the same size and shape, that is, if one could be superimposed exactly on the other to make a perfect fit. If two figures are the same shape but perhaps have different sizes, we say they are *similar*. All circles are similar (the same shape); if their radii are equal in length, the circles are also congruent. Two triangles, $\triangle ABC$ and $\triangle DEF$, are similar if there is a one-to-one correspondence between their vertices so that corresponding angles are congruent (i.e., AAA). Similarity is denoted by $\triangle ABC \sim \triangle DEF$. For two triangles to be congruent, there must also be a correspondence between the congruent sides of the triangles.

However, it is not necessary to compare all three pairs of angles and all three pairs of sides to determine whether two triangles are congruent. It is possible to verify congruence by checking only a few of these six items. You had an opportunity to examine conditions for congruence of triangles in Activity 1. You probably observed that if any two pairs of angles are congruent, the third pair of angles is also congruent. Thus, if one pair of corresponding sides is congruent and two pairs of corresponding angles are congruent, you were unable to construct a pair of noncongruent triangles. Thus, it seems that ASA and AAS are valid criteria to identify a pair of triangles as congruent. On the other hand, if each angle of one triangle is congruent to a corresponding angle in another triangle (AAA), it is fairly easy to construct a pair of noncongruent triangles. In this case, the triangles are similar but not congruent. What did you find in the situations where you had two pairs of congruent sides but only one pair of congruent angles (e.g., in the situations for SAS and SSA)?

Euclid attempted to prove that SAS triangle congruence followed from his five postulates. Most modern versions of Euclidean geometry recognize that Euclid's argument had a logical flaw. Either additional postulates must be assumed or SAS triangle congruence should itself be a postulate. As a result, at least one of the triangle congruence statements is generally added to the list of postulates. We will follow David Hilbert, and consider the SAS criterion for triangle congruence as an axiom. We will study congruence of triangles in greater depth in Chapter 3.

Saying that similar geometric objects have the "same shape" gives a general idea, but we need a more precise definition. The shape of a polygon depends on the size of its angles and the relative proportions of its sides. Thus, there are two requirements to consider for similarity.

DEFINITION 2.1   Two polygons are *similar* if

1. each pair of corresponding angles is congruent; and
2. the ratio of each pair of corresponding sides is the same as all other pairs.

It is not difficult to create pairs of quadrilaterals that satisfy only one of these criteria. For instance, squares can be dissimilar to rhombi, and rectangles can be dissimilar to squares. Triangles are more restricted than quadrilaterals, of course, and we can determine similarity of triangles from less information.

THEOREM 2.1   **AA Criterion for Triangle Similarity**   For two triangles $\triangle ABC$ and $\triangle DEF$, if two pairs of corresponding angles are congruent, then the two triangles are similar.

Proof   Suppose that $\angle A \cong \angle D$ and $\angle B \cong \angle E$. If the side AB is congruent to the side DE, then the two triangles are congruent by ASA, and the congruent triangles are similar with the ratio $\frac{1}{1}$.

Consider the case where the sides AB and DE are not congruent, and suppose that AB is shorter than DE. (See Figure 2.1.) Locate the point A' on DE so that $A'E \cong AB$, and locate the point C' on EF so that $C'E \cong CB$. Thus, the triangle $A'EC'$ is congruent to $\triangle ABC$ by SAS. In other words, we have copied the smaller triangle into a corner of the larger triangle. Notice that because $\angle A \cong \angle D$ and $\angle A \cong \angle EA'C'$, the segments $A'C'$ and DF do not intersect (by a corollary to Euclid's Fifth Postulate).

Now construct the segments $A'F$ and DC'. The triangles $A'C'F$ and $A'C'D$ have the same area. (*Why?*) This tells us that

$$\frac{\text{Area}(\triangle A'C'F)}{\text{Area}(\triangle A'EC')} = \frac{\text{Area}(\triangle A'C'D)}{\text{Area}(\triangle A'EC')}$$

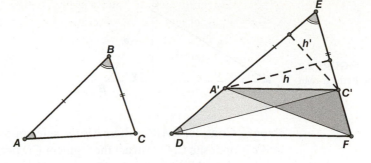

FIGURE 2.1
Proving the AA Criterion for
Similar Triangles

Drop a perpendicular from A' to EF, and label this segment h. Observe that h is an altitude of $\Delta A'EC'$ as well as $\Delta A'C'F$. Now, Area$(\Delta A'C'F) = \frac{1}{2} \cdot h \cdot C'F$ and Area$(\Delta A'EC') = \frac{1}{2} \cdot h \cdot EC'$. Thus

$$\frac{\text{Area}(\Delta A'C'F)}{\text{Area}(\Delta A'EC')} = \frac{\frac{1}{2} \cdot h \cdot C'F}{\frac{1}{2} \cdot h \cdot EC'} = \frac{C'F}{EC'}$$

Similarly, drop a perpendicular from C' to DE, and label this segment h'. Using the altitude h' with $\Delta A'C'D$ and $\Delta A'EC'$, we get a corresponding calculation:

$$\frac{\text{Area}(\Delta A'C'D)}{\text{Area}(\Delta A'EC')} = \frac{\frac{1}{2} \cdot h' \cdot A'D}{\frac{1}{2} \cdot h' \cdot EA'} = \frac{A'D}{EA'}$$

Therefore, $\frac{C'F}{EC'} = \frac{A'D}{EA'}$. Then, since $\frac{EC'}{EC'} = 1 = \frac{EA'}{EA'}$, we can write

$$\frac{EC'}{EC'} + \frac{C'F}{EC'} = \frac{EC' + C'F}{EC'} = \frac{EA'}{EA'} + \frac{A'D}{EA'} = \frac{EA' + A'D}{EA'}$$

so that $\frac{EF}{EC'} = \frac{ED}{EA'}$. Recalling that $\Delta A'EC'$ was constructed congruent to ΔABC, we see that $\frac{EF}{BC} = \frac{ED}{BA}$.

So far this proof has shown that if two sets of corresponding angles are congruent, then two sets of corresponding sides have the same ratio. To finish the proof, copy ΔABC to the vertex D instead of E, and use a similar argument to show that $\frac{DF}{AC} = \frac{DE}{AB}$.

There are other ways to test triangles for similarity. The SSS *criterion* says that if the ratio for each pair of corresponding sides is the same as for all other pairs of corresponding sides, then the triangles will be similar. The *SAS criterion* says that if two pairs of corresponding sides have the same ratio and the corresponding angles between these sides are congruent, then the triangles are similar.

The ratios of similar triangles can be used to prove a famous result.

THEOREM 2.2 **The Pythagorean Theorem** Suppose a, b, and c are the lengths of the sides of ΔABC with a opposite vertex A, b opposite vertex B, and c opposite vertex C. If $\angle C$ is a right angle, then $a^2 + b^2 = c^2$.

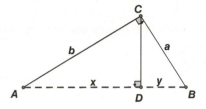

FIGURE 2.2
Proving the Pythagorean
Theorem

Proof   Consider $\triangle ABC$, where a is the side opposite vertex A, b is opposite B, and c is opposite C. Construct the segment CD perpendicular to AB. (So CD is an *altitude* of the triangle.) See Figure 2.2. Using the AA criterion, we find three similar triangles in this figure: $\triangle ABC \sim \triangle CBD \sim \triangle ACD$. Thus, $\frac{BC}{BD} = \frac{AB}{CB}$, or $\frac{a}{y} = \frac{c}{a}$, so that $a^2 = cy$. Moreover, $\frac{AC}{AD} = \frac{AB}{AC}$, or $\frac{b}{x} = \frac{c}{b}$, so that $b^2 = cx$. Notice also that $y + x = c$. Therefore,

$$a^2 + b^2 = cy + cx = c(y + x) = c^2.$$

The converse of the Pythagorean Theorem is also important.

THEOREM 2.3   **Converse of the Pythagorean Theorem**   Suppose a, b, and c are the lengths of the sides of $\triangle ABC$. If $a^2 + b^2 = c^2$, then $\angle C$ is a right angle.

This converse is not difficult to prove; construct a right triangle with legs of lengths a and b, and verify that this new triangle is congruent to the original triangle. You will be asked to write this proof as an exercise.

CONSTRUCTIONS

We have made a distinction between *constructing* a figure and merely *drawing* it. Historically, this distinction indicates whether or not you used only a straight-edge and compass to create the sketch. If you are careful—that is, if you have a steady hand and a good eye—it is possible to make a very nice drawing that looks like the figure you are trying to construct. For example, you could probably draw a fairly believable equilateral triangle. However, the drawing will only be an approx-imation of an equilateral triangle, whereas the construction, made using only the straightedge and compass, will be exact. With GeoGebra, the distinction indicates whether the sketch is robust (i.e., dynamic). That is to say, if you select one of the vertices and drag it, does your sketch maintain its integrity? If you started with an equilateral triangle, will it remain equilateral or will it become scalene? If you have constructed an equilateral triangle, you can select and drag various points, and although your triangle might change size, it will continue to be equilateral.

In Activity 6 of the previous chapter (see page 7), you were asked to construct an equilateral triangle. You had to develop a strategy using circles and intersection points to make your construction robust. One way to construct a pair of equilat-eral triangles is to draw a line segment AB, which will be one side of the equilateral triangle. Then construct a circle centered at A through the point B, and another circle centered at *B* through the point *A*. These two circles will intersect in two points, *C* and *D*. Both triangles, △*ABC* and △*ABD*, are equilateral.

Once you have constructed an equilateral triangle on the segment *AB*, you should also be able to find the midpoint of the segment *AB* as well as to construct the perpendicular bisector of the segment (see Figure 2.3). Can you explain why your construction is correct? Look for congruent triangles in the diagram to help you.

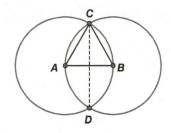

FIGURE 2.3
Constructing an Equilateral
Triangle

From the time of the ancient Greeks up to the nineteenth century, mathematicians were fascinated with the question of whether certain quantities could be constructed using only a compass and an unmarked straightedge (not a ruler). The straightedge is used to construct straight objects—lines, segments, rays—and as such, it represents Euclid's First and Second Postulates. The compass is used to construct circles, and as such, it represents Euclid's Third Postulate. Working strictly from Euclid's Postulates thus meant working only with these two tools. Many quantities can be successfully constructed by straightedge and compass. You have seen a few of these constructions: the midpoint of an arbitrary segment and the bisector of an angle, for instance. It is also possible to construct products and quotients of two given lengths, and square roots as well. However, some problems resisted the best efforts of mathematicians for centuries.

Three construction problems in particular held the attention of mathematicians:

- *Doubling a cube*—constructing a cube with a volume twice that of any given cube

- *Squaring a circle*—constructing a square with the same area as any given circle

- *Trisecting an angle*—constructing an angle that measures one-third the size of any given angle

These three problems were attempted by Euclid and his contemporaries but eluded solution for 2000 years. The last problem, trisecting an angle, is the most famous of the three because of the many, many people who have claimed—incorrectly—to have found a valid construction. In the nineteenth century, it was shown that problems of constructing geometric figures using a compass and straightedge alone could be translated into corresponding problems of finding the solution of algebraic equations [Eves 1976, 410]. For some algebraic problems, there is no solution in real numbers. Thus, the corresponding geometric constructions are impossible to realize in the real plane. By this approach, the three famous problems mentioned above have been proved to be impossible constructions. However, you should not leap too quickly to the conclusion that a particular construction is impossible. Some problems, while possible, are simply very difficult! (It should be noted that these three problems have been solved using methods more advanced than classic straightedge and compass constructions. This is a fascinating topic in the history of mathematics.)

GEOMETRIC LANGUAGE REVISITED

Once you have constructed and selected two or more points in GeoGebra, you can use tools to construct a *line*, a *line segment*, or a *ray* through any two of the points. In English and other natural languages, we do not always make a careful distinction between a line and a line segment. What exactly is the difference? Try to state this as precisely as you can. When you construct a straight object in GeoGebra, the order in which the points P and Q are selected is not important for the line PQ, nor is it important for the segment PQ. However, the order of selection makes a critical difference for the two rays $\overrightarrow{PQ}$ and $\overrightarrow{QP}$. Try these constructions in GeoGebra to be sure that you understand how the order affects the result.

Because a line segment has two endpoints, we can find the middle, or *midpoint*, of the line segment. If a line segment is represented by a piece of string or a fold in a sheet of paper, we could find its midpoint by folding the string or paper in half. GeoGebra has a tool that allows you to construct the midpoint of a line segment. In doing Activity 3, how did you construct the midpoint of the segment RS using only the **Circle with Center through Point** and **Line** tools? Can you use Euclid's postulates to help you construct an argument explaining why this construction works?

A line is a simple one-dimensional object. When we find the midpoint of a line segment, we are locating the middle point of the segment, and it is clear what this means. The question of middle point is less clear for two-dimensional figures. For example, does a figure like a circle or a triangle have a midpoint? The circle does, of course, and this is called the *center* of the circle. How would you find the midpoint of a triangle? There are several ways to answer this question, which use different strategies and give different results—as we will see in the next chapter. Consider polygons with more sides, such as quadrilaterals, pentagons, and hexagons. How could you find a middle point for these figures? Can you think of more than one way to find a middle point? Do different strategies give the same or different middle points for these figures? Does convexity play a role in this?

A line that is *tangent* to a circle will be perpendicular to the radius of the circle at the point of tangency. For a point A on the circle, this suggests an easy way to construct a tangent to the circle at the point A. From the center of the circle, you can construct a radius (that is, the segment from the center to the point A); then you can construct a perpendicular to the radius at point A. However, the construction is a little different if the point A is not on the circle. Can you figure out how to do this? (*Hint*: Use an idea from Activity 5 of the previous chapter (see page 7).) We will let you ponder this question for a while.

An *angle*, ∠PQR, is defined by two rays, $\overrightarrow{QP}$ and $\overrightarrow{QR}$ (or two segments, QP and QR) that share a common vertex (in this case, the point Q). GeoGebra will also allow you to designate an angle by selecting three points; to designate ∠PQR you could select the points P, Q, and R in that order. You can also designate this angle by selecting the two rays (or two segments) that form the sides of the angle. You may find that the order in which you select points, rays, or segments can make a difference in the resulting measurement.

GeoGebra provides a tool that will bisect an angle for you. However, how did you construct the bisector of ∠AOB in Activity 2 using only the **Circle with Center through Point** and **Line** tools? The *angle bisector* is the ray—in this case, $\overrightarrow{OX}$ —that divides ∠AOB into two equal angles. So the question arises of how to locate a suitable point X. One way to do this is to use the **Circle with Center through Point** tool to construct a circle centered at O, and to find the points P and Q where this circle intersects the rays $\overrightarrow{OA}$ and $\overrightarrow{OB}$, respectively. The midpoint of the segment PQ (which you can find using your construction from Activity 3) will be a suitable point X, and $\overrightarrow{OX}$ will bisect ∠AOB.

CONDITIONAL STATEMENTS: IMPLICATION

It is very common in mathematics to make statements of the form *IF certain things are assumed to be true, THEN certain other things must also be true*. In Activity 8, you may have said something like the following:

> IF an exterior angle is formed by extending one side of a triangle, THEN the measure of that exterior angle is greater than the measure of either remote interior angle.

This type of statement is called a *conditional statement* or an *implication*. The pattern is expressed as $P \rightarrow Q$ (read as "P implies Q"). In a conditional statement, the if-clause (or P) is the *hypothesis*, the condition that is being assumed to be true. The then-clause (or Q) is the *conclusion*, the result that is being deduced from the assumptions. It is good practice to write your conjectures in this form, so that you can see clearly what is being assumed (the hypothesis) and what is the result (the conclusion).

An implication statement can be true in several different ways. The fundamental idea is that a true hypothesis always should lead to a true conclusion, and never to a false conclusion. Here is the beginning of a truth table for implication:

| | | P implies Q |
P	Q	$P \rightarrow Q$
true	true	true
true	false	false
false	true	?
false	false	?

As the table shows, we want a true hypothesis to produce a true conclusion. There remains the question of what to do when the hypothesis is false.

If the assumptions in the hypothesis are not true, what can the implication tell us? Does it tell us anything at all when the hypothesis is false? In other words, how should we evaluate the truth values of an implication $P \rightarrow Q$ if P is false? To answer this question, it may help to understand the negation of a statement $P \rightarrow Q$.

Consider what it means to say $\neg(P \rightarrow Q)$: If P does not imply Q, then we can have P be a true statement and have Q be a false statement; that is, $\neg(P \rightarrow Q) \equiv (P \wedge \neg Q)$. Let's apply this to a conditional statement for which P is blatantly false:

If parallel lines intersect, then the diagonals of a rectangle bisect each other.

Recall that if the negation of a statement is false, the original statement must be true. The negation of the statement we are considering is

Parallel lines intersect *and* the diagonals of a rectangle do not bisect each other.

Because parallel lines do not intersect, this statement is false, so the original statement must be true. Thus, a statement of the form $P \rightarrow Q$ where P is false and Q is true must be a true implication. Now consider another statement:

If parallel lines intersect, then diagonals of a rectangle do not intersect each other.

Apply similar reasoning to determine the truth value of this implication—and then you should be able to complete the truth table.

Let's look at another example of a conditional statement that is false:

If *PQRS* is a trapezoid, then the diagonals *PR* and *QS* bisect each other.

It is not difficult to sketch an example showing that this statement is false. How can we rewrite this as a true statement? The goal in writing the negation of this implication is to reverse the truth value; in this case, we want to change *false* to *true*. In formal symbols, we want to write $\neg(P \rightarrow Q)$, and we want to express the new statement in a way that is clear and easy to understand. Think about the completed truth table for $P \rightarrow Q$. There is only one line of this table that is false, namely, the line where P is true and Q is false. This will be the only line that makes the negation true. We can write this symbolically:

$$\neg(P \rightarrow Q) \equiv P \wedge \neg Q,$$

which is read as "The negation of P implies Q is equivalent to P and not Q." (Many people expect the negation of $P \rightarrow Q$ to be a new implication, but that is not the case. The pattern $P \wedge \neg Q$ says it best.)

The negation of our false statement about trapezoids is

PQRS is a trapezoid *and* the diagonals *PR* and *QS* do not bisect each other.

This can be restated in more simply in English as "There can be a trapezoid *PQRS* whose diagonals do not bisect each other." This new statement is true.

USING ROBUST CONSTRUCTIONS
TO DEVELOP A PROOF

By now, you have learned to make a geometric construction in GeoGebra. If your construction is *robust,* you will be able to select any of the vertices or edges of the figure and move them around the GeoGebra window without losing the properties that were constructed. If the figure you have constructed is not robust, it might fall apart when you drag some of the vertices or edges.

The order in which you made your construction is important as well. Some steps must occur before others, and there are reasons for the order in which things happen. Paying careful attention to how one step of your construction depends on the previous steps may help you develop a proof.

In the GeoGebra environment, the allowable constructions are based on Euclid's postulates. (See page 26.) Constructions involving points and lines have their justification in Euclid's first two postulates. Constructions involving circles have their justification in Euclid's third postulate. Constructions involving perpendicular lines are justified by Euclid's fourth postulate, while constructions involving parallel lines are justified by Euclid's fifth postulate. Whenever you construct a diagram in a GeoGebra window, you are using Euclid's postulates implicitly.

As you construct a robust GeoGebra diagram to illustrate a geometric theorem, you are developing a compelling argument that the underlying mathematical statement is true. Since your sketch is dynamic, you have, in a sense, shown that the given relationship holds even when some of the points and lines are moved. Even though your sketch might convince you that the relationship you have constructed always holds, it does not serve as a proof. The term *proof* is reserved for a deductive argument. Euclid, for instance, was not satisfied with providing only a construction; he also provided an accompanying deductive argument. We will follow his example. There are many reasons why we would provide a deductive argument even if we are already convinced that a statement is true. A proof can provide insight into why a statement is true. The method used in the proof can lead to discovering new results. A proof can show about how different concepts and results are related. Perhaps most importantly, a proof allows us to communicate our thinking [de Villiers 2003, 5–10].

We can use the insight gained from constructing a diagram to create a formal proof. Let us now turn our attention to how we might do this. You have been using the GeoGebra environment to construct figures. By this time you may have noticed how using GeoGebra really requires you to make deliberate choices about what you are constructing. For example, when you use GeoGebra to construct a line ℓ, GeoGebra starts with two points and constructs ℓ using these points. If you animate one of these points, it is free to wander all over the plane. If you construct a new point Q *on* ℓ and animate it, Q will be constrained to move only along line ℓ. Having to make these deliberate choices about how to construct a GeoGebra diagram helps us to think more carefully about important ideas as we work to develop proofs. Retracing the steps that you take in developing a robust construction can lead to a robust proof.

For example, here is a construction devised by students in one of our classes to construct a line through a given point P perpendicular to a given line ℓ.

- Construct two points, A and B, on the line ℓ.
- Construct a circle centered at A and passing through P.
- Construct a second circle centered at B and passing through P.
- Construct the intersection points of the two circles. One of these is P; call the other Q.
- Construct the line PQ. This line will be perpendicular to ℓ at the point C.

A proof that PQ is perpendicular to ℓ might go as follows, working from the steps of the construction:

> The circle centered at A, and passing through P and Q, tells us that the segments AP and AQ *are* congruent, for these segments are radii of the circle. Similarly, $BP \cong BQ$. With AB congruent to itself, $\triangle BAP \cong \triangle BAQ$ by SSS. Then $\angle BAP \cong \angle BAQ$. From this, we can conclude $\triangle ACP \cong \triangle ACQ$ by SAS. Hence $\angle ACP \cong \angle ACQ$ and, since these angles together make a straight angle, each must be a right angle.

By the way, this construction is flawed. If the point P lies on the line ℓ, it will not work. What goes wrong with the proof in this situation? A stronger construction begins with a circle centered at P that intersects ℓ at two points, A and B, and continues from there. This approach to the construction will work no matter where P is located.

ANGLES AND MEASURING ANGLES

Angles can be classified into three categories: *right angles*, *acute angles*, and *obtuse angles*. We often say that a right angle has a measure of 90°. But this way of measuring angles is arbitrary. (Some historians have speculated that using 360° in a circle comes from early astronomy and the number of days in a year, but this is not known for certain.) There is nothing special about the size of a degree, and we could develop other systems of measuring angles using other kinds of units. For instance, a *radian* is the size of an angle whose arc measured along the circumference of a circle is the same length as the radius of that circle. In other words, if an angle is subtended by a circular arc, the measure of the angle in radians is the length of the arc divided by the radius of the arc; as a ratio of two lengths, the radian is considered a unitless measure. Euclid avoided reference to measure when he defined right angles. A *right angle* was defined to be an angle formed when a straight angle was divided into two congruent angles, and then *acute* and *obtuse* angles were described as angles less than or greater than a right angle. (It was assumed that a straight angle was the largest angle.)

In highway construction, the angle (incline) of a road is measured by its grade, which is stated as a percentage. A road with 10% grade rises 10 meters for every

100 meters of horizontal distance. How would you express this angle in degrees or radians? It is not necessary to measure an angle to determine whether it is a right angle, an acute angle, or an obtuse angle. For example, you can take a sheet of paper and very easily fold a right angle. (Try it!) If two lines form right angles (in this case, the lines are represented by two folds in the paper), we say that the lines are *perpendicular*.

Activity 9 asks you to work with parallel lines and to measure angles formed by a transversal—a line that lies across (transverses) two parallel lines. To measure an angle ∠*PQR* in GeoGebra, use the **Angle** tool. Select the points *P*, *Q*, *R* in that order. Alternatively, you can select the rays, segments, or lines that make up the angle, again being sensitive to the order of selection. An option on the Style bar will allow you to control the range of the measurement, so that angle measurements greater than 180° can be displayed.

When one line intersects another, two pairs of angles are formed. (See Figure 2.4.) Any adjacent pair of angles in this diagram are supplementary (i.e., they add up to two right angles), while the nonadjacent pairs of angles, called *vertical angles*, are congruent.

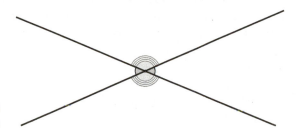

FIGURE 2.4
Two Pairs of Vertical Angles

In Activity 9, you explored the angles created by a transversal of parallel lines. What did you learn (or recall) about parallel lines as you worked on this activity? Some pairs of the angles in the figure you created are called *alternate interior* angles, other pairs are called *alternate exterior* angles, and still others are called *interior* (or *exterior*) *angles on the same side of the transversal*. Some pairs of these angles are congruent—having the same measure—while other pairs are supplementary. What did you observe?

In Activity 10, you were asked to consider the converse of this situation. Given a line ℓ and a line *t* that intersects ℓ, how could you construct a line *m* that is parallel to ℓ? One way of doing this is to measure an angle between ℓ and *t*, and to construct *m* so that the corresponding angle between *t* and *m* has the same measure.

A *parallelogram* is a quadrilateral whose opposite sides are parallel. Use your observations from Activities 9 and 10 to analyze the properties of a parallelogram. For example, based on your observations from these activities, what can you conclude about a pair of opposite angles of a parallelogram?

What are some other characteristics of a parallelogram? There are many things that can be proved from the simple definition of a parallelogram; for instance, the opposite sides of a parallelogram are equal in length. Here is a question you may not have thought about before: Is a parallelogram a cyclic quadrilateral? To decide this, you must use the definition of *cyclic quadrilateral* as well as the definition of *parallelogram*.

CONSTRUCTING PERPENDICULAR AND PARALLEL LINES

GeoGebra has a tool that allows you to construct a line perpendicular to a given line; most of the time, you will be expected to use this tool. But in Activities 3 and 4 you were asked to construct a perpendicular line using only the **Circle with Center through Point** and **Line** tools, and not the full array of tools available. Suppose you want to construct a line through the point P that is perpendicular to the line ℓ. This construction begins, as many compass and straightedge constructions do, by constructing a circle centered at P that intersects ℓ in two points. Then construct two more circles, each circle centered at one of the intersection points and passing through the other intersection point. A line through the intersections of the two circles will pass through P and be perpendicular to the line ℓ. This construction is based on ideas that you used in constructing an equilateral triangle (see Activity 6 of the previous chapter, page 7). How can you use Euclid's postulates to explain why this construction works?

GeoGebra also has a command that allows you to construct a new line through a given point and parallel to a given line. In Activities 9 and 10, you were asked to consider the angles formed when a transversal crosses a pair of parallel lines. If you are given a line ℓ and a point P not on ℓ, you can draw a line t through P that intersects ℓ. Then you can use the observations you made while working on Activities 9 and 10 to construct a line m through P that is parallel to ℓ. Doing these constructions will help you to understand what GeoGebra is doing when you use the **Perpendicular Line** and **Parallel Line** tools.

PROPERTIES OF TRIANGLES

Triangles may be classified as *equilateral* (all three sides are the same length), *isosceles* (at least two sides are the same length), or *scalene* (all three sides have different lengths). A triangle may also be classified as a *right triangle* if it has a right angle. Some right triangles are scalene, and some are isosceles. Could a right triangle be equilateral? Why or why not?

Triangles will be *similar* if corresponding pairs of angles have the same measure. (This is Theorem 2.1.) Corresponding sides of similar triangles have a constant ratio. If two triangles (or any two geometric figures) are congruent, they are also similar. If similar figures are also congruent, the constant ratio will be 1. Congruent figures are identical except for their position.

When we look at a triangle, the angles we usually see are the three interior angles of the triangle. In Activity 8, you were asked to think about the exterior angles of a triangle. Any exterior angle has an obvious relationship to its neighboring interior angle (they are supplementary), but in a triangle, an exterior angle is also related to the other interior angles. As you worked on Activity 8, what observations did you make about the relationship between the exterior angle and the remote interior angles? Here are two possible observations that you might have made:

Observation 1 An exterior angle of a triangle will have a greater measure than either of the remote (or nonadjacent) interior angles.

Observation 2 The measure of an exterior angle of a triangle will be the sum of the measures of the two remote interior angles.

The first observation can be expressed in the form of a conjecture in the following way:

Conjecture 1 If an exterior angle is formed by extending one side of a triangle, then this exterior angle will be larger than the interior angles at each of the other two vertices.

This conjecture is actually a theorem, which means that it has been proved to be true for all triangles. It is called the *Exterior Angle Theorem*. How would you prove this theorem? You will get a chance to do this proof in the exercises.
     The second observation can also be expressed as a conjecture:

Conjecture 2 If an exterior angle is formed by extending one side of a triangle, then the measure of this exterior angle will be the same as the sum of the measures of the two remote interior angles of the same triangle.

Conjecture 2 is a little harder to prove. This may surprise you, for your experience with Activity 3 of the previous chapter (see page 6) and a little algebra seems to prove it quite quickly:

$$\text{exterior angle at } A = 180° - \angle A$$
$$= 180° - (180° - (\angle B + \angle C))$$
$$= \angle B + \angle C.$$

In fact, the sum of the measures of the (interior) angles of a triangle is a more complicated question than you might think, for it depends on Euclid's Fifth Postulate. As you will see when we study hyperbolic geometry in a later chapter, changing Euclid's Fifth Postulate to something else will have an unexpected and powerful impact on the angle sum of a triangle.
     Once we prove the Exterior Angle Theorem, there is another theorem that is very quick to prove. When one theorem follows very easily from another, we often call it a *corollary* to that theorem.

COROLLARY 2.1 **Corollary to the Exterior Angle Theorem** A perpendicular line from a point to a given line is unique. In other words, from a specified point, there is only one line that is perpendicular to a given line.

How would you prove this corollary? One way to begin is to suppose that there are two lines through a point P that are both parallel to the line m. In other words, suppose that on line m there are two points X and Y so that both PX and PY are perpendicular to m. What can you say about $\triangle PXY$? It might be helpful to make a sketch.

Exterior angles are not limited to triangles. Any polygon has both interior angles and exterior angles. Do you think there is an extension of the Exterior Angle Theorem that holds for quadrilaterals? For polygons with even more sides?

You will have an opportunity to prove some properties of triangles in the exercises, and you will study triangles in greater depth in Chapter 3.

EUCLID'S PARALLEL POSTULATE

The whole issue of parallel lines is a very interesting story in the history of mathematics. Euclid and his contemporaries made some fundamental assumptions about the geometry of the plane, which are expressed in Euclid's postulates. *Postulates* (which are also called *axioms*) together with a list of *undefined terms* (which are listed as *definitions* and *common notions* in the *Elements*) are statements to be accepted without proof. They are the beginning of a mathematical theory, and all theorems in that theory are proved—directly or indirectly—from the postulates. In the historical development of geometry, one of Euclid's postulates has generated much controversy—as well as a great deal of study that has led to significant developments in mathematical thinking. This is Euclid's Fifth Postulate, the one related to parallel lines.

Euclid's Fifth Postulate   If a straight line falling on two straight lines makes the sum of the interior angles on the same side less than the sum of two right angles, then the two straight lines, if extended indefinitely, meet on that side on which the angles are less than two right angles.

If this postulate seems deep (or even convoluted) to you, you are not alone. Mathematicians wrestled with this postulate for nearly 2000 years, attempting to simplify it and to prove it. In general, mathematicians prefer to accept as few postulates as possible. For a long time, mathematicians felt that such a complicated statement surely could be proved from the simpler axioms that preceded it. Euclid himself developed as much of his geometry as possible before using this assumption.

One idea that persisted is that parallel lines are everywhere equidistant; that is, if ℓ and m are parallel lines, then the distance from any point on line ℓ to the closest point on line m will be a constant. Working in the sixteenth century, nearly 1900 years after Euclid, Christopher Clavius formulated an axiom that is almost equivalent to Euclid's Parallel Postulate:

Clavius' Axiom   The set of points equidistant from a given line on one side of it forms a straight line [Hartshorne 2000, 299].

Another mathematician, John Playfair, working 150 years after Clavius, formulated a postulate that is equivalent to Euclid's Fifth Postulate in the presence of the first four postulates:

Playfair's Postulate   Given a line ℓ and any point P not on ℓ, there is exactly one line through P that is parallel to ℓ.

Sometimes, Playfair's Postulate has been expressed as "two straight lines that intersect one another cannot both be parallel to the same straight line" [Hartshorne 2000, 300]. Later in this course, we will investigate some non-Euclidean geometries. These are geometric worlds where parallel lines are not equidistant, and where there may be two (or more) lines through a particular point P that are both parallel to a given line ℓ. There are even geometric worlds where parallel lines do not exist! We will leave these matters to later chapters. Hyperbolic geometry, which is one example of a non-Euclidean geometry, will be studied in depth in Chapter 11.

EUCLID'S CONSTRUCTIONS IN THE *ELEMENTS*

One of the reasons that it is worthwhile to study Euclid's *Elements* is that he shows how to carefully argue that certain constructions are possible. He often proves one result, and then uses that result to establish the next one. Here is an example of Euclid's approach. His first proposition is that, given a straightedge and a compass, it is possible to construct an equilateral triangle. He provided both a construction and a deductive argument that the construction worked. Figure 2.3 is repeated here for your convenience, along with a deductive argument that the construction works (Figure 2.5).

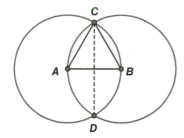

FIGURE 2.5
Constructing an Equilateral
Triangle (Figure 2.3 Repeated)

Construction 1   Equilateral triangles can be constructed with a straightedge and a compass. (This construction is based on Proposition 1 in Euclid's *Elements*.)

Proof   We first use our straightedge to construct a line segment AB. Then we use the compass to construct a circle with center A and passing through B. Next we construct a circle centered at B and passing through A. These circles intersect at a point C. Since both AB and AC are radii of the same circle, they are congruent. Since BA and BC are radii of the same circle, they are congruent.

Since AC and BC are both congruent to AB, they are congruent to each other by the transitive property of congruence. Since all three sides are congruent, $\triangle ABC$ is equilateral by definition of an equilateral triangle.

One of the reasons Euclid chose this as his first result in geometry is that he needed this result to prove his next result, that a compass can be used to copy a shorter line segment onto a larger line segment (Figure 2.6). Here is Euclid's construction and the associated deductive argument.

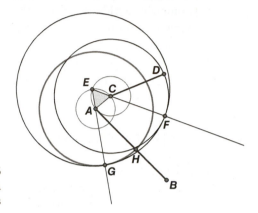

FIGURE 2.6
Copying a Line Segment Using a
Floppy Compass

Construction 2 A line segment can be copied from one location to another with a straightedge and a compass. (This construction is based on Propositions 2 and 3 in the *Elements*.)

Proof We start with line segments AB and CD. (We can assume that AB is the longer segment.) We use Proposition 1 to construct an equilateral triangle, $\triangle ACE$. We use our straightedge to extend the sides EC and EA. Using a compass, we construct a circle centered at C and passing through D. This circle intersects $\overrightarrow{EC}$ at the point F. Since CD and CF are radii of the same circle, they are congruent. We then construct the circle centered at E and passing through F. This circle intersects $\overrightarrow{EC}$ at G. EF and EG, being radii of the same circle, are congruent. Since EC and EA are two sides of an equilateral triangle, they are congruent. Taking these congruent segments away from congruent segments EF and EG leaves us with congruent segments CF and AG.
Finally, construct a circle centered at A and passing through G. This circle intersects AB at H. Since AG and AH are radii of the same circle, they are congruent. We have AH on AB, so that AH is congruent to AG, which is congruent to CF, which is congruent to CD, thus completing this construction.

This result, allowing us to copy a line segment using a compass, is implemented in GeoGebra by the **Circle: Center & Radius** tool.

An interesting sidelight is that the compasses of Euclid's day were "floppy," that is, picking up the compass caused it to collapse so that the radius setting was lost. Many compasses available today are mechanically rigid, so that the radius setting for one circle can be used immediately to create a congruent circle somewhere else. Construction 2 shows that this difference is not important, for a floppy compass can be used to copy a radius used in one location to any other desired location.

After establishing some triangle congruence propositions, the next construction in the *Elements* is of an angle bisector. The construction requires the construction of an equilateral triangle, another reason why Euclid chose the construction of an equilateral triangle as his first proposition. Use the compass to find points on each side of the angle, and then use those points as two of the vertices of an equilateral triangle. A properly constructed equilateral triangle will allow you to construct the angle bisector. The proof that the construction works is based on SSS triangle congruence.

The *Elements* is wonderfully organized, always using established results to develop new results. Once it has been established that an angle can be bisected, Euclid's method for constructing a perpendicular bisector of a segment is to construct an equilateral triangle using the given segment as a side, and then constructing an angle bisector of the angle in the equilateral triangle opposite the given line segment. You will get an opportunity in the exercises to argue that the construction works.

Euclid continues to build upon the results he has already established when he constructs a perpendicular to a line through a point not on the line. He approaches this problem by cleverly creating a line segment on the line whose perpendicular bisector is precisely the perpendicular line we were to construct. This is accomplished by intersecting the given line with a circle centered at the point not on the line.

Having established that angle bisectors, perpendicular bisectors, and perpendicular lines are all constructible with a straightedge and compass, we have confirmed that these tools are allowable tools for any further constructions. It is worth noting that all of these results are based on Euclid's first four postulates. In other words, they are not dependent on Euclid's Fifth Postulate, the parallel line postulate. This will take on added significance in later chapters when we change the parallel postulate.

IDEAS ABOUT BETWEENNESS

In the two millennia since Euclid, mathematicians have wrestled with his five postulates and have come to understand that there are many issues that Euclid took for granted. One of these issues is *order* of points on a line, the notion that given any three collinear points, one of them will be between the other two. This seems pretty obvious, so it is easy to accept this as an axiom. However, it is not stated nor implied by Euclid's five postulates. In the decades around 1900, many alternative sets of axioms were developed for Euclidean geometry by such mathematicians as David Hilbert, George Birkhoff, Oswald Veblen, and Moritz Pasch. Pasch, in particular, developed a careful theory of ordered geometry [Coxeter 1961, 176–182].

Suppose a line ℓ enters ΔABC by crossing the side AB. How can ℓ exit the triangle? There are not many choices: ℓ can intersect a vertex, or it can cross another side. If ℓ does not pass through vertex C, it might intersect BC at a point between B and C. If it does not intersect BC, it must intersect AC at a point between A and C.

Here are two theorems related to order that seem obvious, and that are useful sometimes when you want to show that a line or a ray goes where you expect it to go:

THEOREM 2.4   **Pasch's Theorem**   If A, B, and C are distinct noncollinear points and ℓ is a line that intersects the segment AB, then ℓ also intersects either segment AC or segment BC.

Pasch actually used this statement as one of his axioms, as did Hilbert. We, on the other hand, will make a different assumption, and prove Pasch's statement as a theorem.

Proof   We will assume that any line divides the plane into two separate pieces. In other words, we accept that whenever point A is on one side of the line ℓ and point B is on the other side of ℓ, the segment AB intersects ℓ.
We are given three distinct noncollinear points, A, B, and C, and a line ℓ that intersects the segment AB. Suppose that ℓ does not intersect either BC or AC. Then, the points B and C are on the same side of ℓ. Further, the points A and C are on the same side of ℓ. Therefore, A and B must be on the same side of ℓ, implying that the segment AB does not intersect ℓ. However, our hypothesis is that ℓ does intersect AB. So our assumption that ℓ does not intersect either BC or AC must be incorrect; in other words, ℓ must intersect either AC or BC.

Pasch's Theorem can be used to prove the following useful theorem. This proof will be left to the exercises.

THEOREM 2.5   **Crossbar Theorem**   If ray $\overrightarrow{AD}$ is between rays $\overrightarrow{AC}$ and $\overrightarrow{AB}$, then ray $\overrightarrow{AD}$ intersects the segment BC.

2.3 EXERCISES

Give clear and complete answers to the following problems and questions. Write your explanations clearly using complete sentences. Include diagrams whenever appropriate.

1. What is an axiom (postulate or common notion), and what is its role in a mathematical system?

2. Use Euclid's postulates to prove that your constructions for angle bisector and perpendicular bisector from Activities 2 and 3 are correct. Explain how the proofs of these constructions are linked.

3. Use Euclid's postulates to prove that your constructions for a perpendicular from the point P to a line ℓ from Activity 4 are correct. (Note that these constructions are slightly different depending on whether P lies on ℓ or not.) Explain how these constructions build on the perpendicular bisector construction (Activity 3).

4. Assuming SAS (as an axiom), prove that if a triangle is isosceles then its base angles are congruent.

5. Given $\triangle ABC$ with $\angle A \cong \angle C$.
   a. State the converse of the theorem of Exercise 4.
   b. Here are three possible approaches to proving that $\triangle ABC$ is isosceles. Which of these will give a valid proof and what criterion for congruent triangles would be used in each situation?
      - Let X be the point of side AC so that $BX \perp AC$ and construct the segment BX.
      - Let M be the midpoint of side AC and construct the segment BM.
      - Let D be the point of side AC so that the segment BD bisects $\angle B$ and construct the segment BD.

6. What does it mean for two line segments to be congruent? If two line segments were both on the x-axis, how would you check whether they were congruent? If two line segments were drawn in the xy-plane, how would you check whether they were congruent? What if they were drawn in 3-space? In n-space?

7. A *parallelogram* is a quadrilateral whose opposite sides are parallel. Use your observations from Activities 9 and 10 to analyze the properties of a parallelogram.
   a. Construct a parallelogram using this definition. Explain why your construction is correct.
   b. What can you conclude about a pair of opposite angles of a parallelogram?
   c. Explain why the opposite sides of a parallelogram must be equal in length.
   d. Is a parallelogram a cyclic quadrilateral?
   e. What are some other characteristics of a parallelogram?

8. Explain why vertical angles must be congruent.

9. If several points lie along a common line, they are said to be *collinear*. The corresponding idea for lines is *concurrence*.
   a. Make a sketch showing three collinear points.
   b. Sketch an example of three concurrent lines, and then write a clear, simple definition of what it means for three or more lines to be *concurrent*.

10. Consider the statement, "If parallel lines intersect, then even integers can be written in the form $2k + 1$, where k is an integer." Analyze the truth value of this implication.

11. Complete the truth table that was set up on page 33 to investigate a statement of the form $P \rightarrow Q$.

12. Each of the following statements can be expressed as an implication. Rewrite each statement clearly in an "If ..., then ..." format. If possible, determine whether each statement is *true* or *false*.
    a. If a is not a quadrilateral, then a is not a square.
    b. If T is a right triangle, then T might be an equilateral triangle.
    c. Every right triangle is isosceles.
    d. Every equilateral triangle is isosceles.
    e. Every isosceles triangle is a right triangle.
    f. An octagon has more sides than a dodecagon.
    g. No rhombus is a square.

13. Write the negation of each of the implications from Exercise 12.

14. Use Playfair's Postulate to explain why the interior angles formed by a transversal to a pair of parallel lines must be supplementary.

15. One consequence of Playfair's Postulate is that alternate interior angles on a transversal of two parallel lines must be congruent. Use this result to explain why the sum of the measures of the interior angles of a triangle is two right angles.

16. Prove the Corollary to the Exterior Angle Theorem.

17. What is a parallelogram? What is a minimal set of things you need to show in order to prove that quadrilateral $RSTU$ is a parallelogram? Can you develop more than one strategy for doing this?

18. Is every square a rectangle? Is every rectangle a square? Are some parallelograms rectangles? Draw a Venn diagram that shows the relationships among the various quadrilaterals. Your diagram should make it clear whether you can say "Every X is a Y," "Some Xs are Ys," or "No Xs are Ys."

19. Not all figures in plane geometry are polygons. Find the names of at least three plane figures that are not polygons. Write a definition of each. Make your definitions complete but minimal.

20. We have defined a rectangle as a quadrilateral with four right angles.
    a. Rectangles have many properties that are not mentioned in this definition. List as many of these properties as you can.
    b. Assuming that we are working in the Euclidean plane, would we need to define a rectangle as having four right angles? That is, could we have defined a rectangle as having just three right angles, ... or even just two right angles? What is a minimal definition for a rectangle?

21. Take another look at Activity 6 of the previous chapter (page 7). The context of this activity, a construction involving a point P in the interior of a triangle and the sum of the distances from P to each of the sides of the triangle, led the Italian mathematician Vincenzo Viviani to formulate a theorem.
    a. Formulate a conjecture about the sum of the three perpendicular segments in this situation in which you clearly indicate the hypothesis and the conclusion.
    b. What is *Viviani's Theorem*? Compare your conjecture with a statement of Viviani's Theorem that you find in another geometry textbook or on the Internet.
    c. Does this theorem apply only to equilateral triangles, or can it be extended to other polygons?

22. Take another look at the activity about a quadrilateral and its midpoint quadrilateral. (See Activity 1b, page 4.) In 1731, Pierre Varignon published a theorem about the construction of a midpoint quadrilateral in which he excluded the possibility of the original quadrilateral being self-intersecting.
    a. Formulate your conjecture from Activity 1b, page 4, so that your hypothesis and your conclusion are clearly expressed.

    b. Find a statement of *Varignon's Theorem* in another geometry textbook or on the Internet. Compare your conjecture to Varignon's Theorem.
    c. Does the original quadrilateral have to be convex for this theorem to hold? What if the original quadrilateral is self-intersecting? Explain.

23. Take another look at your investigations in the previous chapter with areas of a quadrilateral and its midpoint quadrilateral. (See Activity 1b, page 4, and Exercise 21, page 19.) Repeat this investigation with a triangle.
    a. What is the ratio of the area of the midpoint triangle to the original triangle? Make a conjecture, and vary the vertices of the triangle. Does your conjecture continue to hold?
    b. Can you explain what is going on? (*Hint*: Look for similar or congruent triangles.)

24. Given $\triangle ABC$. An exterior angle is formed at C by extending side AC. M is the midpoint of side BC. E is the point on $\overrightarrow{AM}$ so that $AM \cong ME$. (See Figure 2.7.) Explain how we can be sure that $\angle BCD > \angle B$. This proves the first part of the Exterior Angle Theorem. How would you prove the other part?

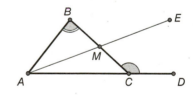

FIGURE 2.7
Figure for Exercise 24

25. Given a scalene triangle $\triangle ABC$.
    a. If $\angle A > \angle B$, would you expect $BC > CA$ or $CA > BC$? Explain your reasoning.
    b. Suppose, on the other hand, that one of the sides is longer than the other, say that $BC > CA$. Would you expect that $\angle A > \angle B$ or that $\angle B > \angle A$? Again, explain your reasoning. (This is the *converse* of the implication in part (a).)

26. In general, is it possible for a parallelogram to be a cyclic quadrilateral? Use a diagram to support your answer.

27. Are the perpendicular bisectors of the sides of a cyclic quadrilateral concurrent? Sketch an example of this in GeoGebra, and make a conjecture. What would you need to know to prove your conjecture?

28. Which of the following statements seem to be "true" and which seem to be "false"? Construct diagrams in GeoGebra to support your answers.
    a. The diagonals of a rectangle bisect each other.
    b. The diagonals of a parallelogram bisect each other.
    c. The diagonals of a cyclic quadrilateral bisect each other.
    d. If the diagonals of a quadrilateral bisect each other, then the quadrilateral is cyclic.
    e. If the diagonals of a quadrilateral bisect each other, then the quadrilateral is a rectangle.
    f. If the diagonals of a quadrilateral bisect each other, then the quadrilateral is a parallelogram.

29. Using GeoGebra, draw an arbitrary triangle. Develop a strategy to construct the center or "midpoint," M, of this triangle. Drag the vertices of the triangle to new positions. Does M continue to be the midpoint of the triangle? Compare your method of constructing the midpoint of a triangle with that of at least one of your classmates. Explain why your method of finding the midpoint of a triangle is (or is not) a robust construction. (*This exercise anticipates concepts that will be discussed in greater depth in the next chapter.*)

30. In this chapter, we have discussed ways of doing each of the following constructions using only a compass and unmarked straightedge (or using only the **Circle with Center through Point** and **Line** tools in GeoGebra). Do each of these constructions, and provide a deductive argument explaining why each construction is correct.
    a. Construct the midpoint M of a line segment AB.
    b. Bisect an angle PQR.

    c. Given a line ℓ and a point P not on ℓ, construct a line through P *perpendicular* to ℓ.
    d. Given a line ℓ and a point P not on ℓ, construct a line through P *parallel* to ℓ.

31. Exterior angles are not limited to triangles. Any polygon has both interior angles and exterior angles. Conduct an exploration using GeoGebra to explore the following questions.
    a. Is there an extension of the Exterior Angle Theorem that holds for quadrilaterals?
    b. For polygons with even more sides?

32. A polygon is called *regular* if all of its sides (and all of its angles) are congruent. A convex polygon is said to be *inscribed in a circle* if each of its vertices lies on the circle.
    a. Find a construction that inscribes a regular hexagon in a circle.
    b. Adapt your construction from part (a) to inscribe an equilateral triangle in a circle.
    c. Find a construction that inscribes a square in a circle.
    d. Adapt your construction from part (c) to inscribe a regular octagon in a circle.

The following problems are more challenging.

33. Draw a circle. (*This exercise anticipates some ideas that will be studied more deeply in Chapter 3.*)
    a. Mark a point P on the circle, and construct a tangent to the circle through P.
    b. Draw a point Q outside the circle, and construct a tangent to the circle from Q. (*Hint*: Use an idea from Activity 5, page 7.)

34. The *midpoint polygon* of a polygon is the polygon formed by the midpoints of the edges, taken in the same order. You have had an opportunity to explore midpoint quadrilaterals (Activity 1, page 4), and midpoint triangles (Exercise 23, page 46). What is the relationship between the area of the midpoint polygon and the area of the original polygon? Suggest (and prove, if possible) generalizations of your observations with midpoint quadrilaterals and midpoint triangles.

35. Here is a construction to inscribe a regular pentagon in a circle. Construct a diameter AB of the circle. At the center C, construct a

perpendicular line and let D be one of its intersections with the circle. Let E be the midpoint of CD. Bisect the angle $\angle AEC$ and let F be the intersection of this bisector with the diameter AB. Construct a line ℓ through F that is perpendicular to AB. The points where ℓ intersects the circle, together with A, begin the pentagon.

   a. Carry out this construction and finish the pentagon.

   b. What would you need to know in order to prove that the construction given here actually creates a regular pentagon?

36. Given an arbitrary angle $\angle RST$. Using only a compass and unmarked straightedge (or using only the **Circle with Center through Point** and **Line** tools in GeoGebra), can you find a way to construct two rays $\overrightarrow{RX}$ and $\overrightarrow{RY}$ that divide the angle $\angle RST$ into three equal parts? How good is your construction? That is, how close do you come to trisecting $\angle RST$?

37. Given a circle, C, with center at O and radius r. Using only a compass and unmarked straightedge (or using only the **Circle with Center through Point** and **Line** tools in GeoGebra), can you find a way to construct a square that has the same area as C? How good is your construction? That is, how close do you come to squaring the circle?

Exercises 38 and 39 are especially for future teachers.

38. In the *Principles and Standards for School Mathematics*, the National Council of Teachers of Mathematics [NCTM 2000, 11] recommends six specific principles for school mathematics that address overarching themes.

   a. Find a copy of the *Principles and Standards*, and study Chapter 2, Principles of School Mathematics (pages 11–27). What are these principles? What do they mean for your future students?

   b. What are specific NCTM recommendations regarding the use of technology in teaching school mathematics?

   c. Find copies of school mathematics texts for the grade levels for which you are seeking teacher certification. How is the NCTM Technology Principle implemented in those textbooks? Cite specific examples.

   d. Write a report in which you present and critique what you learn.

39. Design several classroom activities to introduce a geometric concept using manipulatives or technology that would be appropriate for students in your future classroom. Write a short report explaining how the activities you design reflect both what you have learned in studying this chapter and the recommendations of the NCTM.

Reflect on what you have learned in this chapter.

40. Review the main ideas of this chapter. Describe, in your own words, the concepts you have studied and what you have learned about them. What are the important ideas? How do they fit together? Which concepts were easy for you? Which were hard?

41. Reflect on the learning environment for this course.

   a. Describe aspects of the learning environment that helped you understand the main ideas in this chapter. Which activities did you like? Dislike? Why?

   b. How do you think a deepened understanding about how you learn will impact your own continued approach to learning, and eventually your approach to your professional/personal life in the future?

2.4 CHAPTER OVERVIEW

In these two opening chapters, you have been asked to do a lot of explorations. You have been asked to observe what is going on, to reflect on what you see, and to make conjectures about your observations. This kind of reasoning, which is grounded in your observations and experiences, is called *inductive reasoning*. In mathematics as in the sciences, *exploration leads to conjecture*. Your conjectures may or may not be valid theorems in geometry. As you work with your colleagues in this course, you will be challenged again and again to justify your conjectures. Those conjectures that can be justified—that is, proved—are called *theorems*. If another result follows very quickly from a particular theorem, it is often called a *corollary* to that theorem.

Euclid was a Greek mathematician who lived and worked in Alexandria around 300 BC. In the *Elements*, one of the most influential books in the history of mathematics, Euclid and his colleagues *deduce* principles of what is now known as *Euclidean geometry*. From a small number of definitions, postulates, and common notions, they laid out a theory of mathematics—including geometry, arithmetic, and number theory—in a logically coherent framework. Thus, the *Elements* presents mathematics as a *deductive theory*, a system of reasoning from postulates (or axioms) to theorems (or propositions). This process of deducing conclusions from a few basic assumptions is fundamental to the mathematical way of thinking.

You also have been reminded of a lot of the vocabulary of plane geometry. Much of this geometric language is probably familiar to you, and it has been included here as a review. Some of the geometric terms mentioned in this chapter may be new to you—or may be familiar English words used in a more precise and technical way in geometry.

How do we know the geometric facts that we think we know? What do we need to do to verify or prove our conjectures? Once we have convinced ourselves, how can we convince others that our conjectures are correct? We hope that you are beginning to see the need for some kind of formal or structured way to construct proofs. We will take this up in more depth in Chapters 3 and 4.

We spent a lot of time in this chapter discussing Euclid's postulates and their interpretation in the GeoGebra environment. Each of these postulates can be represented visually, as can the many theorems that can be derived from these postulates. GeoGebra helps us see, literally, what is going on.

Throughout this course, you will be using GeoGebra as a virtual compass and straightedge to *construct* illustrations of many of the ideas that you are studying. We make an important distinction between *drawing* a figure and *constructing* that figure. It is often relatively easy to sketch or draw a picture to represent an idea—and quite a different matter to construct the same figure. Geometric constructions, using only a straightedge and a compass, or using the virtual straightedge and compass in GeoGebra, will challenge you to think more deeply about the underlying geometry of the idea. Often understanding the construction will give insight into why the construction works correctly. In this chapter, you have seen examples of several constructions along with deductive arguments that these constructions are correct.

Although GeoGebra offers tools to do many of the constructions needed for this course, you should be able to do some basic constructions using only the standard tools of compass and straightedge (or equivalently, using the **Circle with Center through Point** and **Line** tools in GeoGebra). Furthermore, you should be able to create deductive arguments that your constructions are correct. The constructions you should master include the following:

- Construct a perpendicular to a line from any point (on or off the line).
- Construct the perpendicular bisector of a given line segment.
- Construct the foot of the perpendicular from a point P to a line ℓ.
- Construct the tangent line to a circle from a point on the circle.
- Construct the tangent line to a circle from a point not on the circle.
- Construct the bisector of a given angle.

Euclid's Fifth Postulate has been the focus of much attention in the history of mathematics. This postulate is a statement about two lines, m and n, with a third line (or *transversal*) t that intersects both m and n. You worked with this situation in Activity 9, page 25.

If m and n are parallel, then eight angles are formed by the intersection of lines m, n, and t. We can label these angles with letters a through h as in Figure 2.8. These eight angles come in two sizes; that is, there are two sets of four congruent angles: a, c, f, and h are in one set and b, d, e, and g are in the other set. Angles a and f are *vertical angles*, formed by a pair of intersecting lines. Vertical angles are congruent to each other. Angles e and d are called *alternate exterior angles,* while angles b and g are called *alternate interior angles*. If lines m and n are parallel, pairs of alternate interior angles will be congruent. The same is true for pairs of alternate exterior angles.

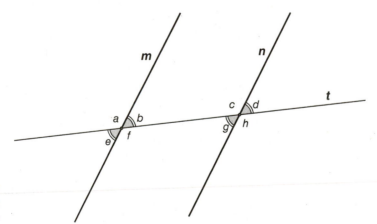

FIGURE 2.8
Parallel Lines m and n Crossed by Transversal t

Angles e and g are *corresponding angles* on the same side of the transversal. Since angles e and b are vertical angles (thus congruent to each other) and angles b and g are alternate interior angles (thus also congruent to each other), we can conclude that angles e and g are congruent. In this way, we can prove that any pair of corresponding angles are congruent.

Angles f and g are *interior angles* on the same side of the transversal. These are the angles referred to in Euclid's Fifth Postulate. If the sum of the measures of these two angles is less than two right angles, Euclid's Fifth Postulate tells us that lines *m* and *n* will intersect on this side of line *t*. Playfair's Postulate is equivalent to Euclid's Fifth Postulate.

Congruent triangles are frequently used as tools in geometric proofs. Modern axiom systems for Euclidean geometry use as an axiom the Side-Angle-Side (SAS) criterion for congruence of triangles. From this assumption, other useful criteria for triangle congruence can be proved: Angle-Side-Angle (ASA), Angle-Angle-Side (AAS), and Side-Side-Side (SSS).

We also discussed the notion of similar polygons, which have congruent angles and for which corresponding sides are in the same ratio. We proved one test for similarity of triangles, the Angle-Angle (AA) criterion. Other criteria for similar triangles are Side-Side-Side and Side-Angle-Side. For SSS and SAS, corresponding sides of the triangle must be in the same ratio. Similar triangles are useful for proofs also. For instance, the proportionality of similar triangles gave us a method to prove the famous Pythagorean Theorem.

Because this overview includes a summary of the chapter, it is appropriate for us to list the named theorems that have been introduced in this chapter. Some of the theorems introduced in this chapter have been left as exercises for you to write out.

Viviani's Theorem   (*Formulation in Exercise 21*)

Varignon's Theorem   (*Formulation in Exercise 22*)

Euclid's Fifth Postulate   If a straight line falling on two straight lines makes the interior angles on the same side less than two right angles, the two straight lines, if produced indefinitely, meet on that side on which the angles are less than two right angles.

Clavius' Axiom   The set of points equidistant from a given line on one side of it forms a straight line.

Playfair's Postulate   Given any line ℓ and any point P not on ℓ, there is exactly one line through P that is parallel to ℓ.

Pasch's Theorem   If A, B, and C are distinct noncollinear points and ℓ is a line that intersects the segment AB, then ℓ also intersects either segment AC or segment BC.

Crossbar Theorem   If ray $\overrightarrow{AD}$ is between rays $\overrightarrow{AC}$ and $\overrightarrow{AB}$, then ray $\overrightarrow{AD}$ intersects the segment BC.

Exterior Angle Theorem   An exterior angle of a triangle will have a greater measure than either of the nonadjacent interior angles.

Corollary to the Exterior Angle Theorem   A perpendicular line from a point to a given line is unique.

Playfair's Postulate (see page 27) is equivalent to Euclid's Fifth Postulate, when the other four axioms are assumed. This means that if we accept Euclid's Fifth Postulate as an axiom, we can prove Playfair's Postulate—and if we accept Playfair's

Postulate as an axiom, we can prove Euclid's Fifth Postulate. Euclid's Fifth Postulate is true if and only if Playfair's Postulate is true. We will accept Euclid's first four postulates as axioms—that is, we will accept them as true and will not attempt to prove them. In a certain sense, these postulates will be part of the implicit hypotheses—the unstated assumptions—in all of our conjectures. For the time being, we will also accept Euclid's Fifth Postulate as an axiom. However, in Chapter 11, when we study *hyperbolic geometry*, we will explore what happens when Euclid's Fifth Postulate is replaced with a different postulate. For more than 2000 years in the history of mathematics, Euclid's Fifth Postulate created a lot of controversy! But we are getting a little ahead of our story.

CHAPTER THREE

Mathematical Arguments and Triangle Geometry

In the first chapter, you were asked to play with a variety of geometric figures—to experiment, to observe, and to make conjectures based on your observations. In doing this, you were engaging in a process of *inductive reasoning*. In the second chapter, you were introduced to proofs through a historical look at Euclid's *Elements*, the book that introduced *deductive reasoning* into mathematics. In these opening chapters, you have been encouraged to express your conjectures in the form of "If . . . , then . . . " statements, or implications. In this chapter, you will combine inductive and deductive reasoning as you explore some interesting properties of triangles.

In Chapter 2, we also looked at the structure of statements you will be using in proofs: simple statements, compound statements, and implications. *Compound statements* are formed from simple statements using the logical operators *and*, *or*, and *not*. An *implication* is formed using the structure "If . . . , then . . . " For an implication $P \rightarrow Q$, there are two closely related implications that we will examine in this chapter: $Q \rightarrow P$ (the *converse*), and $\neg Q \rightarrow \neg P$ (the *contrapositive*).

Chapter 3 also presents an introduction to two important types of proof strategy: direct proof and counterexample. If this is your first course requiring mathematical proofs, you will need to study this chapter carefully—and you will find yourself referring back to this chapter many times throughout this course. If this is your second or third course requiring mathematical proofs, you may find that portions of this chapter are a review for you of ideas you have used in those previous courses.

Do the following activities, paying attention to anything that you observe as you construct each diagram. You will be able to answer many of the questions posed here by typing a sentence or two directly into your GeoGebra diagram. Write your observations clearly in complete sentences. Try to think of explanations for the things you observe, and express your explanations in complete sentences.

Save your work for each activity, as later work sometimes builds on earlier work. Use a button on the Style Bar to hide the axes, for you will not need them in this chapter. You will find it helpful to read ahead into the chapter as you work on these activities.

The first activity does not require the use of the computer.

1. Recall that the *negation* of a statement is a statement whose truth value is the opposite of the original statement. Negate each of these statements. In each case decide which statement is true, the original statement or its negation.
   a. Some students like geometry.
   b. There is a quadrilateral for which the diagonals do not intersect.
   c. All right triangles are isosceles.
   d. No equilateral triangle is a right triangle.

2. a. Which of the following three statements do you think are true? If you think a statement is true, give a reason and construct an example. If you think a statement is false, construct an example to show this.
   - Suppose ABC and DEF are triangles. If $\angle A$ is congruent to $\angle D$, segment AB is congruent to segment DE, and $\angle B$ is congruent to $\angle E$, then these two triangles are congruent.
   - Suppose that ABC and LMN are triangles. If these two triangles are similar, then $\frac{AB}{LM} = \frac{BC}{MN}$.
   - Suppose ABC and XYZ are triangles. If these two triangles have the same perimeter, then they have the same area.

   b. Each statement in part (a) uses an implication, which has the form *If* (P is true) *then* (Q is true). The *converse* of any implication has the form *If* (Q is true) *then* (P is true).

   For each of the implications in part (a), state its converse. If you think the converse is true, give a reason and construct an example. If you think the converse is false, construct an example to show this.

3. Construct a right triangle, ABC. Construct three circles, one on each side of $\triangle ABC$; that is, the diameter of each circle should be one of the sides of $\triangle ABC$. Calculate (or measure) the areas of each of these circles. What do you observe? Vary your right triangle; does your observation still hold? Repeat this experiment with an arbitrary $\triangle DEF$. Make a conjecture. (*Hint*: The Perpendicular Line and Midpoint or Center tools can be helpful in this activity.)

Note that when GeoGebra calculates the area of an object such as a circle, a label appears near the object in the Graphics pane. The number representing that area appears in the Algebra pane and the text of that label appears in another section of the Algebra pane (and is solely a text object). If you want to do computations with these numbers, you can use the names given to the numbers. The Graphics pane can quickly become cluttered with these labels, so you may choose to hide most of them.

You can edit the variable names to help you keep track of what each of the numbers represents. You can edit the objects in either the Graphics pane or the Algebra pane, and corresponding changes are made in the other pane.

4. In a triangle, an *altitude* is a line segment from a vertex perpendicular to the line containing the opposite side. Construct a triangle and the three lines containing the sides of the triangle. (*Suggestion:* Make the segments that form the sides of the triangle solid, and the lines containing these sides dotted. This can be done by selecting the objects and using an option on the Style Bar. To select multiple objects at once, hold down the CTRL key as you make the selections.) Then construct the three altitudes, being sure that each altitude is constructed to the line containing the appropriate side of the triangle. Also construct the line containing each altitude. What do you observe about the lines containing the altitudes? What happens for acute triangles, right triangles, and obtuse triangles?

5. In a triangle, a *median* is a line segment from a vertex to the midpoint of the opposite side. Draw a triangle and construct the three medians. What do you observe about these segments? What happens for acute triangles, right triangles, and obtuse triangles?

6. Draw a triangle and construct the three bisectors of the angles at the vertices. The Angle Bisector tool can be used to do this, but use three points to specify the angle. What do you observe about these rays? What happens for acute triangles, right triangles, and obtuse triangles?

7. Draw a triangle and construct the perpendicular bisectors of the three sides. What do you observe about these lines? What happens for acute triangles, right triangles, and obtuse triangles?

8. Construct a line, ℓ. Then construct a new point Q on ℓ. (Q should not be one of the points you used to construct the line.) Construct a line parallel to ℓ with two points P and R. Use the Polygon tool to draw triangle PQR and then measure its area. Right-clicking on point Q will open a menu of options for this point. Choose Animation On and observe what happens to the area as point Q is animated. (This can also be done on the listing for Q in the Algebra pane. The same steps will stop the animation.) Can you explain what is going on?

9. You are given $\triangle ABC$. QR has been constructed through B so that $QR \parallel AC$. AR intersects the side BC at X, and CQ intersects the side AB at Z. Point P is the intersection of AR and CQ. $\overrightarrow{BP}$ intersects the side AC at Y. Thus, AX, BY, and CZ are concurrent at P. Find all pairs of *similar triangles* in Figure 3.1.

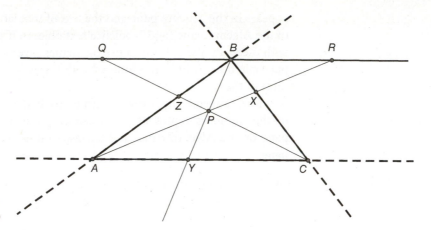

FIGURE 3.1
Figure for Activity 9

10. Draw an arbitrary $\triangle ABC$. Let X be a point on the side BC and Z be a point on the side AB. Lines $\overleftrightarrow{AX}$ and $\overleftrightarrow{CZ}$ intersect at P. Construct line $\overleftrightarrow{BP}$, and find the point Y where $\overleftrightarrow{BP}$ intersects $\overleftrightarrow{AC}$. Calculate the ratios $\frac{AZ}{ZB}$, $\frac{BX}{XC}$, and $\frac{CY}{YA}$, and find their product. What do you observe about this product? Express your observation as a conjecture. Vary some of the points. Does your conjecture still hold?

11. Draw a triangle and construct the altitudes. The three points where the lines containing these altitudes meet the sides of the triangle (or the sides of the triangle extended) are called the *feet* of the altitudes.
    a. Construct the circle through the feet of the three altitudes. (*Hint*: Once the three feet have been located, use the **Circle through 3 Points** tool.)
    b. What other interesting points does this circle contain?

3.2 DISCUSSION

DEDUCTIVE REASONING

As you have worked on the activities that open each chapter, you have frequently been asked to write conjectures in the form of if-then statements about your observations. Each of these conjectures is an *implication*, or conditional statement. Deductive reasoning builds a chain of implications that starts with a set of assumptions—the *hypotheses*—and leads to a final *conclusion*. In deductive reasoning, one statement leads to the next statement, which leads to another statement, and so on until the conclusion is reached. As long as each implication in the chain is logically valid, the assumptions at the beginning inevitably lead to the conclusion at the end. The process of deductive reasoning demonstrates that if certain statements are accepted as true, then other statements can be shown to follow logically from those statements.

The preceding paragraph suggests several important questions. What sort of statements can be used in deductive reasoning? How are statements combined to form implications? What does it mean for an implication to be logically valid? These questions will be addressed below.

A mathematical argument, or any instance of deductive reasoning, is built up from statements, which are declarative sentences that may be either true or false. Chapter 1 introduced the mathematical notion of statement and discussed some basic ways to form statements. Now let us take another look at the contrast between *closed* and *open* statements. A *closed statement* is a sentence that is either true or false, sometimes called a *proposition*. A statement that has a variable is called an *open statement*, sometimes called a *predicate*. Once the variable is specified, an open statement becomes a closed statement and its truth value can be determined. Here are some examples of statements.

- *All triangles are equilateral.* We know from experience that some triangles are equilateral and some are not. This is a closed statement, and its truth value is false.

- *$\triangle ABC$ is equilateral.* This is an open statement. In order to decide whether the statement is true or false, we need to know which triangle is being discussed. Once we know which triangle, we will be able to decide the truth value of this statement. Until we know something about $\triangle ABC$, we treat "$\triangle ABC$" as a variable. Once this variable is specified, the truth value of the statement can be determined.

- *This figure has four vertices.* This is another example of an open statement. In order to determine the truth value of the statement, we need to know which figure is being pointed out. So *figure* is a variable in this statement.

- *Some rectangles have five sides.* We know that *all* rectangles have four sides, so this statement is false.

- *Pentagons have four sides.* A pentagon is a 5-gon, so it has five sides. Since it has five sides, it certainly has four! This makes the statement true. However, the statement "Pentagons have *only* four sides" is false.

If a sentence cannot take on a truth value—that is, if it cannot be evaluated as true or false—then it is a *non-statement*. Some examples of non-statements are:

- *Construct a right angle.* This is a command, an imperative sentence. It is not a declarative sentence, so it is not a statement.

- *Is the triangle isosceles?* This is a question, an interrogative sentence. It is not a declarative sentence, so it cannot be a statement.

- *This sentence is false.* Think about this for a minute. Is it true? What would that mean? ... Is it false? What would that mean? ... What is going on here? (This paradoxical sentence played an important role in the history of mathematical logic. If you are curious, you can consult almost any book on mathematical logic.)

Notice that for non-statements, it does not make sense to ask if the sentence is true or false. The sentence "*PQRS* is a parallelogram" can be evaluated as true or false once the particular quadrilateral *PQRS* is specified, and thus it is a statement. It does not make sense to ask if the command to "Construct a right angle" is true or false. A simple check of whether a sentence is a statement is to ask yourself if it makes sense to talk about the truth value of the sentence.

UNIVERSAL AND EXISTENTIAL QUANTIFIERS

Let us examine more closely the notion of an open statement. An open statement has a variable, or perhaps more than one variable. In order to decide the truth value of an open sentence, we need some further information about the variables; that is, we need to close the statement. There are two ways to close an open statement: *substitution* and *quantification*.

Substitution means replacing the variable or variables by specific values. We have already seen several examples where an open statement can be closed by specifying a particular object that is to be substituted for the variable. Here are a couple more examples of open statements:

- The area of the circle C is 25π. (The circle C is a variable. By substituting a particular circle, we can decide whether this statement is true.)
- $x^2 + 5 = 9$. (This algebraic statement is open. By substituting a numerical value for the variable, x, we close the statement and can determine its truth value. Some values for x will make the statement true, while other values for x will make the statement false. Either way, substituting a value for x closes the statement.)

Another way to close an open statement is quantification. When we quantify a variable from an open statement, we tell what values are candidates for the variable and how strongly the statement applies to the set of those values. So a quantified statement is really talking about a set of values for a variable, not about any one value. Consider, for example, the quantified statement *All squares are rectangles*. In this statement, we are talking about an entire set, the set of squares. Every member of that set is supposed to have the property of being a rectangle—that is, every square is supposed to have four sides and four right angles.

Let us be a little more formal about this. Let S denote the set of all squares, and x can represent a member of that set. Let $P(x)$ mean that the variable x has the desired property of being a rectangle. By itself, $P(x)$ is an open statement called the *predicate*, and x is its variable. The predicate can be used to refer to any item from this set S. Our statement that all squares are rectangles can then be represented by the symbols $(\forall x \in S)\ P(x)$, which is read as "For all x in the set S, P of x." For this statement to be true, every member of the set S must have the property P—that is, every member of the set of squares must have the property of being a rectangle.

In a mathematical sense, an open statement can be viewed as a function that takes in values for the variable and returns a truth value for the statement. That is, if $P(x)$ is an open statement (a predicate), we must supply input values for x in order to determine the truth value—the output—of the predicate statement. For our predicate, $P(x) = x$ *is a rectangle*, the set of possible input values for this function is the set S of squares and the possible outputs are the values *true, false*.

The symbol $\forall$ is called the *universal quantifier*. (It is an upside-down A to help you think of *All*.) It says that all members of the universe—in this case, the universe of squares—must have the specified property. To prove a universally quantified statement, you must show that every possible member of the universe has the property stated by the predicate.

We also can interpret a universally quantified statement as an implication. The statement $(\forall x \in S)\ P(x)$ can be read as "If x is an element of the set S, then x must have the property P." For our example, we can rephrase "For all x in the set of squares, x is a rectangle" as the implication "If x is a square, then x is a rectangle."

Here is another quantified statement: "Some rectangles are not squares." This can be expressed symbolically as $(\exists x \in R)\ \neg P(x)$, which is read as "There is an x in the set R which is not P of x." This uses a different quantifier, a different universe, and a different predicate. Let's consider these in reverse order. The predicate in this situation, $P(x)$, is *x is a square*. The universe is the set, R, of rectangles. The quantifier is the *existential quantifier*. (The existential quantifier symbol is a backward E to help you think of *Exists*.) For the statement $(\exists x \in R)\ \neg P(x)$ to be true, there must be at least one rectangle that is not a square. Existential statements can be easy to prove; it is enough to display one object that has the desired property.

NEGATING A QUANTIFIED STATEMENT

By inductive reasoning, you have formed conjectures based on your observations. The next goal for a conjecture is to find a proof of that conjecture, using deductive reasoning. It may happen, however, that your conjecture is incorrect. In this situation, you will need to prove that the conjecture is false, that is, to prove that the negation of the conjecture is true. So it is important to understand clearly how to negate a particular statement.

We have already seen how to state a negation for conditional statements. Here is a reminder:

$$\neg(P \rightarrow Q) \equiv P \wedge \neg Q$$

For example, the negation of "If the quadrilateral $ABCD$ is a parallelogram, then $ABCD$ is cyclic" is the statement "The quadrilateral $ABCD$ is a parallelogram and $ABCD$ is not cyclic." (Which statement is true?)

Here are the negation patterns for quantified statements:

- *To negate a universally quantified statement:* $\neg(\forall x)\ P(x)$ means the same thing as $(\exists x)\ \neg P(x)$. For example, the negation of the statement "All right triangles are isosceles" is "There is (at least) one right triangle that is not isosceles."

- *To negate an existentially quantified statement:* $\neg(\exists x)\ P(x)$ means the same thing as $(\forall x)\ \neg P(x)$. For example, the negation of the statement "There is a quadrilateral for which the diagonals do not intersect" is "Every quadrilateral has diagonals that intersect."

(In each of these examples, which statement is true: the original or its negation?)

Sometimes, the quantification of a particular statement may not be obvious or explicit. In order to negate a statement, we need to think carefully about what is intended. For example, consider the statement "Students like geometry." Does it mean that "*All* students like geometry"? In this case, the statement is universally quantified, and its negation states that "There is at least one student who doesn't like geometry." On the other hand, if "Students like geometry" is taken to mean that "*Some* students like geometry," then it is existentially quantified, and its negation is "All students don't like geometry" (which can be more simply expressed in English as "No students like geometry").

Notice that the negation of *All* is not *None*. This is a common mistake. For instance, the statement "All triangles are equilateral" is clearly false. However, the statement "No triangles are equilateral" is also false. Try to write the negations of these two statements. Your negations of these statements will be true, of course, and they will state different things.

Statements that use key words such as *all, any,* or *every*—and statements that express an idea about *all, any,* or *every* without using these key words—are universally quantified. You may have noticed in the above examples that the negation of a universal statement may be expressed using words like *not all* or *some do not.* Statements that use key words such as *there exists* or *some*—and statements that express the same idea without using these key words—are existentially quantified.

DIRECT PROOF AND DISPROOF BY COUNTEREXAMPLE

You have been thinking about a particular geometric idea—perhaps a conjecture you're trying to prove. Having experimented with a GeoGebra diagram, you think you understand the construction. Maybe you've even had one of those "*Aha!*" moments of insight, and you feel ready to develop a proof. How do you get started?

Actually, you've already taken the first step—perhaps the most important step. You have a sense that you understand what is going on. Now you feel ready to try to write out a proof, which is a certain kind of explanation of what is going on. The steps you've taken to develop the GeoGebra diagram can be a guide to writing your proof; try to explain in a clear, step-by-step way how your diagram was constructed and why you did each step. The task is to state your steps so that others can follow your reasoning. Your argument must flow from the geometric ideas with justifications for what you claim you can do at each step. Diagrams and tables may be included to help communicate your ideas, but your proof needs to be carried forward in the logical progression of ideas.

Start by being clear about your assumptions. For the present, we are assuming Euclid's postulates (or axioms). The allowable constructions in a GeoGebra worksheet are based on these postulates. Thus, Euclid's postulates are implicit assumptions for all of your conjectures.

Clearly state the conjecture or theorem you are proposing to prove. What are the "givens," that is, what is the *hypothesis* of your conjecture? What things result from the givens, that is, what is the *conclusion* of your conjecture? In general, a *conjecture* or a *theorem* is a statement of the form $P \rightarrow Q$. Express the conjecture or theorem you are trying to prove in the form

If ... [hypothesis] ... **then** ... [conclusion] ....

If you have been able to construct a robust GeoGebra diagram, the steps in your proof might follow in the same order as the steps in your construction. If your construction is robust, it will not fall apart as individual objects are dragged. By reflecting on the steps you took to construct the diagram, you may be able to develop the steps that are needed in the proof. If your proof is robust, it will stand up to the scrutiny of your colleagues. Once you have developed a proof, it is a good idea to talk it through with someone else. Let your colleagues question your justification of each step. A sound proof—like a robust construction—will not fall apart under such questioning.

Constructing a Direct Proof

Just as most of the steps in any construction must be done in a certain order, most of the steps in a proof follow in a certain order from earlier steps. We start with the objects and assumptions given in the hypothesis, and we work step by step toward the conclusion. In a *direct proof*, we work logically forward, one step at a time, toward the desired conclusion. This mimics the development of a GeoGebra construction—starting with a line, a point, a circle, whatever, and building step by step toward the conclusion.

The rule of logic that allows us to move a proof forward in a direct way is the *syllogism*. Here is a formal statement of this rule:

Syllogism If $P \to Q$, $Q \to R$, and $R \to S$ are statements in a proof, then we can conclude $P \to S$.

A direct proof consists of a chain of implications leading directly from the hypothesis to the conclusion. One step implies the next step, and that step implies one further step, and on and on until the conclusion is reached. As long as each implication step is valid, the rule of syllogism says that the proof will be valid.

As an example of a direct proof, let us give a second proof of a famous theorem.

THEOREM 3.1 **The Pythagorean Theorem** Suppose a, b, and c are the lengths of the sides of $\triangle ABC$. If $\angle C$ is a right angle, then $a^2 + b^2 = c^2$.

Proof Consider $\triangle ABC$, where a is the side opposite vertex A, b is opposite B, and c is opposite C. Construct a segment of length $a + b$ and construct a square with $a + b$ as its side. In each corner of this square, construct a congruent copy of $\triangle ABC$. See Figure 3.2.

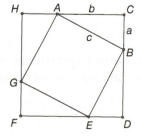

FIGURE 3.2
Another Proof of the
Pythagorean Theorem

Since $AB \cong BE \cong EG \cong GA$, the quadrilateral $ABEG$ is a rhombus. Since $\angle ABC$ and $\angle DBE$ are complementary, $\angle ABE$ is a right angle. Similarly, the angles BEG, EGA, and GAB are all right angles. Thus, $ABEG$ is a square, with side length c. Now calculate the area of the large square in two ways. Because the four triangles are congruent, each has the same area.

$$\text{Area}(HCDF) = \text{Area}(ABEG) + 4 \cdot \text{Area}(\triangle ABC)$$

$$(a + b)^2 = c^2 + 4 \cdot \frac{1}{2} \cdot a \cdot b$$

$$a^2 + 2ab + b^2 = c^2 + 2ab$$

and therefore

$$a^2 + b^2 = c^2.$$

Notice the structure of this proof. Each step leads to the next step, and eventually these steps lead to the conclusion. This is the pattern of a direct proof.

Hundreds of proofs are known for the Pythagorean Theorem, including proofs by Leonardo da Vinci and by James Garfield (before he became President). We encourage you to investigate further. Perhaps you can create a proof of your own!

Using a Counterexample in a Proof

Not every conjecture is a theorem. By this time, you have probably made some conjectures that you have found to be incorrect. In fact, not every statement you are asked to "prove" in the exercises is a legitimate theorem. You must learn to be critical of any statement you are trying to prove. Sometimes as you think about a statement or develop a GeoGebra diagram to illustrate a statement, you will find an example for which all the requirements in the hypothesis hold, but the conclusion does not. Such an example is called a *counterexample*. A counterexample can serve as a *disproof* of a conjecture, that is, a proof that the conjecture is false.

Consider, for example, the conjecture "All right triangles are isosceles." It is not hard to produce an example of a right triangle that is not isosceles, thus showing that this conjecture is not correct.

Counterexamples play an important role in mathematics. A counterexample shows that something is wrong with the statement of the conjecture. Perhaps an additional hypothesis is needed. Perhaps the conclusion should be altered. Understanding why a counterexample refutes the conjecture can suggest ways to improve that conjecture.

STEP-BY-STEP PROOFS

Let us see how we can use the GeoGebra environment to help us construct robust proofs. We will start with carefully constructed step-by-step proofs, which give us a clear way to begin writing correct proofs. As you grow in your confidence in writing mathematical proofs, you may gradually shift from writing step-by-step proofs to writing your proofs in a flowing paragraph form. In a step-by-step proof, each line of the proof presents one new idea or concept, which together with previous steps produces a new result [Maher 1994].

Write out each line of your proof as a complete sentence, clearly justifying the step. In developing a geometric argument, you may use the following types of justifications for each step of the proof:

- Your justification may be based on the conditions given when the problem is posed: "We are given . . .", or "By hypothesis . . .".
- The justification may be based on the definitions, postulates, and axioms of the geometric system we are using: "By definition . . .", "By postulate . . .", or "By axiom . . .".
- The constructions you can do with GeoGebra are implicitly linked to axioms or postulates of geometry. You can make this link explicit by saying "This construction is allowed by . . .".
- Any previously proved theorem can be used as a justification in a proof: "By theorem . . .". We don't expect you to memorize the theorems, but it can be helpful to refer to the theorem by its name or number (if it has one).
- As you develop a proof, one step of your proof may depend directly on a previous step in the argument. The justification can be given simply as "By step . . .".
- In the *Elements*, Euclid listed some "common notions" as allowable justifications in a proof. These common notions include properties of equality and congruence, arithmetic and algebraic computations, and rules of logic. In giving your justification, you can name the property or rule you are using.

Many of the diagrams you have been constructing with GeoGebra—if they are robust diagrams—can be viewed as visual demonstrations of geometric theorems. Consider, for example, the figure you constructed for Activity 8. Recall that you constructed a triangle ΔPQR with the point Q on a line ℓ, which was parallel to the line containing the points P and R. The base of ΔPQR was the fixed line segment PR, and the altitude was the perpendicular distance between the parallel lines ℓ and $\overleftrightarrow{PR}$. If your diagram was a robust construction, the distance between the parallel lines did not change as Q moved along the line ℓ. Your diagram demonstrated very clearly that the area of triangle ΔPQR remained constant no matter how the shape of the triangle changed.

Let's use a similar diagram to prove that the interior angles of a triangle add up to a straight angle. We will develop this proof in a step-by-step format.

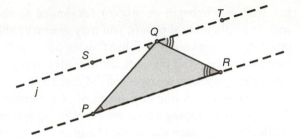

FIGURE 3.3
Angle Sum of a Triangle

THEOREM 3.2 The interior angles of a triangle add up to a straight angle.

Proof Refer to Figure 3.3 as you read this proof.

1. We are given an arbitrary triangle. Let's call it $\triangle PQR$. We are interested in the sum of the angles of $\triangle PQR$. That is, we are interested in the sum

$$m(\angle RPQ) + m(\angle PQR) + m(\angle QRP).$$

2. Construct a line through Q parallel to the side PR, using Playfair's Postulate, which is equivalent to Euclid's Fifth Postulate. Call this line j.

3. Since lines $\overleftrightarrow{PQ}$ and $\overleftrightarrow{RQ}$ are transversals to parallel lines j and $\overleftrightarrow{PR}$, we know that pairs of alternate interior angles are congruent. This is a consequence of Euclid's Fifth Postulate. Construct two additional points, S and T, on line j so that

$$\angle RPQ \cong \angle SQP, \quad \text{and} \quad \angle QRP \cong \angle TQR.$$

4. Substituting equal quantities for equal quantities in the expression given in step 1, we get

$$m(\angle SQP) + m(\angle PQR) + m(\angle TQR).$$

5. Since j is a straight line, we know that

$$m(\angle SQP) + m(\angle PQR) + m(\angle TQR) = \text{straight angle}.$$

6. Thus, again by substituting equal quantities, we can write

$$m(\angle RPQ) + m(\angle PQR) + m(\angle QRP) = \text{straight angle}.$$

So we have proven that *the interior angles of a triangle add up to a straight angle.*

Notice that we have used Euclid's Fifth Postulate (in steps 2 and 3) to prove this theorem. In a non-Euclidean world, it is *not* the case that there is *exactly one* line through P parallel to line j. There may be more than one line, or there may not be any line at all through P that is parallel to j. Changing Euclid's Fifth Postulate would change this proof drastically—and might even change the theorem. We will investigate this situation in greater depth in Chapter 11, Hyperbolic Geometry.

CONGRUENCE CRITERIA FOR TRIANGLES

In Activity 1 of the previous chapter (see page 23), you were asked to give informal explanations for the various combinations of criteria (SAS, AAS, and so on) that guarantee the congruence of two triangles. Now we would like to make these criteria more formal. We will accept one of these combinations as an axiom and develop proofs (or disproofs) of the other combinations.

Congruence Axiom for Triangles (SAS)   If two sides and the included angle of one triangle are congruent, respectively, to two sides and the included angle of another triangle, then the two triangles are congruent.

This is the side-angle-side (SAS) criterion for congruence of triangles. Following the lead of the twentieth-century mathematician David Hilbert, we accept this axiom without proof. Building on this axiom, we will now prove the angle-side-angle (ASA) criterion for triangle congruence.

THEOREM 3.3   **ASA Criterion for Triangle Congruence**   If two angles and the included side of one triangle are congruent, respectively, to two angles and the included side of another triangle, then the two triangles are congruent.

Proof   We are given triangles $\triangle ABC$ and $\triangle DEF$ with $\angle A \cong \angle D$, $AC \cong DF$, and $\angle C \cong \angle F$. (See Figure 3.4.) We want to prove that $\triangle ABC \cong \triangle DEF$. Here is an outline of the proof. Can you justify each step?

If $AB \cong DE$, these triangles would be congruent. (*Why?*) So assume that AB is not congruent to DE. There is a point X on ray $\overrightarrow{DE}$ so that $AB \cong DX$. (*Why?*) By our assumption, the point X is different from the point E. We know that $\triangle ABC \cong \triangle DXF$. (*Why?*) This implies that $\angle C \cong \angle XFD$. But this is impossible since $\angle C \cong \angle EFD$. (*Why?*) So X must be the same point as E; that is, $AB \cong DX = DE$. (Note that we say $DX = DE$ instead of $DX \cong DE$ to emphasize that DX and DE are the same segment.)

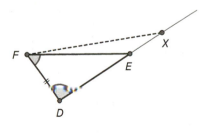
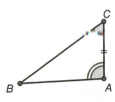

FIGURE 3.4
ASA Criterion for Triangle
Congruence

Consequently, given a pair of triangles with two angles and the included side of one congruent, respectively, to two sides and the included angle of the other, we can establish that another pair of sides must be congruent, making the triangles congruent by SAS. Thus, ASA is a valid criterion for triangle congruence.

Notice the strategy we used in this proof: We needed to say that $AB \cong DE$, but we didn't really know that fact at the beginning of the proof. So we said, "Suppose that $AB \not\cong DE$ . . . ," and we used a point X on $\overrightarrow{DE}$ for which we could say $AB \cong DX$. And then the proof goes on to show that the point X must be the same point as E. This approach, assuming the opposite of what we want and showing that this cannot happen, can be a useful proof-writing strategy, and we will discuss it further in the next chapter.

You will be asked to prove the SSS and AAS criteria for triangle congruence in the exercises. It is interesting to try to argue that SSA is sufficient for triangle congruence. Can you find the point at which the argument breaks down? There are special situations in which SSA is sufficient to guarantee triangle congruence, though it does not work in general. For example, if the triangle is a right triangle, it is sufficient to show that the hypotenuse and one leg of one triangle are congruent to the hypotenuse and one leg of the other triangle. This is the RHL (right triangle-hypotenuse-leg) criterion for triangle congruence. Try making a sketch using RHL to give you insight into why it works.

These congruence criteria play an important role in proving or explaining why the results you found in the activities hold. In doing Activity 6, you probably observed that the three angle bisectors of a triangle are concurrent. Anticipating our proof of this conjecture, we call it a theorem. Let's develop an outline of the proof of this theorem. We will use again the step-by-step format for presenting a proof. In the process, we might identify properties of angle bisectors that are useful beyond this one result.

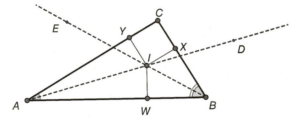

FIGURE 3.5
Angle Bisectors of a Triangle are
Concurrent

THEOREM 3.4   The three angle bisectors of a triangle are concurrent. (See Figure 3.5.)

Proof   (*In the exercises, you will be asked to complete this proof by providing a justification for each step of this proof.*)

1. We are given triangle ABC.

2. Construct $\overrightarrow{AD}$ so that it bisects $\angle A$, and $\overrightarrow{BE}$ so that it bisects $\angle B$.

3. $\overrightarrow{AD}$ and $\overrightarrow{BE}$ intersect at the point I interior to $\triangle ABC$. (Can you come up with an argument for why this has to be the case? This is a subtle argument that has to do with ideas of "betweenness.")
   We must show that ray $\overrightarrow{CI}$ bisects $\angle C$.

4. Construct perpendiculars from the point I to each side of $\triangle ABC$. Let W, X, and Y be the feet of the perpendiculars from I to sides AB, BC, and AC, respectively. Thus, we have

$$IW \perp AB, \quad IX \perp BC, \text{ and } \quad IY \perp AC.$$

5. $\triangle AIY$ and $\triangle AIW$ are congruent.

6. $IY \cong IW$.

7. $\triangle BIW$ and $\triangle BIX$ are congruent.

8. $IW \cong IX$.

9. $IY \cong IX$.

10. $\triangle CIY$ and $\triangle CIX$ are congruent. (*Be careful! The reason for this step is not the same as the reason given for steps 5 and 7.*)

11. $\angle YCI \cong \angle XCI$. In other words, ray $\overrightarrow{CI}$ bisects $\angle C$.
    So—once you have provided the justification for each step of this proof—we have proved that *the three angle bisectors of a triangle are concurrent.*

In this proof, notice that the three perpendicular segments IW, IX, and IY are congruent. This tells us that the point I is the same distance from each side of the triangle. Thus, we can construct a circle centered at I with IW as a radius. This is the *incircle*, the circle that is tangent to all three sides of the triangle.

If you look carefully at the proof of Theorem 3.4, you will see the key components of the proofs of two related results.

THEOREM 3.5 Any point on the angle bisector of an angle is an equal distance from the two sides of the angle.

The converse of this statement is also a theorem:

THEOREM 3.6 Any point that is equidistant from the two sides of an angle lies on the angle bisector of the angle.

This illustrates what we mentioned previously about the role of proofs: A proof may lead you to new results. You will be given an opportunity to prove these two theorems in the exercises.

THE CONVERSE AND THE CONTRAPOSITIVE

When you worked on Activity 6 on page 7, in the first chapter, you were working with the ideas that led to Viviani's Theorem. If you expressed your conjecture for that activity in the form of a conditional statement, you might have written something like the following statement.

THEOREM 3.7 **Viviani's Theorem** If P is a point interior to an equilateral triangle, then the sum of the lengths of the perpendiculars from the point P to each side of the triangle is equal to the altitude of the triangle [Wells 1991, 267].

Suppose that the hypothesis of Viviani's Theorem is false. Perhaps P is exterior to the triangle, or perhaps the triangle is not equilateral. It still might happen that the sum of the lengths of the three perpendiculars equals the length of an altitude. You can use GeoGebra to try an example of a non-equilateral triangle if you wish; see if you can find a point where the sum equals the length of one of the altitudes and another point where it does not. The theorem is valid when its hypothesis is false, but in this case the theorem does not provide any information about the situation.

The *converse* of an implication $P \rightarrow Q$ is the statement $Q \rightarrow P$. Notice that the converse of a statement interchanges the hypothesis and the conclusion. Thus, the converse is the new statement *If Q, then P.*

Since the implication and its converse use the same components, it is easy to confuse them. However, these two patterns do not mean the same thing. You should compare truth tables to see that the statement $P \rightarrow Q$ does not mean the same thing as its converse. The converse of Viviani's Theorem, for instance, is false.

Converse of Viviani's Theorem If the sum of the lengths of the perpendiculars from the point P to the sides of a triangle is equal to the altitude of the triangle, then the triangle is equilateral and P is an interior point of that triangle.

It is not difficult to create a counterexample to this converse.

Activity 2 dealt specifically with the notion of converse. Two of the implications in this activity are true, but only one of the converses is true. Consider the second statement: If the two triangles ABC and LMN are similar, then $\frac{AB}{LM} = \frac{BC}{MN}$. This implication is true, because proportionality of corresponding sides is one of the essential properties of similar figures. The converse means something completely different: If $\frac{AB}{LM} = \frac{BC}{MN}$, then the two triangles ABC and LMN are similar. The hypothesis of this converse is not enough to ensure that the triangles are similar; for instance, $\triangle ABC$ could have $AB = 1$ and $BC = 2$, while $\triangle LMN$ could have $LM = 3$ and $MN = 6$. These values make the two pairs of corresponding sides proportional $\left(\frac{1}{3} = \frac{2}{6} \right)$, but this does not mean that the triangles are similar. The third side CA of $\triangle ABC$ could be any value between 1 and 3, while LN could be any value between 3 and 9. Without knowing the third sides—or knowing the angles between the two given sides of each triangle—the conclusion of the converse is very likely to be false. So not only does the converse of an implication have a different meaning, there is no guarantee that the converse is even true!

There is another variation of a conditional statement that can be very useful. This is the *contrapositive*. The contrapositive of $P \rightarrow Q$ is the statement $\neg Q \rightarrow \neg P$. The contrapositive of a statement means the same thing as the original statement. Again it is a valuable exercise to compare their truth tables. The contrapositive will be a valuable tool for creating indirect proofs, which will be discussed in the next chapter.

CONCURRENCE PROPERTIES FOR TRIANGLES

In each of Activities 4–7 in this chapter, the same sort of thing should have happened. In each activity, three lines were created that had a certain relationship with a triangle, and the three lines intersected at a single point. These lines are said to be *concurrent* at this point. There is nothing particularly special about two lines that intersect. It is much more remarkable, however, for three lines to share a common intersection point.

The analogous situation for points is *collinearity*. Two distinct points are, of course, collinear; this is Euclid's first postulate. It is more significant when three or more points are collinear. We will see an interesting example of this later in this chapter.

An *altitude* of $\triangle ABC$ is a line segment that is constructed from a vertex and is perpendicular to the line containing the opposite side of the triangle. Since a triangle has three vertices, it has three altitudes. The altitudes of $\triangle ABC$ are each perpendicular to one of the sides of the triangle, so they cannot be parallel to each other and consequently must intersect. As you worked on Activity 4, you might have made a conjecture something like: *If AX, BY, and CZ are altitudes of $\triangle ABC$, then AX, BY, and CZ are concurrent.* This works all right if $\triangle ABC$ is acute, but what happens to this point of concurrence if the triangle is obtuse? For obtuse triangles, the altitudes do not intersect because at least one of the altitudes lies outside the triangle and at least one lies inside the triangle. However, the *lines containing the altitudes* are concurrent. This gives rise to the following conjecture:

THEOREM 3.8   The lines containing the three altitudes of a triangle are concurrent. This point, called the *orthocenter* of the triangle, is often denoted by H.

In working on Activity 4, you were asked to observe what happens to the orthocenter of $\triangle ABC$ as you varied the triangle. This tested how robust your construction is, for an altitude can be exterior to the triangle. For your diagram to be robust, you should have constructed a line from each vertex that is perpendicular to the line containing the other two vertices. Each of these lines will contain an altitude. If you then look at the intersection of the lines containing the altitudes, you will see that sometimes the orthocenter is interior to the triangle, and sometimes it is exterior to the triangle. What conjecture can you make about when (under what conditions) the orthocenter is *interior to* (or *on*, or *exterior to*) the triangle? Can you explain why this happens?

A *median* of $\triangle ABC$ is a line segment from a vertex to the midpoint of the opposite side. As you worked on Activity 5, you may have noticed that the three medians of $\triangle ABC$ appear to be concurrent. That is, you may have conjectured that *if AD, BE, and CF are medians of $\triangle ABC$, then AD, BE, and CF are concurrent.* While the sketch may convince you that this is the case, we want to develop a proof of this conjecture.

THEOREM 3.9   The three medians of a triangle are concurrent. The point where they intersect, called the *centroid*, is often denoted as G.

Proof   Here is one way to prove this theorem: Let $\triangle ABC$ be an arbitrary triangle, and D, E, and F the midpoints of their respective sides. Medians AD and BE intersect at point G. We need to show that median CF passes through G. (See Figure 3.6.)

Construct X as the midpoint of CD, and Y as the midpoint of DB. Draw lines EX and FY, and observe that this creates pairs of similar triangles. (*Which pairs of triangles are similar? How do we know that they are similar?*) Thus, lines EX, AD, and FY are parallel. (*Why?*) It is easy to see that segments CX, XD, DY, and YB are congruent. (*Why?*) The segment BE is divided into congruent segments as well (*again, why?*), so the length of BG is twice the length of GE; we can express this symbolically as $|BG| = 2|GE|$. In other words, G is two thirds of the way along the median BE.

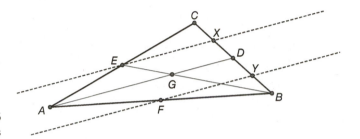

FIGURE 3.6
Concurrence of Medians

Now start again. Let G' be the intersection of medians BE and CF. A similar argument shows that G' is also two thirds of the way along BE. (*You should draw another diagram, and work out the details of this argument.*) Thus, G and G' are the same points, showing that the three medians intersect at a single point.

Unlike the situation of the orthocenter, the centroid is always interior to its triangle. Why does this happen? Also, note how once again, the proof provides us with a new result, that the centroid is two thirds of the way from the vertex to the midpoint of the opposite side. There are additional results to discover about the medians and the centroid, but we will leave that for the exercises.

In Activity 7, you observed that the three perpendicular bisectors of the sides of the triangle appear to be concurrent.

THEOREM 3.10   The three perpendicular bisectors of the sides of a triangle are concurrent. The point where they intersect, called the *circumcenter*, is often denoted as O.

If we look at a proof of this result, we may understand why this is the case and we may learn something new about perpendicular bisectors. We will leave this proof for you to do as an exercise.

The *circumcircle* has its center at O and passes through the three vertices of the triangle. Is the circumcenter always interior to its triangle? Can you explain why or why not?

Look back at your work on Exercise 29, page 47. Which of the points of a triangle could most reasonably be called the "midpoint" of a triangle—the *incenter*, the *circumcenter,* the *orthocenter,* or the *centroid*? Why do you think so? Are there other points that could be candidates for the "midpoint" of a triangle?

It is interesting to construct the *circumcenter*, O, the *orthocenter*, H, and the *centroid*, G, of a triangle in one diagram. If you do so, these three points will appear to be collinear. One way to prove that three points are collinear is to find the line through two of them, and show that the third point also lies on this line. For example, you might start with the line $\overleftrightarrow{OG}$ through the circumcenter O and the centroid G. Then show that there is a point on this line, temporarily called point X, that lies on each of the three altitudes of the triangle. Once you have shown that X lies on all three altitudes, you can conclude that X is indeed H, the orthocenter of the triangle. You will have established that the *circumcenter*, the *orthocenter*, and the *centroid* are collinear; the line containing these three points is called the *Euler line* of the triangle. You will have an opportunity to do this proof in the exercises.

CEVA'S THEOREM AND ITS CONVERSE

A *Cevian* is a segment from a vertex of a triangle to a point on the line containing the opposite side. You have seen several examples of Cevians in this chapter. A median is one example of a Cevian, but not every Cevian is a median. An altitude of a triangle is also a Cevian.

THEOREM 3.11   **Ceva's Theorem**   In $\triangle ABC$, if the Cevians AX, BY, and CZ are concurrent, then

$$\frac{AZ}{ZB} \cdot \frac{BX}{XC} \cdot \frac{CY}{YA} = 1.$$

Sketch of a proof   You saw the beginning of this proof in Activity 9. Look again at Figure 3.1. In that activity, you found pairs of similar triangles. The pairs needed for the proof are

$$\triangle AZC \sim \triangle BZQ$$

$$\triangle BXR \sim \triangle CXA$$

$$\triangle CYP \sim \triangle QBP$$

$$\triangle YAP \sim \triangle BRP.$$

From each similarity, we get equal ratios. From the first pair, we get

$$\frac{AZ}{BZ} = \frac{AC}{BQ},$$

and from the third pair, we get

$$\frac{CY}{QB} = \frac{PY}{PB}.$$

You can derive two more such ratios. With these four equations, it is a simple matter to substitute into the product of the theorem and simplify to 1.

Notice the structure of this proof: Starting with the hypothesis that the Cevians are concurrent, we constructed a diagram to represent this. Then we looked for similar triangles and set up ratios that must be equal by the definition of similarity. Eventually, our calculations led to the conclusion that the product is equal to 1. This proof begins with the assumptions that are expressed in the hypothesis and moves directly toward the conclusion that was stated in the theorem. This is another example of a *direct proof.*

There is an unstated assumption in the hypothesis of this theorem. Consider the possibility that A, Y, and Z are the same point. Then the three Cevians are concurrent at the point A, but the calculation is undefined. A more complete statement would add the requirement that the three ratios are all defined and nonzero. Then the calculation makes sense and will equal 1.

Although the converse of a theorem frequently is not true, the converse of Ceva's Theorem is also a theorem, and we must find a proof for it. Here is a situation where an *indirect proof* can be helpful. This approach to a proof begins by restating the conjecture in its contrapositive form. (Indirect proofs will be discussed in more detail in Chapter 4.)

First we write the converse of Ceva's Theorem:

Converse of Ceva's Theorem   In triangle $\triangle ABC$, if the product $\frac{AZ}{ZB} \cdot \frac{BX}{XC} \cdot \frac{CY}{YA} = 1$, then the Cevians AX, BY, and CZ are concurrent.

Since the contrapositive of a statement means the same thing as the original statement, we rewrite the converse of Ceva's Theorem using its contrapositive form:

Contrapositive of the converse of Ceva's Theorem   In triangle $\triangle ABC$, if the Cevians AX, BY, and CZ are not concurrent, then $\frac{AZ}{ZB} \cdot \frac{BX}{XC} \cdot \frac{CY}{YA} \neq 1$.

To prove this last statement, start by drawing two of the Cevians and locate their intersection point. Construct a new Cevian that includes this intersection point. For this set of three Cevians, the product will equal 1. The product for the original set of Cevians has two of the same factors, with a different third factor. Thus, this product must be different from 1. (You will be asked to write a full proof in the exercises.)

Again, notice the suggested structure for the indirect proof: Express the converse of Ceva's Theorem in its contrapositive form, then prove the contrapositive. Since the contrapositive is equivalent to the original statement, you will have proved the theorem—doing so indirectly.

Using Ceva's Theorem and its converse, it is easy to prove that the medians of a triangle are concurrent. The proof that the altitudes of a triangle are concurrent (see Activity 4 and Exercise 39) requires a bit of trigonometry. Many other special points can be defined from Ceva's Theorem. Many of these have names, such as the Nagel point and the Gergonne point. Some of these will appear in the exercises. Ceva's Theorem is unusual in that both this theorem and its converse are true theorems. When this happens, we can combine the statement and its converse into a single statement using the mathematical phrase "if and only if," which is often abbreviated as *iff.* This kind of statement is called a *biconditional* statement. Thus, we can express the two theorems in a single statement.

THEOREM 3.12   **Ceva's Theorem and its converse**   In $\triangle ABC$ with points X on BC, Y on CA, and Z on AB, the lines AX, BY, and CZ are concurrent if and only if

$$\frac{AZ}{ZB} \cdot \frac{BX}{XC} \cdot \frac{CY}{YA} = 1.$$

You may have noticed that this statement is actually somewhat stronger than our first statement of Ceva's Theorem, because it talks about the lines AX, BY, and CZ, not just the Cevian segments. The proof given earlier is valid for these lines, so the stronger statement is justified. You can see this by redrawing Figure 3.1 with the point P exterior to $\triangle ABC$ and finding the same pairs of similar triangles cited in the proof.

For biconditional statements, the two components are interchangeable; that is, they mean the same thing. We can express the pattern for a biconditional statement symbolically as

$$P \leftrightarrow Q \equiv (P \rightarrow Q) \wedge (Q \rightarrow P).$$

To prove a *biconditional* statement, it is necessary to prove two separate implications: both $P \rightarrow Q$ and $Q \rightarrow P$. So a proof of a statement like the one in Theorem 3.12 requires two major parts: a proof that concurrence implies the product equals 1, and a proof that a product equals 1 implies concurrence.

Get into the habit of expressing your conjectures clearly in the form of conditional statements. This will help you to think clearly about what your hypotheses and your conclusions are. You will find that this will help you to develop robust proofs.

BRIEF EXCURSION INTO CIRCLE GEOMETRY

We say that "two points determine a line," meaning that given any two points, there is exactly one line that goes through these points. This is one of Euclid's postulates. This idea is implemented in GeoGebra as one of the allowable constructions; from two distinct points, you can construct a line. Let us pose another question: *How many points determine a circle?*

- If we designate one point as the center and a second point to lie on the circle, then there is exactly one circle that can be drawn from that center through the specified point. The radius of the circle will be the distance between the two given points. This is Euclid's third postulate.

- Suppose that we stipulate that two points A and B are to lie on a circle. How many different circles can be drawn through A and B? Think carefully about where the center of the circle must lie.

- Suppose that we designate three points A, B, and C, and want to find a circle through these points. How many distinct circles can be drawn through these three points? If A, B, and C are not collinear, it is helpful to think about the triangle formed by these three points. How can you construct a circle through these three specified points?

- Now consider four points A, B, C, and D. Is there a circle through these four points? If so, how would we find the center of this circle?

THE CIRCUMCIRCLE OF ΔABC

If you draw a circle and mark three points on it, these points will not be collinear (unless the circle has infinite radius—which would be a very special case!). So these three points will form the vertices of a triangle. It is interesting to ask the question the other way around: If you start with a triangle, can you construct a circle that goes through three vertices? If so, this would be the *circumcircle* of the triangle. Can you always construct a circumcircle, or is it only possible for certain special triangles? In other words, are triangles cyclic polygons? Is every triangle a cyclic polygon, or just special triangles?

Let's start by making the problem a bit simpler. Given two points A and B, can we construct a circle through these two points? We will have to find a suitable point X for the center of the circle, and X must be equidistant from A as it is from B. (*Why?*) One such point would be the midpoint of the line segment AB. More generally, if X is any point on the perpendicular bisector of the segment AB, then X will be equidistant from the points A and B. Can you prove this? (*Hint*: Look for congruent triangles.)

Returning to the question of constructing the *circumcircle of triangle* ΔABC, we are looking for a point that is equidistant from the points A and B and simultaneously equidistant from the points B and C. Thus, the point we are looking for must be on the perpendicular bisector for the segment AB and on the perpendicular bisector for the segment BC. Can we be sure that these two lines—that is, the perpendicular bisectors of the segments AB and BC—really do intersect? Either they intersect, or they are parallel. If they were parallel, then the segments AB and BC would also be parallel. However, we know that AB and BC intersect at the point B, and that AB and BC are not the same line. Therefore, the perpendicular bisectors of these segments must intersect. This intersection point O will be the center of the circumcircle of ΔABC, and OA or OB can be taken as the radius of this circumcircle. Hence, we can say that every triangle is a cyclic triangle. The circle that passes through the vertices of a triangle is called its *circumcircle*.

THE NINE-POINT CIRCLE: A FIRST PASS

For any ΔABC, the points where the altitudes intersect their opposite sides are called the *feet* of the altitudes. The triangle formed by the feet of the three altitudes is sometimes called the *pedal triangle* of ΔABC, and, of course, it has a circumcircle. This circle—the circumcircle of the pedal triangle—contains quite a few interesting points. As you worked on Activity 11, you might have noticed that not only does it pass through the feet of the altitudes, but it also passes through the midpoints of the sides of ΔABC. We will investigate this triangle more closely in the next two chapters and will see that it is sometimes called the "nine-point circle" because it passes through nine (actually more than nine) interesting points.

As long as you are experimenting with GeoGebra, it will be interesting to compare the length of the diameter of the circumcircle of the pedal triangle with the length of the diameter of the circumcircle for ΔABC. What do you observe? Does this ratio seem familiar? Can you prove your conjecture?

MENELAUS' THEOREM AND ITS CONVERSE

Ceva's Theorem in its stronger form deals with the concurrence of lines drawn from the vertices of a triangle. A much older theorem examines the collinearity of points drawn on the (possibly extended) sides of a triangle.

THEOREM 3.13 **Menelaus' Theorem** In triangle ABC, suppose that the point X is on the line $\overleftrightarrow{BC}$, Y is on the line $\overleftrightarrow{CA}$, and Z is on the line $\overleftrightarrow{AB}$. If the points X, Y, and Z are collinear, then

$$\frac{AZ}{ZB} \cdot \frac{BX}{XC} \cdot \frac{CY}{YA} = -1.$$

If the point X does not lie on the side BC, but rather on the extension of the side BC, we denote the ratio $\frac{BX}{XC}$ as negative, because the rays $\overrightarrow{BX}$ and $\overrightarrow{XC}$ are pointing in opposite directions. Points Y and Z may require a similar treatment, depending on their location.

The converse of Menelaus' Theorem is also a theorem. How would you state the converse of Menelaus' Theorem? You will be invited to explore the geometric situation that underlies this theorem in Exercise 13.

Menelaus' Theorem offers another way to prove Ceva's Theorem. For $\triangle ABC$, as before, let the lines AX, BY, and CZ be concurrent at the point P. (See Figure 3.1.) Consider the triangle ABY and the line CPZ. From Menelaus' Theorem,

$$\left| \frac{AZ}{ZB} \cdot \frac{BP}{PY} \cdot \frac{YC}{CA} \right| = 1.$$

Now consider the triangle BCY and the line APX. This gives

$$\left| \frac{BX}{XC} \cdot \frac{CA}{AY} \cdot \frac{YP}{PB} \right| = 1.$$

Multiplying these expressions together produces the conclusion of Ceva's Theorem:

$$\frac{AZ}{ZB} \cdot \frac{BX}{XC} \cdot \frac{CY}{YA} = 1.$$

3.3 EXERCISES

Give clear and complete answers to the following problems and questions. Write your explanations clearly using complete sentences. Include diagrams whenever appropriate.

1. Negate the following statements. In each case, determine which statement is true, the original statement or its negation.

   a. An angle inscribed in a semicircle is a right angle. (*Hint*: What type of quantifier is used in this statement?)
   b. Every triangle has at least three sides.
   c. Every rectangle is a square.
   d. There are exactly three points on every line.
   e. Through any two distinct points there is at least one line.

f. Every rectangle has three sides, and all right triangles are equilateral.

g. $\triangle XYZ$ is isosceles, or a pentagon is a five-sided plane figure.

2. Negate the following statements:

a. For every shape A, there is a circle D, such that D surrounds A.

b. There is a circle C, such that for every line ℓ, ℓ intersects C.

3. Consider the following two statements: "All rhombi are squares," and "No rhombi are squares." Are these statements negations of each other? Explain your reasoning.

4. Given a right triangle $\triangle ABC$ with right angle at A, prove that the area of the equilateral triangle on the hypotenuse is equal to the sum of the areas of the equilateral triangles on the other two sides.

5. Given a right triangle $\triangle ABC$ with right angle at A, prove or disprove that the area of the semicircle on the hypotenuse is equal to the sum of the areas of the semicircles on the other two sides.

6. Let $\triangle ABC$ be a right triangle, with right angle at A. Rectangles, each of height 3 units, are constructed along each side of this triangle. Prove or disprove that the area of the rectangle on the hypotenuse is equal to the sum of the areas of the rectangles on each of the other two sides.

7. The previous three exercises use the Pythagorean Theorem. That is, you were allowed to assume the Pythagorean Theorem and to use it as a justification for one of the steps in your proof.

a. Find out how Pythagoras (or one of the other ancient Greeks) proved this theorem.

b. Find at least one additional proof of the Pythagorean Theorem in another book or on the Internet.

c. Develop your own proof of the Pythagorean Theorem itself.

8. Prove the converse of the Pythagorean Theorem. (See page 30.)

9. The Indian mathematician Bhaskara gave a proof of the Pythagorean Theorem that consisted of the diagram in Figure 3.7 and the single word

"Behold!" Use this diagram to create a step-by-step proof.

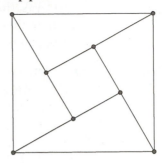

FIGURE 3.7
Bhaskara's Proof; for Exercise 9

10. Consider the sentence "This sentence is false." Is this sentence true? . . . Is it false? Write a short paragraph explaining what is happening here.

11. Set up truth tables to compare a statement of the form $P \rightarrow Q$ with its *converse* and its *contrapositive*.

12. a. State the contrapositive of Euclid's Fifth Postulate.

b. Give an argument that Euclid's Fifth Postulate (or its contrapositive) implies that if two parallel lines are cut by a transversal, then the interior angles on one side of the transversal are supplementary.

c. Suppose that lines ℓ and m are parallel and that t intersects these lines. Assuming Euclid's Fifth Postulate (or Playfair's Postulate), explain why the alternate interior angles must be congruent.

13. The converse of Menelaus' Theorem, like the converse of Ceva's Theorem, is also a theorem. What is the converse of Menelaus' Theorem? Express this converse in its contrapositive form.

14. The converse of Viviani's Theorem is false. Construct a counterexample to prove this.

15. Clearly identify the hypothesis and the conclusion of each statement in Exercise 12 on page 45 of the previous chapter. Then write the converse and the contrapositive of each.

16. Justify each statement in the proof of the ASA criterion for congruent triangles, which begins on page 65.

17. Prove the SSS criterion for triangle congruence: If three sides of one triangle ($\triangle ABC$) are congruent, respectively, to three sides of another triangle ($\triangle DEF$), then the two triangles are congruent. (*Hint*: Use an argument similar to the one we gave for ASA. Assume that $\triangle ABC \not\cong \triangle DEF$. Then a pair of corresponding angles, say A and D, is not congruent. Construct an angle GDE that is congruent to $\angle A$ and shares the side DE with $\angle FDE$. Find a point F' on $\overrightarrow{DG}$ so that $DF' \cong DF$. Also construct the segments EF' and FF'. Show that $\triangle ABC \cong \triangle DEF'$. Now you can use an argument involving isosceles triangles to show that the points F and F' must be the same point.)

18. The angle-angle-side (AAS) criterion for congruent triangles says that: If two angles and a non-included side of one triangle are congruent, respectively, to two angles and a non-included side of another triangle, then the two triangles are congruent. Here is a proof of the AAS criterion for triangle congruence. Justify each step.

Given triangles $\triangle ABC$ and $\triangle DEF$ with $\angle A \cong \angle D$, $\angle C \cong \angle F$, and $BC \cong EF$. We want to prove that $\triangle ABC \cong \triangle DEF$. If $AC \cong DF$, the triangles would be congruent. (Why?) If AC is not congruent to DF, then either $AC < DF$ or $AC > DF$.

Assume $AC < DF$. Then there is a point X on DF so that $AC \cong XF$. This would make $\angle ABC \cong \angle XEF$. So $\angle A \cong EXF$. But this cannot be so since $\angle A \cong \angle D$. (What theorem is violated?) So AC is not shorter than DF.

In a similar way, we can show that AC is not longer than DF. (Write out this argument explicitly.) Since AC is neither shorter than nor longer than DF, AC must be congruent to DF. So $\triangle ABC \cong \triangle DEF$ by SAS. Thus, if two angles and a non-included side of one triangle are congruent, respectively, to two angles and a non-included side of another triangle, then the two triangles are congruent.

19. Given two triangles, $\triangle ABC$ and $\triangle DEF$ with right angles at $\angle A$ and $\angle D$, $AB \cong DE$, and $BC \cong EF$.

Prove that $\angle ABC \cong \angle DEF$. This is the *hypotenuse-leg criterion* for congruence of right triangles. (*Hint*: See Figure 3.8. Construct point X on the ray opposite $\overrightarrow{AC}$ so that $AX \cong DF$. First prove that $\angle ABX \cong \angle DEF$. Then you can argue that $BX \cong EF \cong BC$, so that $\triangle BCX$ is isosceles. Then $\angle C \cong \angle X \cong \angle F$. Finally, you can conclude that $\angle ABC \cong \angle DEF$.)

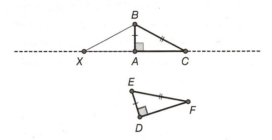

FIGURE 3.8
Figure for Exercise 19

20. Construct a counterexample to show that SSA is not a criterion for congruent triangles.

21. Construct a counterexample to show that AAA is not a criterion for congruent triangles.

22. Suppose that you are given a line segment AB. Construct two circles—one centered at A with radius AB and the other centered at B with radius BA. Let C and D denote the intersection points of these two circles. Draw the line segment CD. Mark the intersection of the segments AB and CD as the point E. Use congruent triangles to prove or disprove each of the following statements:

   a. $\triangle ABC$ and $\triangle ABD$ are equilateral.
   b. E is the midpoint of the segment AB.
   c. E is the midpoint of the segment CD.
   d. $AB \perp CD$.
   e. AB is congruent to CD.
   f. $ACBD$ is a parallelogram.
   g. $ACBD$ is a rhombus.

23. Draw a line m and point P not on m. Construct the perpendicular from P to m, using only a compass and straightedge, or only the Circle with Center through Point and Line tools of GeoGebra. Provide a deductive argument that your construction is correct. (GeoGebra has a command to do this automatically. We want you to figure out how to do it with only these two tools.)

24. Repeat the construction of Exercise 23 with the point P on the line m. Provide a deductive argument that your construction is correct.

25. Given an angle $\angle PQR$, construct the bisector of this angle, using only a compass and straightedge, or only the Circle with Center through Point and Line tools of GeoGebra. Provide a deductive argument that your construction is correct.

26. Prove that a point X is on the perpendicular bisector of a segment AB if and only if X is the center of a circle through points A and B. (*Note*: This requires an argument in both directions. You might want to write the statement as two conditional statements and prove each one separately.)

27. Given a triangle $\triangle ABC$. Let B' and C' be points on sides AB and AC, respectively. Prove that $B'C' \parallel BC$ if and only if

$$\frac{|AB'|}{|AB|} = \frac{|AC'|}{|AC|}.$$

(*Note*: There are two things to prove.)

28. Complete the proof of Theorem 3.4, by supplying the justification for each step of the proof that starts on page 66.

29. The proof of the theorem that the angle bisectors of a triangle are concurrent (Theorem 3.4) includes the key components needed to prove two additional theorems about angle bisectors. This illustrates our comment that developing a proof can lead to new results.
    a. Prove Theorem 3.5, which states that any point on the angle bisector of an angle is an equal distance from the two sides of the angle.
    b. Prove Theorem 3.6, which is the converse of Theorem 3.5.

30. Given a triangle, construct a circle inscribed in the triangle. (*Hint*: You will need to find a point an equal distance from all three sides of the triangle.) This circle is called the *incircle* of the triangle.

31. Given a triangle, construct a circle that passes through the three vertices of the triangle. (*Hint*: You will need to find a point that is an equal distance from all three vertices.) This circle is called the *circumcircle* of the triangle.

32. Given three noncollinear points A, B, and C, prove or disprove that there is exactly one circle through these points. What happens if A, B, and C are collinear?

33. Prove that the circumcenter, O, the centroid, G, and orthocenter, H, lie on a common line, known as the Euler line of the triangle. (*Hint*: One way to approach this proof is to construct the line containing O and G. Then find a point X on $\overleftrightarrow{OG}$ such that G is between O and X, and $2|OG| = |OX|$. Show that this point X is on all three altitudes, and hence X is the orthocenter G.)

34. Write a complete, detailed proof of Ceva's Theorem and of its converse.

35. Prove or disprove that a median divides a triangle into two equal areas.

36. Prove or disprove that an altitude divides a triangle into two equal areas.

37. Use the converse of Ceva's Theorem to prove that the three medians of a triangle are concurrent.

38. Use the converse of Ceva's Theorem to prove that the three angle bisectors of a triangle are concurrent. (*Hint*: Use the Law of Sines.)

39. Use the converse of Ceva's Theorem to prove that the altitudes of a triangle are concurrent. (*Hint*: Use trigonometry.)

40. Let H be the orthocenter of $\triangle ABC$. Where is the orthocenter of $\triangle HBC$? Prove your answer.

41. Prove that the Cevians joining the vertices of a triangle with the points of tangency of the incircle are concurrent. This is the *Gergonne point* of the triangle.

42. Prove that the perpendicular bisectors of the sides of a triangle are concurrent. (*Hint*: Let O be the intersection of two of the perpendicular bisectors. By finding congruent triangles, prove that the line through O perpendicular to the third side is also a bisector.)

43. Prove that the circumcenter of a triangle is the center of a circle that contains all three vertices.

44. Given a triangle, construct a line through each vertex parallel to the opposite side. This forms a larger triangle that surrounds the original. Prove that the lines containing the altitudes of the original triangle are the perpendicular bisectors of the sides of the larger triangle. Use this to prove that the lines containing the altitudes of a triangle are concurrent.

45. Use GeoGebra to make a diagram of an arbitrary triangle ABC, and construct its pedal triangle. In your diagram, verify that the circumcircle of the pedal triangle passes through the midpoints of the sides of $\triangle ABC$. Thus, we see that the pedal triangle contains both the feet of the altitudes of $\triangle ABC$ and the midpoints of its sides. These are the first six points of the so-called "nine-point circle."

The following problems are more challenging.

46. For a triangle $\triangle ABC$, suppose that point X is halfway around the perimeter from A, that Y is halfway around the perimeter from B, and that Z is halfway around the perimeter from C. Prove that the Cevians AX, BY, and CZ are concurrent. This is the *Nagel point* of the triangle.

47. Let P be a point on the circumcircle of $\triangle ABC$. Drop perpendiculars from P to the (possibly extended) sides of the triangle. Prove that the feet of these perpendiculars are collinear. This is the *Simson line* for point P. (*Hint*: Use the converse of Menelaus' Theorem, some trigonometry, and facts about subtended angles.)

48. Construct an example of Menelaus' Theorem in which all three of the ratios are negative. Also, give both a geometric reason and an arithmetic reason why there cannot be an example with exactly two of the ratios negative.

49. Two triangles $\triangle ABC$ and $\triangle A'B'C'$ are said to be *perspective from a point P* if the lines formed by corresponding points (the lines $\overleftrightarrow{AA'}$, $\overleftrightarrow{BB'}$ and $\overleftrightarrow{CC'}$) are concurrent at P. Two triangles are said to be *perspective from a line m* if the intersection points of corresponding sides (the points $\overleftrightarrow{AB} \cap \overleftrightarrow{A'B'}$, $\overleftrightarrow{BC} \cap \overleftrightarrow{B'C'}$, and $\overleftrightarrow{CA} \cap \overleftrightarrow{C'A'}$) are collinear on m. (See Figure 3.9.)

Part of Desargues' Theorem: If two triangles are perspective from a point, then they are perspective from a line.

   a. Create a diagram of Desargues' Theorem in which the point of perspectivity is between the two triangles.

   b. Create another diagram in which the point of perspectivity is interior to both triangles.

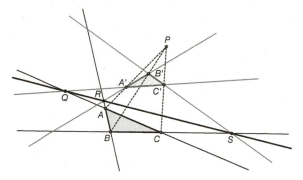

FIGURE 3.9
Figure for Exercise 49

50. Use Menelaus' Theorem to prove the part of Desargues' Theorem stated in the previous exercise. (*Hint*: In Figure 3.9, look at the triangle $\triangle ABP$ and the line $RA'B'$. Then consider the triangle $\triangle BCP$ and the line $B'C'S$. Finally, consider the triangle $\triangle ACP$ and the line $QA'C'$. Combine the Menelaus products from these three situations to get three points on the sides of $\triangle ABC$.) (*The converse of this statement is also true, but is a bit more difficult to prove.*)

51. For a triangle $\triangle ABC$, the angle bisector at A will meet the opposite side BC at the point D. Use the Law of Sines to prove that

$$\frac{|BD|}{|DC|} = \frac{|AB|}{|AC|}.$$

Exercises 52–54 are especially for future teachers.

52. In the *Principles and Standards for School Mathematics* [NCTM 2000, 56], the National Council of Teachers of Mathematics (NCTM) recommends that instructional programs from prekindergarten through grade 12 should enable all students to

- recognize reasoning and proof as fundamental aspects of mathematics;
- make and investigate mathematical conjectures;
- develop and evaluate mathematical arguments;
- select and use various types of reasoning and methods of proof.

What does this mean for your future students?

a. Find a copy of the *Principles and Standards*, and study the discussion of the Reasoning and Proof Standard [NCTM 2000, 56–69]. What are the specific NCTM recommendations with regard to reasoning and proof in school mathematics? What are some expectations that the NCTM has about growth in mathematical reasoning for children and adolescents?

b. In using this textbook to study college geometry, you are engaging in exploration and conjecture, and you are being asked to explain your observations and prove your conjectures. You are engaging in both inductive and deductive reasoning. How is the work you are doing in this course related to the Reasoning and Proof Standard developed by the NCTM? Cite specific examples.

c. Write a report in which you present and critique what you learn in studying the NCTM Reasoning and Proof Standard in light of your experiences in this course. Your report should include your answers to the questions in parts (a) and (b).

53. Find copies of school mathematics texts for one of the grade levels for which you are seeking teacher certification.

a. How is the NCTM Reasoning and Proof Standard reflected in the presentation of mathematics given in those school mathematics texts?

b. Design several classroom activities involving reasoning and proof that would be appropriate for students in your future classroom.

c. Write a short report explaining how the activities you design reflect both what you are learning in this class and the NCTM recommendations on Reasoning and Proof in school mathematics.

54. Find the Common Core State Standards for Mathematics online: http://www.corestandards.org/.

a. Which of the eight Standards for Mathematical Practice have to do with reasoning and proof?

b. Beginning as early as kindergarten, children are expected to reason with geometric shapes and their attributes, analyze and compare two- and three-dimensional shapes, and reason about combining and decomposing shapes. Their skills in reasoning abstractly, constructing viable arguments, and critiquing the reasoning of others are expected to develop in age-appropriate ways throughout the years from kindergarten through grade 8. Study the Common Core Standards for Mathematics Content for three consecutive grade levels (e.g., grade 4, 5, and 6). Write a report summarizing the expectations for children's growth in their ability to reason abstractly and construct viable arguments over this three-year period.

c. "During high school, students begin to formalize their geometry experiences from elementary and middle school, using more precise definitions and developing careful proofs" (*Common Core State Standards for Mathematics*, 74). Study the Common Core State Standards for Mathematics: High School—Geometry. What kinds of proofs are high school students expected to be able to develop? At what times in the high school curriculum, do students develop these skills? What is the responsibility of their high school teachers—your responsibility as a future high school mathematics teacher—to facilitate their learning of these skills of reasoning abstractly, constructing viable arguments, and critiquing the reasoning of others?

Reflect on what you have learned in this chapter.

55. Review the main ideas of this chapter. Describe, in your own words, the concepts you have studied and what you have learned about them. What are the important ideas? How do they fit together? Which concepts were easy for you? Which were hard?

56. Reflect on the learning environment for this course.
    a. Describe aspects of the learning environment that helped you understand the main ideas in this chapter. Which activities did you like? Which did you find challenging? Why?
    b. How do you think a deepened understanding of how you learn will impact your own approach to teaching in your future classroom?

3.4 CHAPTER OVERVIEW

Writing good mathematical proofs is an important theme in this course. Developing a correct proof is a complex skill. First *you must understand the ideas* in the conjecture or theorem you are attempting to prove. Then *good logical reasoning* is needed to clearly lay out the steps of your proof. In this chapter, we presented some of the rules of deductive reasoning that are needed for developing mathematical arguments. We discussed existential and universal quantifiers, $\exists x$ and $\forall y$, and what these quantifiers mean. Deductive reasoning is a process of demonstrating that if certain things are given, then the results you claim in your conjecture follow logically. We will continue to develop these ideas in the next chapter.

Each chapter of this book opens by inviting you to construct diagrams in GeoGebra, and experiment with those diagrams to see (literally) what happens as you manipulate the diagrams. You are then asked to formulate conjectures based on your observations. By now you have probably noticed that expressing your observations in complete sentences and then formulating conjectures as if-then statements can be challenging. In developing the if-part of a conjecture, you need to think carefully about what you need to include in the hypothesis of your conjecture. Constructing a robust diagram of a geometric situation requires you to do things in a particular order. Often the order of the steps you took to construct the diagram will give an indication of the order of steps you will need as you develop your proof.

Step-by-step proofs are similar to the "two-column proofs" you may have used in your high school geometry course. Setting up your proofs in a step-by-step format is a way to begin to organize your thoughts. This will help you to be sure that you are providing a justification for each step in your proof. As you become more skilled at developing proofs, you may begin to write your proofs in a flowing paragraph form, as you may have seen in many mathematics texts.

A sentence such as the one you worked with in Exercise 10, "This sentence is false," is an example of a *paradox*. This sentence appears on the surface to be a simple statement, yet when we try to assign it a truth value, it gets quite complicated. No matter what truth value we try to assign—*true* or *false*—it is not quite right.

Paradoxes such as this are reminders that human thought is rich and complex and not always reducible to simple true/false logic.

Converse and Contrapositive   You have been asked to write your conjectures using an if-then format. Statements of the form "If P, then Q" are called implication statements. Each such implication has two closely related implications: its *converse*, "If Q, then P", and its *contrapositive*, "If not Q, then not P." The contrapositive means the same thing as the original implication, while the converse does not.

Pythagorean Theorem   The Pythagorean Theorem says that the area of the square on the hypotenuse is equal to the sum of the areas of the squares on the other two legs of a right triangle. Our investigations in this chapter have extended this theorem to include several new possibilities. If $\triangle ABC$ is a right triangle, then the area of the circle on the hypotenuse is equal to the sum of the areas of the circles on the other two sides. Squares, circles, and equilateral triangles work in this situation because these are families of similar figures. All circles are similar to each other; that is, they are the same shape even when they have different sizes. Because of this similarity, their areas are proportional. This is why the Pythagorean Theorem can be extended to include circles, but does not work for all situations involving rectangles.

The *area of a triangle* can be measured by calculating one-half the product of the base and the height:

$$\text{area}(\triangle ABC) = \frac{1}{2} \text{ base} \times \text{height}.$$

The length of any side of the triangle can be taken as the base, while the height is measured as the length of the altitude perpendicular to that base. Since a triangle has three sides, there are three different calculations that can be used to find the area—and all three will give the same result.

Congruence Criteria for Triangles   Many proofs can be developed using similar or congruent triangles. Two triangles are similar if all three pairs of corresponding angles are congruent; this is the AAA criterion for similarity. We have accepted the SAS criterion as an axiom for triangle congruence and used this to prove the ASA criterion as a theorem. Exercises 16 through 19 ask you to investigate several additional criteria for triangle congruence.

- **SAS Congruence Axiom for Triangles** If two sides and the included angle of one triangle are congruent, respectively, to two sides and the included angle of another triangle, then the two triangles are congruent.

- **ASA Criterion for Triangle Congruence** If two angles and the included side of one triangle are congruent, respectively, to two angles and the included side of another triangle, then the two triangles are congruent.

Concurrence Properties for Triangles   In the activities that opened this chapter, you investigated some of the concurrence properties for triangles. When three or more lines intersect at a common point, we say that those lines are *concurrent*.

- The three altitudes of a triangle are concurrent at the orthocenter, H, of the triangle.
- The three medians of a triangle are concurrent at the centroid, G, of a triangle.
- The perpendicular bisectors of the three sides of a triangle are concurrent at the circumcenter, O, of a triangle. The point O is the center of a circle that passes through the three vertices of the triangle.
- The angle bisectors of the three angles of a triangle are concurrent at the incenter, I, of a triangle. The point I is the center of a circle that is tangent to the three sides of the triangle.

Three of these special points of a triangle—the orthocenter (H), the centroid (G), and the circumcenter (O)—are collinear; they lie on the *Euler line* of the triangle.

Ceva's and Menelaus' Theorems and Their Converses The theorems of Ceva and Menelaus are closely related. The former involves concurrence of three lines, while the latter involves collinearity of three points. These theorems are unusual in that both the statement and its converse are theorems.

- **Ceva's Theorem** In $\triangle ABC$, the Cevians AX, BY, and CZ are concurrent if and only if

$$\frac{AZ}{ZB} \cdot \frac{BX}{XC} \cdot \frac{CY}{YA} = 1.$$

- **Menelaus' Theorem** In a triangle ABC, suppose that the point X is on the line $\overleftrightarrow{BC}$, Y is on the line $\overleftrightarrow{CA}$, and Z is on the line $\overleftrightarrow{AB}$. The points X, Y, and Z are collinear if and only if

$$\frac{AZ}{ZB} \cdot \frac{BX}{XC} \cdot \frac{CY}{YA} = -1.$$

To make this work, a ratio must be considered negative if the two segments are in opposite directions.

We concluded this chapter by making a brief excursion into circle geometry, and we will continue to investigate properties of circles in the next chapter. A circle can always be constructed that passes through the three vertices of a triangle; this is the circumcircle of the triangle. The pedal triangle of a triangle passes through the feet of the three altitudes of that triangle. As you will see in the next chapter, the circumcircle of the pedal triangle passes through quite a few special points of the triangle.

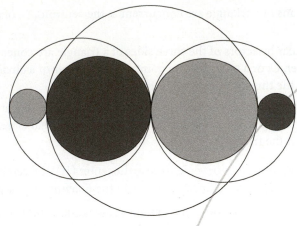

CHAPTER FOUR

*G*eoGebra sees things through Euclidean eyes—that is, the default world view of GeoGebra is the Euclidean plane. Each construction you are allowed to perform on a GeoGebra worksheet is related to Euclid's postulates. As you work on the following activities, think about Euclid's postulates. Which of these postulates are being applied as you use GeoGebra to construct each diagram? If the diagrams you construct are robust, you will be shaping your geometric reasoning according to a Euclidean perspective. After constructing a diagram in GeoGebra, reflect on the steps you needed to take to produce the diagram. This will enable you to begin your proofs.

Circle Geometry and Proofs

Do the following activities, expressing your explanations clearly in complete sentences. Include diagrams whenever appropriate. Save your work for each activity, as later work sometimes builds on earlier work. Use a button on the Style Bar to hide the axes, because you will not need them in this chapter. You will find it helpful to read ahead into the chapter as you work on these activities.

1. A cyclic quadrilateral is a quadrilateral whose vertices lie on a common circle. Construct a cyclic quadrilateral *ABCD*. Extend the side *AB*, creating an exterior angle at *B*. Construct the diagonal *AC*. Measure the exterior angle at *B* and each of the interior angles of the quadrilateral.

   a. What is the relationship between the sizes of $\angle ABC$ and $\angle ADC$? Does your observation still hold if you move the vertices of the quadrilateral, or if you change the size of the circle? What if you move *D* past *C*?

   GeoGebra Reminder: When you put the cursor in the Input bar, a small button appears at the far right end of the input bar. Clicking on this button produces a menu of Greek letters and mathematical symbols.

   b. What is the relationship between the measures of the exterior angle at *B* and the interior angle at *D*? Does your observation still hold if you move the vertices of the quadrilateral, or if you change the size of the circle?

   c. Use an idea from Activity 4 on page 6 to explain what is happening.

2. In the previous chapter, we found that the three perpendicular bisectors of the sides of a triangle are concurrent. (See Theorem 3.10, page 70.) Here we consider an analogous situation with quadrilaterals.

   a. Use the **Polygon** tool to draw an arbitrary quadrilateral *ABCD*. Construct the perpendicular bisector of each of the sides. Are these four lines concurrent?

   b. The perpendicular bisectors of sides *AB* and *BC* intersect at a point; call it *X*. Construct a circle centered at *X* that passes through the point *A*. What do you observe about your circle?

   c. Maneuver the point *D* so that all four perpendicular bisectors are concurrent. Try to find several locations for *D* for which this occurs. What do you observe about the location of *D* when the four lines are concurrent?

   d. Complete the following conjecture: If the perpendicular bisectors of the sides of a quadrilateral are concurrent, then the quadrilateral is ....

   e. Write down the converse of your conjecture from part (d), and explore whether it is true.

3. Construct a cyclic quadrilateral *WXYZ*. Extend the sides *WX* and *YZ* to lines, and label the intersection of these lines as *P*. (*Note that we can rename objects in either the Graphics pane or the Algebra pane.*)

   a. Identify all pairs of similar triangles in this figure.

   b. Create segments *PW*, *PX*, *PZ*, and *PY*. Use the lengths of these segments (displayed in the Algebra pane) to calculate the products $PW \cdot PX$ and

$PZ \cdot PY$. Make a conjecture about these products: "If $WXYZ$ is a cyclic quadrilateral and the lines containing WX and YZ intersect at point P, then ...."

    c. Does your conjecture still hold if the point P is inside or on the circle?

    d. Prove your conjecture.

4. Construct a circle centered at O.

    a. Draw a point A outside the circle. Using the **Tangents** tool on the Perpendicular Line button, construct the tangent lines from A to the circle. Now construct the points B and C where the tangent lines touch the circle. Also, construct the radii OB and OC. What is the measure of the angle between each radius and its respective tangent line? Measure these angles to demonstrate your answer.

    b. Now construct the segment OA and the circle with OA as a diameter. How does this situation relate to Activity 5 on page 7?

    c. Use the **Attach/Detach Point** tool on the Point button to attach point A to your original circle. What happens to the tangent lines? What can you say about the angles?

5. Construct a circle centered at point O. For a point P external to the circle, construct the line $\overleftrightarrow{PO}$ and label its intersections with the circle as points W and X. Construct a new line through P that intersects the circle, and label the points of intersection as Q and R. Also construct the segment PT tangent to the circle at T.

    a. What is the measure of angle $\angle PTO$? (We want the "smaller" angle here, so pay attention to the order in which you select the three points.)

    b. Find an expression for PT^2 in terms of PO and TO. Have GeoGebra do this calculation for your diagram. (*Hint*: Construct the necessary segments. Use the lengths of these segments for a calculation in the **Input** bar. The result of this calculation can be included in a text box by selecting the appropriate item from the Objects list.)

    c. Find an expression for PT^2 in terms of PW and PX. Have GeoGebra do this calculation for your diagram.

    d. Find an expression for PT^2 in terms of PQ and PR. Have GeoGebra do this calculation for your diagram. Does your expression depend on the position of the line $\overleftrightarrow{PQR}$?

    e. Move the point P to the interior of the circle. What do you observe about the values of your three expressions?

6. Given a circle C and a point P, the *power of P with respect to C* is a function that depends only on the radius, r, of C and the distance, d, of P from the center of C. In the previous activity, you have seen three ways to calculate the power of the point P with respect to a given circle.

    a. Draw two overlapping circles, C_1 and C_2, and mark their common chord as AB.

    b. Construct a third circle, C_3, that also has AB as a chord. What can you say about the centers of the family of circles that have AB as a common chord?

c. Construct a point P on $\overleftrightarrow{AB}$. Calculate the powers of P with respect to each of the circles, C_1, C_2, and C_3. Move P along the line $\overleftrightarrow{AB}$. Make a conjecture about the values of power of P with respect to C_k, where k can be 1 or 2 or 3. Prove your conjecture.

7. Draw a circle, C, with diameter AB. (Construct AB so that it is certain to be a diameter of C.)
   a. Construct a point P on the diameter AB, and construct two additional circles with diameters AP and PB.
   b. The region bounded by the three semicircular arcs on one side of the diameter AB is called an *arbelos*. Calculate the area of the arbelos.
   c. Construct a perpendicular to AB at the point P. Mark the intersections of this perpendicular with the circle C as R and S. Construct a circle with diameter PR, and calculate its area.
   d. Make a conjecture about these areas. Prove your conjecture.

8. Draw a triangle $\triangle XYZ$.
   a. Construct the incenter, I, of $\triangle XYZ$. (*Hint*: The **Angle Bisector** tool will be helpful.) Construct the incircle of this triangle.
   b. Extend the sides XY and XZ to lines. Construct the angle bisectors of the exterior angles at Y and Z, and mark their intersection as the point P. Using P as the center, construct a circle that is tangent to the side YZ.
   c. Can you prove that the circle you constructed in part (b) is also tangent to lines $\overleftrightarrow{XY}$ and $\overleftrightarrow{XZ}$? (This circle is called an *excircle* of $\triangle XYZ$. A triangle has three excircles.)

4.2 DISCUSSION

AXIOM SYSTEMS: ANCIENT AND MODERN APPROACHES

Around 300 BC, Euclid and his colleagues set down just five postulates and hundreds of propositions (theorems) that follow from those postulates in the thirteen books of Euclid's *Elements*. Book I of the *Elements* opens with a list of definitions [Heath 1956]:

> A point is that which has no part. A line is breadthless length. The extremities of a line are points. A straight line is a line that lies evenly with the points on itself.

> When a straight line set up on a straight line makes the adjacent angles equal to one another, each of the equal angles is right, and the straight line standing on the other is called a perpendicular to that on which it stands. An obtuse angle is an angle greater than a right angle. An acute angle is an angle less than a right angle.

Parallel straight lines are straight lines that, being in the same plane and being produced indefinitely in both directions, do not meet one another in either direction.

There are actually more definitions in this list. We have included just a few here to give you a bit of the flavor of Euclid.

At the beginning of the twentieth century, David Hilbert, doing research in the foundations of geometry, refined and clarified Euclid's postulates and definitions. He was attempting to clean up weaknesses and ambiguities that had been noticed in Euclid's *Elements,* and to set out very clearly and exactly what Euclid's postulates meant. In building the language for geometry, Hilbert identified certain terms as the basic building blocks of this language. The basic geometric objects are *point, line,* and *plane.* Unlike Euclid, Hilbert called these *undefined terms.* He wanted to avoid the kind of circular reasoning in which the definition of one term depends on the definition of another, which in turn depends on the definition of the first. For instance, in Euclid's definitions of a point, we could ask "What is meant by 'that which has no part'?" The answer could well be "We mean a point." In using these undefined terms to build up the language and theory of geometry, Hilbert was not simply saying "Oh well, we know what points, lines, and planes are, so let's just agree to use these terms without defining them." Rather, he was acknowledging that there needed to be a starting point for the language of geometry and that from these undefined terms, one could rigorously define all other terms. In a sense, undefined terms play a foundational role similar to axioms in systems of theorems. One must assume some basic properties of a system, and then based on those assumptions, other properties of the system can be deductively argued. Hilbert developed sets of axioms to specify the properties of these undefined objects and the relationships that exist among them. In his *Grundlagen der Geometrie* (Foundations of Geometry), published in 1899, Hilbert identified five sets of properties for points, lines, planes, and the relationships possible among them. He organized his axioms into five groups: *incidence, betweenness, congruence, continuity*, and *parallelism.* Hilbert's *axioms of incidence* specify exactly what we mean when we say that a point is "on a line," a line "goes through a point," or a line "lies in a plane." His *axioms of betweenness* address how we know when a point is between two other points, or a ray is between two other rays. The *axioms of congruence* specify exactly what conditions must be met for one object to be congruent to another.

From a purely axiomatic perspective, we should be able to substitute any words—even nonsensical words such as *abba, dabba,* and *jobba*—for the undefined terms *point, line*, and *plane.* For example, Euclid's first postulate says that

Given two distinct *points*, P and Q, there is exactly one *line* ℓ through P and Q.

To underscore the idea that point and line are undefined terms, we might express this postulate as

Given two distinct *abbas*, a and b, there is exactly one *dabba* d incident with a and b.

Since our focus in this course is more constructive than axiomatic, we will leave this discussion of axiom systems for now. In closing, we observe that many contemporary high school and college geometry texts use Hilbert's axioms. In fact, your own high school geometry course may have used axioms of incidence, betweenness, and congruence that were based directly on Hilbert's formulation of these axioms [Eves 1976; Greenberg 1980].

LANGUAGE OF CIRCLES

A *circle* is the set of points at a fixed distance, r, from a fixed point, O; that is, a circle is $\{P : d(P, O) = r\}$. The point O is called the *center* of the circle and the distance r is called the *radius* of the circle. Points whose distance from the center point O is less than r, that is, $\{P : d(P, O) < r\}$, are said to be *interior* to the circle, while points whose distance from P is greater than r, that is, $\{P : d(P, O) > r\}$, are *exterior to* the circle.

A *chord* of a circle is a line segment joining two points on the circle. A chord that passes through the center of the circle is called a *diameter*. Using GeoGebra, we can construct a diameter of a circle by constructing a line through the center of the circle, and then finding the line segment between the points where this line intersects the circle.

While a chord intersects a circle at two points, a *tangent* is a line that intersects a circle at exactly one point. The point where a tangent line touches the circle is called the *point of tangency*. It is not difficult to prove that a tangent line is perpendicular to a radius at the point of tangency.

The *circumference* of a circle is the length of its perimeter. An *arc* of a circle is a piece of the circle. A *sector* of a circle is a pie-shaped portion of the interior of the circle, bounded by an arc of the circle and two radii. If P, Q, and R are three points on a circle with center at O, the angle $\angle POR$ is called a *central angle* of the circle, and the angle $\angle PQR$ is an *inscribed angle*. The angle $\angle PQR$ may also be called an angle *subtended by the chord PR*. We can define the measure of an arc as the measure of the central angle subtended by the arc. This allows us to reword the statement about inscribed angles: The measure of an inscribed angle is half the measure of the arc subtending the inscribed angle. It turns out to be convenient at times to be able to refer to the arc rather than the central angle.

Since a tangent to a circle, C, is a line perpendicular to a radius of C at the point of tangency, it is easy to construct a tangent to the circle C at a point A that is on C. To construct a tangent to C from a point B that is exterior to the circle, use the idea that an angle inscribed in a semicircle is a right angle. Construct a line segment from the point B to the center of C, then construct its midpoint, M. A circle centered at M with radius MB will intersect C at two points, P_1 and P_2. Lines $\overleftrightarrow{BP_1}$ and $\overleftrightarrow{BP_2}$ will both be tangent to the circle C. Why is it impossible to construct a tangent to the circle C from a point interior to C?

INSCRIBED ANGLES

As you worked on Activities 4 and 5, pages 6–7, in Chapter 1, you observed a fixed relationship between a central angle and an inscribed angle that share the same chord: the measure of an inscribed angle is one-half the measure of the corresponding central angle (i.e., the measure of the arc subtending the inscribed angle). You can prove this by working with several isosceles triangles that appear in a diagram of this situation. A consequence of this relationship between the inscribed and central angles is that any angle inscribed in a semicircle will be a right angle. Since the diagonal of a cyclic quadrilateral is a chord of a circle, opposite interior angles of a convex cyclic quadrilateral are supplementary, as you saw in Activity 1 at the beginning of this chapter (page 85). Moreover, an exterior angle of a cyclic quadrilateral will be congruent to the opposite interior angle. Recognizing pairs of such angles is key to seeing the similar triangles in Activity 3 (page 85), and to proving that $PW \cdot PX = PZ \cdot PY$.

MATHEMATICAL ARGUMENTS

In this course, you have been—and will be—asked many times to prove geometric statements. The process of developing a robust mathematical proof will challenge you to think very carefully about many things. Is your conjecture stated clearly and correctly? What exactly are your assumptions (hypotheses)? How are these assumptions related to the conclusion? Do the intermediate steps of your proof follow logically from the earlier steps? Have you overlooked anything? These are critical questions.

The first step in developing a robust proof is to write a clear statement of your conjecture. A conjecture is a conditional statement, consisting of hypothesis and conclusion. If the assumptions you are making in the hypothesis are met, then your proof should demonstrate that the conclusion you are claiming will follow. So it is very important to make your assumptions explicit and to express them clearly. Your assumptions—those stated explicitly and those that are implicitly understood (perhaps in the context of the problem)—form your hypothesis.

Sometimes writing a clear statement of your conjecture will show you the connection between the hypothesis and the conclusion. More often, however, finding this connection is the most difficult part of a proof. Try combining various parts of the hypothesis to see what they tell you. Experiment with diagrams to see how the parts of the hypothesis come into play. Work backward from the conclusion. Rephrase the conjecture, then rephrase it again. Try to prove a special case of your conjecture. Creating proofs is an art that improves with practice, and you will get a lot of practice in this course.

The goal for a robust proof is to develop a *valid* argument. A valid argument is one that uses the rules of logic correctly. Each step must follow logically from what has come before it, whether from part of the hypothesis or from a statement already proved. A proof based on valid arguments will stand up to critical questioning by your colleagues. Like a robust construction, a robust proof can be examined, prodded, and questioned, yet still show how the concepts fit together. Once you have created a robust proof, your reader (or listener) will either have to agree with your conclusion or disagree with your assumptions.

A *conjecture* that has been proved is called a *theorem*. If the hypothesis of the theorem is accepted as *true* and the argument is *valid*, then the conclusion must also be accepted as *true*.

We have seen that the rules of logic give us a way to determine the truth value of complicated statements. Rules of logic also give us strategies for proving (or disproving) conjectures. Here are three ideas from formal logic that provide tools for developing proofs:

Modus ponens: If $P \rightarrow Q$ and P are statements in a proof, then we can conclude Q. If the statement P is part of the hypothesis, or is something that has been previously proved, and you can explain why $P \rightarrow Q$, then you have proved the statement Q. Modus ponens is used to apply theorems to particular situations; for instance, knowing that ΔABC is a right triangle and that side c is the hypotenuse allows us to conclude that $a^2 + b^2 = c^2$. Modus ponens frequently appears within a proof as well, when something verified earlier is combined with an implication to get a new step in the proof.

Syllogism: If $P \rightarrow Q$ and $Q \rightarrow R$ are statements in a proof, then we can conclude $P \rightarrow R$. A direct proof relies on syllogisms, because a direct proof is a chain of implications leading directly from the hypothesis to the conclusion. Other forms of proof often use chains of implications, so syllogisms come into play in many proof situations.

Modus tollens: If $P \rightarrow Q$ and $\neg Q$ are statements in a proof, then we can conclude $\neg P$. In essence, *modus tollens* suggests that you try to prove the contrapositive of the conjecture, $\neg Q \rightarrow \neg P$, which means the same thing as $P \rightarrow Q$. This approach is called an *indirect proof*. It is often an effective proof strategy.

ADDITIONAL METHODS OF PROOF

In Chapter 3, we discussed the direct proof. This is the most straightforward approach to developing a proof, as a chain of implications. It is also a good way to present a written or verbal proof, for each step follows directly from previous steps and the logic is easy to follow. We also discussed the counterexample as a way to disprove a conjecture (i.e., to prove the negation of a conjecture). However, there are other approaches, such as indirect proof and proof by contradiction. A good prover can employ any of these as he or she attempts to develop a proof.

Constructing an Indirect Proof

Sometimes a direct proof does not work. In this case, we can back into the proof using the logic rule of *modus tollens*. *Modus tollens* is based on the fact that the *contrapositive* of a statement ($\neg Q \rightarrow \neg P$) means the same thing as the original statement ($P \rightarrow Q$). The idea here is that we want to prove $P \rightarrow Q$, and we begin by saying "Suppose *not Q*." That is, we consider what the situation would be if Q did not occur. Assuming $\neg Q$, we work through steps as before, and by a chain of implications reach the *negation of P*. If you can show that $\neg Q$ leads to $\neg P$ (i.e., $\neg Q \rightarrow \neg P$), then by contraposition, you can conclude $P \rightarrow Q$.

For example, we used this strategy when we were discussing the construction of the circumcircle of $\triangle ABC$ in Chapter 3. (See page 74.) We were working with a triangle, $\triangle ABC$, and wanted to show that the perpendicular bisectors of the sides AB and BC intersect. Let's call these two perpendicular bisectors ℓ and m. We want to prove that ℓ and m intersect, but what happens if we assume that $\ell \parallel m$? (*So we are assuming ¬Q.*) If $\ell \parallel m$, then $AB \parallel BC$ because ℓ is perpendicular to AB and m is perpendicular to BC. Since AB and BC share point B and are parallel, they must be the same side of the triangle. (*We have ¬P.*) Of course, the original hypothesis was that ABC is a triangle, with AB and BC as distinct sides. The logical combination of $¬Q \rightarrow ¬P$ and P thus allows us to conclude Q, that ℓ and m intersect. This point of intersection turns out to be the center of the circumcircle of triangle $\triangle ABC$.

In summary, an indirect proof uses the following pattern: Assume ¬Q. Show by a direct proof that ¬Q leads to ¬P, that is, $¬Q \rightarrow ¬P$. This is equivalent to $P \rightarrow Q$. The original hypothesis was P. Therefore, we can conclude Q.

Constructing a Proof by Contradiction

A proof by contradiction has somewhat the same flavor as an indirect proof, for it too begins by assuming the opposite of what we are trying to prove. So we assume ¬Q. The goal of a proof by contradiction is to show that ¬Q and the hypothesis P cannot be true simultaneously. The proof proceeds by showing that P and ¬Q together imply something impossible. Since we want the hypothesis P to be true, we must reject ¬Q and accept Q. In symbols, a proof by contradiction follows the pattern $P \wedge ¬Q \rightarrow$ *false*. You should create a truth table to verify that this expression means the same thing as $P \rightarrow Q$.

Here is an example of a proof by contradiction. Suppose that we have a circle of radius r centered at point O. We will prove that a line ℓ that intersects this circle at point T and is perpendicular to the radius OT must be tangent to the circle. The hypothesis is that ℓ contains point T and is perpendicular to OT. Assume the negation of the conclusion; that is, assume that ℓ is *not* tangent to this circle. Since ℓ contains one point of the circle and is not tangent, it must contain a second point S. Then, $\triangle TOS$ is isosceles, with two sides of length r. The base angles of this triangles are congruent, so $\angle OST \cong \angle OTS$. However, $\angle OTS$ is a right angle. Thus, our triangle contains two right angles, which is impossible. Therefore, our assumption was incorrect; ℓ must be tangent to the circle.

What we have done in the preceding paragraph is to demonstrate that the hypothesis, P, and the negation of the conclusion, ¬Q, cannot both be true. Since the statement of the theorem asks us to assume the truth of the hypothesis, we must reject ¬Q and thereby conclude that the conclusion Q is true. This is typical of proof by contradiction.

Proving a Statement of the Form $P \leftrightarrow Q$

Both a statement and its converse may be theorems. This is not always the case, but it does happen. In this special situation, the theorems can be expressed as a single statement in the form

$$P \rightarrow Q \quad \text{and} \quad Q \rightarrow P.$$

Such a theorem may be expressed more compactly as

$$P \text{ if and only if } Q.$$

The expression *if and only if* is used so often in mathematics that we have a special abbreviation to express this idea. *Iff* means *if and only if*, and it can be written in symbolic form as a double-headed arrow ($\leftrightarrow$).

P if and only if Q can be written as P iff Q,   or even as $P \leftrightarrow Q$.

For example, Ceva's Theorem and its converse can be expressed as a single statement, thus:

Given triangle $\triangle ABC$. The Cevians AX, BY, and CZ are concurrent *if and only if*

$$\frac{AZ}{ZB} \cdot \frac{BX}{XC} \cdot \frac{CY}{YA} = 1.$$

Ceva's Theorem and its converse are two theorems. To prove Ceva's Theorem and its converse requires two separate proofs. To prove any statement of the form $P \leftrightarrow Q$, two separate proofs are needed. That is, you must prove *both* (1) $P \rightarrow Q$ *and* (2) $Q \rightarrow P$. These two proofs are independent of each other and may even use different proof strategies [Fenton & Dubinsky 1996; Smith *et al.* 2001].

CYCLIC QUADRILATERALS

Any three noncollinear points form the vertices of a triangle. As you worked on some of the activities for Chapter 3 (particularly Activities 7 and 11, pages 55–56), you found that a circle can always be constructed that goes through the vertices of a triangle. The perpendicular bisectors of the three sides of the triangle will be concurrent at the point O, which is the center of this circumscribed circle.

Quadrilaterals, on the other hand, do not always have all four vertices lying on one circle. Those special quadrilaterals that have this property are called *cyclic quadrilaterals*. Look again at the list of different quadrilaterals you worked with in Exercises 15 and 16, page 18 and Exercise 18, page 45. Where do cyclic quadrilaterals fit into this scheme of quadrilaterals? Every square is a cyclic quadrilateral, since all the angles are right angles. What about parallelograms? . . . trapezoids? . . . kites? . . . rectangles?

In Activity 2, you might have observed that if the perpendicular bisectors of the sides of a quadrilateral are concurrent, then the quadrilateral is cyclic. It turns out that the converse is also true, allowing us to state a biconditional theorem.

THEOREM 4.1   A quadrilateral is cyclic if and only if the perpendicular bisectors of the sides are concurrent.

This follows fairly easily from what we have learned about points on the perpendicular bisector of a line segment (see Exercise 26, page 78):

THEOREM 4.2   A point is on the perpendicular bisector of a line segment if and only if it is an equal distance from the endpoints of the line segment.

When a result follows fairly easily from a previous result, we sometimes refer to the new result as a *corollary* of the first. Thus, we could refer to the result about cyclic quadrilaterals (Theorem 4.1) as a corollary of the result about points on a perpendicular bisector (Theorem 4.2).

Another result you may have observed about cyclic quadrilaterals is that their nonadjacent angles are supplementary. If we recall that the measure of an inscribed angle is half the measure of the corresponding central angle, then we can prove that the result about nonadjacent angles of a cyclic quadrilateral. We outline this proof below, leaving it to the reader to complete the proof as an exercise.

THEOREM 4.3   The nonadjacent (opposite) angles of a convex cyclic quadrilateral are supplementary; that is, their measures sum to 180°.

Note: Because standard notation makes it difficult to distinguish between the two central angles formed by the two points on the circle, we refer to the arc subtending the angles in the following proof.

Outline of a proof   Assume that quadrilateral *ABCD* is cyclic. Consider a pair of nonadjacent angles. Without loss of generality, let those angles be $\angle BAD$ and $\angle BCD$. (See Figure 4.1.) Let $\overparen{BAD}$ (read "arc *BAD*") be the arc subtending the central angle marked by *a*, and $\overparen{BCD}$ be the arc subtending the central angle marked *b*. Note that $a + b = 360°$. Since the measure of an inscribed angle is half the measure of its corresponding central angle (or equivalently, half the measure of the corresponding arc), we get $m\angle BCD + m\angle BAD = \frac{1}{2}a + \frac{1}{2}b = \frac{1}{2}360° = 180°$, so nonadjacent angles of a cyclic quadrilateral are supplementary.

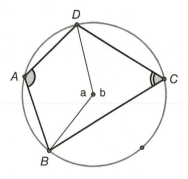

FIGURE 4.1
Nonadjacent Angles of a Cyclic
Quadrilateral are Supplementary

When a preliminary result is needed to prove a particular theorem, that preliminary result is sometimes referred to as a *lemma*. For this theorem about the opposite angles of a cyclic quadrilateral, we could refer to the earlier result about the measure of an inscribed angle (see page 89) as a lemma, since the focus of our discussion in this section was on the opposite angles of a cyclic quadrilateral. Both the terms "corollary" and "lemma" are used to communicate the way in which theorems are related. For this reason, these labels are dependent on the way in which the theorems are organized and presented.

INCIRCLES AND EXCIRCLES

We have seen that the three angle bisectors of the interior angles of a triangle are concurrent at a point that is commonly denoted I. In the proof of that theorem, we saw that the distance from I to a side of the triangle is the same for all three sides. Therefore, the *incenter* I is the center of the *incircle*, a circle interior to the triangle that is tangent to all three sides of the triangle.

We also can consider the angle bisector of an *exterior angle* for a triangle ΔXYZ. Recall that an exterior angle is formed at Y when either side XY or YZ is extended beyond the point Y. (The two exterior angles at Y are congruent because they are vertical angles to each other.) The bisectors of the exterior angles at Y and Z will be concurrent with the bisector of the interior angle at X. That is, if the bisectors of the exterior angles at Y and Z intersect at the point P, the bisector of the interior angle at X also goes through P. Can you prove this? You will have a chance to do this in the exercises. (*Hint*: Look for congruent triangles.)

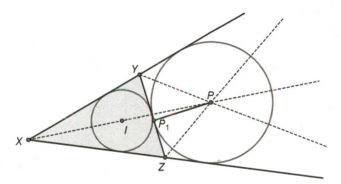

FIGURE 4.2
The Incircle and One of the Excircles of a Triangle

The point P will be the center of an *excircle* of the triangle, a circle exterior to the triangle and tangent to one side and to extensions of the other two sides. (See Figure 4.2.) One way to construct the circle you wanted in Activity 8b is to drop a perpendicular from P to side YZ. Call the foot of this perpendicular P_1. The segment PP_1 will be the radius of the excircle centered at P. When you construct the circle centered at P with radius PP_1, it certainly appears to be tangent to lines $\overleftrightarrow{XY}$ and $\overleftrightarrow{XZ}$. But how can we prove that this is actually the case? Since this circle is tangent to side YZ by construction, we only need to show that it must be tangent to the extended sides $\overleftrightarrow{XY}$ and $\overleftrightarrow{XZ}$ of our triangle. Drop perpendiculars from P to $\overleftrightarrow{XY}$ and $\overleftrightarrow{XZ}$, calling the feet of these perpendiculars P_2 and P_3, respectively. Using a method similar to that used in the proof of the theorem that the three angle bisectors of a triangle are concurrent (see page 66), we can prove that PP_1, PP_2, and PP_3 are congruent segments, so P_1, P_2, and P_3 must be points on the circle centered at P. Thus, the excircle is tangent to the side YZ and to the extensions of the sides XY and XZ [Baragar 2001, 36; Coxeter 1969, 11].

SOME INTERESTING FAMILIES OF CIRCLES

In Activity 6, you were working with another family of circles: circles that share a common chord. All the circles in Activity 6 share the common chord AB. Did you notice that the centers of C_1, C_2, and C_3 are collinear? Perhaps you used this idea to construct the circle C_3. You can choose any point X on the line that passes through the centers of C_1 and C_2, and X will be the center of a circle that has AB as a chord.

Suppose, however, that you start with the segment AB and want to construct a circle that has AB as a chord. That is, suppose that you don't have the circles C_1 and C_2—so that you can't use the line through their centers. How will you find the line where the centers of the family of circles through AB lie? The centers of this family of circles will lie on the perpendicular bisector of AB. To prove this, choose any point X on the perpendicular bisector of AB. (See Figure 4.3.) Triangle ΔXAB is an isosceles triangle with $XA \cong XB$. So the circle centered at X that passes through A will also pass through B. On the other hand, suppose that the point X does not lie on the perpendicular bisector of AB. Then the two segments AX and BX are not congruent, implying that a circle centered at X cannot pass through both A and B.

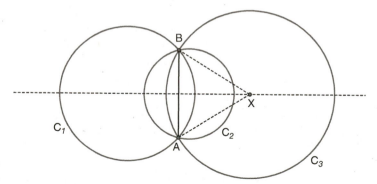

FIGURE 4.3
Circles that Share a
Common Chord

Pause for a moment to think about the proof structure of the last paragraph. First, we gave a direct proof that if X is on the perpendicular bisector of AB, then X can be the center of a circle containing A and B. Then, we gave an indirect proof that if X is the center of a circle containing A and B, then X must be on the perpendicular bisector of AB. These two proofs establish a biconditional statement: X is on the perpendicular bisector of AB if and only if X is the center of a circle containing A and B.

Suppose you are given a circle (or an arc of the circle, or even just a few points on the circle), and you want to find the center of the circle. Or suppose you are given a triangle, and you want to construct the circumcircle of that triangle. How can you use the fact that the center of the circle must lie on the perpendicular bisector of any chord of the circle to solve these problems? You will have a chance to do this in the exercises.

Two circles are said to be *orthogonal* if their tangents are perpendicular at their points of intersection. Let's construct an example of orthogonal circles: Starting with a circle, C_1, centered at A with radius AB, it is easy to construct a tangent line t to C_1 at the point B. (See Figure 4.4.) Choose any point Q on t, and construct the circle centered at Q with radius QB. Call this second circle C_2. Then, the line $\overleftrightarrow{AB}$ is tangent to the circle C_2, and the line $\overleftrightarrow{QB}$ is tangent to the circle C_1. Moreover, $\overleftrightarrow{AB} \perp \overleftrightarrow{QB}$. So circles C_1 and C_2 are orthogonal circles.

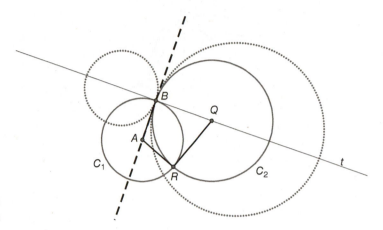

FIGURE 4.4
Orthogonal Circles

Observe also that circles C_1 and C_2 intersect at a second point R. AR is a radius of C_1, and AR will be tangent to the circle C_2. (*How can you be sure that AR and QR really are perpendicular?*) In other words, both of the tangent lines to the circle C_1 from the point Q are perpendicular to the corresponding tangent lines to the circle C_2 from the point A. This makes $ABQR$ a cyclic quadrilateral, although for a new circle that does not appear in this figure. (*Can you prove this?*)

If you animate the point Q, you will see that the circle with center Q grows larger as Q moves away from B, and becomes smaller as Q moves closer to B. In fact, as Q moves across the point B, the radius of C_2 shrinks momentarily to 0, so that the circle C_2 shrinks (momentarily) to a single point.

As Q moves along line t, it is constrained to stay within the GeoGebra window. However, we can imagine the line t as extending far beyond the edges of this window. What happens to the circle C_2 as Q moves off toward ∞ (i.e., toward "infinity")? As the point Q moves farther and farther away from the point B, the radius of the circle C_2 gets larger and larger. If Q were allowed to move off to ∞, the circle would have infinite radius, and its curvature would become very "straight"; in other words, the circle would become a straight line.

THE ARBELOS AND THE SALINON

Archimedes, a significant figure among the Greek mathematicians who followed Euclid, left us a number of interesting problems in his *Book of Lemmas* (or *Liber Assumptorum*). Among these are several problems involving the arbelos (or "shoe-maker's knife") and the salinon (or "salt cellar"). Perhaps part of the fascination of these figures is that they are apparently very simple—being bounded by semicircular arcs—yet they provide a rich source of problems.

You worked with the arbelos in Activity 7. If you constructed the arbelos in a GeoGebra worksheet, you had an opportunity to observe that the area of the arbelos appears to be equal to the area of the circle with diameter PR in Figure 4.5. How can you prove this?

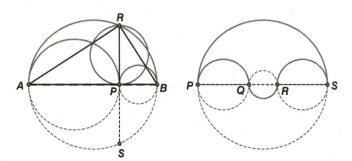

FIGURE 4.5
The Arbelos and the Salinon

To prove that the areas are equal, we can use an algebraic approach. That is, we can express the areas we are looking for using algebraic expressions. The area of the arbelos can be found by calculating the area of the large semicircle, and subtracting the areas of the two small semicircles. Since the point P is on the diameter AB, we know that the diameters of the two smaller semicircles must add up to the diameter of the largest semicircle. So we can find an expression for the area of the arbelos in terms of the lengths of the diameters (or the radii) of the three semicircles.

Let r_1 be the radius of the largest circle, and r_2, r_3 be the radii of the two smaller circles. Note that $r_1 = r_2 + r_3$. So the area of the arbelos is given by

$$\frac{1}{2}(\pi r_1^2 - (\pi r_2^2 + \pi r_3^2)).$$

This can be simplified to

$$\frac{\pi}{2}(r_1^2 - r_2^2 - r_3^2).$$

Since P can be anywhere on the segment AB, how can we find the area of the circle with diameter PR? Observe that $\angle ARB$ is a right angle. (*How do we know this?*) Using this fact and the Pythagorean Theorem, we can find an expression for the area of the circle with diameter PR in terms of the radii of the other three circles.

Let d_1 be the diameter of the largest circle, and d_2, d_3 be the diameters of the two smaller circles. Let d_4 denote the diameter of the circle on PR. Then using the Pythagorean Theorem three times, we have

$$d_1^2 = |AR|^2 + |RB|^2, \quad |AR|^2 = d_2^2 + d_4^2, \quad |RB|^2 = d_3^2 + d_4^2.$$

Substituting for equal quantities, we can write

$$d_1^2 = (d_2^2 + d_4^2) + (d_3^2 + d_4^2).$$

Solving for d_4^2 and simplifying, we get

$$d_4^2 = \frac{1}{2}(d_1^2 - d_2^2 - d_3^2).$$

Since we used radii instead of diameters to calculate the area of the arbelos, we express $d_4{}^2$ in terms of r_i instead of d_i:

$$d_4^2 = \frac{1}{2}\,[(2r_1)^2 - (2r_2)^2 - (2r_3)^2] = \frac{4}{2}\,[r_1^2 - r_2^2 - r_3^2].$$

Finally, the area of the circle on PR is calculated by

$$\pi\left(\frac{d_4}{2}\right)^2 = \frac{\pi}{4}d_4^2 = \frac{\pi}{4}\frac{4}{2}[r_1^2 - r_2^2 - r_3^2]$$

$$= \frac{\pi}{2}(r_1^2 - r_2^2 - r_3^2).$$

This is exactly the result we got when we calculated the area of the arbelos.

The salinon is another interesting figure that can be constructed using semicircular arcs. Given a circle with diameter PS, construct circles with diameters PQ, QR, and RS, setting $PQ \cong RS$. The salinon is formed by taking three semicircular arcs on one side of PS and one arc on the other side of PS as in Figure 4.5. You will have a chance to work with the salinon in the exercises [Eves 1976, 156; Knight 2000; Wells 1991, 5]

POWER OF A POINT

The idea of *function* is an important mathematical idea. A function is a process that takes one or more inputs from a specified set and turns them into an output. You studied functions in your high school or college algebra course. For example, you may have worked with expressions that looked something like

$$y = f(x) = 5x^3 + 4x.$$

In this expression, x is the input, y is the output, and the expression $5x^3 + 4x$ is a rule that tells you how to convert the input into an output of the function. For this example, x can be any real number, so the set of all real numbers is the domain of the function f. The output of this function is also a real number. You may have encountered some functions that required more than one input. For example,

$$g(x, y) = 5x^2 + 2xy + 3y^3$$

is a function that requires two inputs. Here you have to supply two numbers, x and y, then use the expression $5x^2 + 2xy + 3y^3$ to calculate the output. The inputs, x and y, can be any real numbers, and the output of the function g will again be a real number.

In Activity 6, you were working with a different kind of function. This function has two inputs—a point P and a circle C. The process of this function requires you (or GeoGebra) to figure out the radius, r, of C, and the distance, d, of P from the center of C, and then to calculate the value $d^2 - r^2$. So the output of this function is a number.

Given a circle C and a point P, *the power of P with respect to C*, denoted Power(P, C), is a function that depends only on the radius, r, of C and the distance, d, of P from the center of C:

$$\text{Power}(P, C) = d^2 - r^2.$$

So Power is a function that takes two geometric objects (a point and a circle), and returns a number. Notice that if P is interior to C, d will be smaller than r, so that Power(P, C) will be a negative number.

As you worked on Activity 5, you probably observed that if Q and R are points on the circle C and P is collinear with Q and R, then the product $PQ \cdot PR$ gives another way of calculating Power(P, C). But this needs to be proved. You can use the similar triangles you saw in Activity 3 to show that $PQ \cdot PR$ is constant no matter where Q and R are on the circle (as long as P, Q, and R are collinear). But we still need to prove that $PQ \cdot PR = d^2 - r^2$. You will have a chance to do this in the exercises.

So you can calculate the power of the point P with respect to the circle C using either of these methods—and there is a third method involving a tangent that works when P is on or exterior to the circle. If you know the radius of the circle, r, and the distance of P from the center of the circle, d, you can calculate Power(P, C) using the defining formula $d^2 - r^2$. On the other hand, if you have a line through P that intersects the circle at points Q and R, you can calculate the power of P with respect to C using the product $PQ \cdot PR$. If there is a line through P that is tangent to C at the point T, you can calculate the power by PT^2. If P is interior to the circle, we have seen that Power$(P, C) < 0$, since $d^2 < r^2$. If this happens, then Q and R will be on opposite sides of the point P. In other words, the rays $\overrightarrow{PQ}$ and $\overrightarrow{PR}$ will be pointing in opposite directions. In this case, we take the product $PQ \cdot PR$ to be negative [Coxeter 1969, 81; Sved 1991, 15].

THE RADICAL AXIS

One way to think of Power is as a measure of the distance from the point P to the given circle. In fact, if the circle has radius zero—that is, if the circle is a single point—the Power of P with respect to that circle is exactly the square of the distance from P to the center. When two circles are involved, the point P has a power for each of the two circles. At some points, this power will have the same value from both circles. A natural question to ask is this: For two given circles, what set of points has equal power from both circles?

In the case when both circles have radius zero, this question is asking for the points P whose distances from two given points A and B are equal. It is not difficult to prove that the set of possible points P is a line, the perpendicular bisector of the segment AB. A similar thing happens when the radii of the circles are nonzero; the set of points P for which the power is the same value from both circles forms a line called the *radical axis* of the circles. Of course, this statement needs a proof.

THEOREM 4.4   Suppose two circles are given: the first circle C_1 centered at A with radius r_1 and the second circle C_2 centered at B with radius r_2. The set of points P for which $\text{Power}(P, C_1) = \text{Power}(P, C_2)$ forms a line.

Proof   (adapted from [Court 1952, 16–17]) Consider a point P as described in the hypothesis of the theorem. Since the powers of P from the two circles are equal, $PA^2 - r_1^2 = PB^2 - r_2^2$. Construct a line on P that is perpendicular to the line AB, and let these lines intersect at a point C. (See Figure 4.6.) Then $\triangle PAC$ and $\triangle PBC$ are right triangles. Therefore,

$$PC^2 + AC^2 - r_1^2 = PC^2 + CB^2 - r_2^2.$$

Rearranging the terms of this equation gives $AC^2 - CB^2 = r_1^2 - r_2^2$ and thus $(AC - CB)(AC + CB) = r_1^2 - r_2^2$. Since $AC + CB = AB$, this last equation can be expressed as

$$AC - CB = \frac{r_1^2 - r_2^2}{AB}.$$

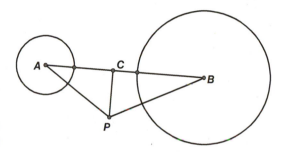

FIGURE 4.6
Point P with Equal Powers

Notice that the right-hand side of this equation is a constant k that is derived solely from the two given circles. Hence $AC = CB + k$, no matter what point P is used. This implies that there is only one possible location for C.

This is a subtle point, and it deserves more explanation. We have established that $AC = CB + k$. On the segment AB, construct a segment AD of length k. (If $k < 0$, AD should be on the line $\overleftrightarrow{AD}$ in the direction away from B.) Then the point C is the midpoint of DB. The critical fact is that C is the same point no matter which P was used.

In addition, notice that every point P for which the two powers are equal lies on the line through C perpendicular to AB. This line is the radical axis.
(If the point C does not lie between A and B, it is necessary to consider directed distances in this proof. You may work out the details for yourself.)

It is not obvious how to construct the radical axis for two particular circles. If the circles intersect, the radical axis is the line through their intersection points.

(You will be asked to prove this in the exercises.) If the two circles do not intersect, the construction is more difficult. It may even be the case that one circle is inside the other! The preceding proof tells us that the radical axis is perpendicular to the line connecting the centers of the two circles, which is helpful but not sufficient. The next theorem will give us a tool to help with this construction.

THEOREM 4.5   Suppose three circles are given for which the centers are not collinear. Each pair of circles determines a radical axis, and these three radical axes are concurrent.

Figure 4.7 shows an example of this theorem in which two of the circles intersect but the third is disjoint from the others. The theorem is not difficult to prove. You might wonder why the hypothesis included the requirement that the three circle centers are not collinear. Suppose these centers were collinear. Then each radical axis would be perpendicular to the line through the centers, and thus the three axes would be parallel.

To construct a radical axis, start with two given circles, C_1 and C_2. Construct a third circle C_3 that intersects both of the given circles. The intersection points for C_1 and C_3 determine a line, which is the radical axis of C_1 and C_3. Similarly, the intersection points of C_2 and C_3 determine the radical axis of C_2 and C_3. The point P where these two axes intersect also lies on the radical axis of C_1 and C_2, because the last theorem says that the three radical axes are concurrent. Also, the desired radical axis is perpendicular to the line between the centers of C_1 and C_2. Therefore, construct the line between the centers of C_1 and C_2, and then construct the radical axis as the line through point P that is perpendicular to the line between the centers.

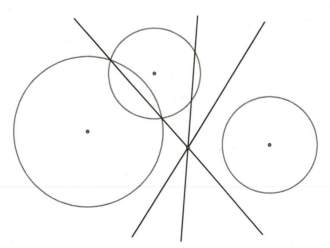

FIGURE 4.7
Radical Axes of Three Circles

THE NINE-POINT CIRCLE: A SECOND PASS

The arbelos and the salinon were figures studied by the Greeks in the third-century BC. Now we turn our attention to an interesting geometric problem of the nineteenth-century AD. In Chapter 3, you began to experiment with the so-called *nine-point circle*. (See Activity 11, page 56.)

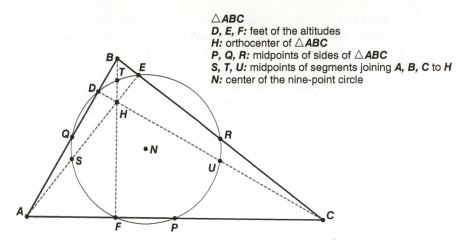

△ABC
D, E, F: feet of the altitudes
H: orthocenter of △ABC
P, Q, R: midpoints of sides of △ABC
S, T, U: midpoints of segments joining A, B, C to H
N: center of the nine-point circle

FIGURE 4.8
The Nine-Point Circle

The circle that passes through the feet of the three altitudes of a triangle contains quite a few interesting points. In 1821 the French mathematicians Charles Julien Brianchon and Jean-Victor Poncelet published a theorem that for any triangle, the *midpoints of the sides*, the *feet of the altitudes*, and the *midpoints of the lines joining the vertices of the triangle to the orthocenter* all lie on a common circle. The English mathematician Benjamin Bevan had posed a very similar problem seventeen years earlier.

In Germany, Karl Wilhelm Feuerbach, proved—by calculating their radii and the distances between their centers algebraically—that the nine-point circle is tangent to the incircle and to each of the three excircles of the triangle. This adds another four special points to the nine-point circle (which is now sometimes called the Feuerbach circle). We will continue our investigations of this special circle in Chapter 5, Analytic Geometry, where you will have an opportunity to use methods of analytic geometry to develop some of the proofs [Thomas 2002, 69; Wells 1991, 76 & 159].

4.3 EXERCISES

Give clear and complete answers to the following problems and questions. Write your explanations clearly using complete sentences. Include diagrams whenever appropriate.

1. The following statements have all appeared in the activities or exercises of this or the previous chapters. You have already constructed GeoGebra diagrams illustrating these statements, and may already have written informal proofs of some of these statements. Write out a careful step-by-step proof for each statement.

a. Let O be the center of a circle, and let P, Q, and R be points on the circle. Prove that the measure of the central angle $\angle POR$ is twice the measure of the inscribed angle $\angle PQR$.

b. Let O be the center of a circle, and let PR be a diameter of this circle. If Q is a point on the circle, prove that angle $\angle PQR$ is a right angle.

c. A median divides its triangle into two equal areas.

d. The three medians of a triangle are concurrent at a point called the centroid, often denoted as G.

e. The three altitudes of a triangle are concurrent at a point called the orthocenter, often denoted as *H*.
f. The perpendicular bisectors of the three sides of a triangle are concurrent at a point called the circumcenter, often denoted as *O*.
g. The circumcenter, *O*, of a triangle is the center of a circle that passes through the three vertices of the triangle.
h. The opposite interior angles of a convex cyclic quadrilateral are supplementary.

2. Create truth tables to verify that the contrapositive, $\neg Q \rightarrow \neg P$, and the method of proof by contradiction, $(P \wedge \neg Q) \rightarrow$ *false*, are each equivalent to the implication $P \rightarrow Q$.

3. Let *AB* and *CD* be chords of a circle that intersect at point *P*. Prove that $AP \cdot PB = CP \cdot PD$.

4. Prove or disprove that
   a. a rectangle is a cyclic quadrilateral;
   b. a parallelogram is a cyclic quadrilateral.

5. Draw a Venn diagram illustrating how cyclic quadrilaterals fit into the set of quadrilaterals. Your diagram should make it clear which quadrilaterals—kites, parallelograms, rectangles, rhombi, squares, and trapezoids—are always cyclic, sometimes cyclic, or never cyclic.

6. Prove that a tangent line to a circle is perpendicular to a radius of that circle at the point of tangency. (This is the converse of the result proved by contradiction on page 92.)

7. Write a short essay explaining why it is impossible to construct a tangent to a circle from a point interior to the circle.

8. Let *ABCD* be a convex cyclic quadrilateral.
   a. Prove that the interior angles at *A* and *C* are supplementary.
   b. Prove that the exterior angle at *B* is congruent to the interior angle at *D*.
   c. How does this situation change if *ABCD* is not convex?

9. Complete the proof that the nonadjacent angles of a convex cyclic quadrilateral are supplementary.

10. State the converse of the statement of Exercise 9. Is this converse true or false? Explain.

11. Prove that the perpendicular bisectors of a quadrilateral are concurrent if and only if the quadrilateral is cyclic. (*Note*: There are two statements to prove.)

12. In Activity 2, page 85, you explored the concurrency of the perpendicular bisectors of the sides of a quadrilateral. Do the same for the angle bisectors of the angles of a quadrilateral. Make conjectures, and present deductive arguments supporting (proving) your conjectures.

13. Let *WXYZ* be a cyclic quadrilateral. (*WXYZ* is not necessarily convex.) Let *P* be the point on the intersection of the lines containing the sides *WX* and *YZ*.
   a. If *P* is exterior to the circle, prove that $PW \cdot PX = PZ \cdot PY$.
   b. Under what conditions will *P* be *interior to* or *on* the circle?
   c. Prove or disprove that

   $$PW \cdot PX = PZ \cdot PY$$

   when *P* is on or interior to the circle.

14. Prove *Ptolemy's Theorem*: If *ABCD* is a cyclic quadrilateral, then the product of the diagonals is equal to the sum of the products of the opposite sides. In symbols, $AC \cdot BD = AB \cdot CD + BC \cdot DA$. (*Hint*: Locate the point *E* on *AC* so that $\angle ABE \cong \angle DBC$ and construct the segment *BE*. Then look for similar triangles.)

15. Given a triangle $\triangle XYZ$, extend sides *XY* and *XZ* creating exterior angles at *Y* and *Z*.
   a. Prove that the bisectors of the exterior angles at *Y* and *Z* are concurrent with the bisector of the interior angle at *X*. Call this point of intersection *R*.
   b. Construct a circle centered at *R*, which is tangent to the line $\overleftrightarrow{YZ}$.
   c. Prove that this circle is also tangent to the lines $\overleftrightarrow{XY}$ and $\overleftrightarrow{XZ}$. This circle is an *excircle* of $\triangle XYZ$.

16. The three excircles of $\triangle ABC$ will be tangent to the (nonextended) sides at three points. Prove that the Cevians joining the vertices of the triangle with these points of tangency are

concurrent. This is the *Nagel point* of $\triangle ABC$. (Compare this to Exercise 46 on page 79.)

17. In GeoGebra, construct two circles. Use the method described in the text to construct the radical axis of these two circles. Vary your original circles and observe how the radical axis behaves.

18. Suppose that two circles intersect at two points P and Q. Prove that the radical axis of these circles is the line $\overleftrightarrow{PQ}$.

19. Suppose that two circles are tangent at the point T. Prove that the radical axis of these circles is the line through T that is tangent to both circles.

20. Prove Theorem 4.5 about the radical axis of three circles.

21. If two circles are congruent—that is, if they have the same radius—prove that the radical axis of these circles is the perpendicular bisector of the segment between the centers of the circles.

22. Prove that if two circles are orthogonal, then they intersect at exactly two points and their tangents are perpendicular at both of those points.

23. Prove that $ABQR$ in Figure 4.4 (page 97) is a cyclic quadrilateral.

24. Given triangle $\triangle ABC$.
    a. Construct the center of the circumcircle of $\triangle ABC$. Prove that your construction is correct.
    b. Explain how you can use this construction to find an entire circle given just an arc of the circle.
    c. What is the smallest number, n, of noncollinear points that determine a unique circle? Explain how you would construct a circle given just n points.

25. Suppose that $\triangle ABC$ is equilateral. Prove that the area of its circumcircle is four times the area of its incircle.

26. A regular hexagon is inscribed in a circle of area 2π. What is the area of the hexagon? (This problem has been adapted from an example given on page 30 of the *Praxis Study Guide for the Mathematics Tests*, ETS, 2003.)

27. Consider circle C with center O and radius r. Let $A_1 A_2$ be a chord of C. Let P be a point on the line $\overleftrightarrow{A_1 A_2}$ and let d denote the distance from P to O.
    a. Assume that P lies outside of C. Let PT be tangent to C at T. Show that $PT^2 = d^2 - r$.
    b. Still assuming that P lies outside of C, show that the product
    $$PA_1 \cdot PA_2 = d^2 - r^2.$$
    (*Hint*: First prove this if $A_1 A_2$ is a diameter. Then show that any other line $\overleftrightarrow{A_1 A_2}$ gives the same value.)
    c. If P lies inside of C, it is not possible to construct the tangent from P to C. However, it still is possible to calculate $PA_1 \cdot PA_2$. Assume that P lies inside of C. Show that the product
    $$PA_1 \cdot PA_2 = d^2 - r^2.$$
    (*Hint*: Use Exercise 3.)
    d. Explain how the power of P with respect to a fixed circle C, Power(P, C), can always be calculated by $d^2 - r^2$.
    e. What is the significance of Power(P, C) being positive, or zero, or negative? That is, if you know that Power(P, C) is
    $$> 0, \quad \text{or} \quad = 0, \quad \text{or} \quad < 0,$$
    what do you know about the point P?

28. Let AB be the diameter of a circle, and let C be another point on this circle. Construct $\triangle ABC$. Let D be the foot of the perpendicular from C to AB.
    a. If $AD = x$ and $BD = y$, prove that the altitude CD of $\triangle ABC$ has length $\sqrt{xy}$.
    b. If x and y are positive numbers, then $\frac{x+y}{2}$ is their *arithmetic mean*, and $\sqrt{xy}$ is their *geometric mean*. Show that $\sqrt{xy} \leq \frac{x+y}{2}$.
    (This problem has been adapted from an example given on page 22 of the *Praxis Study Guide for the Mathematics Tests*, ETS, 2003.)

29. *The Arbelos*: In Figure 4.5 on page 98, let T and U be the points where lines RA and RB intersect the smaller arcs of the arbelos.
    a. Prove that PR and TU are congruent line segments.

b. Prove that *PTRU* is a parallelogram.

c. Prove that line $\overleftrightarrow{TU}$ is an external tangent to the two smaller circular arcs of the arbelos.

30. *The Salinon*: Figure 4.5 (page 98) gives a diagram of a salinon. Points *P*, *Q*, *R*, and *S* are collinear (and in that order) with $PQ \cong RS$. Semicircles with diameters *PQ*, *RS*, and *PS* lie on the same side of the line $\overleftrightarrow{PS}$, while the semicircle with diameter *QR* lies on the other side of $\overleftrightarrow{PS}$.

a. Construct a diagram of a salinon in a GeoGebra worksheet. Make your diagram robust enough that *PQ* stays congruent to *RS* even if you move the points around.

b. Calculate the area of the salinon.

c. The perpendicular bisector of *PS* is the axis of symmetry of the salinon. Construct this axis of symmetry, and let *M* and *N* be the points where this line intersects the semicircles on diameters *PS* and *QR*, respectively. Construct a circle with diameter *MN*.

d. Prove that the area of the salinon is equal to the area of the circle with diameter *MN*.

The following problems are more challenging.

31. Prove that the nine-point circle for triangle $\triangle ABC$ is tangent to the incircle of $\triangle ABC$.

32. Prove that the nine-point circle of triangle $\triangle ABC$ is tangent to one of the excircles of $\triangle ABC$.

33. For any triangle $\triangle ABC$, it is claimed that *the diameter of the nine-point circle is half the length of the diameter of the circumcircle of $\triangle ABC$.*

a. If this claim can be proved, how will the radius of the nine-point circle compare to the radius of the circumcircle? Explain.

b. What impact will this have on the relative *areas* of the nine-point circle and the circumcircle?

c. Prove (or disprove) the claim.

34. Prove that for any triangle $\triangle ABC$, the center of the nine-point circle lies on the Euler line of the triangle, midway between the circumcenter and the orthocenter.

35. We have a method for constructing a tangent to a circle *C* from a point *A*, which may be on or exterior to *C*. (See page 89.) Suppose you have two circles, C_1 and C_2. Develop a strategy for constructing a line that is tangent to both C_1 and C_2. (*Hint*: If r_1 and r_2 are the radii of C_1 and C_2, respectively, it will be helpful to construct a circle with radius $|r_1 - r_2|$.)

36. For triangle $\triangle ABC$, let $a = |BC|$, $b = |CA|$, and $c = |AB|$. (So *a* is the length of the side opposite $\angle A$, etc.) For convenience, let *s* be the *semi-perimeter* $\frac{a+b+c}{2}$.

a. The incircle of the triangle is tangent to the three sides. Label these points of tangency as *D*, *E*, and *F* on the lines *AB*, *BC*, and *CA*, respectively. Find expressions for the lengths of the segments *AD*, *DB*, *BE*, *EC*, *CF*, and *FA* in terms of *a*, *b*, *c*, *s*.

b. Consider one of the excircles for $\triangle ABC$. This circle too is tangent to the three sides, at points *X*, *Y*, and *Z* on the lines *AB*, *BC*, and *CA*, respectively. Find expressions for the lengths of the segments *AX*, *XB*, *BY*, *YC*, *CZ*, and *ZA* in terms of *a*, *b*, *c*, *s*.

Exercises 37 and 38 are especially for future teachers.

37. In the *Principles and Standards for School Mathematics* [NCTM 2000, 56], the National Council for Teachers of Mathematics (NCTM) recommends that

Instructional programs from prekindergarten through grade 12 should enable all students to

- recognize reasoning and proof as fundamental aspects of mathematics;
- make and investigate mathematical conjectures;
- develop and evaluate mathematical arguments;
- select and use various types of reasoning and methods of proof.

What does this mean for your future students?

a. The NCTM has developed specific instructional recommendations for each of four different grade bands: Pre-K–2, 3–5,

6–8, and 9–12. Find a copy of the *Principles and Standards*, and study the discussion of the Reasoning and Proof Standard [NCTM 2000, 56–59] for one of these grade bands. Choose one of the grade levels for which you are seeking certification. What are the specific recommendations with regard to reasoning and proof for your chosen grade band?

b. Find some mathematics textbooks for these same grade levels. How are the NCTM recommendations implemented in these textbooks? Cite specific examples.

c. Write a report in which you present and critique what you learn in studying the NCTM Reasoning and Proof Standard in light of your experiences in this course. Your report should include your answers to parts (a) and (b).

38. Design several classroom activities involving reasoning and proof that would be appropriate for students in your future classroom. Write a short report explaining how the activities you design reflect both the NCTM recommendations and what you are learning about reasoning and proof in this course (in Chapters 1–4).

Reflect on what you have learned in this chapter.

39. Review the main ideas of this chapter. Describe, in your own words, the concepts you have studied and what you have learned about them. What are the important ideas? How do they fit together? Which concepts were easy for you? Which were hard?

40. Reflect on the learning environment for this course.

   a. Describe aspects of the learning environment that helped you understand the main ideas in this chapter. Which activities did you like? Dislike? Why?

   b. How are you growing in understanding your own approach to learning? How do you think this will impact your approach to your professional/personal life in the future?

4.4 CHAPTER OVERVIEW

Two important themes of this course have been highlighted in this chapter: *the concept of a function* and *the development of sound mathematical proofs*.

The function concept is foundational in mathematics. In your experiences prior to this course, functions may have been all about numbers—numbers as inputs and numbers as output. We have investigated a new kind of function in this chapter: *Power*.

Power is a function that takes two inputs, a point and a circle, and returns a number. The number returned by Power(P, C) is a measure of how far P is from C, where both the *distance* (d) of P from the center of C and the *radius* (r) of C are used in computing this measure: Power(P, C) $= d^2 - r^2$. If Power(P, C) is positive, we know that $d > r$, so that P lies outside of C. If Power(P, C) is negative, we know that $d < r$, so that P lies interior to C. If P lies on C, $d = r$; in this case, Power (P, C) $= 0$. We also saw two other methods for computing Power.

When two circles are involved, the Power of a point can be calculated from each circle. The set of points for which Power is equal from both circles forms the *radical axis* of the circles. A set of three circles produces three such axes, and typically these three radical axes are concurrent. This theorem is the basis for construction of the radical axis.

Writing good mathematical proofs is an important theme in this course. In earlier chapters, we introduced some things that you need to consider in developing proofs of your conjectures and theorems. In this chapter, we have continued this discussion by identifying two additional common proof strategies: indirect proof (in which you essentially prove the contrapositive of your conjecture or theorem) and proof by contradiction. With direct proof and disproof by counterexample, these strategies give you an arsenal of strategies for developing your proofs.

The *scientific method,* an important investigative strategy used in the natural sciences, involves experimentation followed by reflection on the results of the experiments. This is an *inductive process.* In this course, you have been encouraged to do a lot of experimentation of geometric ideas using GeoGebra diagrams, and to make conjectures based on your experimentation. This inductive process can be very effective for learning. Part of the reason for this is that working with geometric constructions in a GeoGebra diagram is a hands-on activity. The constructions are concrete objects (in the pedagogical sense), and the way we humans learn tends to move from concrete experiences toward abstract thought.

In general, the *mathematical method* approaches problems in the opposite way. Developing a sound mathematical proof requires you to move from axioms to theorems, from assumptions to results. Mathematicians tend to start with assumptions in the form of *axioms* (or *postulates*) and deduce results (*theorems*) from the axioms. This is a *deductive process.* Getting an idea for a conjecture requires some experimentation and inductive thinking, while developing a proof requires logical reasoning and is a deductive process.

If you have been able to develop a robust construction using GeoGebra, you may be able to translate the steps you took in constructing the diagram into steps in your proof. At the very least, the experimentation you have done in constructing the diagram will have challenged you to think about the ideas you will need as you develop a proof.

In these first several chapters, we have been working with Euclid's axioms. In some later chapters, we will change one of these axioms and observe the effects of that change. This will give us an opportunity to see how much our world view is shaped by our assumptions. (In other words, what we see depends on our axioms.)

The geometric content of this chapter has been focused on properties of circles. You have been reminded of a lot of the terminology used in talking about circles. You have probably also encountered some new and challenging ideas in the geometry of circles. A triangle has many circles associated with it, and this provides a bridge back to the work of the previous chapter. Each triangle has one *incircle* and three *excircles,* which are associated with the bisectors of the internal and external angles of the triangle. The *circumcircle* passes through the three vertices of the triangle, and its center can be found by constructing the perpendicular bisectors of the sides. The *nine-point circle* of a triangle passes through many interesting points. We will continue our investigations of the nine-point circle in the next chapter, where we will be able to use methods of analytic geometry to develop some of the proofs. This chapter also explored *cyclic quadrilaterals* and some of the special properties they possess.

We can construct various families of circles—circles that share particular characteristics. For example, there is a family of circles that all have the same center point *O*, another family of circles that all pass through a point *A*, and a family of circles with the same radius. We have investigated two interesting families of circles in this chapter: circles that share a common chord and circles that are orthogonal to a given fixed circle. While these two families of circles are interesting to study for themselves, they will also be important in investigations that we will take up in later chapters.

Mathematics is a living study. At every age of history, people have been investigating interesting problems. Our investigations of the arbelos and the salinon gave us an opportunity to step back into the early history of mathematics. Although these figures are constructed using just simple arcs of circles, many interesting problems can be posed about them. We have investigated just a few of these problems. The nine-point circle comes from the nineteenth century. We will continue our investigations of the nine-point circle in Chapter 5, where we will be able to use methods of analytic geometry—coordinates and equations—as tools to investigate these problems and to prove our conjectures.

At the end of Chapter 2, we listed a number of constructions that you should master:

- Construct a perpendicular to a line from any point (on or off the line).
- Construct the perpendicular bisector of a given line segment.
- Construct the foot of the perpendicular from a point *P* to a line ℓ.
- Construct the tangent line to a circle from a point on the circle.
- Construct the tangent line to a circle from a point not on the circle.
- Construct the bisector of a given angle.

Now, as you are coming to the end of Chapter 4, you should recognize that each of these constructions depends in a fundamental way on some properties of circles. Each of these constructions can be done by using the intersection points of one, two, or three circles. The geometric idea of a circle is very simple, yet circles have amazingly many applications.

CHAPTER FIVE

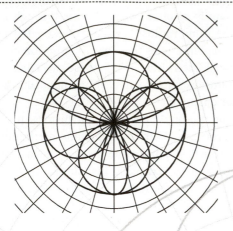

Early seventeenth-century mathematicians established a correspondence between points of the plane and ordered pairs of real numbers, or coordinates. The significance of this development is that geometric lines and curves can be described using equations in two variables, and many problems of geometry can be studied using methods of algebra and analysis. This *analytic geometry* gives us a new tool for solving geometric problems [Eves 1976, 278].

Analytic Geometry

Do the following activities, writing your explanations clearly in complete sentences. Include diagrams whenever appropriate. Save your work for each activity, as later work sometimes builds on earlier work. You will find it helpful to read ahead into the chapter as you work on these activities.

1. Draw a line, and create two new points on it. Label the new points as ZERO and ONE. Then *construct* (don't draw) points to represent 2, $\frac{1}{2}$, -2, and $\sqrt{2}$. Label your points accordingly.

    Now vary the point labeled ONE. What happens to the other points as you do this?

    A challenge: Can you also construct the points for $\frac{1}{3}$ and $\sqrt{3}$?

2. Figure 5.1 shows an unusual coordinate system. As usual, however, you plot a point (x, y) by starting at the origin, O, then moving x units in the x-direction and y units in the y-direction.

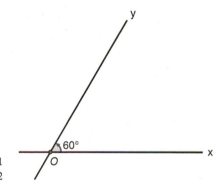

FIGURE 5.1
Coordinate System for Activity 2

    a. On a sheet of paper, make a sketch of this coordinate system, plot the following points, and label them. (You are encouraged to do this activity on paper, rather than using GeoGebra. If you decide to do this using GeoGebra, you will need to label the points with letters or words, instead of numerals.)

    A $(5, 0)$
    B $(0, \sqrt{2})$
    C $(1, 2)$
    D $(0, -4)$
    E $(-\sqrt{3}, \sqrt{3})$

    b. Find the distance between points A and B. (*Hint*: This is equivalent to finding the length of the side AB of $\triangle OAB$.)

    c. Find the distance between points A and E.

3. Open a GeoGebra window with a set of axes and hide the grid. Draw a line that intersects both axes and construct two new points, A and B, on this line. (A and B should not be the points that determine the line.) This activity will

use the individual coordinates of each point. GeoGebra will calculate the *abscissa* (the *x*-coordinate) of the point *A* by the command $x(A)$ and the *ordinate* (the *y*-coordinate) of the point *A* by $y(A)$.

Use the Input Bar to calculate the ratio

$$\frac{y_B - y_A}{x_B - x_A}.$$

Animate the point *A* (by right-clicking on either the point *A* or on the description of *A* in the Algebra pane), and observe the value of this ratio as *A* moves. Now animate the point *B* also and again observe the ratio. Explain what you see happening. Now change your line. Is your observation still valid?

4. Open a GeoGebra window with a set of axes and hide the grid.
   a. Draw a line that intersects the negative *x*-axis and the positive *y*-axis. Find the points of intersection of your line with the axes. Use the coordinates of these intersection points to calculate the slope of your line, as you did in the previous activity.
      Measure the angle between the *x*-axis and your line. This is the *angle of inclination* for this line. You should be able to vary the line and have the calculations update automatically. (*Hint*: For this angle, use a point far to the right on the *x*-axis and use the *x*-intercept point, but do not use the *y*-intercept point.)
   b. How are the slope and the angle of inclination related? (*Hint*: Consider the triangle formed by your line and the two axes.)
   c. Construct another line parallel to your line. Measure both the slope and the angle of inclination for this new line. How are these values related to those values of your original line? Explain why.
   d. Construct a line perpendicular to your original line, and measure its slope and its angle of inclination. How are these values related to the slope and angle of inclination of the original line? Explain why.

5. Suppose you are given a point, *P*, and a line, ℓ. GeoGebra can measure the distance between *P* and ℓ. Precisely what do you think this measurement means? Explain why your idea makes sense as a way to measure the distance from a point to a line.

6. Open a GeoGebra window with a set of axes.
   a. In the Input Bar, define the function $f(x) = 3 + \sqrt{25 - (x - 2)^2}$. Then define the function $g(x) = 3 - \sqrt{25 - (x - 2)^2}$. (*Hint*: The square root can be done as *sqrt* or by an exponent, ^(1/2).)
   b. What is the shape of the figure produced by the graphs of these functions?
   c. Check your answer to part (b) by trying to find the center and radius of the figure.

7. a. In a GeoGebra window with no axes, construct a rectangle, *ABCD*, and its diagonal *AC*. Construct the midpoints *E* of the segment *BC* and *F* of the segment *DA*, then construct the segments *BF* and *DE*. These new

segments cut the diagonal *AC* into three pieces at new points *G* and *H*. Measure the length of each piece of the diagonal. What do you observe? Vary your rectangle; does your observation still hold? Form a conjecture.

b. In the same sketch, show the coordinate system. Place your rectangle on the coordinate system by the following steps: Select point *A* and carefully move it to the origin. (This can be done easily by using the **Attach/Detach Point** tool to attach *A* to the *y*-axis and then moving *A* to the origin.) Next, use the **Attach/Detach Point** tool with point *B* and the horizontal axis. Adjust the vertices of *ABCD* to place the rectangle in the first quadrant. Vertex *C* should lie within the first quadrant, while the other vertices should lie on the axes.

Examine the coordinates of the four vertices of *ABCD*. Also examine the coordinates of the intersection points *G* and *H* on the diagonal AC. How do the coordinates of *G* and *H* compare to those of vertex *C*?

c. Assign *C* the general coordinates (c, d). Of course, vertex *A* has coordinates $(0, 0)$. From this information, find coordinates for the other labeled points in the figure. Then prove your conjecture from part (a).

8. In navigation, it is common to give directions in terms of *distance* and *compass point*.
   a. On a sheet of paper, draw the following points.
      - The origin
      - 2 km east
      - 5 km north
      - 3 km southwest
      - 4 km east–southeast
   b. How should we interpret −3 km west? Add this point to your drawing.
   c. If east = 0° and angles are measured counterclockwise, describe each of the points from parts 8(a) and 8(b) as (*distance, angle°*).
   d. To do graphing in terms of distance and direction, it is necessary to change the axes to *polar coordinates*. To do this, click on the gear icon in the upper-right corner. Select **Graphics**, then **Grid**. Change the Grid Type to Polar and check the box for Show Grid. Also, use **Options**, then **Advanced** to set the Angle Unit to Radians. Now plot the points, as you described them in part 8(c). For example, 5 km north would be typed in the Input Bar as (5; pi/2). Notice that a semicolon is used when working with polar coordinates.
   e. For each point, find a different description in polar coordinates. To do that, you can use negative distances or negative directions. Plot each in GeoGebra to be sure you have described the same points.

9. In the grid of a Cartesian coordinate system, the basic objects are vertical lines and horizontal lines, which can be described by equations such as $x = a$ and $y = b$. What are the basic objects of the grid for a polar coordinate system? How would you describe them by equations?

10. On a polar grid, plot the function $f(\theta) = \sqrt{3}\sin(2\theta)$. You can type this function into the Input line at the bottom of the Graphics pane. How does the $\sqrt{3}$ appear in the graph? Explain why this plot does not go into quadrant II or IV.

11. a. On a polar grid, plot the following functions, one at a time. These functions are called *rose curves*.
    - $r = \sin(3\theta)$
    - $r = \sin(4\theta)$
    - $r = \sin(5\theta)$
    - $r = \sin(6\theta)$

    You can select the function in the Algebra pane, and Hide/Show these plots one at a time or all at once.

    b. For $r = \sin(n\theta)$, how many petals will the rose have?
    c. Create a rose with sixteen petals. Create a rose with seventeen petals. Create a rose with eighteen petals.

    (*Hints*: By double-clicking on either a curve (in the Graphics pane) or its function definition (in the Algebra pane), you can easily edit the function. For eighteen petals, the coefficient of θ does not have to be an integer. You may also need to alter the domain of your function to see more or less of the path.)

5.2 DISCUSSION

Analytic geometry unites geometry and algebra in a powerful way. Coordinate systems allow us to use algebra to answer geometric questions. Because we have a large collection of algebraic tools, this is a valuable connection that works both ways. In the last century or so, much research has been done on what geometry can tell us about algebra. However, this discussion goes well beyond what we plan to cover in this chapter.

In order to use analytic geometry in proofs, we need ways to describe basic geometric concepts in algebraic terms. Let's look at the concepts of point, line, and distance.

POINTS

Activity 1 asks you to create something familiar, a *number line*. By labeling one point as 0 and another point as 1, you have located the *origin* for your number line and have shown how large the *unit length* will be. All other coordinates follow from these two. If you actually constructed each point, then as you varied the location of point 1, the other points should have adjusted accordingly.

The critical idea of a number line is that there is a correspondence between the set of real numbers and the set of points on the line. Each number describes the location of a point, and each point has a unique number describing it. More precisely, there is a *one-to-one correspondence* between these two sets, meaning each real number corresponds to one and only one point on the line, and the point is labeled by this number.

By repeating the unit measure, we can locate the natural numbers on the number line. You might have done this by constructing a sequence of circles and finding their intersections with your number line.

Measuring in one direction from the origin along the number line gives the positive integers, and measuring in the opposite direction from the origin allows us to locate the negative integers. Although it is usual for the negative numbers to go to the left on a number line and the positive numbers to the right, there is no mathematical reason for this; it is merely a convention. The constructions for locating rational numbers are not difficult. Even finding $\sqrt{2}$ and $\sqrt{3}$ is pretty straightforward—though $\sqrt{3}$ takes a bit of thought. A number such as π, however, is a different matter: π is not a *constructible number*. This means we cannot construct a precise location for π using only the standard tools of straightedge and compass. Even so, π has its unique point on the line [Jacobson 1974, 263–277].

With only a single line, we are limited in how much geometry we can do. One important concept is the *distance between two points* on the number line, which is calculated as follows:

$$d(x_1, x_2) = |x_1 - x_2| = \sqrt{(x_1 - x_2)^2}.$$

The second formula may look more complicated than necessary, but bear with us! This pattern will be helpful later.

Things get more interesting when we go to two dimensions. This requires two axes, that is, two number lines set at an angle to each other. Because of the two axes, the coordinate plane is often denoted by $\mathbb{R}^2$, the *Cartesian product* $\mathbb{R} \times \mathbb{R}$ of two number lines. In this situation, the *origin*, the point where two axes intersect, is the zero point for both axes. The origin is the starting point for locating other points in the system.

Activity 2 presents a pair of coordinate axes. These axes are somewhat unusual because they are not perpendicular. However, in this skew coordinate system, positive x-values still go to the right and positive y-values still go upward. To plot the point $(1, \sqrt{2})$, for instance, we would begin at the origin and move a distance 1 to the right and then move upward, parallel to the y-axis, a distance $\sqrt{2}$. The other points in Activity 2 can be located similarly.

In Activity 2, we deliberately did not show what scale to use on these axes. As in the case of a number line, the unit length is arbitrary. With two axes, there can even be two different unit lengths, one for each axis. With any graphing tool, such as a calculator or mathematical software, there is the possibility of distortion resulting from differences in scaling on the two axes. The user must be sensitive to this possibility and must look for ways to compensate.

In GeoGebra, the scaling on the axes of the grid can be adjusted by selecting the gear icon (Preferences) in the upper-right corner, then Graphics and Basic. You can reset the ratio of x Axis:y Axis; the default is 1:1. Another approach is to right-click in the Graphics pane, go to the *x Axis:y Axis* option, and select a ratio.

In GeoGebra, it is possible to zoom in or out on the Graphics pane as well as to move the axes to a convenient viewing position.

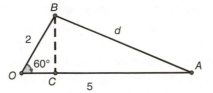

FIGURE 5.2
Distance in a Skew Coordinate System

The distance between point $A(5, 0)$ and point $B(0, 2)$ in Activity 2 can be viewed as the length of one side of $\triangle OAB$. (See Figure 5.2.) Knowing two sides and the included angle, we can use the *Law of Cosines* to find the third side, AB:

$$|AB|^2 = d^2 = |OA|^2 + |OB|^2 - 2 \cdot |OA| \cdot |OB| \cdot \cos(60°)$$

$$|AB| = d = \sqrt{5^2 + 2^2 - 2 \cdot 5 \cdot 2 \cdot \frac{1}{2}} = \sqrt{19}.$$

We could have used the Pythagorean Theorem (twice) to get the same result. In Figure 5.2, how do we know that the coordinates of the point C are $(1, 0)$? We find the length of side BC, then we use this result to find the length of side AB, which is the distance d that we want:

$$BC = \sqrt{2^2 - 1^2} = \sqrt{3},$$

$$d = \sqrt{(\sqrt{3})^2 + 4^2} = \sqrt{19}.$$

A similar calculation will find the distance between points A and E in Activity 2. One approach is to use $\triangle AOE$ with an angle of $120°$ at the origin. Another method is to keep the $60°$ angle and use a longer base, which will keep two sides of the triangle parallel to the two axes (see Figure 5.3).

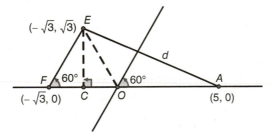

FIGURE 5.3
Another Distance Calculation

The general formula for the distance between two points, $P_1(x_1, y_1)$ and $P_2(x_2, y_2)$, in this $60°$-coordinate system is

$$d = \sqrt{(x_1 - x_2)^2 + (y_1 - y_2)^2 - 2 \cdot |x_1 - x_2| \cdot |y_1 - y_2| \cdot \cos(60°)}.$$

Using this formula, we can calculate the distance between points $A(5, 0)$ and $E(-\sqrt{3}, \sqrt{3})$ as

$$|AE| = d = \sqrt{(5 + \sqrt{3})^2 + (\sqrt{3})^2 - 2 \cdot |5 + \sqrt{3}| \cdot |0 - \sqrt{3}| \cdot \frac{1}{2}}$$

$$= \sqrt{25 + 10\sqrt{3} + 3 + 3 - 5\sqrt{3} - 3}$$

$$= \sqrt{28 + 5\sqrt{3}}.$$

Again, we could also have calculated this distance using two applications of the Pythagorean Theorem. (Having two different strategies gives us a way to check our work.) Notice in Figure 5.3 the location of the point E with respect to the origin. Point C on the x-axis directly below the point E has coordinates $\left(-\frac{\sqrt{3}}{2}, 0\right)$, and EC has length $\frac{3}{2}$. This gives

$$|AE| = \sqrt{\left(5 + \frac{\sqrt{3}}{2}\right)^2 + \left(\frac{3}{2}\right)^2} = \sqrt{25 + 5\sqrt{3} + \frac{3}{4} + \frac{9}{4}} = \sqrt{28 + 5\sqrt{3}},$$

which is the same result we got before.

The presence of the cos 60° in the general distance formula for the 60°-coordinate system makes the calculation a bit messy. When we put the coordinate axes at right angles to each other, the distance formula is the same except that the angle is 90°. This makes the formula much simpler since cos(90°) is simply 0. This is one reason why perpendicular axes are preferred.

Having a formula for distance opens many possible questions. The following theorem presents a useful result.

THEOREM 5.1 The midpoint of the segment between points $P(x_p, y_p)$ and $Q(x_q, y_q)$ is the point

$$\left(\frac{x_p + x_q}{2}, \frac{y_p + y_q}{2}\right).$$

This is straightforward to prove, especially in the case of perpendicular axes. The midpoint should be on the line segment PQ, and the distances from the midpoint to each endpoint of the segment should be equal. The proof will be left to the exercises.

LINES

A point is a zero-dimensional object that has only location. A point's location is described by its coordinate on a number line or by a pair of coordinates in a plane. A line, however, is a one-dimensional object that has both location and direction.

An algebraic description of a line must include both location and direction. Here are three common ways to describe a line, as well as one less common way:

$$y - y_0 = m(x - x_0) \qquad \text{point-slope form}$$

$$y = mx + b \qquad \text{slope-intercept form}$$

$$\frac{x}{a} + \frac{y}{b} = 1 \qquad \text{intercept form}$$

$$Ax + By = C \qquad \text{general form}$$

In the *point-slope form*, the point (x_0, y_0) tells the line's location and the slope m tells its direction. (It is traditional to refer to the slope as m, and we will continue the tradition.) In the *slope-intercept form*, the point $(0, b)$ is the intercept point on the vertical axis. This point tells the line's location, and once again, m tells the direction. In *intercept form*, the points $(a, 0)$ and $(0, b)$ tell the location and indirectly give the direction.

The *general form* is the most powerful of these four ways to describe a line, for it can be used to describe horizontal and vertical lines, as well as any other line. Each of the other forms has limitations, which will be examined in the exercises.

Most of this information should be familiar to you. What we want to do in this section is to carefully examine why we can use these forms to describe a line. To do so, we first need a clear understanding of slope.

In Activity 3, you should have found that the ratio $\frac{y_B - y_A}{x_B - x_A}$ remained constant no matter where A and B were on the line. This formula calculates the *slope* of the line. We often say that the slope is the rise over the run, because slope is a measure of the vertical change (the rise) from point A to point B divided by the horizontal change (the run) from A to B. The vertical change can be denoted by Δy and the horizontal change by Δx. Thus, the calculation for the slope can be written as

$$\frac{\text{vertical change}}{\text{horizontal change}} = \frac{\Delta y}{\Delta x}$$

and can be read as "the change in y divided by the change in x."

Figure 5.4 illustrates one situation that might occur. In this picture, the segments Δx_i and Δy_i are parallel to the x- and y-axes, respectively. Why is the slope from A_1 to B_1 equal to the slope from A_2 to B_2? (*Hint*: Think of similar triangles!) Notice that it really doesn't matter which points we use to calculate the slope of the line, because the triangle for points A_1 and B_1 is similar to the triangle for points A_2 and B_2. Both of these triangles are also similar to the triangle for A_1 and B_2. Since the triangles are similar, ratios of the lengths of corresponding sides will be equal.

Does all this continue to work if either Δx or Δy is 0? We must consider two special cases, the horizontal lines and the vertical lines. For a horizontal line, we cannot draw triangles with vertical and horizontal sides. Instead, think about the coordinates of the points along this line. Each of these points is the same distance from the horizontal axis, so the y-coordinate is always the same. This means that the numerator Δy will always be 0, making the slope equal to 0.

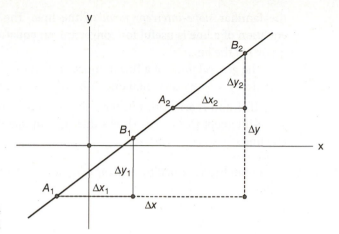

FIGURE 5.4
Slope Is Well Defined

THEOREM 5.2 For a nonvertical line, the slope is well defined. In other words, no matter which two points, $A(x_A, y_A)$ and $B(x_B, y_B)$, are used to calculate the slope, the value

$$\frac{y_B - y_A}{y_B - x_A} = \frac{\Delta y}{\Delta x}$$

will be the same.

There is still the awkward case of the vertical lines. Points along any particular vertical line will all have the same x-coordinate. Thus, we encounter a difficult situation that the denominator $\Delta x = 0$, which makes the fraction undefined. This is our answer: The slope of a vertical line is undefined.

It is not uncommon to hear people say that the slope of a vertical line is infinity. This is not correct, for at least two reasons. First, ∞ is not really a number. It is not part of the real number system, and arithmetic with ∞ does not work in the usual way. Second, there are two contradictory ways to interpret a vertical line. Such a line can be viewed as rising infinitely quickly, and some might call this a slope of $+\infty$. However, the line also can be viewed as falling infinitely quickly, leading to a slope of $-\infty$. If the slope concept is to be well defined, there cannot be one line with two different slopes.

Now suppose that we know a point, (x_0, y_0), on a particular line and that we also know its slope, m. If we let (x, y) stand for any other point on this line, we can write

$$\frac{y - y_0}{x - x_0} = m$$

and simplify to get

$$y - y_0 = m(x - x_0),$$

which is the *point-slope form* of the line. This form of the equation of a line is useful for converting information about a line into an equation for the line. It takes only a little more algebra to rewrite this as

$$y = mx + (y_0 - mx_0) = mx + b,$$

the familiar *slope-intercept form* of the line. The slope-intercept form of the equation of a line is useful for converting an equation of a line into a picture (or graph) of the line.

The *general form* of a linear equation is $Ax + By = C$. If $A = 0$, we have the equation $y = \frac{C}{B}$, a horizontal line. If $B = 0$, we have the equation $x = \frac{C}{A}$, a vertical line. If A and B are both nonzero, the general form can be rearranged into the slope-intercept form. This shows that we can use the general form to represent any line.

THEOREM 5.3   A line can be described by a linear equation, and a linear equation describes a line.

Activity 4 introduces an alternative way to specify the direction of a line, namely, the *angle of inclination*, α. This angle is measured at the point where the line intersects the horizontal axis, and it should have a value $0 \leq \alpha < \pi$. There are, of course, lines that do not intersect the horizontal axis. For convenience later, let us define $\alpha = 0$ for all horizontal lines, whether or not they intersect the horizontal axis. Figure 5.5 shows the relationship between the slope of a line and the angle of inclination. The important relationship is $m = \tan \alpha$. Notice that this relationship holds even for the special cases. For horizontal lines, $m = 0 = \tan 0$. For vertical lines, m is undefined and $\tan \frac{\pi}{2}$ is undefined. This relationship helps us prove some important facts.

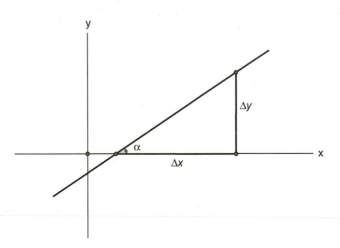

FIGURE 5.5
Slope and Angle of Inclination

THEOREM 5.4   Two lines are parallel if and only if the two lines have equal slopes.

Outline of a proof   It is necessary to deal with the horizontal case separately. However, we will first prove the general case. Figure 5.6 gives a generic picture of the situation.

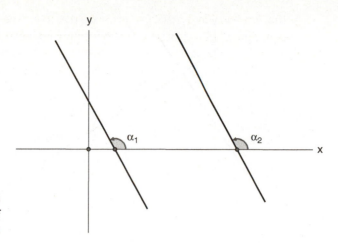

FIGURE 5.6
Parallelism and Angles of
Inclination

Suppose two lines that both intersect the x-axis are parallel. Then, the x-axis is a transversal of the two lines, and the two angles of inclination are equal. Thus, the tangents of the two angles are equal, so the slopes are equal.

The reverse argument also works. Suppose the slopes are equal. Then, the tangents of the two angles are equal, and so the angles of inclination are equal. (Recall that these angles are between 0 and π.) Using the x-axis as a transversal, the two lines are parallel.

The argument just given will not work for horizontal lines, because most horizontal lines do not intersect the x-axis. However, all horizontal lines are parallel, and all horizontal lines have slope $= 0 = \tan 0$. So the theorem is true in this case also.

There are several ways to prove the next theorem. In the proof shown here, we illustrate an approach based on the Pythagorean Theorem.

THEOREM 5.5 Let ℓ_1 and ℓ_2 be two lines, neither one vertical, with slopes m_1 and m_2, respectively. The two lines are perpendicular, written $\ell_1 \perp \ell_2$, if and only if $m_1 \cdot m_2 = -1$.

Proof For the lines in Figure 5.7, $\angle ACB$ is $90°$ if and only if the Pythagorean Theorem holds for $\triangle ACD$. So, we want $|AD|^2 = |AC|^2 + |CB|^2$. This holds

iff $\qquad (b - a)^2 = ((c - a)^2 + (d - 0)^2) + ((b - c)^2 + (0 - d)^2)$

iff $-ab + ac + bc - c^2 = d^2$

iff $\qquad (c - a) \cdot (b - c) = d^2$

iff $\qquad\qquad -1 = \dfrac{d - 0}{c - a} \cdot \dfrac{0 - d}{b - c} = (\text{slope of } \overrightarrow{AC}) \cdot (\text{slope of } \overrightarrow{CB}).$

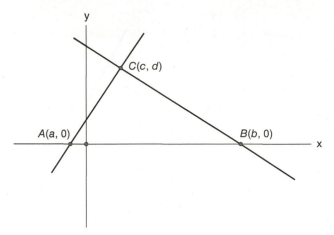

FIGURE 5.7
Perpendicularity and Slope

(You should check our calculations.) If $\overrightarrow{AC}$ is ℓ_1 and $\overrightarrow{CB}$ is ℓ_2, these calculations say that the product of the two slopes, $m_1 \cdot m_2$, is -1.

A consequence of $m_1 \cdot m_2 = -1$ is that $m_1 = \frac{-1}{m_2}$. This means m_1 is the opposite of m_2 in both arithmetic senses: m_1 is both *negative* to and *reciprocal* to m_2.

Here is an example that combines two of the concepts we have just seen: Given a point $A = (a, 0)$ on the horizontal axis and another point $B = (0, b)$ on the vertical axis, find an equation for the perpendicular bisector of the segment AB. To do this, we need to know a location for and the direction of this line. One possible location is the midpoint of AB, which is the point $\left(\frac{a}{2}, \frac{b}{2} \right)$. The slope of AB is $\frac{b}{-a} = -\frac{b}{a}$, so the slope we need for a perpendicular line is $\frac{a}{b}$. Using the point-slope form, an equation for the perpendicular bisector is

$$y - \frac{b}{2} = \frac{a}{b} \left(x - \frac{a}{2} \right).$$

DISTANCE

A circle is a set of points, all of which are the same distance from a fixed center point. So, a circle can be described by its center and its radius—these two pieces of data are enough to let us write an equation for a circle. Let us be more specific: Suppose the center of our circle is the point (a, b) and the radius is r. Any point (x, y) on the circle must be a distance r from the center, and the distance formula gives

$$\sqrt{(x - a)^2 + (y - b)^2} = r.$$

Equations with radical signs can be awkward to use. Fortunately, we can improve this particular equation by squaring both sides to get

$$(x - a)^2 + (y - b)^2 = r^2.$$

Suppose, for example, that you wanted to use an equation to represent a circle with radius 5 units and center at (2, 3). Using the equation form developed above, this circle would be represented by the equation $(x - 2)^2 + (y - 3)^2 = 25$. Solving this for y, we get two equations (because of the square root):

$$y = 3 + \sqrt{25 - (x - 2)^2} \quad \text{and} \quad y = 3 - \sqrt{25 - (x - 2)^2}.$$

These are the two equations you plotted in Activity 6.

We used the formula for the distance between two points to find the equation of a circle because we wanted an equation for the set of all points (x, y) at a fixed distance r from the point (a, b). A harder question is to find the distance between a point and a line. It may not even be clear what we mean by the distance between the point P and the line ℓ, for there are many points on ℓ and many distances could be calculated between P and one of the many points on ℓ. How do we know which of these distances to choose? This is the issue that you had to think about in Activity 5. How did GeoGebra find the distance? By choosing points farther and farther away from P, the distance can be made arbitrarily large. However, there is a limit to how small this distance can be, and that minimum distance is what is meant by the distance from P to ℓ.

So, the problem is to decide which point on ℓ is closest to the point P. One way to solve this problem is to find the circle centered at P that is tangent to line ℓ. This solution is the reverse of some of the problems posed in Chapter 4, where you were trying to find the line through a fixed point that was tangent to a given circle. (See Activity 4a from Chapter 4.) Here we want to find the radius of the smallest circle centered at P and tangent to the line ℓ. It should be clear that the shortest route from P to ℓ is along a line perpendicular to ℓ. This needs a proof, however, and you will be asked to supply one in the exercises.

To find our desired formula, we want the distance from P to the intersection point (labeled Q in Figure 5.8). First, we need some algebraic descriptions. Let P be the point (a, b) and let ℓ be the line $y = mx + c$. (Because we are using b as a

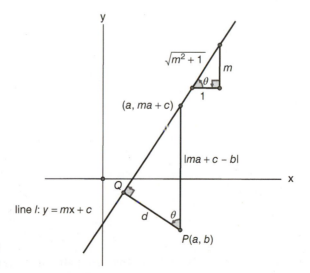

FIGURE 5.8
Distance from a Point to a Line

coordinate for P, we cannot use b in the equation for the line.) The line through P and perpendicular to ℓ is

$$y - b = -\frac{1}{m}(x - a).$$

The point Q is the intersection of this new line with ℓ. To find Q, solve the following system of equations:

$$\begin{cases} y = mx + c \\ y = -\frac{1}{m}(x - a) + b. \end{cases}$$

After solving this system, which you should check, we see that Q is the point

$$\left(\frac{a + bm - cm}{m^2 + 1}, \frac{am + bm^2 + c}{m^2 + 1} \right).$$

Using the distance formula, we now can calculate the distance between the points P and Q. The algebra is tedious, so we will show only portions of the work. You should fill in the missing steps. The distance from P to Q is

$$= \sqrt{\left(\frac{a + bm - cm}{m^2 + 1} - a \right)^2 + \left(\frac{am + bm^2 + c}{m^2 + 1} - b \right)^2}$$

$$= \frac{1}{m^2 + 1} \sqrt{(bm - cm - am^2)^2 + (am + c - b)^2}$$

$$= \frac{1}{m^2 + 1} \sqrt{m^2(am - b + c)^2 + (am - b + c)^2}$$

$$= \frac{1}{m^2 + 1} |am - b + c| \sqrt{m^2 + 1}$$

$$= \frac{|am + c - b|}{\sqrt{m^2 + 1}}.$$

This formula looks somewhat nicer if we use the general form of the line. For the point $P(a, b)$ and the line $Ax + By - C = 0$, we can write the distance from P to this line as

$$\frac{|Aa + Bb - C|}{\sqrt{A^2 + B^2}}.$$

The preceding proof relied on a great deal of algebra, but does not really show why the formula works. Here is an alternative proof that may be more illuminating. In Figure 5.8, a smaller triangle is constructed specifically to show the slope of the line. How do we know that the two angles marked θ are truly equal and that the two triangles are similar? We get

$$\frac{d}{1} = \frac{|am + c - b|}{\sqrt{m^2 + 1}}.$$

There are some issues here that need attention. Why is the absolute value necessary? Recall that the picture is only one of the possible ways that this problem could arise, and P could be above the line. Neither of the preceding explanations deals with the possibility that the line ℓ is vertical. If ℓ is vertical, does the formula still give a correct answer? Obviously, the version with m will not, but what about the version based on the general form of a line?

In mathematics, we are sometimes interested in verifying that a particular calculation gives the correct result. At other times, we are interested in using a calculation to explain what is happening in a particular situation. In the preceding discussion, we used both of these methods to present the idea of calculating the distance from a point to a line. The first method verifies that the calculation works, while the second one explains why it works. Both of these strategies could be called a "proof." Only one of the proofs makes sense for a horizontal line; which one? These issues will appear in the exercises.

USING COORDINATES IN PROOFS

A great benefit of using coordinates is the connection it gives us between geometric ideas and algebraic ideas. Lines and linear equations are a classic example. The geometric ideas of position and direction of a line correspond to the algebraic ideas of the constant term and the leading coefficient of a linear equation in the slope-intercept form. We can now use a wide variety of familiar algebraic tools, such as solving equations and solving systems of equations, to prove geometric facts.

Activity 7 presents a theorem to be proved. Although this is not a particularly important theorem in itself, the activity gave you a chance to try some of the algebraic techniques we have developed so far. To develop this proof, you need to use things such as slope, linear equations, distance between points, and the midpoint formula. One possible picture for Activity 7 is given in Figure 5.9.

First let us discuss this picture. Does it fit the description in the activity? Point A is at the origin and point B is on the positive x-axis. Point C is in the first quadrant and point D is on the positive y-axis. You should realize that there were some arbitrary decisions made about how to put this rectangle on a coordinate system. Vertex B could easily have gone onto the vertical axis, for instance, or C could go into a different quadrant.

To make this a general situation, and not a specific rectangle, the coordinates of the point C were set as arbitrary values (c, d). This information allows us to find coordinates for the other vertices. Notice that there are four 0s among the

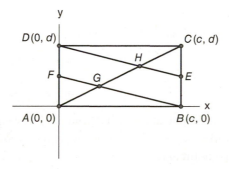

FIGURE 5.9
Graph for Activity 7

coordinates. It is generally a good idea to place the coordinate system to get as many 0s as possible. Here we placed the coordinate system so that the origin and the axes were parts of the rectangle we are examining. Remember that we will be doing algebra with these coordinate values. It is often the case that having lots of 0s will make the algebra easier.

Knowing coordinates for the four vertices makes it easy to find coordinates for points E and F as well.

We hope you noticed that no matter where point C is, the points G and H divide the diagonal AC into congruent segments. How can we prove this? One approach is to compare the distances AG, GH, and HC. These distances are routine to calculate—once we know the coordinates of the points involved.

We will focus on point G. This point is the intersection of the two lines $\overleftrightarrow{AC}$ and $\overleftrightarrow{BF}$. We need to describe those lines algebraically.

$$\text{Line } AC \text{ is } y = \frac{d}{c}x.$$

$$\text{Line } BF \text{ is } y = \frac{-d}{2c}x + \frac{d}{2}.$$

The intersection point G can be found by solving these equations simultaneously, giving the coordinates

$$G = \left(\frac{c}{3}, \frac{d}{3} \right).$$

Now we can use the distance formula to get

$$|AG| = \sqrt{\left(\frac{c}{3}\right)^2 + \left(\frac{d}{3}\right)^2} = \frac{\sqrt{c^2 + d^2}}{3}.$$

Once you have found coordinates for the point H, similar calculations for distance will confirm that the three segments along the diagonal have the same length.

When setting up a coordinate system for a proof, it is always tempting to use the origin as one of the important points. The "double zeros" at the origin often are helpful when writing the equations. In some situations, however, there is an advantage to using points other than the origin. For example, let us prove algebraically that the perpendiculars from the vertices of a triangle to the opposite sides are concurrent (at the orthocenter, remember?). Figure 5.10 shows one way to draw coordinates for a triangle.

By putting B on the vertical axis, we have made the vertical axis one of the altitudes of the triangle. Our desired concurrency point must lie on the vertical axis, where $x = 0$.

The line $\overleftrightarrow{AB}$ is $y = -\frac{b}{a}x + b$. The slope of its perpendicular is then $\frac{a}{b}$ and $\overleftrightarrow{CD}$ is

$$y - 0 = \frac{a}{b}(x - c).$$

$$y = \frac{a}{b}x - \frac{ac}{b}.$$

Now we do a similar thing with the side BC. The equation of the line through the points B and C is $y = -\frac{b}{c}x + b$. So the equation of the line perpendicular to $\overleftrightarrow{BC}$ through the point A is

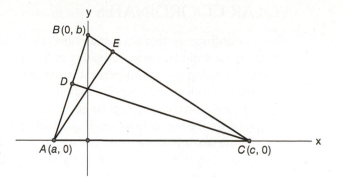

FIGURE 5.10
Proving Concurrence of
Altitudes

$$y - 0 = \frac{c}{b}(x - a).$$

$$y = \frac{c}{b}x - \frac{ac}{b}.$$

Thus, all three perpendiculars pass through the point $(0, -\frac{ac}{b})$. This point, which does lie on the vertical axis, is the orthocenter of the triangle.

If the minus sign looks out of place in the coordinates of the orthocenter, recall that Figure 5.10 shows a as a negative number, while b and c are positive. However, nothing prevents a from being positive. Does the proof still make sense if the point A is to the right of the origin? Where will the orthocenter be in that situation? What happens if A is at the origin?

ANOTHER LOOK AT THE RADICAL AXIS

Cartesian coordinates offer a simple way to prove that the radical axis of two circles is indeed a line. Recall that for two given circles C_1 and C_2, the radical axis is the set of points P for which Power$(P, C_1) = $ Power(P, C_2). We can describe these circles in coordinates as follows:

$$C_1 : (x - a)^2 + (y - b)^2 = r_1^2$$

$$C_2 : (x - c)^2 + (y - d)^2 = r_2^2.$$

Then for point $P = (x, y)$, we have Power$(P, C_1) = (x - a)^2 + (y - b)^2 - r_1^2$ and Power$(P, C_2) = (x - c)^2 + (y - d)^2 - r_2^2$. Setting these powers equal gives

$$(x - a)^2 + (y - b)^2 - r_1^2 = (x - c)^2 + (y - d)^2 - r_2^2.$$

When this is expanded and solved for y, the result is

$$y = \left(\frac{c - a}{b - d}\right)x + \left(\frac{a^2 + b^2 - r_1^2 - c^2 - d^2 + r_2^2}{2(b - d)}\right).$$

This is a bit messy, but it is clearly a linear equation.

POLAR COORDINATES

The *xy*-coordinate system is a comfortable one for people accustomed to city living. With our experiences at navigating in terms of streets and intersections, the notion of moving along two perpendicular directions is quite natural. Indeed, many cities—such as Indianapolis, Indiana; St. Petersburg, Florida; and Milwaukee, Wisconsin—have a rectangular grid for a large portion of their street system. Navigating on the ocean, however, is quite different from navigating in an urban area. On the sea, it is more natural to specify a direction and a distance to travel in that direction. This is the idea underlying the polar coordinate system.

The *polar coordinate system* uses an origin point and a single axis. This axis is actually just a ray, not a line. Typically, this ray is drawn to the right, as though it were the positive portion of the *x*-axis. We can describe a point *P* in the plane by giving two numbers: its distance from the origin *O* and its angle, measured between the polar axis and the ray $\overrightarrow{OP}$. The convention in mathematics is that counterclockwise angles are considered to be positive and clockwise angles are negative; that convention applies here.

It is common to refer to polar coordinates as (r, θ), where *r* is the distance from the origin—the radius of the circle containing this point—and θ is the angle measured counterclockwise from the polar axis. These variables can take on any real number values: positive, zero, or negative. For example, we can plot the points $(3, \pi)$, $(-3, \pi)$, $(-3, -\pi)$ and $(3, -\pi)$. Unlike Cartesian coordinates, however, this list of four ordered pairs actually represents only two distinct points. There are a couple of reasons for this. One difficulty is that π and $-\pi$ are different angles that correspond to the same ray, namely, the negative *x*-axis. So, $(3, \pi)$ and $(3, -\pi)$ are different names for the same point. Similarly, $(-3, \pi)$ and $(-3, -\pi)$ are the same point. However, locating a point whose first coordinate is negative when expressed in polar coordinates can be a little confusing. In Activity 8b, how did you interpret -3 km west? If we think of this as instructions for moving, we should face to the west, then move -3 km—in other words, back up 3 km. On the coordinate system, this point lies on the positive *x*-axis, that is, on the polar ray.

The fact that points do not have unique coordinates in the polar system can cause trouble when analyzing problems algebraically. For example, suppose we want to find the intersection points of the curves described by

$$\begin{cases} r = \sin \theta \\ r = \cos \theta. \end{cases}$$

The standard approach is to set the two expressions for *r* equal and solve for the variable, θ:

$$\sin \theta = \cos \theta$$

$$\tan \theta = 1$$

$$\theta = \frac{\pi}{4}, \frac{5\pi}{4}.$$

Substituting these solutions values into the two functions gives two intersection points: $\left(\frac{\sqrt{2}}{2}, \frac{\pi}{4} \right)$ and $\left(-\frac{\sqrt{2}}{2}, \frac{5\pi}{4} \right)$. However, plotting these shows that they are actually the same point. To make things worse, there are indeed two intersection points. Figure 5.11 shows a plot of two functions. This graph shows these two circles intersecting twice—at the point we found algebraically and also at the origin. What has happened is that the curve $r = \sin\theta$ includes the origin as $(0, 0)$, while the other curve $r = \cos\theta$ includes the origin as $\left(0, \frac{\pi}{2}\right)$. The lesson here is that the algebra is not sufficient. When solving systems of equations given in polar coordinates, you must look at a graph to see (literally) if there are any other intersection points that may have been hidden by alternative descriptions of the points.

$r = \sin(\theta)$

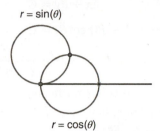

FIGURE 5.11
Intersecting Circles

$r = \cos(\theta)$

The polar grid consists of circles centered at the origin and rays coming from the origin. These circles are represented by equations in the pattern $r = a$. Notice that a could be a negative number or even 0. Once again, however, we have the difficulty of nonunique representations. For example, the equations $r = 5$ and $r = -5$ represent the same circle. The equation $r = 0$ represents the "circle" consisting of just a single point. The lines from the origin also have simple equations, and again these are not unique. The equations $\theta = \frac{4\pi}{3}, \theta = \frac{-2\pi}{3}$, and $\theta = \frac{10\pi}{3}$ represent the same line. In fact, because the point $\left(x, \frac{4\pi}{3}\right)$ lies on the line $\theta = \frac{4\pi}{3}$ for any (positive or negative) value of x, the line $\theta = \frac{\pi}{3}$ is yet another representation for this same line.

Finding an equation for a general line—one that does not go through the origin—is a more difficult question. It is helpful to take an indirect approach. First, let us examine how polar coordinates are related to Cartesian coordinates. The diagram in Figure 5.12 shows this relationship. From basic trigonometry, we know that

$$\begin{cases} x^2 + y^2 = r^2 \\ \tan\theta = \frac{y}{x}. \end{cases}$$

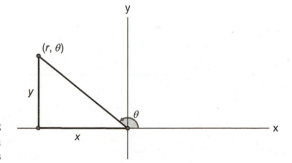

FIGURE 5.12
Converting Between Cartesian
and Polar Coordinates

We also know that

$$\begin{cases} x = r\cos\theta \\ y = r\sin\theta. \end{cases}$$

(We chose a point in quadrant II to remind you that these relationships hold for any angle, not merely acute angles.)

Now consider the general form of an equation for a line and substitute $r\cos\theta$ and $r\sin\theta$ for x and y, respectively:

$$Ax + By = C$$

$$A(r\cos\theta) + B(r\sin\theta) = C$$

$$r = \frac{C}{A\cos\theta + B\sin\theta}.$$

Since A, B, and C are constants (the coefficients of the equation in general form), we see that r is a function of θ, that is, $r = f(\theta)$. However, this is a rather awkward equation for a simple thing like a line!

We have seen that in polar coordinates lines cannot be described by linear equations, except in the special case of lines through the origin. Linear equations in polar coordinates describe a completely different type of curve, called a *spiral*. Try graphing $r = \theta$, for instance, or $r = 2\theta + 1$. Many functions other than linear functions also produce spirals. The function $r = \ln\theta$ is the *logarithmic spiral*, which has many interesting properties. This spiral can be seen in the growth pattern of some sea shells.

It is interesting to see a variety of curves produced by familiar functions when they are graphed in a polar system. You saw examples of this in Activity 11. When plotted on a Cartesian system, the function $r = \sin(3\theta)$ is a sine wave of amplitude 1 and period $\frac{2\pi}{3}$. The period means that in the standard interval $0 \le \theta \le 2\pi$, the wave will occur three times. So it should not be surprising that the polar graph has a maximum distance of 1 from the origin and that there are three petals to the rose. The rose for $r = \sin(4\theta)$ may have surprised you. Do you see why there are eight petals instead of four? (See Figure 5.13.)

It is enlightening to draw the curve $r = \sin(4\theta)$ in GeoGebra, construct a point on the plot, measure its polar coordinates, and then animate the point. Which of the petals are produced by positive r-values and which are produced by negative r-values?

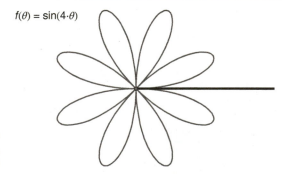

$f(\theta) = \sin(4\cdot\theta)$

FIGURE 5.13
A Rose with Eight Petals,
$r = \sin(4\theta)$

Activity 11c asks for a rose with eighteen petals. This is difficult, for using a coefficient of 9 gives only nine petals and using a coefficient of 18 gives thirty-six petals. Try cutting 18 in half twice for a coefficient of $\frac{18}{4} = 4.5$. The problem with this new function is that $0 \le \theta \le 2\pi$ will not draw the entire rose. You must expand the domain using **Object Properties** for the curve.

THE NINE-POINT CIRCLE, REVISITED

Any $\triangle ABC$ has three altitudes. The point where an altitude intersects the opposite side is called the *foot* of the altitude. In Figure 5.14, the feet of the altitudes are the points D, E, and F. These points are the vertices of the *pedal triangle* for $\triangle ABC$. The circumcircle of this pedal triangle turns out to contain many other important points for $\triangle ABC$.

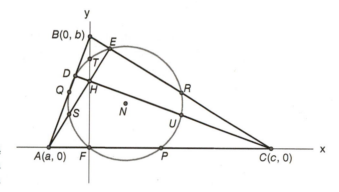

FIGURE 5.14
The Nine-Point Circle on a
Coordinate System

THEOREM 5.6 **The Nine-Point Circle Theorem** For any triangle, the three feet of the altitudes, the three midpoints of the sides, and the three midpoints of the segments from orthocenter to vertex all lie on a common circle, known as the *nine-point circle* of the triangle.

It is possible to prove this theorem without coordinates, as we did in the proofs in the earlier chapters of this book. However, we can use the techniques discussed in this chapter, such as representing lines by linear equations, to give a proof that involves coordinates and algebra. This is called an *analytic proof*.

Proof Let us begin with a list of the general steps needed for the proof.

1. Place the triangle on a coordinate system, preferably in a way that will help the algebra.
2. Find equations for the altitudes of the triangle.
3. Find the coordinates of the feet of the altitudes and the coordinates of the orthocenter.
4. Find the center and radius of the circumcircle of the pedal triangle.

5. Write the equation for the circumcircle of the pedal triangle.

6. Verify (confirm) that the three feet lie on this circle.

7. Verify that the three midpoints of the sides lie on this circle.

8. Verify that the three midpoints of segments from orthocenter to vertex lie on this circle.

As we carry out these steps, we will not show every detail of the algebra. It is good practice to do at least some of this algebra yourself. Here we will include just enough to show you the direction of the proof.

Step 1   Figure 5.14 shows one way to place $\triangle ABC$ on a coordinate system. This placement has the advantage that each vertex has a 0 among its coordinates. Another benefit is that the vertical axis is one of the altitudes; this will be useful in steps 2 and 3. As the triangle is drawn here, it appears that $a < 0$, $b > 0$, and $c > 0$. However, this is not necessarily true, and we must not assume this during our work. For instance, an obtuse triangle could have both a and c with positive values.

Step 2   The altitude through the point A contains the point $(a, 0)$ and is perpendicular to the line $\overleftrightarrow{BC}$. Therefore, by the point-slope form, the altitude on A is described by

$$y - 0 = \frac{c}{b}(x - a).$$

The altitude through the point B is the vertical axis. Therefore, the altitude on B is described by

$$x = 0.$$

The altitude through the point C contains the point $(c, 0)$ and is perpendicular to the line $\overleftrightarrow{AB}$. Therefore, the altitude on C is described by

$$y - 0 = \frac{a}{b}(x - c).$$

Step 3   The foot D is the intersection of the altitude on C with the line $\overleftrightarrow{AB}$. So, we must solve

$$\frac{a}{b}(x - c) = \frac{b}{-a}(x - a).$$

After solving and substituting into either one of the linear equations, we get

$$D = \left(\frac{a(b^2 + ac)}{a^2 + b^2}, \frac{ab(a - c)}{a^2 + b^2} \right).$$

The foot E is the intersection of the altitude on A with the line $\overleftrightarrow{BC}$. By similar work, we get

$$E = \left(\frac{c(b^2 + ac)}{b^2 + c^2}, \frac{bc(c - a)}{b^2 + c^2} \right).$$

Notice that D and E are in the same pattern, except that the roles of a and c are reversed. This is encouraging, for it suggests that we did the algebra correctly! The foot F is the intersection of the altitude on B with $\overleftrightarrow{AC}$: $F = (0, 0)$.

The orthocenter of $\triangle ABC$ can be found by substituting $x = 0$ into one of the equations for a nonvertical altitude: $H = (0, -ac/b)$.

Step 4 We need to find the center of the circumcircle for the pedal triangle *DEF*. From Chapter 3, we know that this center is the intersection of the perpendicular bisectors of the sides of $\triangle DEF$. Look first at the side *DF*. (Do you see why we want to include *F* in our calculations?) The slope of the side *DF* is

$$\frac{b(a - c)}{b^2 + ac}$$

and the midpoint of this side is

$$\left(\frac{a(b^2 + ac)}{2(a^2 + b^2)}, \frac{ab(a - c)}{2(a^2 + b^2)} \right).$$

After some work, this gives the perpendicular bisector of *DF* as

$$y = \frac{b^2 + ac}{-b(a - c)}x + \frac{a(b^2 + c^2)}{2b(a - c)}.$$

Now look at the side *EF*. Here we get that the slope of *EF* is

$$\frac{b(c - a)}{b^2 + ac}$$

and the midpoint of this side is

$$\left(\frac{c(b^2 + ac)}{2(b^2 + c^2)}, \frac{bc(c - a)}{2(b^2 + c^2)} \right).$$

Thus, the perpendicular bisector of *EF* is

$$y = \frac{b^2 + ac}{-b(c - a)}x + \frac{c(a^2 + b^2)}{2b(c - a)}.$$

The circle center we want is the intersection of the perpendicular bisectors of *EF* and *DF*. A good deal of careful algebra gives the following point:

$$N = \left(\frac{a + c}{4}, \frac{b^2 - ac}{4b} \right).$$

This is the *nine-point center*.
The radius of the nine-point circle is the distance from *N* to any of the three feet. Picking the easiest choice, we find that the radius is

$$|NF| = \frac{\sqrt{(a^2 + b^2)(b^2 + c^2)}}{4b}.$$

Step 5 Using the information from step 4, the desired circle can be represented by

$$\left(x - \frac{a + c}{4} \right)^2 + \left(y - \frac{b^2 - ac}{4b} \right)^2 = \frac{(a^2 + b^2)(b^2 + c^2)}{16b^2}.$$

Step 6   If we are confident that we have done the algebra correctly, it should not be necessary to verify that the three feet lie on this circle. After all, the equation in step 5 was developed from these three points. But it is good practice, and it helps confirm that we did the algebra correctly.

Is D on this circle? Substitute the coordinates of D into the circle equation to see if it is satisfied:

$$\left(\frac{a(b^2 + ac)}{a^2 + b^2} - \frac{a+c}{4} \right)^2 + \left(\frac{ab(a-c)}{a^2 + b^2} - \frac{b^2 - ac}{4b} \right)^2 .$$

If you are very patient, and are careful with minus signs, this simplifies to

$$\frac{(a^2 + b^2)(b^2 + c^2)}{16b^2},$$

the correct value for the equation. (If you are not that patient, a computer algebra system can simplify it for you.)

In an equally messy fashion, we can verify that E lies on this circle. Point F is more cooperative:

$$\left(0 - \frac{a+c}{4} \right)^2 + \left(0 - \frac{b^2 - ac}{4b} \right)^2 = \frac{(a+c)^2}{16} + \frac{(b^2 - ac)^2}{16b^2}$$

$$= \frac{(a^2 + b^2)(b^2 + c^2)}{16b^2}.$$

Step 7   Now we need to verify that the three midpoints of the sides of $\triangle ABC$ lie on this circle. In Figure 5.14, these are the points P, Q, and R. The coordinates of P are $(\frac{a+c}{2}, 0)$. So, we get

$$\left(\frac{a+c}{2} - \frac{a+c}{4} \right)^2 + \left(0 - \frac{b^2 - ac}{4b} \right) = \frac{(a+c)^2}{16} + \frac{(b^2 - ac)^2}{16b^2}$$

$$= \frac{(a^2 + b^2)(b^2 + c^2)}{16b^2}.$$

For point $Q = \left(\frac{a}{2}, \frac{b}{2} \right)$, we get

$$\left(\frac{a}{2} - \frac{a+c}{4} \right)^2 + \left(\frac{b}{2} - \frac{b^2 - ac}{4c} \right)^2 = \frac{(a-c)^2}{16} + \frac{(b^2 + ac)^2}{16b^2}$$

$$= \frac{(a^2 + b^2)(b^2 + c^2)}{16b^2}.$$

Verifying point $R = \left(\frac{c}{2}, \frac{b}{2} \right)$ is similar to the work for Q.

Step 8   The three midpoints of segments from the orthocenter to a vertex also lie on this circle. In Figure 5.14, these are the points S, T, and U. The coordinates of S are $\left(\frac{a}{2}, \frac{-ac}{2b} \right)$. So, we get

$$\left(\frac{a}{2} - \frac{a+c}{4} \right)^2 + \left(\frac{-ac}{2b} - \frac{b^2 - ac}{4c} \right)^2 = \frac{(a-c)^2}{16} + \frac{(-b^2 - ac)^2}{16b^2}$$

$$= \frac{(a^2 + b^2)(b^2 + c^2)}{16b^2}.$$

For point $T = \left(0, \frac{b^2 - ac}{2b}\right)$, we get

$$\left(0 - \frac{a+c}{4}\right)^2 + \left(\frac{b^2 - ac}{2b} - \frac{b^2 - ac}{4b}\right)^2 = \frac{(a+c)^2}{16} + \frac{(b^2 - ac)^2}{16b^2}$$

$$= \frac{(a^2 + b^2)(b^2 + c^2)}{16b^2}.$$

Verifying point $U = \left(\frac{c}{2}, \frac{-ac}{2b}\right)$ is similar to the work for S.

Looking at Figure 5.14, you might see an alternative way to attack steps 6 and 8. Instead of substituting these points into the equation of the nine-point circle, we could use the equation of an altitude and find the intersections with this circle. This works out nicely for the altitude $x = 0$:

$$\left(0 - \frac{a+c}{4}\right)^2 + \left(y - \frac{b^2 - ac}{4b}\right)^2 = \frac{(a^2 + b^2)(b^2 + c^2)}{16b^2}.$$

After clearing the denominators, expanding the squared quantities, and canceling lots of terms, this yields

$$y = 0 \ \text{ or } \ y = \frac{b^2 - ac}{2b}.$$

The first solution gives the foot F. The second solution gives the midpoint T of the segment HB.

Unfortunately, the other altitudes do not work this well. For instance, the altitude CD is $y = \frac{a}{b}(x - c)$, which leads us to solve

$$\left(x - \frac{(a+c)}{4}\right)^2 + \left(\frac{a}{b}(x - c) - \frac{(b^2 - ac)}{4b}\right)^2 = \frac{(a^2 + b^2)(b^2 + c^2)}{16b^2}.$$

A computer algebra system will confirm the intersections at D and U, but this equation is quite difficult to solve by hand.

Our proof is not the shortest proof of the nine-point circle, nor is it the clearest. Algebra does not always provide insight into why a theorem is true. However, algebraic methods can be very powerful. The connections between algebraic expressions and geometric objects are still being explored today.

Soon after the discovery of the nine-point circle, the German mathematician Karl Feuerbach proved something more about this circle. Because of his remarkable theorem, it is sometimes called *Feuerbach's Circle*.

Feuerbach's Theorem   The nine-point circle of $\triangle ABC$ is tangent to the incircle and to each of the three excircles of $\triangle ABC$.

Feuerbach proved his theorem by analytic methods, a proof considerably longer and more complex than the proof just shown.

Give clear and complete answers to the following problems and questions. Write your explanations clearly using complete sentences. Include diagrams whenever appropriate.

1. On page 116, there is a general formula for distance in a $60°$-coordinate system. Explain how the distance formula improves if the coordinate axes are perpendicular.

2. The usual distance function (the one that assumes the coordinate axes are perpendicular) is based on the Pythagorean Theorem.
   a. How can we use coordinates to represent points A and B in three-dimensional space?
   b. Extend the Pythagorean Theorem to three dimensions, and prove that this formula is correct.
   c. Given two points, A and B, in three-dimensional space, what is the set of points equidistant from A and B? Prove your answer, using coordinates.
   d. What does your answer for part (c) look like geometrically?

3. Prove the midpoint formula given in Theorem 5.1.

4. a. For the situation in Figure 5.15, prove that the slope between points A_1 and B_1 equals the slope between A_2 and B_2.
   b. Prove that the slope of a horizontal line is zero.

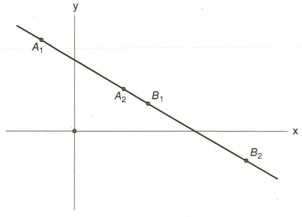

FIGURE 5.15
Figure for Exercise 4

5. Write a detailed step-by-step proof of Theorem 5.4.

6. Use angles of inclination and a trigonometric identity for $\tan(\alpha_1 - \alpha_2)$ to give a different proof of Theorem 5.5. (See Figure 5.7.)

7. Explain why the point-slope and the slope-intercept forms of the equation of a straight line cannot be used to describe a vertical line. Explain why the intercept form cannot be used to describe a vertical line or a horizontal line. Then explain how the general form of the equation for lines can be used to describe any line.

8. Here are general equations for two lines:
$$\begin{cases} y = m_1 x + b_1 \\ y = m_2 x + b_2. \end{cases}$$
   a. Find the x-coordinate for the intersection point of these two lines.
   b. Find the y-coordinate for the intersection point of these two lines.
   c. If Q is the point of intersection of these two lines, for what situation will Q be undefined? Explain.

9. While finding a formula for the distance from a point to a line, we had to solve the system of linear equations
$$\begin{cases} y = mx + c \\ y = -\frac{1}{m}(x - a) + b. \end{cases}$$

Find the intersection point of these two lines.

10. Prove that the shortest distance from a point to a line lies along a segment perpendicular to the line. (Try to do this without using calculus.)

11. Use the similar triangles in Figure 5.8 to give another proof for the formula for the distance from a point to a line.

12. Using coordinates, write a detailed step-by-step proof that the set of points equidistant from two fixed points, A and B, is the perpendicular bisector of the segment AB.

13. a. How many times can a line intersect a circle? Prove your answer algebraically.

b. How many times can a parabola intersect a circle? Prove your answer algebraically. (*Hint*: Pick a specific parabola, perhaps $y = x^2$, and use a general circle $(x - a)^2 + (y - b)^2 = r^2$.)

14. Consider $\triangle ABC$ as shown in Figure 5.10. If $a > 0$, where is the orthocenter H? If $a = 0$, where is H? Justify your answers using the coordinates of H.

15. Using rectangular coordinates, prove that if the diagonals of a parallelogram are congruent, the parallelogram is a rectangle. (This problem has been adapted from an example given on page 29 of the *Praxis Study Guide for the Mathematics Tests*, ETS, 2003.)

16. Using coordinates, prove that the diagonals of a rhombus are perpendicular bisectors of each other. (*Note*: There are two things to prove.)

17. Use coordinates to prove that the midpoint of the hypotenuse of a right triangle is equidistant from all of the vertices.

18. Suppose we draw the line segment connecting the midpoints of the nonparallel sides of a trapezoid. Use coordinates to prove that this segment is parallel to the parallel sides and that its length is the average of their lengths. In addition, prove that the length of this segment times the height of the trapezoid gives its area.

19. a. Using coordinates, prove that the medians of a triangle are concurrent.
    b. If the vertices of a triangle are the points (x_1, y_1), (x_2, y_2), and (x_3, y_3), prove that the centroid of the triangle is the point
    $$\left(\frac{x_1 + x_2 + x_3}{3}, \frac{y_1 + y_2 + y_3}{3} \right).$$

20. For the circles $x^2 + y^2 = 9$ and $(x - 1)^2 + (y + 1)^2 = 1$, find an equation for the radical axis.

21. In the algebraic proof that the radical axis is a line, there is the possibility that $b = d$. This would make the fractions undefined in the final equation. Explain how to fix the proof in the case that $b = d$.

22. A rectangle is constructed in the xy-plane with two vertices on the x-axis at $x = \pm a$. The other

two vertices lie on the parabola with equation $y = 16 - x^2$.
    a. Find the coordinates of all four vertices of this rectangle.
    b. Find the area of this rectangle.
(This problem has been adapted from an example given on page 34 of the *Praxis Study Guide for the Mathematics Tests*, ETS, 2003.)

23. Convert each of the following Cartesian equations to a polar equation:
    a. $3x + y = 5$
    b. $x - 6 = y^2$
    c. $16x^2 + 9y^2 = 144$

24. Convert each of the following polar equations to a Cartesian equation:
    a. $\theta = \frac{\pi}{3}$
    b. $r = 5$
    c. $r \sec \theta = 3$
    d. $r^2 = \cos(2\theta)$

25. Use algebra and a graph to find all points where the curves $r = 3 \sin \theta$ and $r = 3 \cos 2\theta$ intersect.

26. The graph of the equation $r = 2 \cos \theta + 1$ is an example of a *limaçon*. Create a graph of this equation. Now consider the circle $r = a$. Find values of a so that the two curves have the following number of intersection points. In each case, find the coordinates of the intersection points algebraically.
    a. Four intersection points
    b. Three intersection points
    c. Two intersection points
    d. One intersection point
    e. No intersection points

27. In rectangular coordinates, if $y = f(x) = f(-x)$, the graph will be symmetric with respect to the y-axis.
    a. What are the graphical consequences of $f(-x) = -f(x)$ (in rectangular coordinates)?
    b. Now consider the situation in polar coordinates. If $f(\theta) = f(-\theta)$, what can you say about symmetry for the graph of the equation $r = f(\theta)$? Justify your answer and give examples.

c. If $f(-\theta) = -f(\theta)$, what can you say about symmetry for the graph of the equation $r = f(\theta)$? Justify your answer and give examples.

28. The equation $r = f(\theta) = e^{a\theta}$ describes one type of spiral.
    a. Does this spiral include the origin? Explain why or why not.
    b. With a great deal of trigonometry, it can be proved that the angle ψ between a tangent line at a point on $r = f(\theta)$ and the segment from the origin to that point satisfies

    $$\tan \psi = \frac{f(\theta)}{f'(\theta)},$$

    where $f'(\theta)$ is the derivative of the function f. For $f(\theta) = e^{a\theta}$ show that ψ is constant.
    c. Explain the role of the constant a in part (b).
    d. Explain what happens in part (b) if $a = 0$.

29. *Another look at rose curves*: Experiment with various values, positive and negative, for *a, n, b* in the equation $r = a \sin^n(5\theta) + b$. Then describe what effect each of *a, n, b* has on the graph. Also, what would be different if we used cosine instead of sine?

30. Create a diagram in GeoGebra illustrating Feuerbach's Theorem.

31. Use coordinates to prove that the nine-point center is the midpoint of the segment from the orthocenter to the circumcenter. This shows that the nine-point center lies on the Euler Line.

32. Use coordinates to prove that the radius of the nine-point circle is half the length of the radius of the circumcircle.

Exercises 33 and 34 are especially for future teachers.

33. The National Council of Teachers of Mathematics (NCTM) recommends in the *Principles and Standards for School Mathematics* that "Instructional programs from prekindergarten through grade 12 should enable all students to . . . specify location and describe spatial relationships using coordinate geometry and other representational systems" [NCTM 2000, 41]. What does this mean for you and your future students?
    a. Find a copy of the *Principles and Standards*, and study the discussion of the second Geometry Standard [NCTM 2000, 41 & 43]. What are the specific NCTM recommendations with regard to developing a sense of spatial relationships and coordinate geometry as children progress in their study of geometry from prekindergarten though grade 12?
    b. Find some mathematics textbooks for one of the grade levels for which you are seeking teacher certification. How is the second Geometry Standard implemented in those textbooks? Cite specific examples.
    c. Write a report in which you present and critique what you learn in studying the second Geometry Standard in light of your experiences in this course. Your report should include your answers to parts (a) and (b).

34. Design several classroom activities involving coordinate geometry or analytic geometry that would be appropriate for students in your future classroom. Write a short report explaining how the activities you design reflect both the NCTM recommendations and what you are learning about analytic geometry in this class.

Reflect on what you have learned in this chapter.

35. Review the main ideas of this chapter. Describe, in your own words, the concepts you have studied and what you have learned about them. What are the important ideas? How do they fit together? Which concepts were easy for you? Which were hard?

36. Reflect on the learning environment for this course. Describe aspects of the learning environment that helped you understand the main ideas in this chapter. Which activities did you like? Which did you find stretched you beyond your comfort zone? Why?

Analytic geometry gives us a bridge between geometry and algebra. The use of a coordinate system provides a way of representing geometric objects—points, lines, circles, curves—using algebraic tools. It also makes it possible for us to represent algebraic functions visually as graphs. Coordinate systems make it possible to use algebraic tools to prove many theorems about geometric objects.

In this chapter, we have developed a formula for the distance between points P and Q. If $P = (p_1, p_2)$ and $Q = (q_1, q_2)$ are points in the plane, their distance is given by

$$d(P, Q) = \sqrt{(p_1 - q_1)^2 + (p_2 - q_2)^2}.$$

This formula, which is based on the Pythagorean Theorem, actually works for the points P and Q in any number of dimensions. If P and Q are points on a number line (a one-dimensional space), then each point has only one coordinate: $P = (p_1)$ and $Q = (q_1)$. So the distance formula collapses to

$$d(P, Q) = \sqrt{(p_1 - q_1)^2}.$$

If P and Q are points in three-dimensional space—$P = (p_1, p_2, p_3)$ and $Q = (q_1, q_2, q_3)$—we can expand the distance formula to

$$d(P, Q) = \sqrt{(p_1 - q_1)^2 + (p_2 - q_2)^2 + (p_3 - q_3)^2}.$$

In general, if P and Q are points in n-dimensional space with $P = (p_1, p_2, \ldots, p_n)$ and $Q = (q_1, q_2, \ldots, q_n)$, we calculate the distance from P to Q using the formula

$$d(P, Q) = \sqrt{(p_1 - q_1)^2 + (p_2 - q_2)^2 + \cdots + (p_n - q_n)^2}$$

$$= \sqrt{\sum_{i=1}^{n} (p_i - q_i)^2}.$$

In this chapter, we explored the use of several coordinate systems. We used the usual Cartesian coordinate system, in which the coordinate axes are perpendicular to each other. We also looked at a skew coordinate system, in which the coordinate axes meet at an angle of 60°. In this skew coordinate system, we used the *Law of Cosines* to develop a distance formula:

$$d = \sqrt{(x_1 - x_2)^2 + (y_1 - y_2)^2 - 2 \cdot |x_1 - x_2| \cdot |y_1 - y_2| \cdot \cos(60°)}.$$

For the examples given in this chapter, we saw that we could use two applications of the Pythagorean Theorem in place of the Law of Cosines to get the same result. Extending the distance formula to higher dimensions when we are using a skew coordinate system becomes much more complicated, because we must consider the angles between each pair of coordinate axes that do not intersect at right angles.

Lines in the plane require two pieces of information—two parameters—to specify each particular line. The required pieces of information are *location* (which can be specified by giving a point on the line) and *direction* (or slope) of the line. Parallel lines have the same slopes, while the slopes of perpendicular lines are negative reciprocals of each other. We have explored several different forms for representing linear equations. (See page 118.) The choice of a particular form of the linear equation is usually dictated by the situation in the problem we are trying to solve.

The distance from a point P to another point Q can easily be calculated using the Pythagorean Theorem or the Law of Cosines. The distance from a point P to a line ℓ, however, required us to develop a strategy for finding a point Q on the line ℓ that is closest to P. One strategy to do this is to think about the family of circles centered at P. Some of these circles will intersect the line ℓ, and some will not. One of these circles, the smallest one to touch the line ℓ, will be tangent to ℓ at the desired point Q. In other words, the line segment PQ will be a radius of the desired circle, so PQ will be perpendicular to the line ℓ.

Polar coordinates are another example of a coordinate system. The polar coordinate system is probably more familiar to you than the skew coordinate system presented at the beginning of the chapter. In a rectangular coordinate system, such as the familiar Cartesian coordinate system, and even in a skew coordinate system, each point has a unique coordinate representation. This makes it easy to solve problems involving points of intersection by simply solving a system of equations. In a polar coordinate system, each point can be represented in many different ways. In fact, each point has infinitely many different representations! Therefore, it is necessary to continually check the reasonableness of an algebraic solution by looking at the actual geometry of the situation in a graph. Using algebra alone can often lead to missed intersection points.

Polar coordinates are particularly useful in situations where we are interested in representing curves. Circles, spirals, rose-curves, limaçons, and many other curves have polar equations that are much simpler than their corresponding equations in a rectangular coordinate system. The basic components of a rectangular system are lines, which is why equations for lines are simpler in that system. The basic components of the polar coordinate system are circles and rays through the origin. So, curves that loop around the origin—in fact, any kind of motion involving circular movement—can usually be expressed more simply using polar equations.

This chapter closed with a fairly intricate proof of the Nine-Point Circle Theorem. This proof uses many of the tools from the earlier sections of the chapter: coordinates of points, representing lines by linear equations, slopes of perpendicular lines, midpoints of segments, finding intersection points by solving systems of equations, and the equation of a circle. While the algebra involved is not difficult, it takes patience and care to work it out correctly.

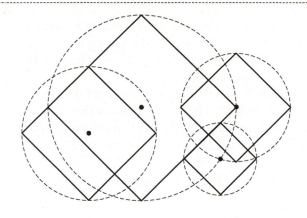

The ordinary Euclidean way of measuring distance makes use of the Pythagorean Theorem. If $P = (x_P, y_P)$ and $Q = (x_Q, y_Q)$, the distance from P to Q is given by the metric formula:

$$d(P, Q) = \sqrt{(x_P - x_Q)^2 + (y_P - y_Q)^2}.$$

We can think of this as the *straight line distance*, or the distance from the point P to the point Q as a crow would fly from one point to the other.

In this chapter, we will examine properties (axioms) for rules or formulas that can be used to measure distance. Such a distance formula is called a *metric*. We will investigate the *taxicab metric*, an alternative to the usual Euclidean metric. In order to see the effect that our assumptions about how distance is measured have on the shape of space, we will look at some familiar curves—circles, ellipses, and parabolas—using both these metrics. These curves can be defined in terms of distances of points from fixed points or lines. Since the taxicab and Euclidean metrics measure these distances differently, these curves will take on different shapes depending on our choice of metric.

Taxicab Geometry

For most of the activities in this chapter, you will be working on a rectangular, or Cartesian, coordinate system. Activities 1–4 will guide your exploration of the conic sections using the ordinary Euclidean distance measure, and then Activities 5–9 will repeat these explorations using the taxicab metric.

It is particularly important for these activities that the scales on the *x*- and *y*-axes be the same—so that circles look like circles. If you notice that these scales are not the same, you can set them to be the same. There are several ways to do this. In the Graphics pane, click on the small triangle to the left of the word "Graphics," and toggle the button to show the axes. One method for setting scales is to go to the **Options** menu, select **Advanced**, then **Preferences|Graphics**, and set the ratio xAxis:yAxis to 1:1. You can lock this setting so that this ratio remains at 1:1 as you interact with the diagram. A second method is to click on the gear icon, select Graphics, then set the xAxis:yAxis ratio to 1:1. A third method is to right-click in open space in the diagram, select xAxis:yAxis, and choose the 1:1 ratio.

Give clear and complete answers to the following problems and questions. Write your explanations clearly using complete sentences, and including diagrams whenever appropriate. Save your work for each activity, as sometimes later work builds on earlier work. It will be helpful to read ahead into the chapter as you work on these activities.

1. Open a new window in GeoGebra. If necessary, in the Graphics pane click on the small triangle to the left of the word "Graphics" and toggle the button to show the axes; toggle the second button to hide the grid.
   a. Click on the **Slider** tool in the Toolbar. Name this slider *r*, and set the minimum value to 0.
   b. Construct a point *C* anywhere on the coordinate plane, and notice that its coordinates are given in the Algebra pane.
   c. Construct a circle centered at *C* with radius *r*, and notice that the equation of this circle is given in the Algebra pane.
   d. Vary the point *C* and the position of *r* on the slider. What do you observe about the equation of the circle?
   e. What is the equation of a circle that is centered at (h, k), and has radius *r*?

2. Open a New Window in GeoGebra. In the Graphics pane, toggle the buttons to show the axes and hide the grid. Construct a slider r_1 ranging from 0 to 10. Using the Input bar, calculate $r_2 = 10 - r_1$. Notice that the sum of these values is constant. (To get subscripts in GeoGebra, use the underscore. That is, naming the object r_1 will make the name appear as r_1.)
   a. Construct two points and label them as F_1 and F_2. Construct a circle centered at F_1 with radius r_1, and a circle centered at F_2 with radius r_2. You will find it helpful to use different contrasting colors for these circles.
   b. Adjust the distance between points F_1 and F_2 (if necessary) so that the circles intersect, and construct these intersections.

c. Trace these intersections as you vary (or animate) the slider. What do you observe?

GEOGEBRA TIP You can turn **Trace** and **Animate** on and off by right-clicking on the appropriate point(s) in the Algebra view.

d. Stop the animation and turn off **Trace** for both intersection points. Gently move the axes; this will erase the traces. Using the **Locus** option on the **Line** tool, select one of the intersection points and the variable point on the slider to construct a curve. Again using **Locus**, select the other intersection point and the slider point to construct the other portion of the curve. Vary the points F_1 and F_2. What do you observe about the shape of this locus?

3. Open a new window in GeoGebra. In the Graphics pane, toggle the buttons to show the axes and hide the grid. In a convenient place near the edge of this window, construct a slider d. (It is convenient to define this slider with values from 0 to 10.)

a. Construct a line k and a point P not on k. We want to construct the locus of points that are equidistant from k and P.

The set of points at a fixed distance from point P will form a circle centered at P. The set of points at a fixed distance from line k will form a pair of parallel lines on either side of k.

Using these ideas, construct the set of points that meet both criteria: they are at a distance of d from k and at a distance of d from P.

b. Using the **Locus** tool, select each of these intersection points in turn with the slider point. Animate the slider to vary the value of d, and observe where these two sets intersect. How would you describe the locus of points that are equidistant from the fixed point P and the fixed line k?

c. Experiment with your diagram, varying both the point P and the line k. How does this affect the locus?

4. Open a new window in GeoGebra. In the Graphics pane, toggle the buttons to show the axes and hide the grid. Construct three points, P, Q, and R. Measure the distances PQ, PR, and QR.

a. Vary the point P. What happens to the distance PQ as P gets closer to (or farther from) Q? How small can you make the distance PQ? What can you say about the points P and Q when the distance between them is as small as you can make it?

b. Does it make a difference if you measure the distance PQ or the distance QP?

c. Calculate $PQ + QR$, and compare this with PR. (*Note*: You can do this by typing PQ+QR into the Input bar. GeoGebra will calculate a number and list this number in the Algebra pane.) What do you observe? Vary the points P, Q, and R. Does your observation continue to hold?

d. Calculate the ratio $\frac{PR}{PQ+QR}$. Vary the points P, Q, and R to make this ratio as large as possible. What do you observe? Can you explain what is going on?

5. The Euclidean distance between the points P and Q is calculated by the distance formula:

$$\sqrt{(x_P - x_Q)^2 + (y_P - y_Q)^2},$$

which is based on the Pythagorean Theorem. The **Distance or Length** tool on the Toolbar calculates the Euclidean distance between two points.

Let's define a new rule for measuring distance, that is, a new *metric*. Open a new window in GeoGebra. In the Graphics pane, toggle the buttons to show both the axes and the grid.

In the *taxicab metric,* distances are measured as though you have to travel like a taxicab, along the streets—either vertically or horizontally, never diagonally. On a coordinate system with a grid, you can measure the taxi-distance easily by counting the blocks from one intersection of the grid to the next.

a. Plot points at $P(3, 4)$, $A(2, 2)$, $B(3, 7)$, $C(2, 5)$, and $D(5, 5)$. By counting the number of blocks from P to A, we find that the taxi-distance PA is 3 units. Find the *taxi-distances PB, PC,* and *PD.* Two of these points are the same taxi-distance from P as A is. Which two?

GEOGEBRA TIP You can use the Input bar to easily define these points. Type P=(3,4) into the Input bar, and the point will appear in the Algebra pane with its coordinates and in the Graphics pane as a point.

b. The set of all points that are at the same taxi-distance from P forms a *taxi-circle* centered at P. In part 5(a), three of the points lie on a taxi-circle of radius 3 centered at P. Find several additional points on this taxi-circle. Describe the set of all points that are at a taxi-distance of 3 units from a fixed point P. How is the shape of a taxi-circle different from (or similar to) the shape of an ordinary Euclidean circle?

c. If you are given a point $Q(x_Q, y_Q)$ and a radius r, how could you quickly sketch a taxi-circle of radius r centered at Q?

d. Experiment with the **Taxi-Tools** on the document that your instructor will provide. To use the **Taxi-Circle**, you need a point for the center of the circle and a number that represents the radius.

GEOGEBRA TIP To use the **Taxi-Circle** tool, open a document that contains this tool. The **Taxi-Circle** tool will be available as an additional button on the Toolbar.

6. Instead of counting blocks by hand, we would like GeoGebra to calculate the taxi-distances for us. There is a **Taxi-Distance** tool on the Taxi-tools document. Also, you can also create your own tool to measure distance according to this new rule.

a. As before, construct two points, P and Q, and find their coordinates. Calculate

$$d_T(P, Q) = |x_P - x_Q| + |y_P - y_Q|$$

by typing this expression into the Input bar at the bottom of the GeoGebra window.

Notice that this rule allows us to find the taxi-distance between points that do not lie at the integer coordinates of the grid. That is, the x- and y-coordinates of a point can be any real numbers.

b. To create your own distance tool, select **Create New Tool** on the **Tools** menu. A pop-up menu will prompt you to select the *output objects* (which in this case is the result of the calculation for $d_T(P, Q)$ that you did in part 6(a)). Click on *Next*, and you will be prompted for the *Input Objects*, the points P and Q. Then click on *Next*, and you will be prompted to name this tool; in the space for Tool Help, say "two points" to remind the user what inputs this tool requires. Finally, click on *Finish*. Now whenever you want to calculate the taxicab distance between two points, select this tool, then click on the two points.

GEOGEBRA TIP A **Custom** tool is associated with the worksheet in which it is created. To save this taxi-distance tool, be sure to save this worksheet.

As you create your own set of customized tools, multiple tools will be saved to the same **Custom Tool** icon in the worksheet. When you select this **Custom Tool** icon, you will be able to choose from the tools that have been stored there.

c. Does *taxi-distance* have the same properties as *Euclidean distance*? Construct another point R on your worksheet, and calculate the taxi-distances $d_T(P, Q)$, $d_T(P, R)$, and $d_T(Q, R)$. Vary the points, and answer the questions of Activity 4 for these taxi-distances. For which of these questions does taxi-distance give results similar to Euclidean distance?

7. Taxi-circles are not round in the ordinary Euclidean sense. In Activity 2, we constructed ellipses by finding the locus of intersection points for particular pairs of circles. We would like to investigate the shape of taxi-ellipses using an adaptation of this method. The shape of taxi-circles will have an impact on the shape of taxi-ellipses.

Open a New Window in GeoGebra. In the Graphics pane, toggle the buttons to show both the axes and the grid. As you did in Activity 2, construct a slider r_1 ranging from 0 to 10 and calculate $r_2 = 10 - r_1$. Of course, the sum of these values is constant.

a. Construct two points in the coordinate plane, and label these as F_1 and F_2. Construct a taxi-circle centered at F_1 with radius r_1, and a taxi-circle centered at F_2 with radius r_2.

b. Adjust the points F_1 and F_2 (if necessary) so that $r_1 + r_2 > d_T(F_1, F_2)$. Construct the points where the taxi-circles intersect.

Each taxi-circle consists of four line segments. To construct the intersection points for a pair of taxi-circles, it is necessary to construct intersections of each pair of intersecting segments.

c. Use the **Locus** tool with one of the intersection points and the variable point on the slider. Repeat this for other intersection points. Continue in this manner until you have constructed the several segments of the locus for a taxi-ellipse. (Depending on the locations of F_1 and F_2, this part of the locus will consist of two or four line segments.)

    d. Unfortunately, this construction does not give the entire taxi-ellipse. Vary the slider, and observe the taxi-circles changing size as their radii get longer and shorter. This construction will give *points* of intersection, but not *segments of intersection*. Can you see what needs to be done to complete the taxi-ellipse?

    e. Vary the points F_1 and F_2. What do you observe about the shape of this locus? What if F_1 and F_2 lie on diagonally opposite corners of a rectangle? What if F_1 and F_2 lie along a vertical line? What if F_1 and F_2 lie along a horizontal line?

8. Recall that in Chapter 5 we investigated what it means to talk about the distance from a point P to a line ℓ. (See Activity 5, page 112, and the discussion on pages 123–125.) We can define the distance from P to ℓ as the radius of the circle centered at P that is tangent to ℓ.

If a Euclidean circle is tangent to a line, it touches the line at exactly one point. But taxi-circles have flat sides. Is there an easy way to find the radius of a taxi-circle centered at P that is tangent to ℓ?

Open a new window in GeoGebra. In the Graphics pane, toggle the buttons to show both the axes and the grid. In a convenient place near the edge of this window, construct a slider d. (Set this slider initially for 0 to 10. After you've experimented a bit, you may decide on a different range of values for d.)

    a. Construct a line ℓ, and a point P not on ℓ. Construct a taxi-circle centered at P with radius d. Vary d to vary the radius of the taxi-circle, and observe whether the taxi-circle is tangent to ℓ. Try to find the radius of the taxi-circle centered at P that is tangent to ℓ.

    b. Vary the line ℓ so that its slope is greater than 1, equal to 1, less than 1. Try some negative values of the slope as well. Formulate a rule for finding the distance from a point P to a line ℓ using the taxi-cab metric.

9. Now let's investigate taxi-parabolas. Open a new window in GeoGebra. In the Graphics pane, toggle the buttons to show both the axes and the grid. In a convenient place near the edge of this window, construct a slider d.

    a. Construct a line k and a point P not on k. We want to construct the locus of points that are equidistant from k and P.

The set of points at a fixed taxi-distance from the point P will form a taxi-circle centered at P.

The set of points at a fixed distance from the line k will form a pair of parallel lines on either side of k. Because taxi-circles have flat sides, you will have to think carefully about how to construct the set of points that are at a distance d from the line k. This construction will depend on whether the absolute value of the slope of the line k is less than, equal to, or greater than 1.

    b. Using these ideas, construct the locus of points that are at a distance of d from k and at a distance of d from P. The taxi-parabola will be composed of several segments, which you will have to construct separately.

To get a complete picture of taxi-parabolas, you will have to consider various cases based on the slope of k. What happens when $|m| < 1$, $|m| = 1$, $|m| > 1$? What if k is vertical or horizontal?

i. Vary the slider d. What do you observe?

ii. Vary the point P. What do you observe?

iii. Vary the line k. What do you observe?

6.2 DISCUSSION

In Chapter 5 we discussed the idea of measuring distance. If the points lie on a line (e.g., a number line), the location of each point can be specified by a single coordinate; for example, P and Q can be specified by coordinates x_P and x_Q, respectively. (See pages 114–115.) Then the distance between these points can be calculated by taking the difference between their coordinates:

$$d(P, Q) = |x_P - x_Q| = \sqrt{(x_P - x_Q)^2}.$$

When the points lie in a plane, we need two coordinates for each point. In Chapter 5, we investigated three different coordinate systems: a skew coordinate system in which the axes were set at 60° to each other; a rectangular coordinate system in which the axes were at right angles; and a polar coordinate system in which the coordinates of a point P tell the distance of P from the origin, and the angle that a ray through P makes with the polar axis.

When the points P and Q are specified by coordinates in either a skew coordinate system or a rectangular coordinate system, the distance $d(P, Q)$ between them can be calculated by the formula

$$\sqrt{(x_P - x_Q)^2 + (y_P - y_Q)^2 - 2|x_P - x_Q| \cdot |y_P - y_Q| \cos(\theta)},$$

where θ is the angle between the axes (measured counterclockwise from the x-axis to the y-axis). In the ordinary rectangular coordinate system, θ is a right angle, so that $\cos(\theta) = 0$, and the distance formula reduces to

$$\sqrt{(x_P - x_Q)^2 + (y_P - y_Q)^2}.$$

This is the usual Euclidean distance formula, and is based on the Pythagorean Theorem.

AN AXIOM SYSTEM FOR METRIC GEOMETRY

A formula or a rule for measuring distance is called a *metric*. The formula for measuring distance in a skew coordinate system and the ordinary Euclidean distance formula are examples of metrics.

We have certain expectations about distance. For instance, we expect the distance between two different points to be positive. There are certain situations where we might allow a negative number to be given for distance with the understanding that the negative sign means that one is backing up or going in the other direction. For example, in a coordinate system, the sign—positive or negative—of the coordinate tells us on which side of the origin a particular point may lie; that is, the signed number gives information about the *direction* as well as the *distance*. We are not considering such directed distances in this chapter.

The idea of distance from point P to point Q is closely related to the idea of the length of the line segment PQ. GeoGebra uses the notation PQ for the distance between points. In this text, we have been using PQ to designate the line segment from P to Q. When we want to emphasize that we are talking about the distance between points, we will use $d(P, Q)$. In Activity 4, you may have noticed that we used the simpler notation PQ for $d(P, Q)$, following the notation in the GeoGebra worksheet.

As you worked on Activity 4, you probably observed that $d(P, Q)$ is usually positive, and $d(P, Q) = 0$ only when P and Q are in the same location. We ordinarily expect the distance from P to Q to be the same as the distance from Q to P. As you worked on Activity 4c, did you observe that $d(P, Q) + d(Q, R) \geq d(P, R)$? This is called the *triangle inequality*. If PQ, QR, and PR are considered line segments, then the points P, Q, and R might be collinear, or they might form the vertices of a triangle. The sum of the lengths of two sides of a triangle cannot be smaller than the length of the third side. In fact, if $d(P, Q) + d(Q, R) = d(P, R)$, the three points P, Q, and R are *collinear* with Q *between* P and R. As a consequence of the triangle inequality, the ratio $\frac{PR}{PQ+QR} \leq 1$. If this ratio equals 1, the points P, Q, and R are collinear and Q lies on the line segment PR.

These ideas about distance are so important, so fundamental to the geometry of spaces where distances can be measured, that we formulate a set of axioms for a metric space:

Let P, Q, and R be points, and $d(P, Q)$ denote the distance from P to Q.

Metric Axiom 1 $d(P, Q) \geq 0$, and $d(P, Q) = 0$ if and only if $P = Q$.

Metric Axiom 2 $d(P, Q) = d(Q, P)$.

Metric Axiom 3 $d(P, Q) + d(Q, R) \geq d(P, R)$.

We will examine several different rules for measuring distance. In each case, we must be sure that the rule we propose meets these three criteria before we can call it a metric.

The Euclidean Distance Formula

THEOREM 6.1 The ordinary Euclidean distance formula,

$$d(P, Q) = \sqrt{(x_P - x_Q)^2 + (y_P - y_Q)^2},$$

satisfies all three of the metric axioms. Hence, the Euclidean distance formula is a metric in $\mathbb{R}^2$.

1. The expression $(x_P - x_Q)^2 + (y_P - y_Q)^2$ is the sum of numbers that have been squared. By convention, when we take the square root of a number we consider the positive square root. So the expression $\sqrt{(x_P - x_Q)^2 + (y_P - y_Q)^2}$ will always give a result greater than or equal to zero. The only way that $\sqrt{(x_P - x_Q)^2 + (y_P - y_Q)^2}$ can equal zero is for both $(x_P - x_Q)^2 = 0$ and $(y_P - y_Q)^2 = 0$, in which case both $x_P = x_Q$ and $y_P = y_Q$; in other words, $P = Q$. So the first metric axiom is satisfied.

2. Observe that $(x_P - x_Q)^2 = (x_Q - x_P)^2$ and $(y_P - y_Q)^2 = (y_Q - y_P)^2$. So $d(P, Q) = d(Q, P)$, satisfying the second metric axiom.

3. Finally,

$$d(P, Q) + d(Q, R) = \sqrt{(x_P - x_Q)^2 + (y_P - y_Q)^2} +$$

$$\sqrt{(x_Q - x_R)^2 + (y_Q - y_R)^2}$$

$$\geq \sqrt{(x_P - x_R)^2 + (y_P - y_R)^2}$$

$$= d(P, R).$$

So the third axiom is also satisfied. Since all three metric axioms are satisfied for points in the plane, the Euclidean distance formula is a metric in $\mathbb{R}^2$.

The **Distance or Length** tool in GeoGebra calculates the Euclidean distance between two points. To verify this, construct two points, P and Q, and find their coordinates. Calculate

$$\sqrt{(x_P - x_Q)^2 + (y_P - y_Q)^2} \; ,$$

and compare this with the distance PQ as calculated by GeoGebra. Vary the points P and Q to see if your observation continues to hold.

The Taxi-Distance Formula

DEFINITION 6.1   The taxi-distance from $P(x_P, y_P)$ to $Q(x_Q, y_Q)$ is given by the formula

$$d_T(P, Q) = |x_P - x_Q| + |y_P - y_Q|.$$

In Activity 6, you created a tool to measure the taxi-distance between two points. Does taxi-distance satisfy all three of the metric axioms?

1. The expression $|x_P - x_Q| + |y_P - y_Q|$ is the sum of absolute values, and so is always greater than or equal to zero. The only way that $|x_P - x_Q| + |y_P - y_Q|$ can equal zero is for both $|x_P - x_Q| = 0$ and $|y_P - y_Q| = 0$, in which case $P = Q$. So $d_T(P, Q) \geq 0$, and $d_T(P, Q) = 0$ iff $P = Q$, and the first metric axiom is satisfied.

2. Observe that $|x_P - x_Q| = |x_Q - x_P|$ and $|y_P - y_Q| = |y_Q - y_P|$. So $d(P, Q) = d(Q, P)$, satisfying the second metric axiom.

3. Finally,

$$d_T(P, Q) + d_T(Q, R) = |x_P - x_Q| + |y_P - y_Q| + |x_Q - x_R| + |y_Q - y_R|$$

$$= (|x_P - x_Q| + |x_Q - x_R|) + (|y_P - y_Q| + |y_Q - y_R|)$$

$$\geq (|x_P - x_Q + x_Q - x_R|) + (|y_P - y_Q + y_Q - y_R|)$$

$$= (|x_P - x_R| + |y_P - y_R|)$$

$$= d_T(P, R).$$

So $d_T(P, Q) + d_T(Q, R) \geq d_T(P, R)$, and the third axiom is also satisfied.

Since taxi-distance satisfies all three of the metric axioms, we can call this formula a metric.

So we have proven the following theorem, which we now state formally:

THEOREM 6.2 The taxi-distance formula is a metric in $\mathbb{R}^2$.

CIRCLES

DEFINITION 6.2 A *circle* is defined as the set of all points at a given distance, r, from a fixed center, C. We can express this symbolically as

$$\text{Circle} = \{P : d(P, C) = r, \text{ where } r > 0, \text{ and } C \text{ is fixed}\}.$$

The fixed point C is the *center* of the circle, and the length r is its *radius*.

This definition describes a circle in terms of distances from a fixed point, but it does not tell us which metric to use. If we choose the Euclidean metric, we get ordinary round circles. (See page 122.) As you worked on Activity 1, you probably observed that a Euclidean circle centered at (h, k) with radius r is described by the equation

$$(x - h)^2 + (y - k)^2 = r^2.$$

Taxi-Circles

Let's see what happens when we choose the taxicab metric. In Activity 5, you worked with an example of a taxi-circle centered at $P(3, 4)$ with a radius of 3 units. You probably observed—to your surprise!—that this circle has flat sides, line segments with slopes of ± 1. Let's analyze this carefully.

We can simplify the algebra by choosing C at the origin. The taxi-circle centered at $C = (0, 0)$ with radius $r > 0$ is the set

$$\{P : d_T(P, C) = r\} = \{(x_P, y_P) : |x_P - 0| + |y_P - 0| = r\}$$

$$= \{(x_P, y_P) : |x_P| + |y_P| = r\}.$$

What does this look like graphically? The expression $|x_P| + |y_P| = r$ is a linear equation (four linear equations, actually). We can rewrite these in the slope-intercept form as $|y_P| = r - |x_P|$. This gives us

$$y_P = \pm(r - |x_P|) = \pm(r \mp x_P).$$

Let's consider one of these lines. The line $y_P = r - x_P$ has a y-intercept of $+r$ and a slope of -1. The set of points on this line that are at a taxi-distance from the origin of r will be the points on the line segment from $(0, r)$ to $(r, 0)$. A similar analysis can be carried out for each of the other four equations, giving three additional line segments: from $(r, 0)$ to $(0, -r)$, from $(0, -r)$ to $(-r, 0)$, and from $(-r, 0)$ to $(0, r)$. In other words, these equations give us four lines, and the requirement that $d_T(P, C) = r$ limits both x_P and y_P, so that $-r \le x_P \le +r$ and $-r \le y_P \le +r$. So a taxi-circle is formed by four line segments, forming a diamond shape standing on one vertex.

If the center of the circle is at $C = (a, b)$, the calculations are similar, just a little more complicated. You will have an opportunity to work out these calculations in the exercises.

ELLIPSES

DEFINITION 6.3   An *ellipse* is defined as the set of points, P, the sum of whose distances from two fixed points, F_1 and F_2, is constant. We can write this symbolically as

Ellipse $= \{P : d(P, F_1) + d(P, F_2) = d, \;\; \text{where } d > 0, \;\; \text{and } F_1, F_2 \text{ are fixed points}\}$.

The fixed points are called the *foci* (singular, *focus*) of the ellipse.

This definition describes an ellipse in terms of distances from two fixed points, but it does not tell us which metric to use. If we choose the Euclidean metric, we get ordinary rounded ellipses. As you experimented with your diagram in Activity 2, you probably observed that as you moved the foci closer together the ellipse became rounder, more like a circle; as you moved the foci farther apart, the ellipse became more elongated. At one extreme case, if $d(F_1, F_2) = 0$ so that $F_1 = F_2$, the ellipse is a circle centered at F_1 with radius $\frac{d}{2}$. At the other extreme case, if $d(F_1, F_2) = d$, the ellipse shrinks (or collapses) to the line segment $F_1 F_2$.

What happens if we choose the taxicab metric? This is what you were investigating in Activity 7. Instead of being rounded, taxi-ellipses are either octagonal or hexagonal. One or two pairs of sides of the ellipse will be horizontal and/or vertical, and the remaining four sides will follow the sides of taxi-circles, which are line segments with slopes of ± 1. If the foci lie on diagonally opposite corners of a rectangle whose sides are parallel to the axes, the taxi-ellipse will be octagonal. However, if the foci lie on the same vertical or horizontal line, one pair of horizontal or vertical segments disappears and the ellipse is hexagonal. (See Figure 6.1.)

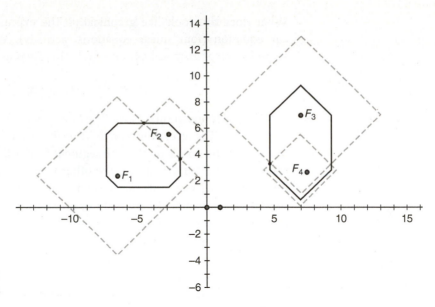

FIGURE 6.1
Taxi-Ellipses

MEASURING DISTANCE FROM A POINT TO A LINE

In order to measure the distance from a point P to a line ℓ, we need a strategy for finding the point on ℓ that is closest to P. As we discussed in Chapter 5 (see pages 122–123), one possible strategy is to think about the family of circles centered at P. When r is very small, the circle around P will not intersect ℓ. As r increases, eventually the circle and the line intersect.

We are used to the idea that in the ordinary Euclidean plane, a circle can intersect a line at two points, one point, or no points. In Euclidean space, when we drop a perpendicular from a point P to a line ℓ (or equivalently when we find the foot of the perpendicular from P to ℓ), we are finding the point X on ℓ that is as close as possible to P. A circle centered at P with radius PX will be tangent to ℓ.

What happens in the taxicab plane? This is the question you were investigating in Activity 8. A taxi-circle might still intersect a line in two points, one point, or no points. But because the sides of a taxi-circle are segments with slope ± 1, it is also possible for a taxi-circle to intersect a line in a segment along one of its sides. So after locating points of intersection, we also have to look for segments of intersection.

In the taxicab plane, if we are looking for a point X on line ℓ that is as close as possible to the point P (which is assumed not to be on ℓ), there are essentially three cases to consider: (1) situations where the slope of ℓ is between -1 and $+1$, (2) situations where the slope of ℓ is equal to ± 1, and (3) situations where the absolute value of the slope of ℓ is greater than 1. Let's consider each of these cases separately: suppose that we are given a line ℓ with slope m and a point P in the taxicab plane.

- **Case 1:** If $-1 < m < +1$, then a taxi-circle centered at P will first touch ℓ at a point directly above or below P. To find the point, X, on ℓ which is closest to

P, construct a vertical line through P. X will be the point where this vertical line intersects ℓ.

- **Case 2:** If $m = \pm 1$, then the point, X, on ℓ that is closest to P is not unique; there will be a whole line segment containing points, X, for which $d_T(P, X)$ is a minimum. To find this line segment, construct a vertical (or horizontal) line through P and find the point Y where this vertical (horizontal) line intersects ℓ. Construct the taxi-circle centered at P with radius $d_T(P, Y)$. Since the sides of this circle have slopes ± 1, one of its sides will lie along line ℓ.

- **Case 3:** If $|m| > 1$, then a taxi-circle centered at P will first touch ℓ at a point directly to the left or right of P. To find the point, X, on ℓ that is closest to P, construct a horizontal line through P. X will be the point where this horizontal line intersects ℓ.

PARABOLAS

You may be familiar with parabolas from your study of high school or college algebra. The graph of a quadratic equation, $y = ax^2 + bx + c$ (where a, b, and c are constants), will have the shape of a parabola. If $b = 0$, the parabola will be symmetric with respect to the y-axis and intersect the y-axis at the point $(0, c)$. If a is positive, the parabola will open up (so that it could hold water), and if a is negative, the parabola will open down (or be shaped like a hill). By varying the size of a, you can make the parabola narrower and steeper, or wider with a more gradual slope.

In this course, we are considering the parabola as a geometric object, rather than as a graph of an algebraic equation. In other words, we are considering the parabola as a locus of points with a specific relationship to a given line and a given point.

DEFINITION 6.4   Given a fixed line, k, and a fixed point F, a *parabola* is defined as the set of points P that are equidistant from k and F. We can write this symbolically as

$$\text{Parabola} = \{P : d(P, F) = d(P, k)\}.$$

The line k is called the *directrix* of the parabola, and the point F is called the *focus* of the parabola.

This definition describes a parabola in terms of distances from two fixed objects, and again it does not tell us which metric to use. If we choose the Euclidean metric, we get an ordinary rounded parabola. As you experimented with your diagram on Activity 3, you probably observed that as you moved the focus closer to the directrix the parabola became narrower, and as you moved the focus further from the directrix the parabola became wider.

In geometry, we think of a parabola as a locus of points, while in algebra we think of a parabola as a graph of a quadratic function. Geometry and algebra are two different lenses through which we can view the same object, in this case, parabolas. You will have an opportunity to investigate this more deeply in the exercises.

In Activity 9, you investigated what happens if we choose the taxicab metric. Let point F be the focus and line k be the directrix. We are interested in the locus of points that are the same distance from F as from k. Let m denote the slope of the line k. Figure 6.2 illustrates the case for $|m| < 1$. In this case, the taxi-parabola consists of two segments and two rays. The corners (or turning points) of the parabola occur where the point of the locus is formed at one of the vertices (or corners) of the circle centered at P. If $|m| > 1$, the parabola will open horizontally to the right or to the left depending on the location of P with respect to the line k.

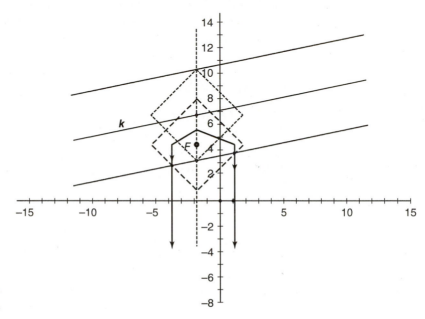

FIGURE 6.2
A Taxi-Parabola

If $|m| = 1$, the parabola will consist of one segment and two rays. The segment will be parallel to k as it will be formed by the side of a taxi-circle centered at F whose radius is one-half the taxi-distance from F to k.

HYPERBOLAS

Hyperbolas are defined similarly to ellipses, with one very small difference—a change in sign. This change in sign, from positive to negative, makes a lot of difference in the shape of the figure.

DEFINITION 6.5 A *hyperbola* is defined as the set of points, P, the difference of whose distances from two fixed points, F_1 and F_2, is constant. We write this symbolically as

$$\text{Hyperbola} = \{P : |d(P, F_1) - d(P, F_2)| = d, \text{ where } d > 0, \text{ and}$$

$$F_1, F_2 \text{ are fixed points}\}.$$

Notice that after subtracting, we take the absolute value, and this gives rise to two branches of the hyperbola. As with ellipses, the fixed points are called the *foci* (singular, *focus*) of the hyperbola.

You will have an opportunity to investigate both Euclidean hyperbolas and taxi-hyperbolas in the exercises.

AXIOM SYSTEMS

A distinctively mathematical way of thinking is to express our assumptions in a formal way, and then use rules of logical reasoning to develop proofs (or dis-proofs) of conjectures that may have been based on observations of particular phenomena. This is a process of *deductive reasoning*, and it is what you have been invited to do throughout this course.

An *axiom system* is a formal statement of our most basic expectations about a particular concept. As you worked on Activity 4, you may have wondered why we were asking such a basic question as "Is the distance PQ the same as the distance QP?" Yet, in an urban setting with one-way streets, the taxi-distances $d_T(P, Q)$ and $d_T(Q, P)$ may be very different. So Metric Axiom 2 (see page 148) is more restrictive than it may appear at first.

So far in this course, you have seen Euclid's postulates, which are basic assumptions—axioms—about the nature of a plane. The metric axioms on page 148 are another example of an axiom system. These metric axioms formalize our ideas about distance, so that we can study our assumptions and investigate the effect that these assumptions have on the shapes of elementary curves in the plane.

There are other concepts that we might formalize axiomatically. For example, what do we mean when we say that point B is *between* points A and C? In the real world, is there a gas station between your home and the grocery store? What exactly would this mean? In other words, what are your most basic assumptions—your axioms—about the concept of betweenness? You will have a chance to explore this question in the exercises.

6.3 EXERCISES

Give clear and complete answers to the following problems and questions. Write your explanations clearly using complete sentences. Include diagrams whenever appropriate.

1. The equation $x^2 - 4x + y^2 + 6y = 12$ describes a Euclidean circle. Find the center and the radius of this circle.

2. Which of the following equations describe a Euclidean circle? If the equation describes a circle, find its center and radius; if the equation does not describe a circle, explain what is going on.
   a. $x^2 - 6x + y^2 + 2y - 6 = 0$
   b. $x^2 - 2x + y^2 + 4y + 12 = 0$
   c. $x^2 - 3x + y^2 + 5y = 0$
   d. $x^2 - 6x + y^2 + 2y + 10 = 0$

3. Prove that the formula for distance in a skew coordinate system meets the conditions specified by the metric axioms.

4. Let $g(P, Q) = \max(x_P, x_Q) + \max(y_P, y_Q)$.
   (*Note*: $\max(a, b)$ denotes the larger of the two numbers a and b.)
   a. Prove or disprove that g is a metric.
   b. If g defines a metric, sketch a unit circle centered at the origin using this metric.
   c. In general, what do circles look like using this metric?

5. Let $h(P, Q) = \min(x_P, x_Q) + \min(y_P, y_Q)$.
   (*Note*: $\min(a, b)$ denotes the smaller of the two numbers a and b.)
   a. Prove or disprove that h is a metric.
   b. If h defines a metric, sketch a unit circle centered at the origin using this metric.
   c. In general, what do circles look like using this metric?

6. Suppose that you have a finite set of points $S = \{a, b, c, d, e\}$. Let $g(x, y)$ be defined on S so that

$$g(x, y) = \begin{cases} 1 & x \neq y \\ 0 & x = y \end{cases}$$

   a. Prove or disprove that g is a metric on S.
   b. If g defines a metric, sketch a unit circle centered at the point e using this metric.
   c. In general, what do circles look like using this metric?

7. Define a function $f(x, y)$ on the infinite plane as follows:

$$f(x, y) = \begin{cases} 1 & x \neq y \\ 0 & x = y \end{cases}$$

   a. Prove or disprove that f is a metric.
   b. If f defines a metric, describe a unit circle centered at the origin using this metric.
   c. In general, what do circles look like using this metric?

8. A court case in Louisville, KY, involved two bars located on opposite sides of a busy street. ("Court aids Bambi Bar bid for liquor permit." *The Courier-Journal*, Louisville, KY, 12 December 2006). The city attorney said that the bars were too close together, that is, the distance between the two bars was less than the legal separation requirement. The attorney for one of the bars argued that legal pedestrian travel between the two bars—without jay-walking—requires patrons to go to the nearest intersection and use the crosswalk. By measuring the distance between the bars using this pedestrian travel distance, the attorney argued that the bars were far enough apart to be in compliance.

   Does the definition of pedestrian travel distance satisfy the three metric axioms? Be sure to consider all possible cases when investigating the triangle inequality. (By the way, the bar won its case.)

9. Starting with the definition of a taxi-circle, find the equations of the four line segments that describe the taxi-circle centered at $C = (a, b)$, and having radius r.

10. The mathematical constant π is defined as the ratio of the circumference of a circle to its diameter. What is the value of π in the taxicab metric?

11. Explain in detail why a taxi-circle consists of four *line segments*, and not of four lines.

12. In the discussion of ellipses, we pointed out two extreme cases for Euclidean ellipses. (See page 151.) Carefully describe the analogous extreme cases for taxicab ellipses.

13. Consider the line segment AB in the plane.
    a. Prove that every point P on the perpendicular bisector of the segment AB is the same Euclidean distance from A as from B.
    b. For what kinds of line segments will this hold if you are using the taxicab metric?
    c. Let us call the set of points that are equidistant from fixed points A and B the *midset* of A and B. Thus, in the Euclidean plane, the perpendicular bisector of the segment AB is the midset of A and B. In general, what does the midset of A and B look like in the taxicab plane?

14. In the Euclidean plane if the point Q lies between the points P and R, then Q lies on the line segment PR. What can you say about the set of points that lie between the points A and B in the taxi-plane?

15. Think about the concept of *betweenness*.
    a. What does it mean for a point B to lie between the points A and C? Formalize your assumptions as a set of axioms for *betweenness of points*.
    b. What does it mean for a ray $\overrightarrow{AD}$ to lie between rays $\overrightarrow{AB}$ and $\overrightarrow{AC}$? Formalize your assumptions as a set of axioms for *betweenness of rays*.

16. After formulating your own *Axioms for Betweenness*, use the Internet or another geometry text to find statements for Hilbert's Axioms for Order (or Betweenness). Compare your set of Axioms for Betweenness with Hilbert's, and discuss any differences between these sets of axioms. In particular, do your Axioms for Betweenness address the same concerns as Hilbert's did?

17. Develop a method to investigate Euclidean hyperbolas, similar to the one you used in Activity 2. In this case, you will need to construct a pair of segments whose lengths maintain a constant difference while one of their endpoints is varied.

    One way to do this is to construct three points in a line j, and label the points A, B, and X. Construct two circles centered at X, one with radius XA and the other with radius XB. As you vary X (but neither A nor B), $|d(X, A) - d(X, B)|$ should remain constant.

18. Repeat Exercise 17 using the taxicab metric.

19. Open a GeoGebra window, and define a coordinate system with a square grid. In a convenient place near the edge of the Graphics pane, construct a line segment AB. Construct a point P on AB and construct the segment AP. This segment will act as a slider for this exercise.
    a. Construct a point F on the y-axis. F will be the focus of a parabola.
    b. Use the Input bar to plot the point $F' = (0, -y(F))$. This new point F' is the reflection of the point F across the x-axis.
    c. Construct a line through F' perpendicular to the y-axis. This will be the directrix of the parabola; label it k. Notice the equation of k in the Algebra pane.

    d. Use the method of Activity 3, with the segment AP as the slider, to construct the parabola with focus F and directrix k. This will give a parabola through the origin opening up or down (depending on the location of the point F). Once you are satisfied that the construction is working properly, you may wish to hide some of the objects.
    e. Use the Input bar to create the function $f(x) = \frac{1}{4}x^2$. This, too, will give a parabola through the origin.
    f. Vary the point F, and try to make the two parabolas—the one created as a locus of points and the one created as the graph of a function—coincide. What are the coordinates of F when this happens?
    g. Experiment with different functions, $g(x) = ax^2$, each time observing the coordinates of F for the particular value of a when the locus and the graph coincide. Some good values of a to try might be $\frac{1}{3}, \frac{1}{5}$, and $\frac{1}{8}$. What is the relationship between the value of a and the coordinates of F?

20. The parabolas you experimented with in Exercise 19 open up or down (depending on the sign of a). Parabolas can also open to the right or left, in which case the form of the equation is $x = f(y)$. Repeat Exercise 19, investigating this type of parabola.

Exercises 21 and 22 are especially for future teachers.

21. The National Council of Teachers of Mathematics (NCTM) recommends in the *Principles and Standards for School Mathematics* that "Instructional programs from prekindergarten through grade 12 should enable all students to . . . specify locations and describe spatial relationships using coordinate geometry and other representational systems" [NCTM 2000, 41]. Furthermore, these instructional programs "should enable all students to . . . understand measurable attributes of objects and the units, systems, and processes of measurement" [NCTM 2000, 44]. What does this mean for you and your future students?

a. Find a copy of the *Principles and Standards for School Mathematics*, and read through the overview of the Geometry Standard and the Measurement Standard (pages 41–47). Then study the specific recommendations for one grade band (i.e., pre-K–2, 3–5, 6–8, or 9–12). What are the specific recommendations of the NCTM regarding coordinate geometry and ideas about measurement for that grade band?

b. Find copies of school mathematics textbooks for these same grade levels. How are the NCTM standards implemented in those textbooks? Cite specific examples.

c. Write a report in which you present and critique what you learn.

22. Design several classroom activities involving coordinate geometry and/or measurement which would be appropriate for students in your future classroom. Write a paragraph or two explaining how the activities you design reflect both what you have learned in studying this chapter, and the recommendations of the NCTM.

Reflect on what you have learned in this chapter.

23. Review the main ideas of this chapter. Describe, in your own words, the concepts you have studied and what you have learned about them. What are the important ideas? How do they fit together? Which concepts were easy for you? Which were hard?

24. Reflect on the learning environment for this course.

a. Describe aspects of this learning environment that helped you understand the main ideas in this chapter. Which activities did you like? Which did you find challenging? Why?

b. How will your experiences in this course influence the kind of learning environment you set up for your future students?

6.4 CHAPTER OVERVIEW

In this chapter, we have investigated some ideas of metric geometry. A metric space is a set of points with a rule or formula for measuring distance that satisfies three metric axioms:

Let P, Q, and R be points, and $d(P, Q)$ denote the distance from P to Q.

Metric Axiom 1 $d(P, Q) \geq 0$, and $d(P, Q) = 0$ if and only if $P = Q$.

Metric Axiom 2 $d(P, Q) = d(Q, P)$.

Metric Axiom 3 $d(P, Q) + d(Q, R) \geq d(P, R)$.

We have approached the concept of a metric space by investigating some familiar curves, using two different rules for measuring distances: the ordinary Euclidean metric and the taxicab metric. We investigated circles, ellipses, parabolas, and hyperbolas using their metric definitions, and found that these ordinary curves have surprisingly different shapes in taxicab space from what they have in ordinary Euclidean space.

By using their metric definitions, we have treated these curves as geometric objects—as sets of points with specified distances from certain fixed points or fixed lines. Using the analytic tools of Chapter 5, we are able to develop formulas for these geometric objects. As you continue your study of geometry, you will be able to use either geometric tools or algebraic tools to study the properties of these and other curves. In this book, we have restricted our study to objects in the plane, that is, two-dimensional objects. With very little additional machinery, it would be possible to extend your investigations to three dimensions (and to even higher dimensions!).

In Chapters 2 and 4, we discussed Euclid's postulates, which are axioms that express our basic assumptions about the nature of space. In this chapter, we have used axioms to express our most basic expectations about what we need to do in measuring distances from one point to another. Perhaps you are beginning to get some insight into how mathematicians think about problems. We try to express our most basic assumptions—those things that we want to take for granted—as axioms. Axioms give mathematicians a way of formalizing our assumptions about a particular situation. Working from the axioms, we build theorems—and eventually a whole theory. In this chapter, we have just touched the very beginnings of a theory of metric spaces. By investigating some unexpected results about some very familiar curves, we hope that we have opened your mind to some new vistas in geometrical reasoning!

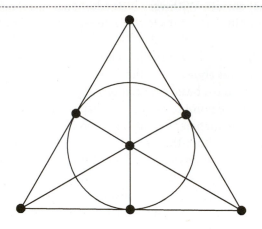

CHAPTER SEVEN

Finite Geometries

H istorically, mainstream mathematics was concerned with infinite sets: natural numbers, integers, real numbers, the number line, the Euclidean plane, and so on. In the nineteenth and twentieth centuries, mathematicians began to investigate finite sets: finite number systems, finite algebras, and finite geometries. In the late nineteenth century, Gino Fano constructed some particularly interesting examples of finite geometries, one of which now bears his name—the Fano plane. In this chapter, we will examine two basic families of finite geometries: affine geometry and projective geometry. Although these two kinds of geometries share some features in common, affine geometries allow the existence of parallel lines while projective geometries do not.

As a prelude to this chapter on finite geometries, we invite you to engage in a simple tactile exploration using pipe cleaners. We begin with an axiom system. The basic (undefined) terms in this system are *moe* and *fuzzy*. The axioms tell us what we can assume about moes and fuzzies.

Axiom 1 There exists at least one fuzzy.

Axiom 2 There are exactly three moes on every fuzzy.

Axiom 3 Not all moes are on the same fuzzy.

Axiom 4 There is exactly one fuzzy on any two distinct moes.

Axiom 5 There is at least one moe on any two distinct fuzzies.

Build a model of this system using pipe cleaners to represent the moes and fuzzies. You will need 8–10 long, white pipe cleaners to represent the fuzzies, and 4–5 colored pipe cleaners, cut in half and each piece twisted into a loop, to represent the moes. Use this pipe-cleaner model to help you answer the following questions:

1. Axiom 5 tells us that there is at least one moe on any two distinct fuzzies. Could there be more than one? That is, can two distinct fuzzies be on more than one moe?

2. Axiom 2 tells us that there are exactly three moes on every fuzzy. How many fuzzies are on each moe?

3. Axiom 1 tells us that there is at least one fuzzy. How many fuzzies are there in this system?

4. How many moes are in this system?

5. In this system, are there any fuzzies that do not share a moe? (If so, we could call this a pair of parallel fuzzies.)

6. In this system, are there any moes that do not share a fuzzy? (If so, we could call this a pair of parallel moes.)

Investigating this finite geometry using your pipe-cleaner model will prepare you for the more abstract ideas presented in this chapter on finite geometries.

The activities that open this chapter can be done without using GeoGebra. Following the activities, we present axiom systems for affine and projective geometries, which describe the fundamental assumptions of these geometries. We will explore some interesting consequences of these axioms and develop some elementary theorems of finite affine and projective geometries. We will show how these two geometries are related and how they are different from each other. Finally, we will use coordinates to explore some additional properties of these geometries.

7.1 ACTIVITIES

Give clear and complete answers to the following problems and questions. Write your explanations clearly using complete sentences, and including diagrams whenever appropriate. Save your work for each activity, as sometimes later work builds on earlier work. It will be helpful to read ahead into the chapter as you work on these activities.

1. Here is a collection of six sets based upon four elements:

$$\left\{ \begin{matrix} a \\ b \end{matrix} \right\}, \left\{ \begin{matrix} a \\ c \end{matrix} \right\}, \left\{ \begin{matrix} a \\ d \end{matrix} \right\}, \left\{ \begin{matrix} b \\ c \end{matrix} \right\}, \left\{ \begin{matrix} b \\ d \end{matrix} \right\}, \left\{ \begin{matrix} c \\ d \end{matrix} \right\}.$$

Which of the following statements does this collection of sets satisfy? Justify your answers.

   a. Any two elements have exactly one set in common.

   b. Any two sets have at least one element in common.

   c. Any element x not in a set S appears in exactly one set disjoint from S.

2. Look again at the elements and sets of Activity 1.
   a. Create a diagram of this situation in which the elements a, b, c, d are represented by points and the sets are represented by lines. Label your diagram.
   b. Now create a diagram in which the elements are represented by lines and the sets are represented by points. Label your diagram.
   c. How are your diagrams similar? How are they different?

3. In Activity 1, the sets $\left\{ \begin{array}{c} a \\ b \end{array} \right\}$ and $\left\{ \begin{array}{c} c \\ d \end{array} \right\}$ do not intersect. Let the values $a, b,$ c, d represent points. If these two sets represent lines, we would say that the lines are parallel. Suppose that we force these two lines to intersect by adding a third point, like this:

$$\left\{ \begin{array}{c} a \\ b \\ e \end{array} \right\} \text{ and } \left\{ \begin{array}{c} c \\ d \\ e \end{array} \right\}.$$

   a. Find all other pairs of parallel lines from Activity 1 and do the same thing. That is, add a new point at which the parallel lines intersect.
   b. Create a diagram showing all points and lines in this new geometric system. Clearly label your diagram.

4. Look again at the collection of sets you created in Activity 3. Which of the properties listed in Activity 1 are satisfied by your collection?

5. To use a coordinate system for a finite geometry, we need a finite arithmetic system. A convenient system is *modular arithmetic*. The basic idea of modular arithmetic is that $x \bmod n$ gives the remainder when x is divided by n. For instance, $18 \bmod 7 \equiv 4$ and $15 \bmod 12 \equiv 3$. Any calculations are done with the remainders only.
   In $\mathbb{Z}_2$, the integers mod 2, here are some sample calculations:

$$0 + 1 \equiv 1, \; 1 + 1 \equiv 0, 0 \cdot 1 \equiv 0, 1 \cdot 1 \equiv 1.$$

   a. Complete the addition and multiplication tables for $\mathbb{Z}_2$. These tables will use only the values 0 and 1.

$+_2$	0	1		$\times_2$	0	1
0				0		
1				1		

   b. Now create the addition and multiplication tables for $\mathbb{Z}_3$. These tables will use only the values 0, 1, and 2.
   c. Simplify the following linear combinations of points, working in $\mathbb{Z}_3$ arithmetic:

$$2 \cdot (1, 2, 0) + 1 \cdot (2, 2, 1)$$

$$1 \cdot (2, 0, 2) + 2 \cdot (0, 2, 1) + 1 \cdot (1, 1, 2)$$

6. In Activity 3, you created the sets

$$\left\{ \begin{array}{c} a \\ b \\ e \end{array} \right\}, \left\{ \begin{array}{c} c \\ d \\ e \end{array} \right\}, \left\{ \begin{array}{c} a \\ c \\ f \end{array} \right\}, \left\{ \begin{array}{c} b \\ d \\ f \end{array} \right\}, \left\{ \begin{array}{c} a \\ d \\ g \end{array} \right\}, \left\{ \begin{array}{c} b \\ c \\ g \end{array} \right\}$$

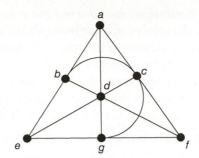

FIGURE 7.1
The Fano Plane

(perhaps with slightly different letters). Suppose that we also collect the three new elements into a seventh set $\left\{\begin{array}{c} e \\ f \\ g \end{array}\right\}$. Figure 7.1 shows a diagram of this situation in which the elements are represented by points and the sets by lines (though we had to cheat by bending one of the lines).

Create a diagram in which the elements are represented by lines and the sets by points. How does your diagram compare to Figure 7.1?

7. Suppose that the points e, f, g and the line $\left\{\begin{array}{c} e \\ f \\ g \end{array}\right\}$ are removed from Figure 7.1.

Create a diagram of the geometry that remains. How does this diagram compare to other diagrams in these activities?

7.2 DISCUSSION

AN AXIOM SYSTEM FOR AN AFFINE PLANE

Axiom systems are an old idea in mathematics. The best-known example is Euclid's set of five axioms (postulates) for plane geometry, which we discussed in Chapter 2. From these five assumptions, Euclid and his contemporaries developed a long list of theorems. As long as his five axioms are accepted as true, all of these theorems must also be true. In Chapter 6, we introduced axioms for metric geometry, and you had the opportunity of exploring the impact that changing the way we measure distance has on the shapes of familiar objects such as circles, ellipses, and parabolas. Another example of an axiom system is the set of axioms for a group, which we will present and develop in Chapters 8 and 10. The short list of axioms for a group yields a surprisingly rich set of theorems, and group theory is an active research area even today.

One of the major issues of Euclidean geometry is parallelism. While the basic notion is not difficult—parallel lines are those lines that do not intersect—the statement of Euclid's Fifth Postulate is far more complicated than the other four. This was a source of concern for hundreds of years, and many mathematicians felt that it should be possible to find a proof of this elaborate statement. However, the search for a proof turned out to be fruitless. In fact, there are geometries in which the Fifth Postulate is false. (We will see some examples in this chapter.) In Chapter 11, we will explore some consequences of altering this axiom.

Affine geometry focuses on the role of parallel lines but does not deal with direction or angles. This may seem like a limited view of geometry; however, many interesting things can be proven even in this simplified situation. This focus also opens up the possibility of a geometry that uses only a finite collection of objects.

Let us begin with a short list of axioms for an affine plane.

Affine Axiom 1   A line lies on at least two points.

Affine Axiom 2   Any two distinct points have exactly one line in common.

Affine Axiom 3   Any point P not on a line ℓ lies on exactly one line not intersecting ℓ.

Affine Axiom 4   There exists a set of three noncollinear points.

It is Axiom 4 which guarantees that the geometry contains anything! This axiom says that there are points, and then Axiom 2 guarantees that there will be lines as well. Notice that these axioms say nothing about betweenness, order, continuity, or many other ideas. Incidence of points and lines is the only issue, at least in the axioms. Axiom 3 asserts that there are parallel lines in this system. Since we do not have the notions of angle or side, we cannot discuss parallelism the way Euclid stated it. Instead, Axiom 3 is adapted from Playfair's Postulate.

A *model* of an axiom system is a situation in which all of the axioms hold true. In the introduction to this chapter, you were invited to construct a model of an axiom system using pipe cleaners to represent the undefined terms *moe* and *fuzzy*. The axioms of the affine plane use *point* and *line* as the undefined terms; the axioms tell us what we can assume about points and lines. To construct a model of the affine plane, we must identify a set of things called *points* and another set of things called *lines*. Further, there must be some interpretation of what *lies on* means. It is very common to talk of points lying on a line, but it is less common to talk of lines lying on a point. Phrases such as "line through a point" or "line containing a point" can be used to convey the same idea. Sometimes, the term *incident* is used, as in the phrases "points incident on a line" and "lines incident on a point." The symmetry of the expressions "a point is incident with a line" and "a line is incident with a point" will be helpful later in this chapter when we discuss the concept of duality. The particular choice of word to be used is not as important as the interpretation given to the concepts expressed in the axioms.

The *undefined terms* of this particular axiom system are *point*, *line*, *lies on* (or *incident with*). In some models, the undefined terms will mean what you are accustomed to, but not always! If a model can be found that implements the axioms, the axiom system is said to be *consistent*, meaning that the axioms do not contradict each other.

Notice also that these axioms say nothing about whether the geometry is finite or infinite. The Euclidean plane satisfies all four affine axioms, so the Euclidean plane is an infinite model of the affine axiom system. The collection of sets in Activity 1 is a finite model for this same axiom system. In these models, Axioms 1 and 4 are clearly true, and with a little thought Axiom 2 is not hard to see either. Axiom 3 is a bit more challenging to verify; here is a typical situation.

The point c of Activity 1 does not lie on the line $\left\{\begin{matrix} a \\ b \end{matrix}\right\}$. The line $\left\{\begin{matrix} c \\ d \end{matrix}\right\}$ is the only line that contains c and is disjoint from $\left\{\begin{matrix} a \\ b \end{matrix}\right\}$.

There are twelve ways to pair a point with a line, and all twelve need to be checked. (We did check these ourselves, and all twelve choices do satisfy Axiom 3. You should check several additional choices on your own so that you see how this works.) Axiom 3 does hold in the setting of Activity 1.

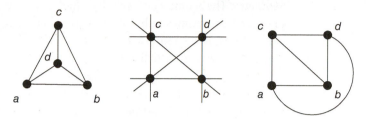

FIGURE 7.2
The Affine Geometry of Order 2

Activity 2a asked you to draw the geometry of Activity 1. There are many ways to draw this geometry. Figure 7.2 shows three possible diagrams. Remember that "point" and "line" do not necessarily have the usual meanings. So we can draw a line that bends or two lines that cross without intersecting if necessary. All that is required is that the axioms are satisfied. If you use GeoGebra to construct a diagram of this geometry, it may be clearer if you make the points of the geometry larger. These four larger points are less likely to be confused with points or pixels in the diagram that are not points of the geometry. In the system involving moes and fuzzies that was given at the beginning of this chapter, a pair of fuzzies "intersect" if they share a moe.

THEOREM 7.1   All lines in a finite affine plane have the same number of points.

Proof   By Affine Axiom 1, each line has at least two points. If each line has exactly two points, then the theorem is true. So suppose ℓ_1 is a line with at least three points. Let ℓ_2 be any other line. (It may be helpful to create a diagram showing the steps of this proof.)
Consider the possibility that ℓ_1 and ℓ_2 contain all the points of the geometry. Let a_1, b_1, and c_1 be three distinct points on the line ℓ_1 and let a_2 and b_2 be distinct points on ℓ_2. Pick point a_2 of ℓ_2 but not ℓ_1. According to Axiom 3, there is a line m containing a_2 that is parallel to ℓ_1. Any other point of m cannot lie on ℓ_1, so it must lie on ℓ_2 (under the assumption that ℓ_1 and ℓ_2 contain all the points of the geometry). Axiom 2 then implies that m and ℓ_2 are the same line. Hence, ℓ_1 and ℓ_2 must be parallel.
Axiom 2 gives lines $b_1 b_2$ and $c_1 b_2$, as well as $a_1 a_2$. The two lines $b_1 b_2$ and $c_1 b_2$ both contain the point b_2 and both lines are parallel to $a_1 a_2$. This contradicts Axiom 3. Thus, it is impossible for ℓ_1 and ℓ_2 to contain all the points of the geometry.
So far we have shown that the two lines ℓ_1 and ℓ_2 do not contain all of the points in the geometry. Let p be any point not on either line. By Axiom 2, there

is a line through p and each point of ℓ_1. In addition, there is a unique line through p that is parallel to ℓ_1. Thus, if there are k_1 points on ℓ_1, the total number of lines through the point p is $k_1 + 1$. Using the same reasoning with p and ℓ_2 and assuming that there are k_2 points on ℓ_2, the total number of lines incident with the point p is $k_2 + 1$. Therefore, $k_1 = k_2$. Thus, we have shown that ℓ_1 and ℓ_2 have the same number of points.

The number of points on a line in an affine geometry is called the *order* of the geometry. The geometry of Activity 1 has order 2. Figure 7.3 shows an affine plane of order 3, sometimes called *Young's geometry*. This geometry has nine points and twelve lines. It is good practice to identify all the triples of parallel lines in this figure. One way to visualize these parallel lines is to draw the nine points, and the "horizontal" and "vertical" lines from Figure 7.3 on a plastic transparency, then curl the transparency into a cylinder. The remaining lines can be drawn as diagonals, making the parallel lines easier to see.

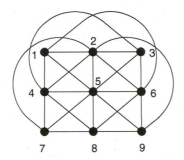

FIGURE 7.3
The Affine Geometry of Order 3

Knowing that an affine plane of order k has k points on every line, we are ready to investigate the question of how many lines are incident with each point.

THEOREM 7.2   Each point in an affine plane of order k lies on $k + 1$ lines.

You will be asked to prove this theorem in the exercises. The key idea you will need for this proof was used in the proof of Theorem 7.1.

Now that we have information about the number of points per line and the number of lines per point, it is possible to determine the total number of points in the geometry.

THEOREM 7.3   An affine plane of order k has k^2 points.

Sketch of a Proof   Pick a point P. This point is collinear with every other point. (*Why?*) Each line incident with P contains $k - 1$ points other than P. (*Why?*) There are $k + 1$ lines incident with P. (*Why?*) Finally, count all the points: the $k - 1$ points on each of the $k + 1$ lines incident with P, plus the point P itself. How many points are there in the affine plane of order k?

This theorem agrees with the examples we have seen thus far. In Figure 7.2 of order 2, there are four points. Also, in Figure 7.3 of order 3, there are nine points. The question of how many lines are in an affine plane of order k is a bit harder. First, we need to be able to count parallel lines.

THEOREM 7.4   In an affine plane of order k, each line is parallel to k lines.

For instance, look again at Figure 7.3. The horizontal line {1, 2, 3} at the top is parallel to two other horizontal lines—plus we will say that this line is parallel to itself. The diagonal line {1, 5, 9} is parallel to itself and to the lines {2, 6, 7} and {3, 4, 8}. You should locate the other trios of parallel lines.

Let us be clear about this notion of parallelism before we prove the theorem. Axiom 3 does not use the term "parallel." Instead, it talks about lines that do not intersect. This is the common meaning of parallel. However, we shall also say that a line is parallel to itself. In the statement of Theorem 7.4, one of the k lines being counted is the original line. (We use a notion from analytic geometry to justify this meaning of parallelism. On a Cartesian coordinate system, lines with the same slope are parallel. Since a line has the same slope as itself, it is reasonable to say that any line is parallel to itself.)

Proof of Theorem 7.4   This proof uses the idea of a transversal. We will show that every line parallel to a given line will intersect the transversal and that every point on the transversal lies on a line parallel to the given line.

Pick any line ℓ_1. Let m be any line that intersects ℓ_1 and let a be the point of intersection. Suppose that ℓ_2 is a line parallel to ℓ_1. The line ℓ_2 must intersect m, or else point a would be on lines ℓ_1 and m, with both lines parallel to ℓ_2. This would violate Axiom 3.

Now consider any point b on the line m, aside from a. By Axiom 3, there is a unique line ℓ_b that contains b and is parallel to ℓ_1. Of course, ℓ_1 lies on a and is parallel to itself.

We have shown that every point on m corresponds to a line parallel to ℓ_1. Since m contains k points, there are k lines parallel to ℓ_1.

Using this theorem, it is not difficult to count the total number of lines. Start with one particular line ℓ, count the lines that intersect ℓ, and then count the lines that are parallel to ℓ. You will be asked for a proof in the exercises.

THEOREM 7.5   An affine plane of order k has $k^2 + k$ lines.

AN AXIOM SYSTEM FOR A PROJECTIVE PLANE

Many axiom systems have been developed for projective geometry. Some of these systems were written to describe only the real projective plane, which is an extended version of the usual Euclidean plane. (This will be discussed in Chapter 12.) In this chapter, we present a very general set of axioms [Batten 1986, 23 and 41–44]. As in the case of affine geometry, these axioms do not say whether the geometry is finite or infinite.

Projective Axiom 1   A line lies on at least two points.

Projective Axiom 2   Any two distinct points have exactly one line in common.

Projective Axiom 3   Any two distinct lines have at least one point in common.

Projective Axiom 4   There is a set of four distinct points, no three of which are collinear.

You should compare these to the affine axioms on page 164. Once again, it is Axiom 4 which guarantees that the geometry contains anything. This axiom says that there are points, and then Axiom 2 guarantees that there will be lines as well. As in the affine situation, the axioms say nothing about angles, betweenness, order, or continuity. A dramatic difference from the affine axioms is that Projective Axiom 3 specifically prohibits parallel lines in projective geometry. Any two lines in a projective plane will intersect.

How can we be sure that a geometry satisfying these axioms even exists? It is conceivable that the axiom system is *inconsistent*, that the assumptions contradict each other in some way. One way of being sure that an axiom system is consistent is to find a *model* of the axioms. In this situation, a model is an example of a geometry in which all of the projective axioms are true.

Figure 7.1 shows a famous example of a projective geometry, the *Fano plane*. Let us check that the projective axioms hold in this model. All lines in this geometry lie on at least two points, even the "curved" line $\left\{\begin{matrix} b \\ c \\ g \end{matrix}\right\}$. Clearly, any two distinct points have exactly one line in common. There are a lot of pairs of lines to check, but it is not hard to see that any two distinct lines have at least one point in common (exactly one, in fact). The diagram shows that no three of the distinct points a, b, c, d are collinear. So, the Fano plane satisfies all four axioms and is a projective plane.

In general, we can prove something stronger than Axiom 1.

THEOREM 7.6   A line in a projective plane lies on at least three points.

Proof   The basic idea is shown in Figure 7.4. Given a line ℓ, Axiom 1 guarantees that there are two points P and Q on ℓ. By Axiom 4, there are two more points R, S not collinear with P, Q. Axiom 3 says that the line $\overleftrightarrow{RS}$ must intersect ℓ at a point T. Now, T must be a new point on ℓ, for R, S, T are collinear, and P and Q are not collinear with R, S.

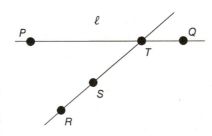

FIGURE 7.4
Proof That a Line in a Projective Plane Contains At Least Three Points

Axiom 3 also can be strengthened.

THEOREM 7.7 In a projective plane, any two distinct lines have exactly one point in common.

The proof of this is easy; suppose that two lines intersect twice and apply Axiom 2.

Axiom 3 and Theorem 7.7 tell us that there are no parallel lines in projective geometry. We are so accustomed to thinking in terms of the Euclidean plane that this may seem hard to accept. However, there are situations in everyday life that agree with Axiom 3. Consider parallel railroad tracks. As they recede into the distance, they appear to get closer and closer and eventually to intersect. It is not difficult to imagine an intersection point at the horizon. This is a basic concept of drawing in perspective; parallel lines, whether the sides of a road or the edges of a building, will intersect on the horizon line. This intersection is called the "vanishing point" by artists. Mathematicians sometimes call this point a "point at infinity" or an "ideal point," and this interpretation will be important when we relate affine planes to projective planes.

For affine geometry, we discussed several facts about the number of points. There are similar facts about the number of points in projective geometry.

LEMMA 7.1 In a projective plane, the points on one line can be put into one-to-one correspondence with the points on any other line.

Sketch of a Proof Pick two lines ℓ_1 and ℓ_2. Using points on these lines, create two new lines and their intersection at point P, which is not on either of the original lines. (*Why?*) For every point X on ℓ_1, the line PX intersects ℓ_2. (*Why?*) This creates the one-to-one correspondence. (You will be asked to give a more complete proof in the exercises.)

COROLLARY 7.1 If a projective plane is finite (i.e., it has a finite number of points), every line has the same number of points.

We can say something similar about the collection of lines incident with any given point. The proof uses another one-to-one correspondence, this time between points and lines.

THEOREM 7.8 If a projective plane is finite, every point lies on the same number of lines. Further, this number of lines per point is the same as the number of points per line.

Proof Let P be any point and let ℓ be any line not containing P. (*Which axioms guarantee that there is such a line?*) Suppose the line ℓ has $k + 1$ points. Each point on ℓ creates a line with P, so P lies on at least $k + 1$ lines. In addition, any line incident with P must intersect ℓ, so P lies on at most $k + 1$ lines.

The number k in the proof of this theorem is the *order* of the projective plane. The theorem says that a projective plane of order k will have $k + 1$ points on every line and $k+1$ lines on every point. This is our first hint of a symmetry between points and lines that will prove to be very important.

Knowing the number of points per line and the number of lines per point allows us to calculate the total number of points.

COROLLARY 7.2 A finite projective plane of order k will have $k^2 + k + 1$ points and will have $k^2 + k + 1$ lines.

Proof Consider a single point P. This point lies on $k+1$ lines, each of which has $k+1$ points—one of which is P. Every point of the projective plane is collinear with P, so every point is included on this set of lines. Thus, we have

(number of lines on P) $\times$ (number of points other than P on a line) + (P itself)
$= (k+1) \times k + 1$.

A similar argument works if we start with a single line.

It is not hard to prove that the Fano plane is the only possible way to create a projective plane of order 2. In fact, it has been proven that there are unique projective planes of order 2, 3, 4, 5, 7, and 8. You will be asked to draw the projective plane of order 3 in the exercises. This is a challenging exercise. How many points are needed? How many points lie on each line, and how many lines lie on each point? It may help if you use numbers to represent the points and list the sets that make up the lines before you start drawing, and you may need several attempts to produce a good drawing. There is no projective plane of order 6 and there are at least four different projective planes of order 9. In 1991, a proof was announced that there is not a projective plane of order 10 [Lam 1991]. This proof involved checking hundreds of smaller questions and was assisted by a computer. The existence and uniqueness of projective planes having large order is still an unanswered question, and there is a general theorem waiting to be discovered.

Is the axiom system for moes and fuzzies given at the beginning of this chapter more like an affine geometry or a projective geometry? Which of the undefined terms—moe or fuzzy—seems to be more like a line and which seems to be more like a point? Could you change the pipe-cleaner model so that the long, white pipe cleaners represent the moes, and the colored, twisted pipe cleaners represent the fuzzies? If you do this, how does that change your answers to these questions?

DUALITY

Look again at the axioms for a projective plane. Axioms 2 and 3 are very similar. The resemblance is even stronger between Axiom 2 and Theorem 7.7. Axiom 2 says "Any two distinct points have exactly one line in common" and Theorem 7.7 says "Any two distinct lines have exactly one point in common." The pattern of the statements is the same. The only difference between the statements is that the words *point* and *line* have been switched. This is the idea of *duality*: If two major terms are interchanged in a statement, the new statement could also be true. In the case of projective geometry, the two terms are *point* and *line*, two of the undefined terms in this system. In this section, we show that switching these terms in any theorem of projective geometry will indeed produce a new theorem, so projective geometry has the duality property.

Euclidean geometry does not have the duality property, nor does affine geometry. In both of those axiom systems, two distinct points determine a line. However, both Euclidean and affine geometry include the notion of parallelism. Two distinct lines do not necessarily determine a point in those settings, for it is possible that two distinct lines might not intersect. So duality does not work for Euclidean or for affine geometry. On the other hand, projective geometry includes an axiom stating that two distinct lines will intersect, which is very different from Euclidean or affine geometry.

Here again are the axioms for a projective plane:

Projective Axiom 1   A line lies on at least two points.

Projective Axiom 2   Any two distinct points have exactly one line in common.

Projective Axiom 3   Any two distinct lines have at least one point in common.

Projective Axiom 4   There is a set of four distinct points, no three of which are collinear.

We have already looked at the dual of Axiom 2. What happens if the terms *point* and *line* are interchanged in all four of the axioms? Here is what we would get:

Dual Axiom 1   A point lies on at least two lines.

Dual Axiom 2   Any two distinct lines have exactly one point in common.

Dual Axiom 3   Any two distinct points have at least one line in common.

Dual Axiom 4   There is a set of four distinct lines, no three of which are concurrent.

Recall that *concurrent* lines are those that lie on a common point, while *collinear* points are those that lie on a common line. So *concurrent* and *collinear* are dual concepts.

Figure 7.5 shows a different way to draw the Fano plane. Check the dual axioms. Every point lies on at least two lines (three, in fact). Any two lines intersect

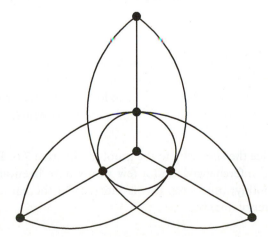

FIGURE 7.5
Another Way to Draw the
Fano Plane

at exactly one point. Any two distinct points are connected by a line. With a little searching, it is possible to find four lines that make a quadrilateral, so no three of these lines are concurrent. Thus, all four dual axioms work in the Fano plane.

In fact, these dual statements are true in a general projective plane. We have proved some things that will confirm this. Dual Axiom 2 is Theorem 7.7, and Dual Axiom 3 is a weaker form of Axiom 2, so they are both true statements. As for Dual Axiom 1, suppose we begin with a point P. By Axiom 4, there are at least three more points A, B, C such that no three of P, A, B, C are collinear. Pair P with each of these points and apply Axiom 2 to get at least two lines incident with the point P. Dual Axiom 4 also can be proved from Axioms 4 and 2.

This shows that a projective plane has the *duality* property. If the terms *point* and *line* are interchanged in any true statement about a projective plane, we get another true statement. Of course, this interchange must occur for any term that is derived from the concepts of point and line; for instance, we must interchange the terms *concurrent* and *collinear*. Duality works for the axioms, as we have just shown, but it also works for any theorem of the projective plane. The reason for this is that writing the dual proof also works. Suppose that we have a proof of some theorem, a proof derived from the four projective axioms. By writing the dual statements for every line of the proof, we get a proof of the dual theorem and this dual proof is based on the dual axioms. Since we know that these dual axioms are true in a projective plane, we know that this dual proof is also valid. So anything derived from the dual axioms also will be true in a projective plane.

It is important to recognize that duality does not hold in an affine plane. We can certainly make the dual statements of the affine axioms, but these duals are not all true in an affine plane. So we cannot use the duality principle in an affine system.

In Activity 6, you were asked to draw the dual of the Fano plane. The diagram of Figure 7.1 shows the points a, b, c, d, e, f, g with the lines listed as sets in the activity. Your challenge was to consider the elements a, b, c, d, e, f, g as the lines and the listed sets as the points. So the roles of the components of the diagram were reversed. Your diagram should look basically the same, except for how things are labeled. The Fano plane is self-dual, as are all projective planes.

Here is an example of a dual theorem and its dual proof:

THEOREM 7.9   **(Dual to Theorem 7.6)**   A point in a projective plane lies on at least three lines.

Proof   Given a point L, Dual Axiom 1 guarantees that there are two lines p and q on L. By Dual Axiom 4, there are two more lines r, s not concurrent with p, q. Dual Axiom 3 says that the point where r and s intersect (which can be denoted as $r \cap s$) will join with point L to form a line t. Now, t must be a new line on L, for r, s, t are concurrent, and p and q are not concurrent with r, s.

Notice the similarity to the proof of Theorem 7.6. The terms *point* and *line* have been interchanged, and a few words have been altered to make it read more smoothly; otherwise, this is identical to the earlier proof. This illustrates the power of duality.

We have already seen some dual results. For instance, the order k of a finite projective plane refers to both the number of points on a line and the number of lines on a point, with $k^2 + k + 1$ of each in the plane. Here is a more general result:

THEOREM 7.10   **Dual to Lemma 7.1**   The lines on one point can be put into one-to-one correspondence with the lines on any other point.

As in the original theorem, the proof consists of defining a mapping (a function) and verifying that it is one-to-one and onto. In the exercises, you will be asked to prove the original theorem and then to write the dual proof.

Duality can also be used when making definitions. For example, a *triangle* is defined as a set of three noncollinear points and the lines connecting them. (Remember that projective geometry deals only with incidence. Since the concept of betweenness is not available, we cannot discuss line segments.) The dual definition is the *trilateral*, a set of three nonconcurrent lines and the points connecting them, that is, the points where lines intersect. But this is the same thing! The triangle is a *self-dual* concept.

What can be created with more points? In Euclidean geometry, you have seen many objects created from four points and line segments of differing lengths. Projective geometry does not deal with length, only incidence, so there is not the same kind of variety of objects. In the projective plane, a *quadrangle* is defined as a set of four points, no three collinear, and the lines connecting them. You drew a quadrangle in Activity 3b, with six lines on these four points. These lines also intersect at three additional points, which create the *diagonal triangle* of the quadrangle. In the Fano plane, the vertices of the diagonal triangle will lie on a single line. For example, consider the quadrangle $bdge$ in Figure 7.1 of Activity 6. The lines bd and ge intersect at f; the lines be and dg intersect at a, and the lines bg and de intersect at c. Thus, the diagonal triangle is acf, which is a line.

Now for the dual of this definition: A *quadrilateral* is a set of four lines, no three concurrent, and the points connecting them. This is sometimes called a *complete quadrilateral*. This is the diagram you created for Activity 2b. How many intersection points were there from the four lines? Notice that a quadrilateral is not the same thing as a quadrangle. In particular, the numbers of points and lines are different. There are six points on the four lines of a quadrilateral. (Compare to the quadrangle to see the duality in these numbers.) The six intersection points of the lines in a complete quadrilateral can be connected to make three additional lines. These lines form a diagonal triangle (trilateral) here as well.

RELATING AFFINE PLANES TO PROJECTIVE PLANES

Making an Affine Plane from a Projective Plane

As we noted earlier, the Fano plane shown in Figure 7.1 is a famous example of a projective plane. In Activity 7, you were asked to look at the geometry created by removing the points e, f, g and the line $\left\{ \begin{array}{c} e \\ f \\ g \end{array} \right\}$. What remains is no longer a projective geometry because Projective Axiom 3 is no longer true. For instance, the lines $\left\{ \begin{array}{c} a \\ b \end{array} \right\}$ and $\left\{ \begin{array}{c} c \\ d \end{array} \right\}$ do not intersect. Their former point of intersection, e, has been removed from the geometry. So the lines $\left\{ \begin{array}{c} a \\ b \end{array} \right\}$ and $\left\{ \begin{array}{c} c \\ d \end{array} \right\}$ are now parallel. Figure 7.6 shows the effect of removing this line and the affine plane of order 2 that remains.

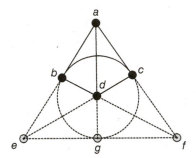

FIGURE 7.6
An Affine Plane from the
Fano Plane

In fact, the four-point geometry remaining is the geometry you drew in Activity 2a. This is an affine geometry, for it satisfies all four of the affine axioms. Axioms 1, 2, and 4 are true because the corresponding projective axioms were true in the Fano plane. For Axiom 3, a line ℓ in the four-point plane came from a line ℓ^* in the Fano plane, so ℓ^* contained one of the deleted points. For the sake of argument, let's assume the point was e. Then points P and e lie on exactly one line in the Fano plane, which we can call m^*. Then the affine line m created by removing e from m^* is parallel to ℓ and every other line on P must intersect ℓ at a point other than e.

There was nothing special about the line $\left\{ \begin{array}{c} e \\ f \\ g \end{array} \right\}$ in this process. Any line of this projective plane could be removed to create an affine geometry.

This process works in general. In any projective plane, select one line to be the *ideal line*. Remove this line and all its points. What remains is an affine geometry. Lines that used to intersect on the ideal line become parallel in the affine situation. In general, however, choosing different lines could lead to different affine geometries.

How are the order theorems affected by this removal? In a projective plane of order k, every line has $k+1$ points, there are $k^2 + k + 1$ points in the plane, and there are $k^2 + k + 1$ lines in the plane. Once the ideal line is removed, there is one fewer point on each line, $k+1$ fewer points in the plane, and one fewer line in the plane. So the corresponding affine plane of order k has k points on each line, k^2 points in the plane, and $k^2 + k$ lines in the plane. These are exactly the values in the theorems we proved earlier.

Making a Projective Plane from an Affine Plane

If we start with a particular affine plane, we can make a projective plane by reversing the process described above: Put in another line in such a way that the projective axioms are satisfied. Let us do this carefully.

For any line in the affine plane, there will be a collection of lines that are parallel to it. The lines in this collection are *equivalent* to each other in a very strong way, for parallelism is an *equivalence relation*. This means three things: Any line ℓ is parallel to itself (the *reflexive* property); if ℓ is parallel to m, then m is parallel to ℓ (the *symmetric* property); and if ℓ is parallel to m and m is parallel to n, then ℓ is parallel to n (the *transitive* property). In the sense of parallelism, all these lines are essentially the same; they are equivalent. (As before, we say that a line is parallel to itself. This convention gives us the reflexive property.)

Equivalence relations are useful tools in many areas of mathematics. The most important theorem about equivalence relations says that any such relation separates its set of objects into disjoint *equivalence classes*. Each equivalence class is a set containing all the objects that are related to each other. In our situation of affine lines related by parallelism, every line belongs to exactly one of these equivalence classes.

As you did in Activity 3, let us add a common point to each line in each equivalence class. For example, lines {1, 2, 3}, {4, 5, 6}, and {7, 8, 9} are parallel to each other in Figure 7.7, so they belong to one equivalence class. We add the new point 10 to each of these lines to make them concurrent at point 10.

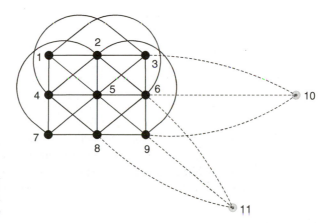

FIGURE 7.7
Adding Ideal Points to an
Affine Plane

To distinguish the new point from the original points on these lines, we call it the *ideal point* of these lines. Similarly, the lines {1, 5, 9}, {2, 6, 7}, and {3, 4, 8} are made concurrent at the ideal point 11. There are two more ideal points to add to the diagram, and the four ideal points together make up *the ideal line* for this extended plane. Thus, each trio of parallel lines in the affine plane of order 3 now intersects at an ideal point (or point at infinity) in the projective plane of order 3. Two lines that are parallel in the affine plane are in the same equivalence class, so they share a common ideal point in the corresponding projective plane. The set of all ideal points forms the *ideal line*. A line is now one of two types: an affine line plus its ideal point or the ideal line.

Projective Axiom 1 is clearly true in this extended geometry, for it was true before ideal points were added. Projective Axiom 2 is true if the two points are ordinary points or if the two points are ideal points; we must check more carefully in the case of one ordinary point and one ideal point. So let P be the ordinary point and I be the ideal point. Suppose there are two lines on this pair of points. Pick any line ℓ that contains I but not P. (Affine Axiom 4 comes into play here.) Then there are two lines on the point P that are parallel to ℓ in the affine geometry, violating Affine Axiom 3.

To verify that Projective Axiom 3 is true in this extended plane, we must examine two cases: When the two lines are affine lines with an ideal point added or when one of the two lines is the ideal line. You will get a chance to do this in the exercises.

Projective Axiom 4 can be proved using just the affine axioms. By Affine Axiom 4, there are three noncollinear points: call them A, B, and C. By Axiom 2, there is a line ℓ_1 containing A and B. By Axiom 3, there is another line ℓ_2 containing C and parallel to ℓ_1. By Axiom 1, there is an additional point D on ℓ_2. Because ℓ_2 does not intersect ℓ_1, no three of the points A, B, C, or D can be collinear. (Since D does not have to be an ideal point, this result is true in the original affine plane as well as in the extended projective plane.)

Look again at the order theorems. In an affine plane of order k, a line has k points. So the corresponding projective line with an ideal point added has $k+1$ points. An affine plane has $k^2 + k$ lines; now we add the ideal line to give $k^2 + k + 1$ lines in the projective plane. An affine plane has k^2 points, so with the ideal line added, the projective plane has $k^2 + k + 1$ points. These values agree with the theorems.

Notice that the projective axioms say nothing about the ideal line. It is merely one line among many lines. This can be a great advantage when proving theorems. A proof that is based solely on the projective axioms avoids any concern about special cases that involve parallel lines.

This technique of forming equivalence classes of parallel lines to create ideal points and then adding an ideal line to the plane can also done with the Euclidean plane. Lines with the same slope form an equivalence class (including the case of undefined slope). Thus, each slope value corresponds to an ideal point, a "point at infinity" for those lines. When these ideal points are added to the Euclidean plane, the result is the *real projective plane*. This is the subject of Chapter 12.

COORDINATES FOR FINITE GEOMETRIES

Activity 5 asked you to experiment with two small number systems. One of them is $\mathbb{Z}_2$, the integers mod 2. The mod 2 calculation divides an integer by 2 and tells what the remainder is. Of course, there are only two possibilities: 0 if the integer is even and 1 if the integer is odd. (Another way to think of mod 2 arithmetic is *even* + *even* = *even*, *even* + *odd* = *odd*, etc.) To do arithmetic in $\mathbb{Z}_2$, do the normal operations, then do the mod 2 step to simplify the result to either a 0 or a 1.

The slightly larger number system $\mathbb{Z}_3$ is the integers under mod 3 calculations. There are only three possible remainders: 0, 1, or 2. So every calculation will give an answer of 0, 1, or 2. This leads to unusual arithmetic facts: $1 + 2 = 0$, $2 + 2 = 1$, $2 \cdot 2 = 1$, etc. These finite number systems, and others like them, will be just what is needed to place coordinates on finite affine or projective planes.

In an abstract algebra course, you will learn that $\mathbb{Z}_2$ and $\mathbb{Z}_3$ are examples of *finite fields*. A field satisfies a long list of properties: closure, commutativity, distributivity, identity elements, inverses, and so on. Whenever the mod calculation involves a prime number p, the system $\mathbb{Z}_p$ will be a finite field. However, not every mod situation creates a finite field. For instance, $\mathbb{Z}_4$ is not a field, for it fails the inverse property for multiplication. There does exist a finite field of size 4, but it is more difficult to describe.

Finite fields behave very much like real numbers—aside from being finite. One property that finite fields do not share with real numbers is order. The relation "less than," $<$, does not make sense for a finite field. For example, adding 1 to a value would normally give a larger number. However, in $\mathbb{Z}_2$, $0 + 1 = 1$, which makes 1 seem greater than 0 (as we might expect), while $1 + 1 = 0$, which makes 0 seem greater than 1 (which is jarring to our sense of order). Because $\mathbb{Z}_2$ is finite, there is no consistent way to order its elements.

The finite field $\mathbb{Z}_2$ can be used to place coordinates on the affine plane of order 2. Look at the second image in Figure 7.2. Suppose we assign coordinates as follows:

$$a = (0, 0)$$
$$b = (1, 0)$$
$$c = (0, 1)$$
$$d = (1, 1).$$

The line ab can be described by the equation $y = 0$ and the line ad can be described by $y = x$. For the line bc, we can use the equation $y = x + 1$. This may require a little thought. Point c satisfies this equation because $0 + 1 = 1$. Point b satisfies the equation because $1 + 1 = 0$ in $\mathbb{Z}_2$. Since we can only use coefficients from $\mathbb{Z}_2$, there are only a few possible linear equations to consider. You should find an equation to match each line.

We saw earlier that the affine geometry of order 2 can be extended to the projective geometry of order 2, namely, the Fano plane, by adding three ideal points and one ideal line. A challenge is that with the finite field $\mathbb{Z}_2$, there are not enough ordered pairs to describe seven points. So the coordinates will need three components. By convention, the triple $(0, 0, 0)$ will not be used. That leaves seven possible triples, the precise number needed for seven points.

Let each point from the affine geometry keep its previous components but include a third component of 1:

$$a = (0, 0, 1)$$
$$b = (1, 0, 1)$$
$$c = (0, 1, 1)$$
$$d = (1, 1, 1).$$

To find coordinates for the ideal points, we first need to understand how the coordinates (x, y) are related to the new coordinates (x_1, x_2, x_3). The key is to see that the calculations $x = \frac{x_1}{x_3}$ and $y = \frac{x_2}{x_3}$ can be used to convert the new coordinates (x_1, x_2, x_3) back to their original form (x, y).

The ideal points will be marked by having their third component equal to 0. To decide on the other components, look at the equations for the various lines. The line ab, for instance, is $y = 0$; thus the second coordinate for the ideal point on this line must be 0. Since $(0, 0, 0)$ is not used, the ideal point e on the line ab must have coordinates $(1, 0, 0)$. Similarly, $f = (0, 1, 0)$ and $g = (1, 1, 0)$.

These new coordinates for the projective plane are called *homogeneous coordinates*. Notice that the homogeneous coordinates of an ideal point cannot be converted into affine coordinates. With the point $f = (0, 1, 0)$, for instance, the calculation would give $x = \frac{0}{0}$ and $y = \frac{1}{0}$, neither of which is possible. This is not a serious problem, because the ideal points are not part of the affine geometry.

Homogeneous Coordinates

Consider a more challenging problem: how to assign coordinates to the points of the affine plane of order 3 (shown in Figure 7.3) and then how to assign coordinates to the points of the associated projective plane of order 3. Here, we should work in the field $\mathbb{Z}_3$. There are nine ordered pairs that can be made from $\mathbb{Z}_3$ and there are nine points in this plane. Furthermore, there are twelve linear equations using $\mathbb{Z}_3$:

$$x = 0, \ x = 1, \ x = 2$$
$$y = 0, \ y = 1, \ y = 2$$
$$y = x, \ y = x + 1, \ y = x + 2$$
$$y = 2x, \ y = 2x + 1, \ y = 2x + 2.$$

In the exercises, you will be asked to assign coordinates, (x, y), to the points and equations to the lines of the affine plane of order 3.

To find the corresponding coordinates for the points in the projective plane of order 3, we can use the same substitutions as before:

$$x = \frac{x_1}{x_3} \ \text{and} \ y = \frac{x_2}{x_3}.$$

For instance, the line $y = 2x + 1$ in the affine plane contains the points $(0, 1)$, $(1, 0)$, and $(2, 2)$. In the projective plane, this equation becomes

$$\frac{x_2}{x_3} = 2\frac{x_1}{x_3} + 1 \ \text{or} \ x_2 = 2x_1 + x_3.$$

Now the points $(0, 1, 1)$, $(1, 0, 1)$, and $(2, 2, 1)$ satisfy this equation. Notice, however, that $(0, 2, 2)$ gives exactly the same affine point as $(0, 1, 1)$, for the ratios are the same. In homogeneous coordinates, then, any (nonzero) multiple of a point is considered to be the same point. So a triple (x_1, x_2, x_3) in which not all coordinates are 0 is equivalent to any other triple (ax_1, ax_2, ax_3) as long as $a \neq 0$. The triple $(0, 0, 0)$ is not used.

For the ideal point on the line $x_2 = 2x_1 + x_3$, we use $x_3 = 0$. This gives two possibilities: $(1, 2, 0)$ and $(2, 1, 0)$, since $(0, 0, 0)$ is never used. Notice, however, that $2 \cdot (1, 2, 0) = (2 \cdot 1, 2 \cdot 2, 2 \cdot 0) = (2, 1, 0)$ in mod 3 calculations. So these two possibilities are really the same point.

Coordinates and Duality

Look again at the equation $x_2 = 2x_1 + x_3$. This equation describes a line in the projective plane of order 3 and it uses coefficients from the finite field $\mathbb{Z}_3$. By adding $2x_2$ to both sides, we get the new equation

$$2x_1 + 2x_2 + x_3 = 0.$$

If you have studied linear algebra, you may recognize this as a dot product of two vectors:

$$[2, 2, 1] \cdot (x_1, x_2, x_3) = 0.$$

The second vector (x_1, x_2, x_3) represents a point on the line. The first vector $[2, 2, 1]$ represents *coordinates of the line*. It may seem surprising that a line can have coordinates, but it fits with the duality of a projective plane. If points have coordinates, so must lines!

The general statement is that the equation $Ax_1 + Bx_2 + Cx_3 = 0$ corresponds to the line $[A, B, C]$ and the points (x_1, x_2, x_3) that satisfy this equation lie on that line. This is very useful for assigning coordinates.

Here is another example. We are used to writing the equation $y = 0$ to represent the x-axis in the Euclidean plane. As we move from the affine plane of order 3 to the projective plane of order 3, $y = 0$ becomes $\frac{x_2}{x_3} = 0$. This simplifies to $x_2 = 0$ or $0x_1 + x_2 + 0x_3 = 0$. So the coordinates of the line $y = 0$ are $[0, 1, 0]$. In a similar manner, the coordinates of what we might call the y-axis, the line $x = 0$ are $[1, 0, 0]$. The ideal line is $x_3 = 0$ so it has coordinates $[0, 0, 1]$.

Homogeneous Coordinates for the Fano Plane

It may be helpful to examine one example in thorough detail. The Fano plane is a good choice for this, because it is small enough that pictures can guide our work. Refer back to Figure 7.1 for one possible picture of the Fano plane. The Fano plane is the smallest projective plane, having merely seven points and seven lines. Since it is a finite system, we must have a finite list of possible coordinates. So we must restrict ourselves to a finite number system. For the coordinates of the Fano plane, we will use the number system $\mathbb{Z}_2$ with only the two values 0 and 1. The points will be of the form (x_1, x_2, x_3) and, as always, $(0, 0, 0)$ will not be used. With only two options for each coordinate, this leaves seven triples to use.

There is some arbitrariness in how these coordinates are assigned. For instance, any of the seven points could be the "origin" $(0, 0, 1)$. Let us choose a at the top to be $(0, 0, 1)$. Then any line not containing the origin could be the ideal line, that is, the set of the "points at infinity." Let us choose the line $\left\{ \begin{array}{c} e \\ f \\ g \end{array} \right\}$

at the bottom. The points on this line must have $x_3 = 0$, so there are only three possibilities: (1, 0, 0), (0, 1, 0), and (1, 1, 0). The coordinates of this ideal line are [0, 0, 1]. Let us choose $e = (1, 0, 0)$ and $f = (0, 1, 0)$, leaving $g = (1, 1, 0)$.

This ends the arbitrary selections. Consider the line ae. Substituting the point a into the general pattern gives $A \cdot 0 + B \cdot 0 + C \cdot 1 = 0$, so $C = 0$. Substituting the point e into the equation gives $A \cdot 1 + B \cdot 0 + C \cdot 0 = 0$, so $A = 0$. Since the line [0, 0, 0] does not exist, ae must be [0, 1, 0]. (An interesting side note: Projective Axiom 2 says that any two distinct points have exactly one line in common. We just used the coordinates of two distinct points to find the coordinates of their common line.) The third point b on ae must satisfy the equation $0x_1 + 1x_2 + 0x_3 = 0$ and must be distinct from a and e, so $b = (1, 0, 1)$.

We can continue in this way to find the coordinates of every other line and every other point. For instance, the point d is (1, 1, 1) and the curved line $\left\{ \begin{array}{c} b \\ c \\ g \end{array} \right\}$

is [0, 1, 1].

7.3 EXERCISES

Give clear and complete answers to the following problems and questions. Write your explanations clearly using complete sentences. Include diagrams whenever appropriate.

1. Prove Theorem 7.2, that each point in an affine geometry of order k lies on $k + 1$ lines.

2. Give a detailed proof of Theorem 7.3, that an affine geometry of order k has k^2 points.

3. In Figure 7.3, find several examples of Affine Axiom 3.

4. Prove Theorem 7.5, that an affine geometry of order k has $k^2 + k$ lines.

5. In an affine plane of order k, prove that any line intersects k^2 other lines.

6. Suppose you wish to play Tic-Tac-Toe on the affine plane of order 3, shown in Figure 7.3. As usual, the goal of the game is to get three of your symbols, Xs or Os, on a common line. Explain why the player who goes first can always win.

7. From the projective geometry axioms, prove that two distinct lines have exactly one point in common.

8. Complete Figure 7.7 to draw the finite projective plane of order 3. Recall that the "lines" do not have to be straight in your picture. (A harder question: draw the finite projective plane of order 4.)

9. Is the axiom system for moes and fuzzies given at the beginning of this chapter more like an affine geometry or a projective geometry? Explain why you think so. Which of the undefined terms—moe or fuzzy—seems to be more like a line, and which seems to be more like a point?

10. Suppose that the fuzzies (long, white pipe cleaners) correspond to lines, and moes (twisted, colored pipe cleaners) correspond to points. Show that by interchanging fuzzies and moes in this model, you get a dual system in which fuzzies correspond to points and moes correspond to lines.

11. a. Prove that the points on one line in a projective plane can be put in a one-to-one correspondence with the points on any other line. (This is Lemma 7.1.)

    b. State the dual of the statement you proved in part (a). (This is Theorem 7.10.) Then write the dual proof and check that this proves the dual statement.

12. Prove Dual Axiom 4, using the axioms of the projective plane.

13. State the duals of the affine axioms. Which of these dual statements is true in an affine plane?

14. Find four lines in Figure 7.5 (page 171) that form a quadrilateral. Verify that no three of these lines are concurrent.

15. Construct examples of a quadrangle and a quadrilateral. Identify the diagonal triangle in each of your examples.

16. Consider Figure 7.1. Draw the geometry that remains when the line $\begin{Bmatrix} b \\ c \\ g \end{Bmatrix}$ and its points are removed. Verify that this new geometry satisfies the affine axioms.

17. For the affine plane in Figure 7.3, list all equivalence classes of parallel lines.

18. In the Euclidean plane, prove that parallelism is an equivalence relation for lines.

19. Prove that an affine plane extended by ideal points and an ideal line will satisfy Projective Axiom 3.

20. Find an equation to describe each line of the affine plane of order 2.

21. Page 178 lists twelve linear equations for the lines of the affine plane of order 3, shown in Figure 7.3.
    a. Use these lines to assign coordinates to each point in this plane. (You should work in the number system $\mathbb{Z}_3$.)
    b. Verify that lines with the same slope (in the usual sense of a linear equation) are parallel in this diagram.

22. Refer to Exercise 21. Consider how to create the corresponding projective plane.
    a. Convert the coordinates of this affine plane into homogeneous form.
    b. Each set of parallel lines has one ideal point. Give the coordinates of these ideal points.
    c. Find the coordinates of the ideal line.
    d. Find the coordinates of the other lines in the projective plane. (There should be $3^3 + 3 + 1 = 13$ lines in all.)

23. Continue the discussion of the Fano plane on pages 179–180 until you have found coordinates for every point and every line.

24. Consider the drawing of the Fano plane in Figure 7.5. Assign coordinates to this drawing so that the point in the center is the origin and the "circle" is the ideal line.

25. Can the point (a, b, c) ever lie on the line $[a, b, c]$? Either give an example in some model or explain why not.

Exercises 26 and 27 are especially for future teachers.

26. The National Council of Teachers of Mathematics (NCTM) recommends in the *Principles and Standards for School Mathematics* that "Instructional programs from prekindergarten through grade 12 should enable all students to . . . analyze characteristics and properties of two- and three-dimensional geometric shapes and develop mathematical arguments about geometric relationships" [NCTM 2000, 96].

    How has your study of finite geometries in this chapter challenged your understanding of points, lines, and planes? What impact might this experience have on your preparation to teach strange, new, and difficult concepts to your own future students?

27. This chapter began with an unusual prelude, a hands-on activity with *moes* and *fuzzies*, intended to give you some concrete experiences with abstract concepts of finite geometries. Think about students at a grade level for which you are seeking teacher certification. Choose a topic or concept in the mathematics curriculum at that grade level that you anticipate your future students will find strange, difficult, and abstract. Design several explorations that you could use to give your future students a concrete hands-on experience with this topic or concept prior to introducing the concept through direct instruction.

Reflect on what you have learned in this chapter.

28. Review the main ideas of this chapter. Describe, in your own words, the concepts you have studied and what you have learned about them.

What are the important ideas? How do they fit together? Which concepts were easy for you? Which were hard?

29. Reflect on the learning environment for this course.

   a. Describe aspects of the learning environment that helped you understand the main ideas in this chapter. Which activities did you like? Which were more challenging? Why?

   b. Euclid defined a *line* as "breadthless length," and a *straight line* as "a line which lies evenly with the points on itself." More than 2000 years later, David Hilbert called *line* an *undefined term* and developed sets of axioms to describe the properties he wanted to assume about lines.

   One of our goals in this chapter was to challenge your concept of what a *line* is, and to invite you to think more deeply about what you mean when you talk about "points" and "lines." How well did we succeed? Cite specific examples of ways we challenged your thinking.

7.4 CHAPTER OVERVIEW

In this chapter, we have presented two systems of geometry that are very different from Euclidean geometry. In both cases, we considered geometric systems with only a finite number of points and lines. Some axioms were similar to the familiar Euclidean axioms, while some other axioms were quite different. The issue of parallel lines was the key difference between the two systems. Affine geometry allows the existence of lines parallel to a given line, while in projective geometry there are no parallel lines at all! The axiom systems for an affine plane or for a projective plane are very short and simple, but they lead to surprisingly strong results.

After a discussion of these axioms, a few basic theorems about points and lines were presented. Here we proved that every line contains the same number of points and that every point is on this same number of lines. From this information, we found a formula for the total number of points in a finite affine plane or a finite projective plane.

For these axioms and theorems to be meaningful, of course, there must be mathematical situations (models) to which they apply. We examined some smaller models. The Fano plane is the finite projective plane of smallest possible order.

A remarkable property of any projective plane is duality. The notions of point and line are interchangeable in the axioms and hence are interchangeable in any theorem proven from those axioms. Duality does not hold in an affine plane.

To introduce coordinates into finite geometric systems, we needed finite number systems such as $\mathbb{Z}_2$ and $\mathbb{Z}_3$. As usual, affine points are described by coordinates, and lines in an affine plane are described by equations. The notion of homogeneous coordinates brought algebraic tools to the study of projective geometry as well. Because of duality, in projective geometry, we can have coordinates for a line as well as for a point.

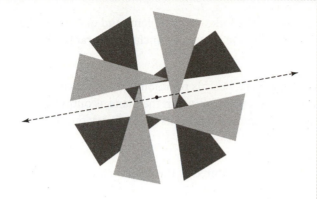

CHAPTER EIGHT

From your work in previous courses, you are familiar with functions whose inputs and outputs are real numbers. In this chapter, you will be working with functions that use points of the plane as inputs and outputs. If a set of points forms a geometric figure in the plane, the functions we will study in this chapter will transform that figure in various ways. A figure may simply be moved from one place to another, or it may be deformed in some way—perhaps stretched or twisted.

Of particular interest are transformations of the plane that do not alter the distances between points. These special functions, called *isometries*, are the main topic of this chapter. We introduce the four basic types of isometry and prove that every isometry is one of these basic types. We show how isometries can be used to study congruence of geometric figures. As functions, isometries can be combined by composition. This leads to notions of *closure*, *identity*, *inverse*—and eventually to the important concept of *group*.

Transformational Geometry

Give clear and complete answers to the following problems and questions. Write your explanations clearly using complete sentences. Include diagrams whenever appropriate.

1. Consider the function $f_1(x, y) = (x, \frac{1}{y})$. This function takes points in the coordinate plane as inputs and returns points in the plane as outputs. Let us examine the effect this function has on its input. Carry out the following steps:

   - Create an xy-coordinate system.
   - Construct a circle of radius 2 centered at the origin.
   - Construct a point P on this circle.
   - Use the Input bar to plot the new point $P' = (x(P), 1/y(P))$.
   - Drag the original point P around the circle and watch what happens to the new point P'. It may be helpful to set **Trace On** for P' as you drag P. To turn the trace on, right-click on point P (in the Graphics pane) or on its description (in the Algebra pane) and select the **Trace On** option. Do the same thing to turn the trace off. An easy way to erase traces is to zoom in or out with the mouse wheel. In a similar way, you can select the point P and toggle **Animation On** (and off).

   Now answer the following questions about f_1.

   a. Does every point on the circle have an image point, that is, an output? Use the expression for the function to explain why or why not.

   b. Which points from this circle are unchanged by the function; that is, which points are in the same location on the output as on the input?

   c. What does the function do to a point if its y-value is large—near 2? What happens to a point if its y-value is small—near 0? Use the expression of the function to explain your answers.

   d. Now try to answer these questions when the domain is the entire plane. Use the expression of the function to justify your answers. Discuss the domain and range of the function as well as its geometric effects. (You may wish to select the point P, then use **Attach/Detach Point**, which is on the Point button. This will allow you to observe P' as you move P about the entire GeoGebra window.)

2. Repeat Activity 1 for each of the following functions:
   - $f_2(x, y) = (0, y)$
   - $f_3(x, y) = (x + 2y, y)$
   - $f_4(x, y) = (x - 2, y + 1)$
   - $f_5(x, y) = (x, y^3 - y)$.

3. Using the entire plane as domain and as target, which of the five functions in Activities 1 and 2 are *one-to-one*? Which are *onto*? Explain why. See page 187 for definitions of the one-to-one and onto concepts.

4. When a set of points is put through a function such as those in Activities 1 and 2, a variety of things can happen. Figures can move and stretch and

twist in many ways. One kind of function that behaves better than others is the *isometry*, a transformation that preserves distances. If f is a distance-preserving function, then $|AB| = |f(A)\,f(B)|$; that is, the distance between the points A and B is the same as the distance between points $f(A)$ and $f(B)$.

Which of the functions from Activities 1 and 2 are isometries? Justify your decisions.

5. In this activity, you will see some basic isometries.
   a. Using GeoGebra, draw a scalene triangle. Draw a line not intersecting the triangle. Use the **Reflect about Line** tool to reflect the triangle across the line. Select the original triangle, drag it, and observe what happens.
   b. In a new sketch, again draw a scalene triangle. Use the **Vector** tool on the Line button to create a vector somewhere in the sketch. Then, use the **Translate by Vector** tool to translate your triangle by this vector. Drag your original triangle and observe what happens.
   c. In a third sketch, draw a scalene triangle. Draw a new point and use the **Rotate around Point** tool to rotate the triangle by some angle. As before, drag your original triangle and observe what happens.
   d. How is the result in part (a) different from the results in parts (b) and (c)?

6. A *fixed point* for a transformation is a point that is not changed by the transformation. In other words, the output point from the function is in exactly the same position as the input point. What are the fixed points of a reflection? Of a translation? Of a rotation?

7. Create a point C. Use the **Polygon** tool to create a triangle to the side of point C.
   a. Use the **Slider** tool to create a slider somewhere in the sketch, with values from -5 to 5. Notice the variable name for the slider.
   b. Use the **Dilate from Point** tool with your triangle, the point C, and the variable from the slider as the factor.
   c. Vary the slider and observe what happens. What happens as the slider value gets close to zero? What happens as the slider value is far from zero? What happens when the slider value is negative?
   d. Reposition your triangle so that the point C is in the interior. Vary the slider. What do you observe?
   e. Repeat these steps with a different polygon. Do your observations still hold?

8. Every isometry is either *direct* or it is *opposite*. (This is the difference in Activity 5.) Every isometry either has fixed points or it doesn't. This leads to four possibilities. List the four possibilities, and decide what kind of isometry each represents. (You need to know that there is a fourth kind of isometry, the *glide reflection*, which is a reflection followed by a translation parallel to the mirror line.)

9. Since isometries are functions, it is possible to form compositions of isometries in which one transformation is followed by another.

   a. Draw a scalene triangle. Reflect it across one line ℓ, then reflect this image across a second line m that is parallel to ℓ. (It will be helpful to make the three triangles different colors.) Drag the original triangle and observe what happens. What kind of isometry is produced by this composition? Explain how you decide this.

   b. Draw a scalene triangle. Reflect it across one line ℓ, then reflect this image across a second line m that intersects ℓ. Drag the original triangle and observe what happens. What kind of isometry is produced by this composition? Explain how you decide this.

   c. Draw a scalene triangle. Rotate it 180° around one point P, then rotate this image 180° around a second point Q. Drag the original triangle and observe what happens. What kind of isometry is produced by this composition? Explain how you decide this.

   d. Draw a scalene triangle. Rotate it 90° around one point P, then rotate this image 90° around a second point Q. Drag the original triangle and observe what happens. What kind of isometry is produced by this composition? Explain how you decide this.

10. Can you find an isometry that is the inverse of a translation, that is, an isometry that has the reverse effect of a translation? If so, what kind of isometry is it? If not, why not? Repeat this question for reflections, for rotations, and for glide reflections.

8.2 DISCUSSION

You are accustomed to functions that use a real number as input and produce a unique real number as output. However, the definition of function allows any kind of mathematical object to be used as input or as output. These objects could be numbers, points, lines, sets, or even other functions. In this chapter, we are interested in functions that use points of the plane as both inputs and outputs.

Let us review the idea of *function*. A function is a mapping from a set A (which can be called the *source* of the function) to a set B (sometimes called the *target* of the function). In order to be called a function, this mapping must take each element of A to a unique element of B. In other words:

1. Every element of A is allowable as an input for the function.

2. Each input generates a unique output.

The set of allowable inputs is called the *domain*. Most of the time, the domain of a function is the same as its source, but it can happen, as in Activities 1 and 2, that some elements of the source cannot be used. In these activities, we asked you to think of the entire *xy*-plane as possible inputs and possible outputs for these functions. That is, both the source and the target for each of these functions are the set $\mathbb{R}^2$. In Activity 1, none of the points on the *x*-axis can serve as an input for f_1. So although the set $\mathbb{R}^2$ is the source, the x-axis is not part of the domain. Similarly, the output of f_1 cannot be on the x-axis, so in this case the set of possible outputs is a subset of the target. The target of f_1 is the set $\mathbb{R}^2$, while the *range* of f_1 is $\mathbb{R}^2$ minus the x-axis.

TRANSFORMATIONS

In Activities 1 and 2, you saw several functions that take a point from the plane as input and return another point in the plane. What does f_1 do visually? Because the x-coordinate is unchanged by f_1, the output does not move horizontally from the input, only vertically. However, $\frac{1}{y}$ has drastic effects on the y-coordinate. Small values are changed into large ones; large values are changed into small ones. Visually, this means that points near the horizontal axis are moved away from this axis, while points away from the axis are moved close to it. Points above the horizontal axis stay above the axis, and points below stay below. Only those points with $y = \pm 1$ are unaffected by the function f_1.

Because there are points of the plane that are not in the range of f_1, this function is not *onto*. Informally, a function is *onto* if every point in the target occurs as an output of the function. Here is a more formal statement of this definition.

DEFINITION 8.1   A function $f: D \to T$ is *onto* if for every $Y \in T$ there is an X in the domain D, so that $f(X) = Y$. In symbols, we write that f is onto if $(\forall Y \in T)\,(\exists X \in D)\,(f(X) = Y)$.

Being onto means that the range is the same as the target. Since there are points in the plane that cannot be obtained as outputs of f_1, this function is not onto. The function f_3, however, is onto, as are two other functions in Activity 2.

Another property of functions is that of being *one-to-one*. This property says that different inputs must produce different outputs. Consider the function f_1. The input point (x_1, y_1) gets mapped to $(x_1, \frac{1}{y_1})$, and the point (x_2, y_2) gets mapped to $(x_2, \frac{1}{y_2})$. If the outputs are the same, $\left(x_1, \frac{1}{y_1}\right) = \left(x_2, \frac{1}{y_2}\right)$, then $x_1 = x_2$ and $\frac{1}{y_1} = \frac{1}{y_2}$. So clearly, $(x_1, y_1) = (x_2, y_2)$; in other words, the inputs must have been the same. Here is a more formal statement of the one-to-one property.

DEFINITION 8.2   A function $f: D \to T$ is *one-to-one* if $X_1 \neq X_2$ implies that $f(X_1) \neq f(X_2)$. Another way to say this, using the contrapositive, is that a function is one-to-one if $f(X_1) = f(X_2)$ implies $X_1 = X_2$.

Three of the functions $f_1, \ldots, f_5$ are one-to-one. A function on the plane that is both one-to-one and onto is called a *transformation* of the plane. Only two of the functions $f_1, \ldots, f_5$ are transformations.

ISOMETRIES

One of the two transformations among the functions of Activities 1 and 2 has an additional property; it preserves distances. This means that the distance between the points A and B is the same as the distance between their images $f(A)$ and $f(B)$.

DEFINITION 8.3 A function $f: \mathbb{R}^2 \to \mathbb{R}^2$ is a *distance-preserving* function if for any points A and B, the distance between A and B is the same as the distance between the images $f(A)$ and $f(B)$. That is, f preserves distances if $|AB| = |f(A)f(B)|$.

For a given function, this is not hard to check. Suppose (a, b) and (c, d) are two points. The distance between them is $\sqrt{(a-c)^2 + (b-d)^2}$. Now consider the function f_2 as an example:

$$f_2(a, b) = (0, b) \quad \text{and} \quad f_2(c, d) = (0, d).$$

The distance between the images $f_2(a, b)$ and $f_2(c, d)$ is $\sqrt{(0-0)^2 + (b-d)^2}$, which is not the same as the distance between the original points. So f_2 does not preserve distances.

A function with all three of these properties—onto, one-to-one, and distance preserving—is called an *isometry*. Figures that are put through an isometry emerge looking the same, without stretching, twisting, or any other distortion. However, they may come out in a different position. This word, *iso-metry*, literally means "same measure." Other names for isometries are *rigid motions* and *Euclidean motions*.

Activity 5 introduced three basic kinds of isometry. The first is the *reflection*. For a reflection, one line ℓ acts as the mirror. For any input point A, the output point $f(A)$ is directly across the line and is the same distance from ℓ as A is. In more precise terms, ℓ is the perpendicular bisector of the segment between A and $f(A)$. An object, such as a triangle, drawn on one side of the line ℓ will be reflected to its mirror image on the other side of ℓ. What happens if an object touches or overlaps the mirror line?

The isometry in Activity 5b is a *translation*. This is simpler; an input point is moved (dragged) to a new location by translation. This motion is always in a constant direction and for a constant distance. Thus, a vector is an ideal way to represent the motion of a translation.

Activity 5c introduces the *rotation*, a third kind of isometry. You should experiment with the cases where the center of rotation is inside your triangle or outside your triangle. In either case, an input point does not change its distance from the center, but its angle with respect to the center is changed. Using the language of polar coordinates, if the center of rotation is at the origin, the r-coordinate of a particular point is not changed by the rotation, but a constant is added to (or subtracted from) the θ-coordinate.

In Figure 8.1, one of the triangles is the original (the input) and the other three are the results of a translation, a reflection, and a rotation. Which is which?

Finally, Activity 5d asks how the reflection is different from the translation and the rotation. It may help if you label the vertices of your triangle as A, B, C in a clockwise manner. Then decide what the isometry does to each vertex and label the images accordingly. Sometimes the orientation of the image points will also be clockwise, and sometimes it will reverse. Translations and rotations keep the same orientation, and so they are called *direct* isometries. However, a reflection reverses the orientation; for this reason, reflections are called *opposite* isometries.

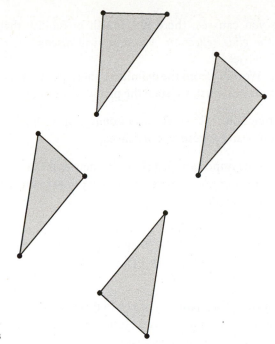

FIGURE 8.1
The Basic Isometries

Here is a physical interpretation that may help you understand this distinction. Imagine that your triangle is cut from cardboard and is lying on a table. Label the vertices if you wish. You can translate the triangle without picking it up; simply drag it along the surface. You also can rotate the triangle without picking it up (although this is a bit tricky if the center is not inside the triangle). But to reflect the triangle, you must pick it up and turn it over. This extra motion in a third dimension causes the opposite orientation of the vertices.

Now you should be able to sort out Figure 8.1. Look at the orientations of the triangles. (Need a hint? The original triangle is on the upper right.)

Another way to classify isometries is to consider their *fixed points*. In mathematics, *fixed* means constant or unchanging. So we are looking for points X for which $f(X) = X$. A translation does not have fixed points; every point moves the same distance and direction. (For the moment we will ignore the trivial case of a translation using the zero vector.) A rotation has only one fixed point: its center. (Again, we will ignore the trivial cases of a rotation through angles of 0, 2π, and multiples of 2π.) A reflection, however, has an entire line of fixed points. Any point on the mirror line is unchanged by the reflection.

If we combine the last two concepts—direct versus opposite, fixed points or no fixed points—we see that there are four possibilities. These are shown in the following table:

	Has fixed points	Has no fixed points
Direct	Rotation	Translation
Opposite	Reflection	?????

As you can see, there is a fourth possibility that has not appeared yet. This is the *glide reflection*, which we will discuss after we examine composition of isometries.

Working from the definition, there are some useful things we can prove about isometries. First, we state the precise definition.

DEFINITION 8.4   A function $f: \mathbb{R}^2 \to \mathbb{R}^2$ is an *isometry* of the Euclidean plane if f is one-to-one, f is onto, and f preserves distances.

One important fact about isometries is that we need only a little information to figure out exactly what an isometry does to the whole plane. In fact, three points tell us enough.

THEOREM 8.1   In the Euclidean plane, the images of three noncollinear points completely determine an isometry. In other words, if we know the outputs for three noncollinear points A, B, C, we can figure out what the isometry does to any point X.

Outline of a Proof   The key to this proof is the distance-preserving property. A picture may make it clear (see Figure 8.2). Point X is a certain distance from point A, so $f(X)$ must be that same distance from $f(A)$. This compels $f(X)$ to lie on a circle centered at $f(A)$ with radius $|AX|$. Furthermore, X is a certain distance from point B, so $f(X)$ must lie on a circle centered at $f(B)$ with radius $|BX|$. These two circles intersect at two points. However, we also know that $f(X)$ must lie on a third circle, centered at $f(C)$ with radius $|CX|$. The three circles will have exactly one common intersection point.

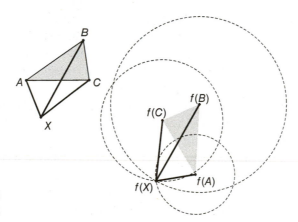

FIGURE 8.2
$f(X)$ Is Uniquely Determined

There are some details of this proof that we have glossed over. How can we be sure that the first two circles intersect at all? Is it possible that the first two circles intersect only once, and how would that affect the proof? Can we be sure that the third circle shares an intersection point with the first two and that it does not share both intersection points? These are not difficult questions, but they deserve some thought.

It is natural to visualize three noncollinear points as the vertices of a triangle. This is why you were asked to use triangles in Activity 5. It is important to use scalene triangles, to avoid any confusion that might be caused by accidental symmetries of the triangle.

THEOREM 8.2 An isometry preserves collinearity. In other words, three points that are collinear will still be collinear after going through an isometry.

Proof First, recall the Triangle Inequality:

For any three points A, B, C, we have $|AB| + |BC| \geq |AC|$.

If the three points are collinear, there will be one way to list the points along their line that makes this an equality. Suppose A, B, C is that correct ordering, so that $|AB| + |BC| = |AC|$. Because the isometry f preserves distances, we have

$$|f(A)f(B)| + |f(B)f(C)| = |f(A)f(C)|.$$

Therefore, the three points $f(A)$, $f(B)$, and $f(C)$ must also be collinear.

We can also use the triangle inequality to prove that the order of the points along the line must stay the same.

THEOREM 8.3 An isometry preserves betweenness. In other words, if the point B is between the points A and C along a line, then the point $f(B)$ will be between the points $f(A)$ and $f(C)$ along their line.

Proof By Theorem 8.2, we know that $f(B)$ is collinear with $f(A)$ and $f(C)$. Suppose that $f(A)$ is between the other two points. This makes

$$|f(A)f(B)| + |f(B)f(C)| > |f(A)f(C)|.$$

However, since B is between A and C, we know that $|AB| + |BC| = |AC|$, which implies that

$$|f(A)f(B)| + |f(B)f(C)| = |f(A)f(C)|.$$

Hence, $f(A)$ cannot be the middle point. A similar argument shows that $f(C)$ cannot be the middle point either, leaving $f(B)$ in the middle.

Together, Theorems 8.2 and 8.3 give us a very important fact.

COROLLARY 8.1 Under an isometry, the image of

a line segment		line segment
a triangle	is a congruent	triangle
an angle		angle
a circle		circle

You should think carefully about why each part of this corollary is true.

Corollary 8.1 says that isometries are another way to study congruence. The image of a geometric figure under an isometry will be congruent to the original figure.

OTHER TRANSFORMATIONS

Some of the functions in Activities 1 and 2 are not isometries. Nevertheless, each of these functions has an effect on points and on geometric shapes. The function f_5 twists and folds the plane in a complicated way because the cubic calculation in the y-coordinate is not one-to-one. The functions f_2 and f_3 are better behaved because their calculations use linear functions, but they still have interesting features.

The function f_3 is an example of a *shear*. This function stretches shapes, but only in one direction. For f_3, objects are stretched horizontally but not vertically, and the farther a point is from the horizontal axis, the more drastic the stretching. When put through the function f_3, the circle of Activity 2 should become an ellipse tilted away from the vertical, with points in the upper half-plane shifted to the right and points in the lower half-plane shifted to the left. This function f_3 is a transformation, for it is both one-to-one and onto. However, it is not distance-preserving. To see this, compare two points such as $A = (0, 0)$ and $B = (0, 2)$. We can calculate $f_3(A) = (0, 0)$ and $f_3(B) = (4, 2)$. Then $|AB| = 2$ but $|f(A)f(B)| = \sqrt{20}$.

The function f_2 is a *projection*. Every point is projected horizontally to an image point on the vertical axis. We can think of this image as a "shadow" of the original point. A shape in the plane will be projected to a line segment by f_2 unless the shape is unbounded, in which case the projection could be a ray or even the entire axis. The function f_2 projects to the vertical axis, but projections in the plane can happen to the horizontal axis, or indeed to any line. Notice that projection is not truly a transformation of the plane, for projection is neither one-to-one nor onto. However, projection is a useful tool in many settings. For instance, determining the domain for an integral involves a projection of a function's graph onto an axis.

Activity 7 presented another type of transformation, *dilation*. For GeoGebra, the dilation tool asks for a fixed dilation factor. Using a slider allows us to vary this factor. Each factor value creates a different transformation.

While each dilation is both one-to-one and onto, dilation is not distance-preserving. Figure 8.3 shows a triangle XYZ and its image under a dilation. Clearly, the distances are changed by the dilation. However, all distances change in the same proportion, so shape is preserved but not size. Thus, dilation is related to *similarity*. Every triangle you saw in Activity 7 was similar to the original triangle.

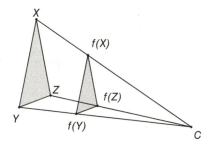

FIGURE 8.3
Dilation of a Triangle

A specific dilation f uses a center C and a ratio r. The three points X, $f(X)$, and C are collinear, and these points satisfy the equation $|f(X)C| = r \cdot |XC|$. So the distance from the output point $f(X)$ to the center C is a constant multiple of the distance from the input X to the center. This ratio r can be large, causing an increase in size, or small, causing a decrease in size. The ratio can even be negative; if we think of directed distances, a negative ratio would use segments in opposite directions, meaning that $f(X)$ would be on the opposite side of the center from X.

COMPOSITION OF ISOMETRIES

Because isometries are functions—even though they use types of inputs and outputs that are different than what you are accustomed to—we can combine isometries by composition. Here is a quick review of how composition works. Suppose we have two functions, f and g, for which the range of f is a subset of the domain of g. This means that an output value $f(x)$ makes sense as an input for g. The composition $(g \circ f)(x)$ means that we are to compute $g(f(x))$; that is, we start with the input x, perform the function f, then use the output value $f(x)$ as an input to perform the function g. We can represent this process in a diagram:

$$x \rightarrow f(x) \rightarrow g(f(x)).$$

It is, of course, necessary that the output of f be a legitimate input for g, so that $f(x)$ is in the domain of g. Otherwise the composition is undefined. For isometries of the plane, this is not a problem, because any output is a point in the plane and can serve as an input for the next function.

In Activity 9, you investigated some of the things that can happen with a composition of two isometries. Consider, for example, a reflection across a line followed by a second reflection across a line parallel to the first line. Each reflection reverses the orientation of a triangle; this double reversal results in a direct isometry. Further, this composition of reflections has no fixed points. (Can you explain why?) Therefore, the composition of two reflections in parallel lines is a translation.

The preceding paragraph was not really a proof, but rather a plausibility argument. Here is a more formal proof that the composition of two reflections in parallel lines is a translation.

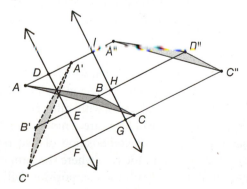

FIGURE 8.4
A Composition of Two
Reflections

Proof By Theorem 8.1, we know that it will be enough to show what happens to three noncollinear points. In Figure 8.4, the first reflection uses the line on the left as its mirror and the second reflection uses the line on the right. Point A is reflected to point A' and then to A''; points B and C are reflected similarly. Notice that the first line of reflection is the perpendicular bisector of segment AA' and that the second line of reflection is the perpendicular bisector of the segment $A'A''$. Thus, the point A moves in a direction perpendicular to the mirrors and the total distance it moves, $|AA''|$, equals

$$|AD| + |DA'| + |A'I| + |IA''| = 2(|DA'| + |A'I|) = 2|DI|,$$

which is twice the distance between the two mirrors. For the point B between the mirrors, we have the same phenomena of perpendicular bisectors. In this case, the motion is again perpendicular to the mirrors. The total distance can be calculated as follows:

$$|BB''| = |BH| + |HB''|$$
$$= |BH| + |B'H|$$
$$= |BH| + |B'E| + |EB| + |BH|$$
$$= |BH| + |EB| + |EB| + |BH|$$
$$= 2(|EB| + |BH|) = 2|EH|.$$

As happened with the point A, the composition of these reflections moves the point B in the direction perpendicular to the mirror lines, and the distance that B moves is twice the distance between the mirrors. The argument for the point C is similar to this. Notice that we have omitted the two special cases when the images fall on a line; these are easily dealt with.

We will not give formal proofs for every possible pairing of isometries. Let us look at some other compositions, however, and decide what type of isometry should result.

Consider another composition from Activity 9—a reflection in one line followed by a reflection in a second line intersecting the first. Each reflection reverses the orientation, so the double reversal produces a direct isometry. Also, the point where the two mirror lines intersect is a fixed point, for it is unchanged by either reflection. Thus, this composition will be a rotation.

What happens when a translation is followed by another translation? The net effect is a translation whose vector is the sum of the vectors of the two original translations. Another easy composition to think about is a rotation followed by a rotation around the same center, which produces a rotation around this center through an angle equal to the (directed) sum of the given rotation angles.

What about two rotations with different centers? Activity 9 showed two examples of this. This will be a direct motion, so it must be either a rotation or a translation. Usually, the composition of two rotations with different centers will be a rotation, but in the case where the sum of the two angles of rotation is an integer multiple of 360°, the composition will be a translation. This is what happened in Activity 9c. (The matrix techniques you will learn in Chapter 9 can be used to prove this.)

One composition warrants a special mention. Suppose that we compose a reflection with translation parallel to the mirror line. The result will be an opposite isometry because of the reflection, and it will have no fixed points because of the translation. This is called a *glide reflection*. It fits the missing category in the table on page 189.

We now have four different types of isometry in the Euclidean plane. As the following important theorem shows, these are the only possibilities.

THEOREM 8.4   In the Euclidean plane, there are only four types of isometry: translations, rotations, reflections, and glide reflections.

To prove this, we need a preliminary result (or lemma) [Coxeter 1969, 40].

LEMMA 8.1   For four points A, B, A', and B' with $|AB| = |A'B'|$, there are exactly two isometries that give $f(A) = A'$ and $f(B) = B'$.

Proof of the Lemma   Pick any point C not collinear with A and B. This creates a triangle, $\triangle ABC$. Since $|AB| = |A'B'|$, there are two ways to construct a triangle $A'B'C'$ that is congruent to $\triangle ABC$. (See Figure 8.5.) Thus, there are only two isometries that give $f(A) = A'$ and $f(B) = B'$.

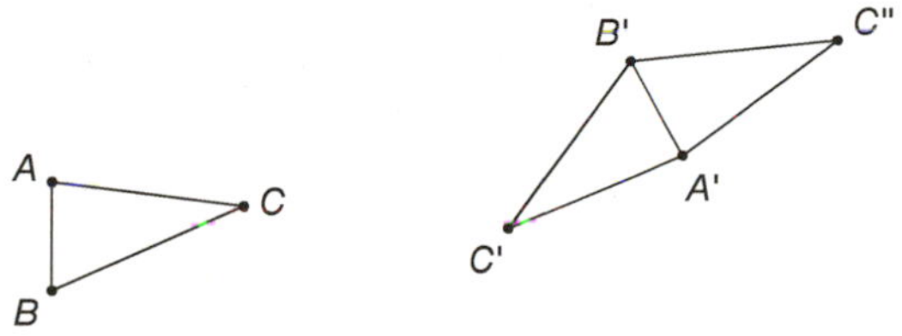

FIGURE 8.5
Only Two Possible Isometries

It is interesting to observe that this proof also shows that one of the two isometries will be direct and the other isometry will be opposite.

Proof of Theorem 8.1   The approach for this proof is to examine all possible situations and describe two isometries that fit each situation. Since the lemma says that there are only two possibilities, we will have described everything that can happen.

Suppose f is an isometry and A is a point for which $f(A) \neq A$. If there is no such point A, that means that every point is a fixed point for f. This is an isometry—rather dull but legitimate—that can be interpreted either as a translation by the zero vector or as a rotation through an angle of $0°$. Suppose there is an A for which $f(A) \neq A$. We need to decide what happens to three points; let's choose points B and C so that $B = f(A)$ and $C = f(B)$.

Case 1 Suppose $A = C$. Let M be the midpoint of the segment AB, and let ℓ be the perpendicular bisector of this segment. The reflection in line ℓ takes A to B and B to C. The 180° rotation around M does as well. These two isometries are the only possibilities in this case.

Case 2 Suppose $A \neq C$ and A, B, C are collinear on line m. Then a translation by the vector $\overrightarrow{AB}$ works, as does a glide reflection in the line m with the vector $\overrightarrow{AB}$.

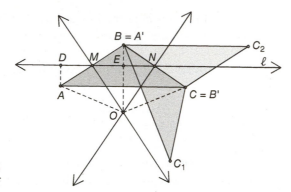

FIGURE 8.6
Case 3 of the Proof

Case 3 Suppose A, B, and C are three noncollinear points. Let M be the midpoint of AB and N be the midpoint of BC. Then let ℓ be the line through M and N, and let O be the intersection point of the perpendicular bisectors of the segments AB and BC. Drop perpendiculars from A and B to ℓ, and label the feet of A and B in ℓ as D and E, respectively. (See Figure 8.6.) The isometry in this situation is either a rotation around the point O through $\angle BOC$, or a glide reflection in the line ℓ with the vector $\overrightarrow{DE}$. (In Figure 8.6, the image of $\triangle ABC$ under the rotation is $\triangle A'B'C_1'$. The image of $\triangle ABC$ under the glide reflection is $\triangle A'B'C_2$.)

Thus in every case, both possible isometries can be described by one of the four known types. Therefore, these are the only possible types of isometry.

INVERSE ISOMETRIES

Activity 10 asks you to find an isometry that reverses a translation. If we think of translation as moving a geometric object a certain distance in a certain direction, the reverse motion is pretty obvious: move the geometric object the same distance in the opposite direction. Thus, if $\overrightarrow{v}$ is the vector for the original translation, the inverse isometry is a translation by the vector $-\overrightarrow{v}$. A rotation also has an easy inverse: rotate around the same center with the same angle, but in the opposite direction. Thus, a rotation through angle α would have an inverse rotation through angle $-\alpha$. (Equivalently, we could say that the new rotation is through the angle $360° - \alpha$.)

Composing an isometry with its *inverse* has the effect of undoing the original isometry and moving everything back to its starting point. We say that $f \circ f^{-1}$

produces the identity isometry. The *identity* is the isometry i that leaves every point fixed, so that $i(X)$ always equals X. It can be thought of as a translation using the zero vector or as a rotation using an angle of 0°. We can write $f \circ f^{-1} = i$.

The inverse of a reflection may be a surprise: It is the same reflection! In other words, any reflection composed with itself produces the identity. Now can you describe the inverse of a glide reflection?

The set of isometries in the Euclidean plane is an example of an important mathematical concept called a *group*.

DEFINITION 8.5   A *group* is a set with a binary operation that satisfies four properties: closure, associativity, identity, and inverses.

For the set of isometries, the operation is composition. This is a binary operation, because we combine two isometries at a time. Earlier we started to verify closure when we showed that some compositions of two isometries produced another isometry. Rather than check every possible pairing, let us do a general proof.

LEMMA 8.2   The composition of any two isometries is an isometry. In other words, isometry is closed with respect to composition.

Outline of a proof   If f and g are isometries, then they preserve distances and are one-to-one and onto. The composition $f \circ g$ is also one-to-one and onto. (You will have an opportunity to prove this in the exercises.) Because $|AB| = |g(A) g(B)|$ and $|g(A) g(B)| = |f(g(A)) f(g(B))|$, we have $|AB| = |f(g(A)) f(g(B))|$, showing that $f \circ g$ preserves distances.

Composition of functions is always associative. (What do we need to show in order to prove this?) The function i that fixes all points is the identity, and we just explained what the inverse of each type of isometry will be. This gives us the following theorem.

THEOREM 8.5   The set of all isometries in the plane is a group.

Notice that the operation—composition—is not commutative. That is, it typically matters very much in what order you perform the isometries. For instance, the composition of two reflections in parallel lines will produce two different translations, depending on the order of the composition. Although some groups have a commutative operation, such as the group of integers with the addition operation, the group of isometries does not.

Suppose we focus our attention on the set of translations, which is a subset of the set of all isometries in the plane. The set of translations is also a group—the composition of two translations is a translation (closure), associativity still works, the identity is a translation by the zero vector, and the inverse of a translation is another translation. Thus, the set of translations forms a *subgroup* of the group of all isometries.

The set of rotations about a fixed center point is another subgroup of isometries. However, we cannot make a subgroup of reflections or of glide reflections. First of all, the identity isometry is not a reflection, because it is direct; thus, the identity property fails. Also, the closure property fails, because the composition of two opposite isometries will be direct and, hence, not a reflection.

Another way to form a subgroup of isometries is to restrict the domain and range to a particular geometric figure. For instance, suppose we use only the points of a given square. There are isometries that map points of a square to points of that same square. Certain rotations will use the points of the square as input and produce only that same set of points as output. Some reflections will do this also. However, no translations will, and no glide reflections will either. As we will see in more detail in Chapter 10 on symmetry, the small subset of isometries that map a square to itself forms a subgroup.

USING ISOMETRIES IN PROOFS

Isometries can be useful as tools for proving various geometric facts. Recall that an isometry preserves congruence; therefore, finding an isometry between two objects is one way to verify the congruence of those objects. Sometimes a proof using isometries can provide a different insight from a more traditional proof. For example, here is a transformational proof of a standard result—a proof that gives a visual sense of why the theorem is true.

THEOREM 8.6   **(ASA criterion for congruent triangles)**   Suppose ΔABC and $\Delta A'B'D$ satisfy $|AB| = |A'B'|$, $\angle ABC \cong \angle A'B'D$, and $\angle BAC \cong \angle B'A'D$. Then the two triangles are congruent.

Proof   Because $|AB| = |A'B'|$, there are exactly two isometries that map A to A' and B to B'. Let f_1 be the one that sends C to the point C' on the side of $A'B'$ that is opposite D. (See Figure 8.7.)

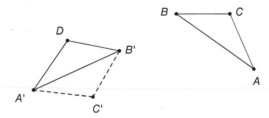

FIGURE 8.7
Proof of ASA

Now use an isometry, r, to reflect $\Delta A'B'C'$ across the line $A'B'$ and denote $r(C')$ $= X$. Recall that isometries preserve congruence of angles. Thus,

$$\angle XA'B' \cong \angle C'A'B' \cong \angle CAB \cong \angle DA'B',$$

showing that the point X is on the line DA'. Similarly,

$$\angle XB'A' \cong \angle C'B'A' \cong \angle CBA \cong \angle DB'A',$$

showing that the point X is on the line DB'. Therefore, $X = D$. Because the composition $(r \circ f_1)$ is an isometry taking $\triangle ABC$ to $\triangle A'B'D$, the two triangles are congruent.

To complete this proof, we need to consider the other isometry, f_2, that sends C to the point C^* on the same side of $A'B'$ as D. Can you show that $C^* = D$? (You will have an opportunity to do this in the exercises.)

There are no simple rules about when to use isometries in a proof. Isometries are simply another way of thinking about geometric problems. These motions give us another tool that can be useful in understanding a particular situation.

ISOMETRIES IN SPACE

The idea of isometry can be extended to three or even more dimensions by requiring the same properties we saw in two dimensions—a function that preserves distances and is one-to-one and onto. The distance between points A and B in $\mathbb{R}^n$ can be calculated by using an extension of the Pythagorean Theorem:

$$distance = \sqrt{(a_1 - b_1)^2 + (a_2 - b_2)^2 + \cdots + (a_n - b_n)^2}.$$

With this formula, we can check whether a function preserves distances. For example, in $\mathbb{R}^3$ define a function $f(x_1, x_2, x_3) = (x_2, x_3, x_1)$. Notice that this defines a function that takes a point in space, (x_1, x_2, x_3), as input and returns a point that has the same three coordinates in a different order. Will this be an isometry? It is not difficult to check the properties.

As you might expect, there are more possible types of isometry in 3-space than those we saw earlier. Translations, rotations, reflections, and glide reflections still occur in $\mathbb{R}^3$, though they must be adapted to work with the additional dimension. However, there are completely new types of isometry in three dimensions. We will not work with these new isometries; we merely list and briefly describe them here [Coxeter 1969, 96–101].

Translation   Points are moved along a constant vector. This is a direct isometry without fixed points.

Rotation   Points are rotated around a given line: This is a direct isometry, and the axis of rotation is made up of fixed points.

Reflection   This isometry is like reflection in an ordinary mirror. The mirror is a plane that reflects three-dimensional space. The points in the plane are fixed, and the isometry is opposite. (Orientation is more complicated to define in $\mathbb{R}^3$ but the general idea is the same.)

Glide Reflection   Points are reflected in a plane and then translated using a vector parallel to the plane. This is an opposite isometry with no fixed points.

Screw   This isometry is also called **twist**. It is a rotation followed by a translation along the axis of rotation. The name may make more sense if you imagine the rotation and translation happening simultaneously. This is a direct isometry and, though there are no fixed points, the axis line is transformed into itself.

Rotary Reflection This is a reflection followed by a rotation around an axis perpendicular to the mirror plane. It is an opposite isometry, with a single fixed point where the axis intersects the mirror.

Central Inversion Given a center point, O, the image of a point P is the point P' on line $\overleftrightarrow{PO}$ for which O is the midpoint of the segment PP'. This isometry is opposite, and the center is the only fixed point. Central inversion is sometimes called *reflection in a point*.

Just as in $\mathbb{R}^2$, isometries can be combined by composition. The identity isometry takes every point to itself, and each isometry has an inverse. Thus the set of isometries in $\mathbb{R}^3$ forms a group. There are many possible subgroups. Can you think of some examples?

8.3 EXERCISES

Give clear and complete answers to the exercises, expressing your explanations in complete sentences. Include diagrams whenever appropriate.

1. Consider $\triangle ABC$ with vertices at $(3, 4)$, $(-1, 2)$, and $(2, -2)$. What happens to this triangle when it is put through each of the five functions f_1, f_2, f_3, f_4, f_5 in Activities 1 and 2? Either calculate the vertices of $\triangle A'B'C'$, or explain why they cannot be calculated. Then draw the result of each set of calculations.

2. Consider $\triangle RST$ with vertices at $(5, 0)$, $(0, 3)$, and the origin. What happens to this triangle when it is put through each of the five functions f_1, f_2, f_3, f_4, f_5 in Activities 1 and 2? Either calculate the vertices of $\triangle R'S'T'$, or explain why they cannot be calculated. Then draw the result of each set of calculations.

3. For each of the five functions f_1, f_2, f_3, f_4, f_5 defined on the plane in Activities 1 and 2, either prove that f_n is an onto function or prove that it is not.

4. For each of the five functions f_1, f_2, f_3, f_4, f_5 in Activities 1 and 2, either prove that f_n is a one-to-one function or prove that it is not.

5. For each of the five functions f_1, f_2, f_3, f_4, f_5 in Activities 1 and 2, prove or disprove that f_n is distance-preserving.

6. If a function $f\colon \mathbb{R}^2 \to \mathbb{R}^2$ preserves distances, does f have to be one-to-one? Does f have to be onto? If you answer yes, give a proof; if you answer no, give a counterexample.

7. In Figure 8.1, one of the triangles is the original, and the other three are the result of a translation, a rotation, and a reflection. Write a paragraph explaining how you determined which triangle is which.

8. Suppose that AB is a line segment.
   a. If f is a translation, when will $f(AB)$ be parallel to AB? Justify your answer.
   b. If f is a rotation, when will $f(AB)$ be parallel to AB? Justify your answer.
   c. If f is a reflection, when will $f(AB)$ be parallel to AB? Justify your answer.

9. Write out a careful detailed proof of Theorem 8.1. (See page 190.)

10. Write a paragraph explaining why each part of Corollary 8.1 on page 191 is true.

11. Consider a triangle ABC with its vertices at $A = (2, 5)$, $B = (1, 9)$, and $C = (7.5, 8.5)$.
   a. If $\triangle ABC$ is projected to the y-axis, what is the result? Be as specific as possible in your answer.

b. If $\triangle ABC$ is projected to the x-axis, what is the result? Be as specific as possible in your answer.

c. If $\triangle ABC$ is projected to the diagonal line $y = x$, what is the result? Be as specific as possible in your answer.

12. Consider the function $f_3(x, y) = (x + 2y, y)$ of Activity 2. As noted in the discussion, this function is a *shear*.

    a. What are the fixed points of f_3? Describe the set of fixed points geometrically.

    b. Create an example of a shear function with the vertical axis as its set of fixed points.

13. In Figure 8.3, the dilation ratio is 2/3. Prove that the original triangle XYZ is similar to the image triangle $f(X)f(Y)f(Z)$.

14. Explain how to interpret a dilation ratio of -2.

15. Prove that a dilation with a fixed center, C, and a constant ratio, r, is both one-to-one and onto.

16. Is dilation a direct transformation or an opposite transformation? Are there any fixed points? Justify your answers.

17. Suppose that f and g are isometries. Prove that the composition $f \circ g$ is also an isometry. (There are three things to prove.)

18. Investigate the following compositions of isometries. Decide what type of isometry is produced and explain why you think so. Consider orientation and fixed points in your explanations.

    a. A reflection followed by a translation that is not parallel to the mirror

    b. A reflection followed by a rotation

    c. A rotation followed by a reflection

    d. A rotation followed by a translation

19. Give an example of two specific isometries to show that composition is not commutative. Give another example of two specific isometries that do commute.

20. A glide reflection can be thought of as a composition of a translation and a reflection. Does this pair of isometries commute, that is, does the order in which they are performed affect the result? Explain.

21. Sometimes a composition of two reflections has fixed points, and sometimes it doesn't. Write a paragraph in which you identify when it has fixed points, and explain why this happens.

22. Central inversion through a point (see page 200) can also be done in the plane $\mathbb{R}^2$. Draw a triangle and its image under this type of reflection. How else could you describe this transformation? Is this an isometry? Is it direct or opposite?

23. Consider $\triangle PQR$ with vertices at $(3, 5)$, $(-2, 1)$, and $(4, -2)$.

    a. Reflect this triangle through the origin, and calculate the vertices of the image, $\triangle P'Q'R'$.

    b. Is this transformation an isometry? If so, which of the four types of isometry is it? If not, why not?

24. Consider $\triangle ABC$ with vertices at $(1, 5)$, $(3, 0)$, and $(-2, -2)$.

    a. Reflect this triangle through the origin, and calculate the vertices of the image, $\triangle A'B'C'$.

    b. Is this transformation an isometry? If so, which of the four types of isometry is it? If not, why not?

25. Suppose that f is an isometry.

    a. If f is a translation, describe f^{-1}.

    b. If f is a rotation, describe f^{-1}.

    c. If f is a reflection, describe f^{-1}.

    d. If f is a glide reflection, describe f^{-1}.

    e. Prove that, in general, f^{-1} is also an isometry.

26. Prove that composition of isometries is associative. In other words, prove that

$$(f \circ g) \circ h = f \circ (g \circ h).$$

Which of the properties of isometry did your proof use: function, onto, one-to-one, distance-preserving?

27. Prove that the set of translations is a group.

28. Prove that the set of integers under addition is a group. Is the set of integers under subtraction a group? Why or why not?

29. Consider the set of rotations around one particular point. Prove that this set is a subgroup of the group of isometries in the plane.

30. Prove or disprove that the set of rotations about the points $(1, -1)$ or $(-3, 3)$ is a group.

31. Suppose that f is an isometry. Prove that $\triangle ABC$ is congruent to $\triangle f(A)f(B)f(C)$.

32. Complete the transformational proof of the ASA criterion of triangle congruence. (See page 198.)

33. Develop a transformational proof that the vertical angles formed by two intersecting lines are congruent.

34. Develop a transformational proof that the base angles of an isosceles triangle must be congruent.

35. Suppose that the diagonals of a quadrilateral are perpendicular bisectors of each other. Use isometries to prove that the quadrilateral must be a rhombus.

36. Let $P_1, \ldots, P_k$ be points on a circle with center O. Suppose that these points are evenly spaced in order around the circle. This means that the central angles

$$\angle P_1 OP_2, \angle P_2 OP_3, \ldots, \angle P_k OP_1,$$

are all congruent. Prove that the polygon

$$P_1 P_2 \ldots P_k P_1$$

formed by these points is regular, that is, all sides of the polygon are congruent and all angles of the polygon are congruent. (It may be helpful to try some small examples first, such as $k = 3$ and $k = 4$.)

37. In GeoGebra, draw two points A, B on the same side of a line ℓ and let X be a point on ℓ. Locate X so that the total distance $|AX| + |XB|$ is a minimum. Then find the reflection B' of B across ℓ and draw AB'.

    What conjecture can you make? Vary the points A, B and adjust the location of X. Does your conjecture still work? Prove your conjecture. (This is *Heron's Theorem*.)

38. Create a triangle, $\triangle ABC$, and measure its three angles. Translate the triangle by the vector $\overrightarrow{AB}$. The two triangles should now be connected at the point B. How do the three angles at the point B compare to the angles of $\triangle ABC$? Vary the triangle and compare angles again.

What is the sum of the three angles at B? What can you conclude about $\triangle ABC$? Prove your statement.

39. Let H be the orthocenter of $\triangle ABC$. Show that when H is reflected across the three sides of $\triangle ABC$, the three image points will lie on the circumcircle of the triangle [Yaglom vol. I, 1962, 45].

40. Consider points A and B in $\mathbb{R}^3$. Let

$$A = (a_1, a_2, a_3) \quad \text{and} \quad B = (b_1, b_2, b_3).$$

Prove that

$$|AB| = \sqrt{(a_1 - b_1)^2 + (a_2 - b_2)^2 + (a_3 - b_3)^2}.$$

41. For each of the following functions in $\mathbb{R}^3$, determine whether it is an isometry or not. If it is an isometry, prove it; if not, explain why.
    a. $g_1(x, y, z) = (y, x, z)$
    b. $g_2(x, y, z) = (x, y, 3)$
    c. $g_3(x, y, z) = (2x, 2y, 2z)$
    d. $g_4(x, y, z) = (x, 2y, 3z)$
    e. $g_5(x, y, z) = (x + 2, y + 2, z + 2)$
    f. $g_6(x, y, z) = (x + y, 2y, z + y)$

42. Prove or disprove that the set of translations in $\mathbb{R}^3$ is a group.

43. Prove or disprove that the set of rotations about the x-axis in $\mathbb{R}^3$ is a group.

44. The list of isometries given on pages 199–200 is a group. Identify three different subgroups of this group.

Exercises 45–47 are especially for future teachers.

45. The National Council of Teachers of Mathematics (NCTM) recommends in the *Principles and Standards for School Mathematics* that "Instructional programs from prekindergarten through grade 12 should enable all students to . . . apply transformations and use symmetry to analyze mathematical situations" [NCTM 2000, 41]. What does this mean for you and your future students?
    a. Study the Geometry Standard for one grade band (i.e., pre-K–2, 3–5, 6–8, or 9–12). What are the recommendations of the NCTM regarding transformational geometry?

b. Find copies of school mathematics textbooks for these same grade levels. How are the NCTM standards implemented in those textbooks? Cite specific examples.

c. Write a report in which you present and critique what you learn.

46. Design several classroom activities involving transformational geometry which would be appropriate for students in your future classroom. Write a paragraph or two explaining how the activities you design reflect both what you have learned in studying this chapter, and the recommendations of the NCTM.

47. Find the Common Core State Standards for Mathematics online: http://www.corestandards.org.

a. How is transformational geometry spread through the mathematics curriculum from kindergarten through grade 12?

b. In high school, the Common Core presents congruence in terms of transformations in the plane and rigid motions. What skills and understandings are high school students expected to develop through their study of congruence?

c. What kinds of theorems are high school students expected to be able to prove using their understanding of congruence? Specifically, how is an understanding of congruence required for proving statements about lines and angles, triangles, and parallelograms?

Reflect on what you have learned in this chapter.

48. Review the main ideas of this chapter. Describe, in your own words, the concepts you have studied and what you have learned about them. What are the important ideas? How do they fit together? Which concepts were easy for you? Which were hard?

49. Reflect on the learning environment for this course. Describe aspects of the learning environment that helped you understand the main ideas in this chapter. Which activities did you like? Which did you find more challenging? Why?

8.4 CHAPTER OVERVIEW

In this chapter, we very likely stretched your understanding of *function* to include functions whose inputs and outputs are points in the coordinate plane. A function, f, whose source and target are the set of points in the coordinate plane performs some kind of action on the plane; that is, f transforms the plane.

Some transformations of the plane will stretch or shrink the plane. The function f_1 of Activity 1 pulled (or stretched) the plane away from the lines $y = \pm 1$. Some functions of the plane project the entire plane onto a single line. The function f_2 in Activity 2 projected the entire plane onto the y-axis. Functions of this type change the distances between points. Consequently, the distance between the original points A and B will not be the same as the distance between the images $f(A)$ and $f(B)$. Such functions are interesting, but they were not the primary focus of our study in this chapter.

In this chapter, we focused our attention on transformations of the plane that preserve distances and are one-to-one and onto. Transformations that meet all three of these criteria are called *isometries*. An isometry is classified according to whether it is direct or opposite and whether or not it has fixed points. *Rotations* and *translations* are direct isometries, while *reflections* and *glide reflections* are opposite isometries. A reflection has a whole line of fixed points, and this line is the mirror line of the reflection. A rotation has a single fixed point, namely, the center of the rotation. Neither a translation nor a glide reflection has any fixed points. We showed that every isometry of the plane is one of these four types.

Because an isometry is a distance-preserving function, it can be used as a powerful proof tool. If we can find an isometry between two figures, we know that they are congruent. We showed how isometries can be used to develop another proof of the ASA criterion for triangle congruence.

An isometry is a function. Consequently, we can use composition to combine two (or more) isometries to construct a new isometry. We can also think about undoing the action of an isometry by means of an *inverse* isometry. By considering a set of isometries and the operation of composition, we can ask whether the set is closed with respect to composition. We can check whether the identity isometry is in the set, and we can check to see whether the inverse of each isometry is also in the set. Function composition is associative. Therefore, if a given set of isometries is closed, includes the identity, and includes the inverse of each isometry in the set, we have a *group* of isometries. This idea of a *group* is an important mathematical concept, which is typically studied at greater depth in a course on abstract algebra.

In this chapter, we focused on isometries of the plane. All of these concepts can be extended to three-, four-, and even higher-dimensional space. We will leave an exploration of these ideas to another book in another course!

We have developed a number of theorems in this chapter. They are listed here again for your convenience:

Theorem 8.1   In the Euclidean plane, the images of three noncollinear points completely determine an isometry. In other words, if we know the outputs for three noncollinear points A, B, C, we can figure out what the isometry does to any point X.

Theorem 8.2   An isometry preserves collinearity. In other words, three points that are collinear will still be collinear after going through an isometry.

Theorem 8.3   An isometry preserves betweenness. In other words, if point B is between points A and C along a line, then point $f(B)$ will be between points $f(A)$ and $f(C)$ along their line.

Corollary 8.1   Under an isometry, the image of

a line segment		line segment,
a triangle	is a congruent	triangle,
an angle		angle,
a circle		circle.

Lemma 8.1   For four points A, B, A', and B' with $|AB| = |A'B'|$, there are exactly two isometries that give $f(A) = A'$ and $f(B) = B'$.

Theorem 8.4 In the Euclidean plane, there are only four types of isometry: translations, rotations, reflections, and glide reflections.

Lemma 8.2 The composition of any two isometries is an isometry. In other words, isometry is closed with respect to composition.

Theorem 8.5 The set of all isometries in the plane is a group.

Theorem 8.6 (ASA criterion for triangle congruence) Suppose $\triangle ABC$ and $\triangle A'B'D$ satisfy $|AB| = |A'B'|$, $\angle ABC \cong A'B'D$, and $\angle BAC \cong \angle B'A'D$. Then the two triangles are congruent.

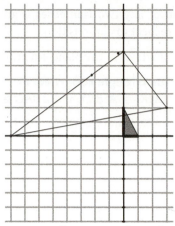

I n this chapter, we examine how to combine the ideas of coordinates and isometry, thus bringing together the analytic and transformational approaches to the geometry of the plane. To do this, it is necessary to describe in algebraic expressions what an isometry does to the *x*-coordinate and *y*-coordinate of a point. This can be done using a system of equations. Matrix notation is a convenient way to represent systems of equations, and thus to describe isometries. Facts about matrices provide additional insights into isometries.

CHAPTER NINE

Isometries and Matrices

Give clear and complete answers to the following problems and questions. Write your explanations clearly using complete sentences, and including diagrams whenever appropriate. Save your work for each activity, as sometimes later work builds on earlier work. It will be helpful to read ahead into the chapter as you work on these activities.

1. In this chapter, we will represent points (x, y) as column vectors $\begin{bmatrix} x \\ y \end{bmatrix}$.

   a. In GeoGebra, use a coordinate system. Draw a vector from the origin to the point $\begin{bmatrix} -2 \\ 3 \end{bmatrix}$.

   b. Create an arbitrary point P and translate it by the vector of part (a). Measure the coordinates of P and of its image P'. Move P and observe how these coordinates change.

   c. Complete the following equation to describe this situation:

   $$P' = \begin{bmatrix} x' \\ y' \end{bmatrix} = \begin{bmatrix} x \\ y \end{bmatrix} + \begin{bmatrix} ? \\ ? \end{bmatrix}.$$

2. In GeoGebra, use a coordinate system.
   a. Construct the standard unit circle. (Recall that this is the circle centered at the origin with radius 1.) Construct an arbitrary point P on this circle.

   b. Use the **Rotate around Point** command to rotate point P by 60° around the origin to get the new point P'.

   c. Measure the coordinates of both P and P'. Also, calculate the values of $\sin(60°)$ and $\cos(60°)$. Drag P and observe the coordinates of P and P'. It will be particularly helpful to observe what happens at the locations $\begin{bmatrix} 1 \\ 0 \end{bmatrix}$, $\begin{bmatrix} 0 \\ 1 \end{bmatrix}$, $\begin{bmatrix} -1 \\ 0 \end{bmatrix}$, and $\begin{bmatrix} 0 \\ -1 \end{bmatrix}$.

   d. Describe the relationship between P and P' by a matrix equation in the following pattern:

   $$\begin{bmatrix} x' \\ y' \end{bmatrix} = \begin{bmatrix} a & b \\ c & d \end{bmatrix} \begin{bmatrix} x \\ y \end{bmatrix}.$$

   In other words, find values for a, b, c, d that describe this relationship.
   e. Use the command **Detach Point** to detach point P from the unit circle. Vary P, and observe P' and their coordinates. Does your matrix equation from part (d) still describe this rotation correctly?

3. Describe in words the inverse of the rotation in Activity 2. Then write a matrix equation to describe this inverse.

4. In a new sketch, create a coordinate system and an arbitrary point P.
   a. Using the vertical axis as a mirror, reflect P across this mirror.
   b. Measure the coordinates of P and of P'. Drag P and observe these coordinates.
   c. Write a matrix equation to describe this reflection.

5. Repeat Activity 4, this time using the horizontal axis as the mirror.

6. In a new sketch, create a coordinate system and an arbitrary point P.
   a. Construct a line ℓ through the origin O. Measure its angle of inclination.
   b. Reflect the point P across ℓ to get the point P_1. Measure the coordinates of P and of P_1. Drag P and observe these coordinates. What relationship do you see between the coordinates of P and those of P_1?

   GEOGEBRA TIP In labeling the point P_1, type P_1.

   c. Now reflect P across the horizontal axis to get the point P_2. Measure the angle $\angle P_1 O P_2$. It may be helpful to construct segments showing this angle. What do you observe? How is this angle related to the angle of inclination? Drag P; do your observations still hold?
   d. Now vary the line ℓ and drag P again. Do your observations hold in this new situation? How could you explain this?

7. The general pattern of the matrix equations in these activities is

$$\begin{bmatrix} x' \\ y' \end{bmatrix} = \begin{bmatrix} a & b \\ c & d \end{bmatrix} \begin{bmatrix} x \\ y \end{bmatrix} + \begin{bmatrix} e \\ f \end{bmatrix}.$$

Suppose we know three specific input points and their images, as follows:

$$\begin{bmatrix} 0 \\ 0 \end{bmatrix} \rightarrow \begin{bmatrix} -2.4 \\ 0.7 \end{bmatrix} \quad \begin{bmatrix} 2.5 \\ 0 \end{bmatrix} \rightarrow \begin{bmatrix} 0 \\ 0 \end{bmatrix} \quad \begin{bmatrix} 3 \\ 1 \end{bmatrix} \rightarrow \begin{bmatrix} 0.2 \\ -1.1 \end{bmatrix}.$$

   a. Use this information to find values for a, b, c, d, e, f in the matrix equation.
   b. In a new sketch, create a coordinate system and an arbitrary point P. Notice the abscissa and the ordinate of the point P.
   c. Using the x- and y-coordinates of P, calculate in GeoGebra the value of x' according to your equation in part (a). Also calculate y'.

   GEOGEBRA HINT $x(P)$ is the x-coordinate of the point P.

   d. In the Input bar, create the point (x', y'). Label this image as P'.
   e. Drag the point P to the locations

$$\begin{bmatrix} 0 \\ 0 \end{bmatrix}, \quad \begin{bmatrix} 2.5 \\ 0 \end{bmatrix}, \quad \begin{bmatrix} 3 \\ 1 \end{bmatrix}$$

   to verify that your calculations in part (a) are correct.
   f. Which of the four types of isometry is this? Explain why you think so.

8. In the activities so far there have been many square matrices. Find the determinant of each of these matrices. What pattern do you see?

9. Here is the equation for a transformation that does not fit the pattern of the earlier activities.

$$\begin{bmatrix} x' \\ y' \end{bmatrix} = \begin{bmatrix} 3 & -4 \\ -4 & -3 \end{bmatrix} \begin{bmatrix} x \\ y \end{bmatrix} + \begin{bmatrix} 0 \\ 6 \end{bmatrix}.$$

a. In a new sketch, create a coordinate system and an arbitrary point P. Measure the abscissa and the ordinate of P. Calculate the coordinates of the image P' under this transformation and plot the point. (This is similar to what you did in Activity 7.)

b. Here are three points. Construct a triangle, and its interior, using these three points as the vertices.

$$A = \begin{bmatrix} 0 \\ 0 \end{bmatrix}, \quad B = \begin{bmatrix} 1 \\ 0 \end{bmatrix}, \quad C = \begin{bmatrix} 1 \\ 2 \end{bmatrix}.$$

c. Use **Attach Point** to attach point P to the interior of $\triangle ABC$.

d. Select point P' (only) and trace it. Then move the point P around the boundary of the triangle. Describe what happens.

e. Is this transformation an isometry? Is it direct or opposite?

f. What is the ratio of the areas for the triangles? What is the determinant of the matrix?

9.2 DISCUSSION

In this chapter, we will examine how to work with isometries analytically, that is, by using coordinates and algebra. In Chapter 5, you explored how to set up coordinates, and you learned (or reviewed) some basic facts about equations and their relation to geometric objects. Now we will explore how to use matrix equations to represent geometric functions (transformations). The algebra of vectors and matrices will allow us to better understand isometries and their properties. We will work only in $\mathbb{R}^2$, although this same approach can be applied in any number of dimensions.

USING VECTORS TO REPRESENT TRANSLATIONS

Recall what a translation does: Each input point is moved a constant distance in a constant direction to its new location. This idea of constant distance and constant direction can be well described by a vector. The vector could be written in polar coordinates, for polar coordinates are based on exactly these two quantities, distance and direction. However, it is more common to work in Cartesian coordinates and we do so in this chapter.

Your GeoGebra diagram in Activity 1 shows both the beginning and ending points of the translation. The input point and its image point are always the same distance apart and are always in the same relative position to each other. The vector for this translation is $\begin{bmatrix} -2 \\ 3 \end{bmatrix}$. This vector says to start at the input point $\begin{bmatrix} x \\ y \end{bmatrix}$, go two units to the left, and then go three units up. Your diagram in Activity 1a should show this vector beginning at the origin. However, a vector can begin anywhere; it is the distance and direction of the vector that are critical, not its location. If the beginning point for the vector is $\begin{bmatrix} x \\ y \end{bmatrix}$, where is the ending point? This will be the image point of the translation.

You have probably noticed that we are using the same notation for points as for vectors. So the notation $\begin{bmatrix} x \\ y \end{bmatrix}$ can be interpreted as either the vector or as the point (x, y). This ambiguity is deliberate. Using the same notation for both meanings allows us to write expressions such as

$$\begin{bmatrix} x' \\ y' \end{bmatrix} = \begin{bmatrix} x \\ y \end{bmatrix} + \begin{bmatrix} -2 \\ 3 \end{bmatrix} = \begin{bmatrix} x - 2 \\ y + 3 \end{bmatrix}.$$

In this expression, $\begin{bmatrix} x \\ y \end{bmatrix}$ is a point and $\begin{bmatrix} -2 \\ 3 \end{bmatrix}$ is the translation vector. The combined expression describes how this translation works.

USING MATRICES TO REPRESENT ROTATIONS

To perform a rotation, we must know two things: the point to use as the center of the rotation and the angle θ through which to turn. This angle θ can be positive or negative, small or huge. The angle can even exceed 360°. The center of rotation can be any point in the plane. In Activity 2, you examined the situation with the rotation center at the origin. As you might expect, this situation is simpler than the general rotation.

Since rotations involve angles, it is convenient for the moment to work in polar coordinates. The starting point is (r, α), which says that the input is distance r from the rotation center and at an inclination of α from the horizontal axis. The image point is the same distance from the center, r, but the angle has changed to $(\alpha + \theta)$. So the image has polar coordinates $(r, \alpha + \theta)$. See Figure 9.1. How do we express this in rectangular coordinates? The input point can be written as

$$\begin{bmatrix} x \\ y \end{bmatrix} = \begin{bmatrix} r\cos(\alpha) \\ r\sin(\alpha) \end{bmatrix}.$$

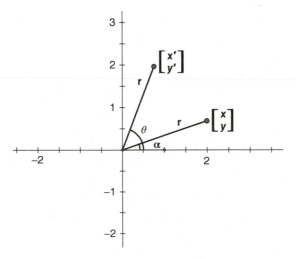

FIGURE 9.1
Rotation Around the Origin

You should examine Figure 9.1 and convince yourself that this is correct. Similarly, the image point can be written as

$$\begin{bmatrix} x' \\ y' \end{bmatrix} = \begin{bmatrix} r\cos(\alpha + \theta) \\ r\sin(\alpha + \theta) \end{bmatrix}.$$

Our challenge is to figure out how the right-hand side of this equation is related to the input point $\begin{bmatrix} x \\ y \end{bmatrix}$.

By using an identity from trigonometry, the upper coordinate can be rewritten as

$$r\cos(\alpha + \theta) = r(\cos(\alpha)\cos(\theta) - \sin(\alpha)\sin(\theta))$$

$$= \cos(\theta)r\cos(\alpha) - \sin(\theta)r\sin(\alpha)$$

$$= \cos(\theta)x - \sin(\theta)y.$$

Since the angle of rotation θ is a constant, the factors $\cos(\theta)$ and $-\sin(\theta)$ are also constants. These are the values for the first row of the matrix in Activity 2d. A similar calculation with $r\sin(\alpha + \theta)$ will produce the values for the second row of the matrix.

Once you have completed the matrix for the rotation through angle θ, finding the matrix for the inverse rotation is easy. There are (at least) two approaches to solving this problem: We can use trigonometry, or we can use linear algebra. The inverse rotation uses the same center, namely, the origin, but the direction of rotation is reversed; that is, the angle of rotation is $-\theta$. The trigonometric approach to finding the matrix for rotation in the opposite direction is to simply replace θ by $-\theta$ everywhere in the matrix and use even/odd identities to simplify the results. The approach using linear algebra is to find the inverse matrix.

Of course, any point can be the center of a rotation, not just the origin. We could find the more general matrix pattern by setting the point (h, k) as the center and doing similar work with trigonometric identities. It is a messy calculation. An alternative approach is to think of this rotation in three steps: translate the rotation center (h, k) to the origin, perform a rotation there, then translate the origin back to (h, k). The composition of these three steps will perform the rotation around (h, k), and the composition of the three matrix functions will calculate this rotation. We will examine this in more detail when we discuss composition of isometries.

USING MATRICES TO REPRESENT REFLECTIONS

The action of a reflection uses a line. Points are reflected across this mirror line to their counterparts on the other side, in a very specific way. Recall from Chapter 8 that the mirror is the perpendicular bisector of the line segment between any point and its reflected image.

Let us use this idea to examine what is going on in Activity 4. Suppose we have a point $\begin{bmatrix} x \\ y \end{bmatrix}$. To begin with, let us suppose that $x > 0$. A positive value for x puts the point in the right side of the plane. With the y-axis as the mirror, the segment between this point and its image must be horizontal. Furthermore, the image is the same distance to the left of the y-axis as the original point is to the right. In coordinates, this means that the image has the same y-coordinate as the input point and that its x-coordinate has the same magnitude but the opposite sign. In vector notation,

$$\begin{bmatrix} x' \\ y' \end{bmatrix} = \begin{bmatrix} -x \\ y \end{bmatrix}.$$

Does this vector equation still work for points of the form $\begin{bmatrix} 0 \\ y \end{bmatrix}$, that is, for points that lie on the reflection line? Does the equation still work for points that have $x < 0$?

This vector equation can be written as a matrix equation, similar to those you wrote for rotations. We need to have

$$\begin{bmatrix} -x \\ y \end{bmatrix} = \begin{bmatrix} a & b \\ c & d \end{bmatrix} \begin{bmatrix} x \\ y \end{bmatrix}.$$

By multiplying out the right side and comparing the coordinates, it is easy to see that reflection across the vertical axis is represented by the matrix equation

$$\begin{bmatrix} x' \\ y' \end{bmatrix} = \begin{bmatrix} -1 & 0 \\ 0 & 1 \end{bmatrix} \begin{bmatrix} x \\ y \end{bmatrix}.$$

In Activity 5, you examined reflections across the x-axis. The pattern is similar. Here, the segment between a point P and its image P' must be vertical, and the distance from P to the horizontal axis is the same as the distance from P' to the horizontal axis. It is not difficult to write this reflection as a matrix equation.

Reflections in other lines are more complicated to represent. In Activity 6, you examined the situation where the mirror line ℓ passes through the origin. The point P_1 is the reflection of the point P across ℓ. What did you observe about the relationship between the coordinates of P and those of P_1? It can be difficult to describe this relationship—unless you were very lucky in how you picked the line ℓ. To find a matrix description of this relationship, it is helpful to consider an alternative way of performing this reflection. You should be able to prove that the reflection across any line ℓ that passes through the origin can be broken into two steps: first reflect across the horizontal axis and then rotate around the origin. (Examine your sketch for Activity 6 and look for congruent triangles.) Activity 6c suggests that the angle $\angle P_1 O P_2$ is twice the angle of inclination for ℓ. Your proof should show that the angle of rotation will be twice the angle of inclination for the mirror line [Wallace & West 1992, 229].

Now we can think of the reflection across ℓ as two steps. We know how to represent each of these two steps as a matrix equation. The first step, the reflection across the horizontal axis, is

$$\begin{bmatrix} x' \\ y' \end{bmatrix} = \begin{bmatrix} 1 & 0 \\ 0 & -1 \end{bmatrix} \begin{bmatrix} x \\ y \end{bmatrix}.$$

The second step, rotating around the origin through an angle of 2α, is

$$\begin{bmatrix} x'' \\ y'' \end{bmatrix} = \begin{bmatrix} \cos(2\alpha) & -\sin(2\alpha) \\ \sin(\alpha) & \cos(2\alpha) \end{bmatrix} \begin{bmatrix} x' \\ y' \end{bmatrix}.$$

The challenge is how to combine these steps into a single matrix. This combination can be accomplished by a substitution; replace the intermediate point $\begin{bmatrix} x' \\ y' \end{bmatrix}$ in the second equation by $\begin{bmatrix} 1 & 0 \\ 0 & -1 \end{bmatrix} \begin{bmatrix} x \\ y \end{bmatrix}$. This creates the following somewhat messy expression:

$$\begin{bmatrix} x'' \\ y'' \end{bmatrix} = \begin{bmatrix} \cos(2\alpha) & -\sin(2\alpha) \\ \sin(2\alpha) & \cos(2\alpha) \end{bmatrix} \left(\begin{bmatrix} 1 & 0 \\ 0 & -1 \end{bmatrix} \begin{bmatrix} x \\ y \end{bmatrix} \right).$$

By carrying out the matrix multiplication, we can simplify this expression. Bear in mind that multiplication of matrices is associative.

COMPOSITION OF ISOMETRIES

Isometries are functions that use points as input and output. Combining isometries, then, means combining functions. There are many ways to combine functions, and you have seen many combinations of functions in other courses. However, some of the standard ways to combine functions do not always produce an isometry. For instance, the sum of two nonzero translations is no longer an isometry. (Can you verify this?) In Chapter 8, we saw that the *composition* of two isometries will always produce another isometry. Remember that in composing isometries we must perform the isometries in sequence, with the output of the first being used as the input for the next. The usual function notation for composition of functions underscores this fact:

$$(f \circ g)(P) = f(g(P)).$$

The right-hand side of this equation tells us how to proceed: the input point P is put into the function g, then the result of that process is used as input for the next function f.

The discussion on pages 212–213 dealt with a two-step composition. The goal was to find a single matrix that represents reflection across the line $y = mx$. This reflection was broken into two steps: reflection across the x-axis followed by rotation around the origin. Each of these steps was represented by a matrix. The first step, reflection across the x-axis, can be calculated by multiplying a matrix and a vector:

$$\begin{bmatrix} 1 & 0 \\ 0 & -1 \end{bmatrix} \begin{bmatrix} x \\ y \end{bmatrix}.$$

This product then replaces the input for the second multiplication, which is the rotation. Doing the substitution gave us the rather complicated expression shown earlier. Fortunately, multiplication of matrices and vectors is associative. Thus, the expression equals

$$\begin{bmatrix} x' \\ y' \end{bmatrix} = \left(\begin{bmatrix} \cos(2\alpha) & -\sin(2\alpha) \\ \sin(2\alpha) & \cos(2\alpha) \end{bmatrix} \begin{bmatrix} 1 & 0 \\ 0 & -1 \end{bmatrix} \right) \begin{bmatrix} x \\ y \end{bmatrix}.$$

By multiplying the two matrices, we can get a much simpler expression for reflection across $y = mx$.

The important idea here is that we can calculate compositions by multiplying their matrices. Therefore, knowing the matrix patterns for some basic isometries can help us create the matrices for much more complicated motions.

You may recall from linear algebra that multiplication of matrices is not commutative, except in a few special circumstances. This tells us that composition of isometries is not commutative in general. We already knew that from Chapter 8, and the implementation of isometries using matrices confirms this fact again in another way. So it is important to write the matrices in the correct order, right-to-left in the way compositions are always written.

Here is a specific example of a composition. Suppose we want to perform the reflection across the x-axis followed by the reflection across the line $y = x$. What is the resulting composition? First we need to write the matrix for each step.

$$\text{Reflection across the } x\text{-axis: } \begin{bmatrix} 1 & 0 \\ 0 & -1 \end{bmatrix}$$

$$\text{Reflection across } y = x: \begin{bmatrix} 0 & 1 \\ 1 & 0 \end{bmatrix}.$$

The matrix for the composition is the product of these two matrices:

$$\begin{bmatrix} 0 & 1 \\ 1 & 0 \end{bmatrix} \begin{bmatrix} 1 & 0 \\ 0 & -1 \end{bmatrix} = \begin{bmatrix} 0 & -1 \\ 1 & 0 \end{bmatrix}.$$

Notice the order of the multiplication; the matrix for the first step is on the right.

Look carefully at this result. The upper-left and lower-right entries are the same, and the lower left and upper right are negatives of each other. This is like the matrix pattern for a rotation around the origin discussed earlier. With an angle of 90°, we get precisely this matrix. (You should compare this to the product in the reverse order. The reversed product will still be a rotation around the origin, but not the same one.)

Matrix algebra can be used to find equations for compositions using translations also. Suppose we want an equation that describes a rotation around a point other than the origin, say around the point (h, k). This can be done in three steps: translate (h, k) to $(0, 0)$, do the rotation around the origin, and then translate the origin back to (h, k). Here is an expression for this.

$$\begin{bmatrix} x' \\ y' \end{bmatrix} = \left(\begin{bmatrix} \cos(\theta) & -\sin(\theta) \\ \sin(\theta) & \cos(\theta) \end{bmatrix} \left(\begin{bmatrix} x \\ y \end{bmatrix} - \begin{bmatrix} h \\ k \end{bmatrix} \right) \right) + \begin{bmatrix} h \\ k \end{bmatrix}.$$

Do you see how each of the three steps is represented in this expression? Matrix multiplication is distributive, so with some work this expression can be simplified.

We have not discussed glide reflections yet precisely because a glide reflection is defined as a composition: a reflection followed by a translation. You should have some idea how this works by now:

Image = reflection matrix × input + translation vector.

Suppose we want to do a glide reflection using the diagonal line $y = x$ and a translation of 2 units in the northeast direction. You should convince yourself that this is

$$\begin{bmatrix} x' \\ y' \end{bmatrix} = \begin{bmatrix} 0 & 1 \\ 1 & 0 \end{bmatrix} \begin{bmatrix} x \\ y \end{bmatrix} + \begin{bmatrix} \sqrt{2} \\ \sqrt{2} \end{bmatrix}.$$

THE GENERAL FORM OF A MATRIX REPRESENTATION

Activity 7 gives three inputs and their images under some isometry. Since the three input points are not collinear, a theorem from Chapter 8 tells us that this is enough information to completely determine the isometry. In other words, knowing what happens to these three points is enough information to figure out what the isometry does to any other point. Similarly, the coordinates of these three points and their images are enough information to figure out the matrix equation for the isometry. It just takes a little algebra.

Even though the equation given in Activity 7 contains six parameters—the values a, b, c, d, e, f—you should find that only four numbers are actually involved: -2.4, 0.7, 0.96, and 0.28 (with a few negative signs tossed in). In particular, the matrix has an important pattern. The upper-left and lower-right entries are the same value (except for perhaps a negative sign), and the lower-left and upper-right entries are the same (again, except for perhaps a negative sign). Look back at the other matrices from the previous activities; all of them should have this same pattern.

Another important fact comes from the determinant of the isometry matrix. In Activities 2–7, there were five square matrices. Every determinant was either $+1$ or -1. The matrices in Activity 1 were also square matrices. If we write the translation of Activity 1 as a matrix equation, it is

$$\begin{bmatrix} x' \\ y' \end{bmatrix} = \begin{bmatrix} 1 & 0 \\ 0 & 1 \end{bmatrix} \begin{bmatrix} x \\ y \end{bmatrix} + \begin{bmatrix} -2 \\ 3 \end{bmatrix}.$$

Here the matrix is the identity matrix, for the translation is done by the addition of the vector. The determinant is again $+1$.

But there is more; think about which type of isometry produced each value:

$$\text{translation} \rightarrow \text{determinant} = 1$$

$$\text{rotation} \rightarrow \text{determinant} = 1$$

$$\text{reflection} \rightarrow \text{determinant} = -1$$

$$\text{glide reflection} \rightarrow \text{determinant} = -1.$$

(The isometry in Activity 7 was a glide reflection.) The direct isometries have a determinant of $+1$, while the opposite isometries have a determinant of -1. To prove this, we will use a tool from multivariable calculus.

THEOREM 9.1   Suppose that an isometry is represented by the equation

$$\begin{bmatrix} x' \\ y' \end{bmatrix} = \begin{bmatrix} a & b \\ c & d \end{bmatrix} \begin{bmatrix} x \\ y \end{bmatrix} + \begin{bmatrix} e \\ f \end{bmatrix}.$$

Then the determinant of this matrix, $ad - bc$, equals $+1$ if the isometry is direct, and -1 if the isometry is opposite.

Proof   First recall the *cross product* and some basic facts about it.

- Let $\vec{u}$ and $\vec{v}$ be vectors in three-dimensional space $\mathbb{R}^3$. Then the three vectors $\vec{u}, \vec{v}, \vec{u} \times \vec{v}$, in that order, form a right-handed triple.
- If A, B, C are three points, then the area of the triangle $\triangle ABC = \frac{1}{2} |\overrightarrow{AB} \times \overrightarrow{AC}|$.
- $\vec{v} \times \vec{u} = -(\vec{u} \times \vec{v})$.

Now, consider what this isometry does to three special points:

$$A = \begin{bmatrix} 0 \\ 0 \end{bmatrix} \rightarrow \begin{bmatrix} e \\ f \end{bmatrix} = A'$$

$$B = \begin{bmatrix} 1 \\ 0 \end{bmatrix} \rightarrow \begin{bmatrix} a + e \\ c + f \end{bmatrix} = B'$$

$$C = \begin{bmatrix} 0 \\ 1 \end{bmatrix} \rightarrow \begin{bmatrix} b + e \\ d + f \end{bmatrix} = C'.$$

The cross product can only be used in three-dimensional space, so think of these points A', B', C' as lying in the plane $z = 0$. Thus, their full coordinates are

$$A' = \begin{bmatrix} e \\ f \\ 0 \end{bmatrix}, \quad B' = \begin{bmatrix} a + e \\ c + f \\ 0 \end{bmatrix}, \quad C' = \begin{bmatrix} b + e \\ d + f \\ 0 \end{bmatrix}.$$

We will be interested in the vectors $\overrightarrow{A'B'}$ and $\overrightarrow{A'C'}$, which are

$$\begin{bmatrix} a \\ c \\ 0 \end{bmatrix} \quad \text{and} \quad \begin{bmatrix} b \\ d \\ 0 \end{bmatrix},$$

respectively. The cross product of these two vectors is

$$\overrightarrow{A'B'} \times \overrightarrow{A'C'} = \begin{vmatrix} \vec{i} & \vec{j} & \vec{k} \\ a & c & 0 \\ b & d & 0 \end{vmatrix}$$

$$= (ad - bc)\vec{k}.$$

Thus, this cross product will point either upward or downwards depending on the sign of $ad - bc$.

The area of the triangle, $\triangle A'B'C'$ is $\frac{1}{2}|\overrightarrow{A'B'} \times \overrightarrow{A'C'}| = \frac{1}{2}|ad - bc|$. Because we are working with an isometry, this area equals the area of $\triangle ABC = \frac{1}{2}$. Thus $|ad - bc| = 1$.

What about the orientation? Will this computation tell us if it is direct or opposite?

Notice that the points A, B, C were labeled in counterclockwise order around their triangle. Thus, the angle from $\overrightarrow{AB}$ to $\overrightarrow{AC}$ is positive. Let us consider what happens with the three vectors $\overrightarrow{A'B'}$, $\overrightarrow{A'C'}$, $\overrightarrow{A'B'} \times \overrightarrow{A'C'}$. If the angle from $\overrightarrow{A'B'}$ to $\overrightarrow{A'C'}$ is positive, then this is a right-handed triple in three dimensions and $\overrightarrow{A'B'} \times \overrightarrow{A'C'}$ points upward. Thus $ad - bc > 0$, making the determinant equal to $+1$. So the orientation of $\triangle A'B'C'$ is the same as the orientation of $\triangle ABC$, confirming that the isometry is direct.

On the other hand, if the angle from $\overrightarrow{A'B'}$ to $\overrightarrow{A'C'}$ is negative, then the right-handed triple will be $\overrightarrow{A'C'}$, $\overrightarrow{A'B'}$, $\overrightarrow{A'C'} \times \overrightarrow{A'B'}$ with the cross product $\overrightarrow{A'C'} \times \overrightarrow{A'B'}$ pointing upward. Therefore, $\overrightarrow{A'B'} \times \overrightarrow{A'C'}$ points downward. This means $ad - bc < 0$, so the determinant equals -1, confirming that the orientation of $\triangle A'B'C'$ is opposite that of $\triangle ABC$.

Here are the two possible patterns for the equation of an isometry:

$$\begin{bmatrix} x' \\ y' \end{bmatrix} = \begin{bmatrix} a & -b \\ b & a \end{bmatrix} \begin{bmatrix} x \\ y \end{bmatrix} + \begin{bmatrix} e \\ f \end{bmatrix}$$

for direct isometries, and

$$\begin{bmatrix} x' \\ y' \end{bmatrix} = \begin{bmatrix} a & -b \\ -b & -a \end{bmatrix} \begin{bmatrix} x \\ y \end{bmatrix} + \begin{bmatrix} e \\ f \end{bmatrix}$$

for opposite isometries. In either situation, we must have $a^2 + b^2 = 1$ so that distances are preserved by the transformation. You should also verify that the sign of each determinant matches its orientation.

USING MATRICES IN PROOFS

How can we be certain that the patterns just mentioned actually represent isometries? The isometries in the activities seem to fit these equations, but will every such matrix equation represent an isometry? Recall the definition from Chapter 8.

DEFINITION 9.1   A function f on the plane is an *isometry* if it is one-to-one, onto, and preserves distances.

Using techniques from linear algebra, you should be able to prove that matrix functions such as those in our patterns are indeed one-to-one and onto. This is what is meant by calling them *transformations* of the plane. We still have to resolve the question of preserving distances. Let us look first at the first pattern, the one for direct isometries.

Here are two points: $\begin{bmatrix} x_1 \\ y_1 \end{bmatrix}$ and $\begin{bmatrix} x_2 \\ y_2 \end{bmatrix}$. The distance between them is, of course,

$$\text{distance} = \sqrt{(x_1 - x_2)^2 + (y_1 - y_2)^2}.$$

Now we need to calculate the image of each point and compute the distance between their image points. The first point is transformed by the matrix equation in this way:

$$\begin{bmatrix} a & -b \\ b & a \end{bmatrix} \begin{bmatrix} x_1 \\ y_1 \end{bmatrix} + \begin{bmatrix} e \\ f \end{bmatrix} = \begin{bmatrix} ax_1 - by_1 + e \\ bx_1 + ay_1 + f \end{bmatrix}.$$

Similarly, the image of the second point is $\begin{bmatrix} ax_2 - by_2 + e \\ bx_2 + ay_2 + f \end{bmatrix}$.

Now calculate the distance between these images:

$$\sqrt{((ax_1 - by_1 + e) - (ax_2 - by_2 + e))^2 + ((bx_1 + ay_1 + f) - (bx_2 + ay_2 + f))^2}.$$

There is more than one way to do the algebra; we will leave the details for the exercises. It is important that $a^2 + b^2 = 1$. Eventually, this simplifies to the same value for distance as calculated earlier.

In Chapter 8, we found that one of the characteristics of an isometry is whether it has any *fixed points*. We observed that a rotation has a fixed point at the center of rotation, and a reflection has a line of fixed points along the mirror line. Translations and glide reflections have no fixed points. With matrix equations, we can now prove these statements.

Consider a nonzero rotation around the origin. The matrix equation of this transformation is

$$\begin{bmatrix} x' \\ y' \end{bmatrix} = \begin{bmatrix} \cos(\theta) & -\sin(\theta) \\ \sin(\theta) & \cos(\theta) \end{bmatrix} \begin{bmatrix} x \\ y \end{bmatrix}.$$

For a fixed point, $\begin{bmatrix} x' \\ y' \end{bmatrix} = \begin{bmatrix} x \\ y \end{bmatrix}$. So we need to solve the equation

$$\begin{bmatrix} x \\ y \end{bmatrix} = \begin{bmatrix} \cos(\theta) & -\sin(\theta) \\ \sin(\theta) & \cos(\theta) \end{bmatrix} \begin{bmatrix} x \\ y \end{bmatrix}.$$

This is equivalent to the following system, which we must solve for the variable θ:

$$\begin{cases} x = x\cos(\theta) - y\sin(\theta) \\ y = x\sin(\theta) + y\cos(\theta). \end{cases}$$

Solving the first equation for y and substituting into the second equation leads us to the statement $(2 - 2\cos(\theta))x = 0$. If the first factor $(2 - 2\cos(\theta)) = 0$ then $\theta = 0$, and we have the identity isometry, for which every point is fixed. If $\theta \neq 0$, however, x is 0 and the equations say that y must be 0 also. Hence, the origin, the center of the rotation, is the only fixed point.

Other questions about fixed points will appear in the exercises.

There are many propositions about composition of isometries that can be proven by matrix calculations. For instance, what sort of isometry is produced by a composition of two reflections? This depends on whether the mirror lines intersect, and the answers can be proven by matrix calculations. With some facts from linear algebra, we can prove a much more general theorem about composition.

THEOREM 9.2   The composition of two direct isometries is direct. The composition of two opposite isometries is also direct. However, the composition of a direct and an opposite isometry is opposite.

Proof   Suppose the two isometries are represented by the expressions

$$\vec{x}' = M_1\vec{x} + \vec{v}_1$$

$$\vec{x}' = M_2\vec{x} + \vec{v}_2.$$

Here M_1, M_2 are the matrices and $\vec{v}_1, \vec{v}_2$ are the vectors. The composition of these isometries is

$$\vec{x}' = M_2(M_1\vec{x} + \vec{v}_1) + \vec{v}_{12}$$

$$= M_2M_1\vec{x} + (M_2\vec{v}_1 + \vec{v}_2).$$

The quantity $(M_2\vec{v}_1 + \vec{v}_2)$ represents the translation component of the composition. The direct/opposite decision comes solely from the product M_2M_1. Since $det(M_2M_1) = det(M_2)det(M_1)$, the theorem follows by comparing $+$ and $-$ signs.

SIMILARITY TRANSFORMATIONS

From your diagram in Activity 9d, it should be obvious that this transformation is *not* an isometry. It is a legitimate transformation, for it is both one-to-one and onto. However, distances are not preserved. For example, the distance from $A = \begin{bmatrix} 0 \\ 0 \end{bmatrix}$ to $B = \begin{bmatrix} 1 \\ 0 \end{bmatrix}$ is 1, while the distance between their image points, $A' = \begin{bmatrix} 0 \\ 6 \end{bmatrix}$ and $B' = \begin{bmatrix} 3 \\ 2 \end{bmatrix}$, is 5. When we compare other distances in Activity 9, we see this number 5 again: $BC = 2$ and $B'C' = 10$; $CA = CA = \sqrt{5}$ and $C'A' = 5\sqrt{5}$. The transformation increases the length of each of these line segments by a factor of 5.

As you no doubt saw in your diagram, the triangle $\triangle ABC$ is similar to $\triangle A'B'C'$. The image is the same shape as $\triangle ABC$ but is a different size and in a different position. The matrix function of Activity 9 shows the precise relation between the two triangles. This function is called a *similarity*. Similarities behave much like isometries. There are direct similarities and opposite similarities. Some similarities have fixed points, while others do not. The important difference between isometries and similarities is that similarities have a factor that gives the size change.

The pattern for a matrix equation of a similarity is very much like that of an isometry.

$$\begin{bmatrix} x' \\ y' \end{bmatrix} = \begin{bmatrix} a & -b \\ b & a \end{bmatrix} \begin{bmatrix} x \\ y \end{bmatrix} + \begin{bmatrix} e \\ f \end{bmatrix}$$

for direct similarities, and

$$\begin{bmatrix} x' \\ y' \end{bmatrix} = \begin{bmatrix} a & -b \\ -b & -a \end{bmatrix} \begin{bmatrix} x \\ y \end{bmatrix} + \begin{bmatrix} e \\ f \end{bmatrix}$$

for opposite similarities. What is different from isometries is that in a similarity, $a^2 + b^2$ does not have to equal 1.

The equation in Activity 9 fits the pattern for an opposite similarity. We saw that 5 is an important number for this similarity. Suppose we separate a 5 from the matrix as follows:

$$\begin{bmatrix} x' \\ y' \end{bmatrix} = 5 \begin{bmatrix} \frac{3}{5} & -\frac{4}{5} \\ -\frac{4}{5} & -\frac{3}{5} \end{bmatrix} \begin{bmatrix} x \\ y \end{bmatrix} + \begin{bmatrix} 0 \\ 6 \end{bmatrix}.$$

This gives us another way to write the similarity:

$$\begin{bmatrix} x' \\ y' \end{bmatrix} = \begin{bmatrix} \frac{3}{5} & -\frac{4}{5} \\ -\frac{4}{5} & -\frac{3}{5} \end{bmatrix} \left(5 \begin{bmatrix} x \\ y \end{bmatrix} \right) + \begin{bmatrix} 0 \\ 6 \end{bmatrix}.$$

Written this way, the expression shows the two steps of the similarity. The new matrix is an isometry matrix, with its determinant equal to 1. The factor of 5 is the size change. We can understand this similarity as first increasing the sides of triangle $\triangle ABC$ to five times their original size, then performing a glide reflection (i.e., a reflection and a translation).

Here is another interesting observation about this similarity matrix: Its determinant is $-25 = -5^2$. The negative sign, as before, tells us that this is an opposite transformation, one that reverses orientation. The reappearance of 5 is not a coincidence; the size factor affects both dimensions of the plane and thus it causes the area to change by a factor of 25. The factor of 5 affects both rows of the matrix, so it multiplies the determinant twice and causes a change by a factor of 25. (The linear algebra is more technical than that, but this is the general idea. (See [Lay 1997, 201–204] for the details.) This is true for any similarity in the plane; the determinant of its matrix tells the square of the size change.

9.3 EXERCISES

Give clear and complete answers to the following problems and questions. Write your explanations clearly using complete sentences. Include diagrams whenever appropriate.

1. Every isometry for the Euclidean plane can be written in one of the following two patterns.

$$\begin{bmatrix} x' \\ y' \end{bmatrix} = \begin{bmatrix} a & -b \\ b & a \end{bmatrix} \begin{bmatrix} x \\ y \end{bmatrix} + \begin{bmatrix} c \\ d \end{bmatrix}$$

or

$$\begin{bmatrix} x' \\ y' \end{bmatrix} = \begin{bmatrix} a & -b \\ -b & -a \end{bmatrix} \begin{bmatrix} x \\ y \end{bmatrix} + \begin{bmatrix} c \\ d \end{bmatrix}$$

with the requirement that $a^2 + b^2 = 1$. Prove algebraically that the second pattern keeps distances invariant.

2. Write the general matrix equation for a rotation through angle θ around the origin.
   a. What is this matrix if $\theta = 90°$? What is it if $\theta = 180°$?
   b. Find the general matrix equation for the inverse of this rotation.

3. Write the matrix equation for the identity isometry. Is this direct or opposite? Is this a translation? Is it a rotation? Is it a reflection? Is it a glide reflection? Explain why or why not for each answer.

4. Verify that reflection across the line $y = x$ is represented by the equation

$$\begin{bmatrix} x' \\ y' \end{bmatrix} = \begin{bmatrix} 0 & 1 \\ 1 & 0 \end{bmatrix} \begin{bmatrix} x \\ y \end{bmatrix}.$$

5. Here are equations for two translations:

$$T_1\left(\begin{bmatrix} x \\ y \end{bmatrix}\right) = \begin{bmatrix} x \\ y \end{bmatrix} + \begin{bmatrix} a \\ b \end{bmatrix}$$

$$T_2\left(\begin{bmatrix} x \\ y \end{bmatrix}\right) = \begin{bmatrix} x \\ y \end{bmatrix} + \begin{bmatrix} c \\ d \end{bmatrix}.$$

Show that the transformation $(T_1 + T_2)\left(\begin{bmatrix} x \\ y \end{bmatrix}\right)$ is not an isometry.

6. Find matrix equations for
   a. a reflection in the line $x = h$,
   b. a reflection in the line $y = k$.

7. Suppose that the line $y = mx$ has an angle of inclination α. Prove that a reflection in this line is equivalent to a reflection across the x-axis followed by a rotation around the origin through an angle of 2α.

8. a. Prove analytically that two reflections in parallel lines create a translation. (You may assume that the lines are vertical.)
   b. Prove analytically that two reflections in intersecting lines create a rotation. (You may assume that the lines intersect at the origin. The x-axis and an arbitrary line $y = mx$ are good choices.) What is the angle of rotation in this situation?

9. Find a matrix that represents a reflection across the y-axis followed by reflection across the x-axis. Verify that this composition is a rotation about the origin. What is the angle of this rotation?

10. Verify that the matrix equation

$$\begin{bmatrix} x' \\ y' \end{bmatrix} = \begin{bmatrix} 0 & 1 \\ 1 & 0 \end{bmatrix} \begin{bmatrix} x \\ y \end{bmatrix} + \begin{bmatrix} \sqrt{2} \\ \sqrt{2} \end{bmatrix}$$

represents a glide reflection along the diagonal line $y = x$ with a translation of 2 units in the northeast direction.

11. Find a matrix representation for a glide reflection across the line $y = -x$, with a translation by 3 units in a direction parallel to this line.

12. An alternative way to understand a reflection across the line $y = mx$ is by the following three steps: Rotate the line to the horizontal axis; reflect across the horizontal axis; and rotate the

line back to its original position. Use this idea to find a matrix equation for reflection across $y = mx$. Simplify your answer.

13. Triangle A has vertices at $(-1, 2)$, $(3, 4)$, and $(-2, 4)$. Triangle B has vertices at $(3, 1)$, $(7, 3)$, and $(4, -1)$. Create accurate drawings of these triangles. Find an isometry to prove that they are congruent and give the matrix equation for your isometry. Identify the kind of isometry you use.

14. If an isometry has fixed points, they will satisfy the equation $\begin{bmatrix} x' \\ y' \end{bmatrix} = \begin{bmatrix} x \\ y \end{bmatrix}$.
   a. Prove analytically that a nonzero translation has no fixed points.
   b. Prove analytically that a reflection has a line of fixed points. (*Hint*: Use a line through the origin. You may need double-angle formulas from trigonometry.)

15. A nonzero translation will not have fixed points. However, a line parallel to a translation vector will be invariant, meaning that the image of any point on this line will also be on the line. Prove this analytically.

16. Give a simplified expression for the rotation through angle θ around point (h, k). (Follow the hint on page 211.) What does this simplify to if $\theta = 90°$ or if $\theta = 180°$?

17. Pick a point P on the x-axis and a point Q on the y-axis. Consider the following operation: Rotate $90°$ around P, then rotate $90°$ around Q. Find a matrix equation for this composite operation. Then find any fixed points and tell what kind of isometry this is.

18. For two lines ℓ and m, let Ref(ℓ) and Ref(m) stand for the reflections across the lines. We can form two compositions from these: Ref(ℓ) $\circ$ Ref(m) and also Ref(m) $\circ$ Ref(ℓ). When are these compositions equal? Experiment with various lines to find a conjecture, then prove your conjecture analytically.

19. Pick three points P, Q, R. Define the isometry H_P as the half-turn on P, a rotation of $180°$ around P. H_Q and H_R are defined similarly. How does the composition $H_P \circ H_Q \circ H_R$ compare to $H_R \circ H_Q \circ H_P$? Prove your answer analytically.

20. Write a matrix equation for reflection in the line $y - 1 = -2(x - 3)$.

21. It takes three points and their images to completely determine an isometry. Suppose that we know that an isometry g does the following:

$$\begin{bmatrix} 2 \\ 0 \end{bmatrix} \rightarrow \begin{bmatrix} 1 \\ 2 \end{bmatrix} \qquad \begin{bmatrix} 0 \\ -1 \end{bmatrix} \rightarrow \begin{bmatrix} -1 \\ 1 \end{bmatrix}.$$

There are two possibilities for this isometry. Find the matrix equation for each possible isometry, and identify what type of isometry each is.

22. Give an example of two isometries that do not commute. Find the matrix representations of these isometries. Then compute both possible compositions, thus showing analytically that these isometries do not commute.

23. Consider the similarity of Activity 9.
   a. Does this similarity have any fixed points? If so, find them; if not, explain why not.
   b. Find a matrix equation for the inverse of this similarity. Calculate the determinant of the matrix for this inverse and compare this to the determinant you calculated in Activity 9.

24. Suppose that a similarity has two fixed points. Prove that it must be an isometry.

25. Let M represent the matrix of a similarity.
   a. Give a geometric reason to explain why

   $$det(M^{-1}) = \frac{1}{det(M)}.$$

   b. Now give a linear algebra explanation for this.

26. Consider the following equation.

$$\begin{bmatrix} x' \\ y' \\ 1 \end{bmatrix} = \begin{bmatrix} a & b & e \\ c & d & f \\ 0 & 0 & 1 \end{bmatrix} \begin{bmatrix} x \\ y \\ 1 \end{bmatrix}.$$

Explain how all four types of isometry can be represented by this pattern. Discuss the determinant in your explanation. Give a specific example for each type.

Exercises 27 and 28 are especially for future teachers.

27. In *Principles and Standards for School Mathematics*, the National Council of Teachers of Mathematics (NCTM) recommends that "Instructional programs from prekindergarten through grade 12 should enable all students to . . . apply transformations and use symmetry to analyze mathematical situations." In particular, students in grades 9–12 should be able to "understand and represent translations, rotations, and dilations of objects in the plane by using sketches, coordinates, vectors, function notation, and matrices" [NCTM 2000, 308]. Expectations for high school students build directly on experiences these students have in the middle grades. What does this mean for your future students?
   a. Study the Geometry Standard for Grades 9–12. What prerequisite content knowledge and skills do students need to acquire in the middle grades in order to continue their study of transformational geometry in high school? Cite specific examples.
   b. Study the Geometry Standard for Grades 6–8. What content knowledge and skills are students expected to learn in the middle grades? Find some mathematics textbooks for middle school grade levels. How are the NCTM recommendations regarding transformational geometry implemented in these textbooks? Cite specific examples.
   c. Find some high school mathematics textbooks. How are the NCTM recommendations regarding vector and matrix transformations of objects in the plane implemented in these textbooks? Cite specific examples.
   d. Write a report in which you present and critique what you learn. Your report should include your responses to parts (a)–(c).

28. Study the Geometry Standard for one particular grade band. Design several classroom activities involving transformations of objects in the plane that would be appropriate for students in that grade band. These activities should engage students in using a variety of representations of

geometric motions. Write a report explaining how the activities you design reflect both the NCTM recommendations and what you are learning in this course.

Reflect on what you have learned in this chapter.

29. Review the main ideas of this chapter. Describe, in your own words, the concepts you have studied and what you have learned about them. What are the important ideas? How do they fit together? Which concepts were easy for you? Which were hard?

30. Reflect on the learning environment for this course.

   a. Describe aspects of the learning environment that helped you understand the main ideas in this chapter. Which activities did you like? Which stretched you beyond your comfort zone? Why?

   b. How will you use what you are learning about your own learning of geometry in setting up the learning environment in your own future classroom?

9.4 CHAPTER OVERVIEW

In this chapter, we combined the notion of coordinates with that of isometry. This allowed us to represent geometric functions in algebraic form, specifically in matrix notation. Matrix tools provide new ways to understand isometry and similarity.

Translation is represented by adding a vector. Rotation around the origin is represented by multiplying by a certain pattern of matrix. Reflection in a line through the origin is also represented by matrix multiplication. Thus, isometries can be represented as functions in matrix notation.

Composition of isometries can now be accomplished through matrix operations. Multiplying matrices is an important part of this process. Composition allows us to find matrix expressions for more general rotations and reflections, as well as for glide reflections.

After a variety of examples, we saw two general patterns for isometry in the plane:

$$\begin{bmatrix} x' \\ y' \end{bmatrix} = \begin{bmatrix} a & -b \\ b & a \end{bmatrix} \begin{bmatrix} x \\ y \end{bmatrix} + \begin{bmatrix} c \\ d \end{bmatrix}$$

or

$$\begin{bmatrix} x' \\ y' \end{bmatrix} = \begin{bmatrix} a & -b \\ -b & -a \end{bmatrix} \begin{bmatrix} x \\ y \end{bmatrix} + \begin{bmatrix} c \\ d \end{bmatrix}$$

with the requirement that $a^2 + b^2 = 1$. The first pattern is for direct isometries and the second pattern is for opposite isometries.

The determinant of the matrix in the matrix expression for an isometry tells whether it is direct or opposite by its sign. A determinant of $+1$ indicates a direct isometry, while -1 indicates an opposite isometry.

Matrix expressions offer powerful tools for proofs that involve isometries, proofs such as verifying that two triangles are congruent or finding the result of a composition of isometries.

A *similarity* is a transformation in two steps: a size change followed by an isometry. Similarities have many features in common with isometries, including the distinction between direct and opposite. Matrix representations are useful for studying geometric similarity as well.

CHAPTER TEN

Symmetry in the Plane

In Chapter 8, we studied congruence by looking at ways to move one figure on top of another figure. Congruent figures are identical in the measure of their sides, the arrangement of their vertices, the measure of their angles, and so on. If two figures are congruent, the only difference between them is the position of the figures. Using isometries, we can change the position of one figure to make it correspond to its congruent partner; that is, an isometry can move one congruent figure on top of its partner.

We saw that there are four types of isometries in the plane: *translations, rotations, reflections,* and *glide reflections.* We also saw that the composition of two isometries will again be an isometry. Recall that translations and rotations are *direct isometries* and reflections and glide reflections are *opposite isometries.*

The *identity isometry* leaves every point exactly where it is. Because of the identity isometry, any geometric figure is congruent to itself. However, many geometric figures are congruent to themselves in more interesting ways. The purpose of this chapter is to study the ways in which a figure can be self-congruent and to use these self-congruences to classify figures. As we do so, we again will encounter the concept of a mathematical *group.*

Give clear and complete answers to the following problems and questions. Write your explanations clearly using complete sentences, and including diagrams whenever appropriate. Save your work for each activity, as sometimes later work builds on earlier work. It will be helpful to read ahead into the chapter as you work on these activities.

1. Construct a square. The objective of this activity is to find all ways in which this square can be congruent to itself.
   a. Construct a vector near your square. Use the **Translate by Vector** tool to translate the square by this vector. (It may be easier to keep track of things if you label the vertices or if you make the image a different color from the original square.) Vary the vector until the image of the square lies on top of the original square. Find all ways in which this can be done.
   b. Construct the center of your square. Create an angle near the square and measure your angle. Use **Rotate around Point** to rotate the square around its center. (For the angle of rotation, specify the symbol for the measured angle. You should be able to vary the angle and see the image move.) Vary the angle so that the image of the square lies on top of the original square. Find all ways in which this can be done.
   c. Draw a line near your square. Use **Reflect about Line** to construct the reflection of the square in this line. Then vary the position and direction of the mirror line so that the image of the square lies on top of the original square. Find all the ways this can be done.
   d. Look back at your results in this activity. Summarize all the ways in which a square can be congruent to itself. You may use diagrams, symbols, or words to do so.

2. Some terminology: A *figure* is a set of points in the plane. Typically, a figure is a familiar object such as a square or a triangle, but any collection of points will do.

   A *symmetry* of a particular figure S is an isometry f for which $f(S) = S$. This means that the image of the figure lies on top of the original figure. It does not mean that each point is in the same place; the points can shift while the overall figure looks the same, as you saw in Activity 1.

   List the symmetries for each of the figures in Figure 10.1. How are your two lists similar and how are they different?

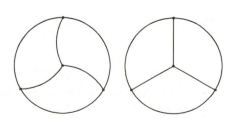

FIGURE 10.1
Figures for Activity 2

3. Each of the symmetries you listed for the second figure in Activity 2 is an isometry, and thus each has an inverse isometry. Are these inverses also symmetries for the second figure? Explain why or why not.

4. Here are the capital letters of the English alphabet, in a *sans serif* font. Sort these letters into disjoint sets so that every element in the same set has the same symmetries.

   A, B, C, D, E, F, G, H, I, J, K, L, M, N, O, P, Q, R, S, T, U, V, W, X, Y, Z

5. Figure 10.2 shows an equilateral triangle. For this activity, you may find it helpful to cut out a paper triangle, label its vertices as in Figure 10.2, and use it to perform the isometries. Be careful when you label the back side of the triangle!

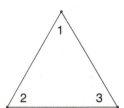

FIGURE 10.2
An Equilateral Triangle

The triangle in Figure 10.2 has six symmetries:

R_0 a rotation through $0°$

R_{120} a rotation through $120°$

R_{240} a rotation through $240°$

V a reflection across a vertical line through the uppermost vertex

L a reflection across a diagonal line through the lower-left vertex

R a reflection across a diagonal line through the lower-right vertex.

Do the following:

a. Sketch the triangle, showing the lines of reflection and the center of rotation.

b. These symmetries can be combined by composition. For instance, $V \circ R_{120} = L$. Complete the following table. (Recall that composition is not commutative!)

	R_0	R_{120}	R_{240}	V	L	R
R_0						
R_{120}						
R_{240}						
V			L			
L						
R						

c. Based on your table, which symmetry is the identity? What is the inverse of each symmetry?

6. A *frieze* is a pattern that is infinite along one line. Wallpaper borders are friezes; they have a pattern that repeats as the border goes around the room. Here is another example of a frieze:

... P P P P P P P P P P P P P P P P P P P P P P P...

This particular frieze has a translation as its only symmetry.

Create at least three more examples of friezes with a different set of symmetries for each of your examples. Mark the initial pattern used to create each frieze and tell what symmetries each example has. (*Hint*: It may help to use a Cartesian coordinate system and a square grid.)

7. A pattern that is infinite in two directions is often called a *wallpaper pattern*. Figure 10.3 shows a portion of a wallpaper pattern based on reflections in both the vertical and the horizontal directions. Notice the darker scalene triangle that is the basis for the pattern.

Using a Cartesian coordinate system and a grid, construct vertical and horizontal lines to divide the plane into squares, as done in Figure 10.3. The **Snap to Grid** option will be helpful for this, but be sure to turn it off once your lines have been drawn. (**Snap to Grid** is in a menu on the Style Bar in the Graphics pane.) In one of the squares, create a nonsymmetric figure. (This does not have to be a triangle.)

   a. Using only translations, create a wallpaper pattern based on your figure.

   b. Using reflections in one direction and translations in another, create a wallpaper pattern based on your figure.

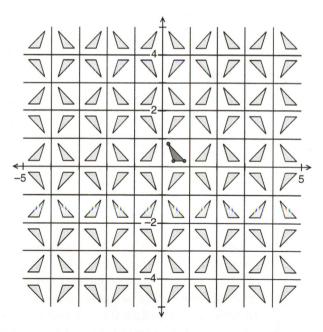

FIGURE 10.3
A Wallpaper Pattern

8. A *tiling* of the plane is a finite collection of polygon patterns that can be assembled to fill the plane completely. Sometimes this collection can consist of a single shape repeated over and over.

Draw a quadrilateral. Use this to begin a tiling of the plane. Show at least sixteen copies of the quadrilateral in your picture and mark the original quadrilateral. Print your tiling. Then vary the original quadrilateral to create a new tiling and print that one also. (Coloring the regions can enhance your pictures.)

9. A polygon is called *regular* if all its sides are the same length and all its angles are congruent. The equilateral triangle and the square are familiar examples of regular polygons.

   Can a plane be tiled by equilateral triangles? Can a plane be tiled by squares? By regular pentagons? By regular hexagons? In each case, either draw an example or explain why it cannot be done.

10.2 DISCUSSION

The term *figure* is not a precise one in geometry. For our purposes, a figure can be any collection of points in the plane: finite or infinite, bounded or unbounded, solid or hollow, etc. For instance, Figure 10.4 shows three figures, all based on a familiar constellation.

FIGURE 10.4
The Constellation Orion the Hunter

The first figure of Orion is a finite collection of points, arranged in a way that suggests the shape of a hunter. The second figure consists of points and line segments, and the shape can be seen more clearly. (Do you see the belt and the sword?) The third figure shows the hunter and how the stars fit within his shape. Any of these figures could be studied geometrically.

In Activity 6, we used another instance of imprecise language. The phrase "infinite along one line" is intended to suggest a pattern that continues indefinitely in one particular direction, without ever coming to an end. However, "infinite" is the wrong term to use. After all, the second figure of Orion contains an infinite number of points on its line segments. The proper term for a pattern that extends indefinitely is *unbounded*. This means that there is no boundary to stop the pattern. The figures for Orion are *bounded*, for we can draw a circle around any of them to act as a boundary.

SYMMETRIES

Activity 1 asks you to find various ways in which a square can be congruent to itself. In a trivial sense, the identity isometry does this; $i(square) = square$ because $i(P) = P$ for every point P. No doubt you discovered some more interesting ways to have $f(square) = square$. One way is to use a rotation of 180° around the center of the square. This isometry will produce an image identical to the original square, not only in shape but also in location. This does not, however, mean that each point is in its original position. For instance, this rotation moves the upper-right vertex to the lower-left corner. Overall, however, the rotated image of the figure uses precisely the same points as the original figure. This 180° rotation is one way in which the square is self-congruent. There are two other rotations as well as four reflections that show self-congruence. Thus, a square is self-congruent in eight ways. This demonstrates that a square is a very symmetric figure.

DEFINITION 10.1   A *symmetry* of a figure S is an isometry f for which $f(S) = S$.

If S is the domain of an isometry, the notation $f(S) = S$ means that the range $f(S)$ is exactly the same set of points as the domain. Individual points do not have to be fixed, but the overall set will be.

The figures in Activity 2 share some symmetries: the identity (of course), a rotation of 120°, and a rotation of 240°. The second figure has three additional symmetries, reflections across certain lines. Thus, the second figure with its straight segments has more symmetry than the first figure with its curved segments.

The regular polygons are very symmetric figures. (See Figure 10.5.) Each regular polygon has rotations and reflections as its symmetries. How many symmetries of each type are there for a regular n-gon?

A circle is an extremely symmetric figure. Which rotations are symmetries for the circle? Which reflections?

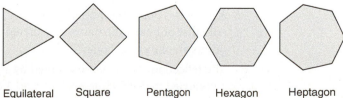

FIGURE 10.5
Some Regular Polygons

Equilateral triangle   Square   Pentagon   Hexagon   Heptagon

GROUPS OF SYMMETRIES

In Chapter 8 we saw that the set of isometries on the plane, together with the operation of composition, forms a mathematical structure called a *group*. This requires that four properties must be satisfied by the set and its operation: closure, associativity, identity, and inverse.

DEFINITION 10.2   A *group* is a set G together with a binary operation $\circ$ such that

- For any two elements x, y of G, $x \circ y$ is in G (the *closure* property).
- For any elements x, y, z of G, $x \circ (y \circ z) = (x \circ y) \circ z$ (the *associative* property).
- There is an element i of G so that $i \circ x = x \circ i = x$ (the *identity* property).
- For any element x of G, there is an element x^{-1} also in G so that $x \circ x^{-1} = x^{-1} \circ x = i$ (the *inverse* property).

The operation for a group can be addition, multiplication, or some other operation. The operation must be *binary*, meaning that the operation combines only two elements at a time. The difficulty is knowing what to do with expressions such as $x \circ y \circ z$. Should it be computed at $x \circ (y \circ z)$ or as $(x \circ y) \circ z$? This is why the associative property is important; it says that we can pair the elements in either way, and still get the same result. The symbol $\circ$ in the definition was chosen to remind you of composition of functions, because that is the operation we use for isometries in general and for symmetries in particular.

An important fact about symmetries is that the set of symmetries for any figure will be a group. Activity 3 is a small step toward proving this. The full proof is not difficult and will appear in the exercises.

Notice that the definition of group says nothing about commutativity. Composition of functions is seldom commutative. A few special combinations of functions commute, but the huge majority do not. This is true for isometries and symmetries as well. In Activity 5, for instance, you were told that $V \circ R_{120} = L$. You should have found that $R_{120} \circ V = R$.

Calculating these compositions can be confusing. It may help to label the three vertices on the equilateral triangle, as in Figure 10.2, and then to write each symmetry in its *cycle notation*. Here is an example:

> The rotation of 120° can be represented by $R_{120} = (1\ 2\ 3)$. The notation $(1\ 2\ 3)$ denotes the cycle $1 \rightarrow 2 \rightarrow 3 \rightarrow 1$, and tells us that the function R_{120} carries point 1 to point 2, point 2 to point 3, and point 3 to point 1. All other points of the figure are carried along also, but these three points are the critical ones.
>
> The reflection V can be represented by $V = (1)(2\ 3)$. This says that point 1 is carried to itself while points 2 and 3 change places. For the composition, we can write
>
> $$V \circ R_{120} = (1)(2\ 3) \circ (1\ 2\ 3).$$

Observe that the transformation that we applied first, R_{120}, appears as the *rightmost* transformation in this expression. Recall that V and R_{120} are functions being applied to points in the plane. $V \circ R_{120}$ is thus a composition of functions.

If P is a point in the plane, we can calculate $V \circ R_{120}(P)$. This can also be written as $V(R_{120}(P))$, showing that we work from the inside outward. That is, the point P is the input to the transformation R_{120}, and the output of this transformation (a point) is the input to the transformation V. The final output (again a point) is the result of these two steps: first applying R_{120} to the point P, and then applying the transformation V to its result.

To simplify a composition given in cycle notation, start at the right and see what happens to each of the points. For example, in the composition $(1)(2\ 3) \circ (1\ 2\ 3)$, point 1 goes to point 2, which then goes to point 3. We can begin to write this as $(1\ 3\ \ldots)$. Now, what happens to point 3? It is carried to point 1 and then left alone. So we close off the cycle, thus: $(1\ 3)$. Point 2 remains; it is carried to point 3, which goes back to point 2. The simplified composition is therefore written as $(1\ 3)(2)$. From the picture, we can see that this result says to interchange points 1 and 3 while keeping point 2 fixed. This is the reflection L.

In reverse order, the composition is

$$R_{120} \circ V = (1\ 2\ 3) \circ (1)(2\ 3) = (1\ 2)(3) = R.$$

Look at the group table you made for the symmetries of an equilateral triangle in Activity 5. There are six symmetries involved; which one is the identity? It is somewhat traditional to place the identity in the first row and the first column of a group table, and this row and column are easy to complete. Now look at the second row of your table; how many different symmetries appear in this row? Is this true in the other rows? What about the columns?

We hope you observed in Activity 5 that every row of the group table contains all six symmetries, and so does every column. In other words, each element of a finite group will appear exactly once in each row and once in each column. This is a very useful fact, and it is not difficult to prove. Suppose that two entries in the row for element a are equal, specifically the entries in the columns for b and for c. This means that

$$a \circ b = a \circ c$$

for certain elements a, b, c. Since a has an inverse, we can calculate

$$a^{-1} \circ a \circ b = a^{-1} \circ a \circ c,$$

and see that $b = c$. Thus, the two equal entries are, in fact, in the same column and must be the same entry! This implies that the elements in a row are all different, and since the number of entries equals the number of elements, every element must be used. A similar proof shows that each element of a group will appear exactly once in each column. These facts can greatly reduce your work when completing a group table.

CLASSIFYING FIGURES BY THEIR SYMMETRIES

In Activity 5, you completed a group table for the symmetries of an equilateral triangle. Each figure in Activity 2 has its own set of symmetries. The group table for one of these is exactly the same as that for an equilateral triangle. (Which one?) When two sets have the same group table, we say that the groups are *isomorphic*.

A set of symmetries for a figure with the operation of composition forms the *symmetry group* of the figure. This is true for the equilateral triangle, for each of the figures in Figure 10.1, and for the letters of the alphabet in Activity 4. Each letter has a corresponding symmetry group. However, these twenty-six letters represent only four symmetry groups. There is the group consisting of just the identity isometry; this is represented by F, G, and so on. There is the group containing the identity and one other rotation; this is represented by N, S, and Z. The group with the identity and one reflection goes with A, B, and lots of other letters. The letters H, I, and X have the largest symmetry group, and hence have the most symmetry. What symmetries does this group contain?

Though the symmetry groups for the alphabet are small groups, they illustrate the two basic types of symmetry groups. One type of symmetry group is the *cyclic group C_n*. This group contains only rotations. The name comes from the fact that every member of the group is a power of the smallest rotation in the group, and these powers occur in a cycle. For instance, the left figure of Activity 2 has R_{120} as its smallest (nontrivial) rotation. If we take powers of this rotation, we get

$$R_{120}^1 = R_{120}$$

$$R_{120}^2 = R_{240}$$

$$R_{120}^3 = R_{360} = R_0$$

$$R_{120}^4 = R_{480} = R_{120}$$

and so on. Continuing the list of powers will not create any new rotations. The cycle is of length 3 and the symmetry group of this figure is C_3. (In this situation, the powers of R_{240} also create a cycle of length 3 so we could use R_{240} to generate the same symmetry group. This is not true in general.)

The right figure of Activity 2 has these three rotations, and it also has three reflections. Its symmetry group is called D_3, a *dihedral group*. The term dihedral refers to the two sides of a reflection line. Notice that the dihedral group D_3 has six elements, half of which are rotations and the other half of which are reflections. So D_3 contains C_3 as a subgroup. This is true in general; D_n has twice as many elements as C_n, and D_n contains C_n as a subgroup. (This statement needs a proof, of course. You will be asked to develop a proof for it in the exercises.)

A major theorem about symmetry groups is credited to Leonardo da Vinci, who discovered it during his architectural work [Bix 1994, 134].

THEOREM 10.1   **Leonardo's Theorem**   A finite symmetry group for a figure in the plane must be either the cyclic group C_n or the dihedral group D_n.

This theorem says that the size of the symmetry group can vary, but that there are only two options for its type: symmetry based solely on rotations or symmetry with both rotations and reflections. The figures of Activity 2 are typical examples of these two types.

To prove Leonardo's Theorem, we need a preliminary result [Sibley 1998, 185–186].

LEMMA 10.1   A finite symmetry group has a point that is fixed for every one of its symmetries.

Proof of Lemma 10.1   We must be clear about the meaning of this statement. The lemma is saying that every symmetry of the figure fixes the same point P. So we must locate P and then, no matter which symmetry we choose, we must prove that $f(P) = P$.

The proof will use coordinates. Suppose the finite symmetry group is $\{f_1, f_2, \ldots, f_n\}$, and for convenience let f_1 be the identity. Pick any point P_1 and calculate

$$f_1(P_1) = P_1$$

$$f_2(P_1) = P_2$$

$$f_1(P_1) = P_3$$

$$\vdots$$

$$f_n(P_1) = P_n.$$

Form the new point

$$P = \frac{P_1 + P_2 + \cdots + P_n}{n}.$$

P is called the *center of gravity* for this collection of points.

Now, $f_1(P) = P$ because f_1 is the identity isometry. What happens for $f_2(P)$? First think about what f_2 does to the list of points.

$$f_2(P_1) = f_2(f_1(P_1)) = (f_2 \circ f_1)(P_1)$$

$$f_2(P_2) = f_2(f_2(P_1)) = (f_2 \circ f_2)(P_1)$$

$$f_2(P_3) = f_2(f_3(P_1)) = (f_2 \circ f_3)(P_1)$$

$$\vdots$$

$$f_2(P_n) = f_2(f_n(P_1)) = (f_2 \circ f_n)(P_1)$$

Earlier we proved that the compositions $(f_2 \circ f_1)$, $(f_2 \circ f_2)$, $\ldots$, $(f_2 \circ f_n)$ are all different from each other. This list of compositions fills the f_2 row of the group table with n different results. Therefore, the list $f_2(P_1), f_2(P_2), \ldots, f_2(P_n)$ contains all of the original n points, though in a different order. Calculating the center of gravity for the points $f_2(P_1), f_2(P_2), \ldots, f_2(P_n)$ is thus the same as calculating the original center of gravity P. So the center of gravity remains fixed for f_2, that is, $f_2(P) = P$.

The same reasoning works for $f_3, \ldots, f_n$, showing that this particular point P is fixed for every symmetry in this group.

Since the members of a finite symmetry group have at least one fixed point, they must be either rotations or reflections. Even the identity falls into these categories, for the identity isometry can be interpreted as a rotation of $0°$. Later we will examine symmetry groups that include translations and glide reflections. Because of this lemma, we know that these will be infinite groups.

Proof of Theorem 10.1   Let us start small and work upward.

Case 1   Suppose the finite symmetry group has a single rotation—which must be the identity—and has no reflections. This is the cyclic group C_1.

Case 2   Suppose the finite symmetry group has a single rotation and has one reflection. This is the dihedral group D_1.

Case 3   Suppose the finite symmetry group has a single rotation and has more than one reflection. Let us focus our attention on two of the reflections. Since these two reflections share a fixed point, their mirror lines intersect. Recall that the composition of two reflections in intersecting lines is a rotation. This cannot be the identity rotation (*Why not?*) so this case is impossible.

Case 4   Suppose the finite symmetry group has more than one rotation and has no reflections. Let R_α be the rotation with the smallest angle, modulo $360°$. It turns out that every other rotation in this group can be generated by a power of R_α. To prove this claim, assume that R_θ is a rotation in the symmetry group but that R_θ is not a power of R_α. This means that θ is not a multiple of α. Consequently, θ lies between two consecutive multiples of α. Expressed algebraically, there is a nonnegative integer k so that $k\alpha < \theta < (k + 1)\alpha$. Then $0 < (\theta - k\alpha) < \alpha$. However, having R_θ in the symmetry group means that the rotation $R_{(\theta - k\alpha)}$ is in the group, since $R_{(\theta - k\alpha)} = R_\theta \circ (R_\alpha^{-1})^k$. This contradicts the choice of α as the smallest positive angle for a rotation, and shows that θ must be a multiple of α.
Let n be the smallest power of R_α that equals the identity. This symmetry group is the cyclic group C_n.

Case 5   Suppose the finite symmetry group has more than one rotation and has at least one reflection. Call this reflection F_1 and once again let R_α be the rotation with the smallest angle, with $R_\alpha^n = identity$. Notice that $R_\alpha^j \circ F_1$ is an opposite isometry, so it must be a reflection. Every choice of j produces a reflection, and every choice produces a different reflection. (Why is this true? Think about a column in a group table.)
Are these all of the reflections? Assume F_2 is a reflection not equal to F_1. The reflection F_2 has the same fixed point as F_1, and their mirror lines intersect there, so the composition $F_2 \circ F_1$ is a rotation, say $R_{k\alpha}$. Then $F_2 = R_{k\alpha} \circ F_1$, which is already accounted for.
Thus, there are n reflections in addition to the n rotations. This is the dihedral group D_n.

Finite symmetry groups are very common. As Leonardo noticed, architects often use small dihedral groups such as D_1 and D_2 when designing a building. Can you find some examples on or near your campus? Some very interesting buildings use other symmetry groups. The Pentagon in Washington, D.C., uses D_5. (See Figure 10.6.) The famous Opera House in Sydney, Australia, has C_1 as its symmetry group when considered as a whole, though each individual component of the building uses D_1. (See Figure 10.7.)

FIGURE 10.6
The Pentagon in Washington, D.C., an Example of D_5 Symmetry
(Frontpage/Shutterstock.com)

Examples of symmetry appear frequently in nature. The leaves of trees usually have D_1 as their symmetry group. Maple leaves are familiar examples. The leaves of the poplar tree are strikingly symmetric. However, the sassafras tree is an exception; its asymmetric leaves have C_1 as their symmetry group. Flowers may have D_4, D_5, or even D_6 as a symmetry group. Snowflakes are famous for having D_6 symmetry.

Commercial logos often will exhibit symmetry. It is fun to look through the Yellow Pages and classify the logos by their symmetries. Hub caps on cars are another interesting source of finite symmetry groups.

FIGURE 10.7
The Opera House in Sydney,
Australia, an Example of D_1
Symmetry
(John Carnemolla/Getty Images)

FRIEZES AND SYMMETRY

The symmetry groups discussed so far have been finite groups. Furthermore, the figures they describe have been *bounded*, meaning that these figures do not continue indefinitely. (A more technical definition for bounded says that the figure can be surrounded by a circle.) Also, these finite symmetry groups have used only rotations and reflections. There is an easy explanation for why translations have not been used. If a figure has a translation T as one of its symmetries, then T^2, T^3, etc., must all be symmetries of the figure also. (The inverse T^{-1} and all its powers must be symmetries too.) Thus, the figure must be unbounded in the direction of the translation and the symmetry group will be infinite.

Let us look more closely at this situation. Suppose that a pattern has translations as symmetries and that all its translation symmetries use parallel vectors. This sort of pattern is called a *frieze*. A frieze will be infinite along a single line parallel to the vectors of its translations. Frieze patterns are often seen in architecture, as ornamentation along the top of a building.

Activity 6 gave a simple example of a frieze. This frieze uses the letter P as its base pattern and has translations as its only symmetries. Other letters suggest other types of patterns, such as these three:

$$\ldots\ \text{N N N N N N N N N N N N N N N N N N N N N N N}\ \ldots$$

$$\ldots\ \text{W W W W W W W W W W W W W W W W W W W W}\ \ldots$$

$$\ldots\ \text{X X X X X X X X X X X X X X X X X X X X X}\ \ldots$$

The N pattern has both translations and 180° rotations in its set of symmetries. The W pattern has translations and reflections across vertical lines. The X pattern is a busy one: it has translations, 180° rotations, reflections in vertical lines, and a reflection in a horizontal line. The X pattern also has glide reflections, formed by the composition of the horizontal reflection and the translations.

Figure 10.8 shows some more examples of friezes. Try to identify the symmetries of each.

Notice that a frieze pattern follows a line, which we can call the *midline* of the pattern. For convenience, assume that the midline is horizontal.

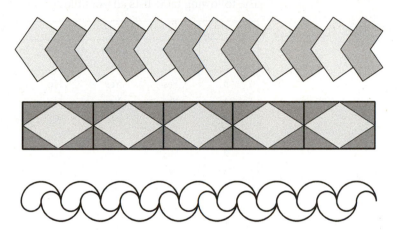

FIGURE 10.8
Examples of Friezes

THEOREM 10.2   The only possible symmetries for a frieze pattern are horizontal translations along the midline, rotations of 180° around points on the midline, reflections in vertical lines perpendicular to the midline, a reflection in the horizontal midline, and glide reflections using the midline.

Proof   [Sibley 1998, 191] The midline must be fixed by any symmetry of the frieze. Now consider what various isometries would do to the midline. Translations that are not parallel to this midline change the position of the midline. Rotations that are not 180° or 0° change the inclination of the midline. Rotations of 180° that are not centered on the midline produce a line parallel to but different from the midline. Reflections in a line that is not parallel or perpendicular to the midline change the inclination of the line. Reflections in a horizontal line other than the midline change the position of the midline. The same is true for glide reflections in other horizontal lines. Thus, we have eliminated all possibilities except those listed in the theorem.

By definition, any frieze will have an infinite number of translational symmetries along its midline. We can use the other possible symmetries to classify and count the frieze groups.

THEOREM 10.3   There exist exactly seven symmetry groups for friezes.

Proof   Since all friezes have translations, let us consider the other types of symmetries and the various combinations of symmetries. We will see that many of these combinations cannot occur. We will use the following abbreviations:

- H is the reflection in the horizontal midline.
- V is a reflection in a vertical line.
- R is a rotation of 180° about a center on the midline.
- G is a glide reflection using the midline.

The following table lists all possible combinations:

	H	V	R	G	Result
1.	Yes	Yes	Yes	Yes	X pattern
2.	Yes	Yes	Yes	No	not possible
3.	Yes	Yes	No	Yes	not possible
4.	Yes	Yes	No	No	not possible
5.	Yes	No	Yes	Yes	not possible
6.	Yes	No	Yes	No	not possible
7.	Yes	No	No	Yes	E pattern
8.	Yes	No	No	No	not possible
9.	No	Yes	Yes	Yes	VΛ pattern
10.	No	Yes	Yes	No	not possible
11.	No	Yes	No	Yes	not possible
12.	No	Yes	No	No	W pattern
13.	No	No	Yes	Yes	not possible
14.	No	No	Yes	No	Z pattern
15.	No	No	No	Yes	Γ L pattern
16.	No	No	No	No	P pattern

In this table, we have shown seven frieze patterns, each having a different combination of symmetries. Why are there no others? Think about some of the possible compositions. If a frieze has the horizontal reflection H and we compose that with a translation along the midline, the result is G, a glide reflection. This eliminates options 2, 4, 6, and 8. If a frieze has H and has vertical reflections, the compositions $H \circ V$ are 180° rotations (because the composition of two such reflections is direct and is not the identity). This eliminates option 3 (and 4 again). The composition $G \circ R$ is opposite so is either H or V. However, the upper half of the pattern will end up on top again, so the composition must equal V. This eliminates option 13 (and 5 again). Composing $V \circ R$ equals either H or G, depending on whether or not the mirror for V passes through the center for R. Either result eliminates option 10. The composition $G \circ V$ is direct, so equals either R or a translation. However, the upper half of the pattern ends up on the bottom this time, so the composition must equal R. This eliminates option 11 (and 3 again). Therefore, we are left with only options 1, 7, 9, 12, 14, 15, and 16, and we have shown friezes to match each of these possibilities.

WALLPAPER SYMMETRY

Allowing translations as symmetries creates patterns that must be unbounded. The friezes have translational symmetries along one line, with all the translation vectors in the same direction. Activity 7 introduces the possibility of translational symmetry in more than one direction. Such a pattern will, of course, use the entire plane. For obvious reasons, these are called *wallpaper patterns*. Translations are not the only possible types of symmetry for wallpaper, however. Rotations, reflections, and glide reflections can occur as well.

If you have ever looked at a book of wallpaper samples, or at the patterns on wrapping paper, you may have noticed that 90° angles are not the only patterns used. It is quite common to see patterns utilizing 60° and 120° rotations. An important fact about these patterns is the following, which we will not prove.

THEOREM 10.4 **The Crystallographic Restriction**   The minimal angle of rotation for a wallpaper symmetry is 60°, 90°, 120°, 180°, or 360°. All other rotation angles for a symmetry must be multiples of the minimal angle for that pattern [Sibley 1998, 194].

This theorem arose in the study of crystals. It can also be seen in the network of cracks in drying mud; the cracks always occur at angles of 90° or 120° [Shorlin *et al.* 2000].

How many symmetry groups are there for wallpaper patterns? The proof is more complicated than that for the frieze groups; see [Bix 1994] for a full treatment, including the classification scheme used by crystallographers. We will merely give the answer.

THEOREM 10.5   There are exactly seventeen wallpaper groups.

The Alhambra is a Moorish palace built in Spain during the 13th and 14th centuries. It is well known among mathematicians for the elaborate tiling patterns on its walls. All seventeen wallpaper groups are represented in the Alhambra.

The study of crystals is concerned with symmetry in three dimensions, not just two. The three-dimensional *crystallographic groups* describe the possible symmetries in 3-D. There are 230 groups for unbounded symmetry in three dimensions. It is possible to study symmetry in four, five, and even higher dimensions by using the same ideas of isometry and symmetry group. For instance, it has been proven that in four dimensions, there are 4,783 possible symmetry groups for unbounded patterns [Bix 1994, 134].

TILINGS

One method for creating symmetric patterns in the plane is to make a *tiling* of the plane. A tiling is a collection of nonoverlapping polygons, laid edge-to-edge to cover the entire plane. *Edge-to-edge* means that an edge of one polygon must also be an edge of the adjacent polygon. The usual way of stacking bricks, staggered for greater stability, is not a tiling. (It is, however, a *tessellation*.) The hexagonal pattern in a honeycomb is a tiling.

When you ask GeoGebra for a coordinate system and it displays the grid, this collection of squares or rectangles is a tiling. There are a great variety of tilings. Figure 10.9 shows a tiling based on the Greek cross [Wells 1991, 89].

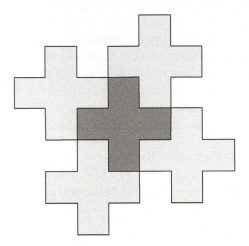

FIGURE 10.9
The Greek Cross Tiling

The artist M. C. Escher is famous for his tilings. He created elaborate interlocking figures that fill the plane: horsemen, fish, birds, etc. In his *Circle Limit* works, he also developed several tilings of the Poincaré disk. To the viewer of these striking works, it appears that the figures shrink to microscopic size as they get nearer to the boundary circle. However, using the unusual method of measuring distance in the Poincaré disk, all the figures in the series of *Circle Limit* illustrations are exactly the same size; that is, they are congruent figures. (See Figure 10.10.)

FIGURE 10.10
A Tiling of the Poincaré Disk
(Fine Art Images/AGE
Fotostock)

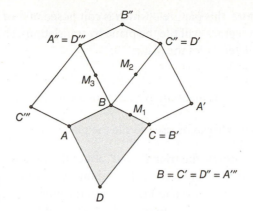

FIGURE 10.11
Any Quadrilateral Will Tile

This will make more sense after you explore hyperbolic geometry in the Poincaré disk. (See Chapter 11.)

Elementary and middle school mathematics classrooms often have a set of pattern blocks. These plastic polygons can be assembled to form multicolored patterns. It is intriguing to watch young children work with these blocks. They often create highly symmetric patterns, without being aware of doing so. These patterns are often the beginnings of tilings.

In an *elementary* tiling, all the regions are congruent to one basic shape [Kay 1994, 246]. The Greek cross tiling is elementary, as is the collection of squares in a grid. In Activity 8, you were asked to create an elementary tiling using a quadrilateral. By rotating and translating your quadrilateral, you should be able to completely fill the computer screen—and, in theory, completely fill the plane.

THEOREM 10.6   Any quadrilateral can be used to create an elementary tiling of the plane.

Proof   We will use the notation of Figure 10.11. Here $ABCD$ is the initial quadrilateral. Let M_1 be the midpoint of the side BC. Rotate $ABCD$ through $180°$ around M_1. This creates the quadrilateral $A'B'C'D'$, where $B' = C$ and $C' = B$. Now let M_2 be the midpoint of $C'D'$ and rotate $A'B'C'D'$ through $180°$ around M_2 to create the quadrilateral $A''B''C''D''$, where $C'' = D'$ and $D'' = C' = B$. Lastly, let M_3 be the midpoint of $D''A''$ and rotate $A''B''C''D''$ through $180°$ around M_2 to create the quadrilateral $A'''B'''C'''D'''$, where $A''' = D'' = C' = B$ and $D''' = A''$. Notice that the four angles at B are congruent to the four different angles of the original quadrilateral. These angles sum to $360°$, so the four quadrilaterals fit together at B without overlapping.

Now, the angle $\angle C'''AD$ is congruent to $\angle B''D'A'$. Also, $\angle C''A''B''$ is congruent to $\angle DCA'$. Thus, we can translate this entire picture by the vector $\overrightarrow{AD'}$ and the image will fit exactly onto the existing copy. This is also true for the inverse translation. In addition, we can translate the entire picture by the vector $\overrightarrow{CA''}$ or by its inverse and the image will fit exactly onto the existing copy.

Therefore, this picture—which is composed of four copies of the original quadrilateral—will tile the plane by translations, showing that the original quadrilateral tiles the plane.

With this theorem, we can prove a similar fact about triangles.

COROLLARY 10.1   Any triangle can be used to tile the plane.

Proof   Rotate the triangle 180° about the midpoint of one of its sides. The resulting figure, two congruent triangles sharing an edge, is a parallelogram. Tile the plane with this parallelogram in the obvious way, then divide each parallelogram to create congruent copies of the original triangle.

This corollary holds for any triangle: scalene, isosceles, equilateral. So we have seen that any triangle and any quadrilateral can be used to make a tiling. A natural question arises: Can a pentagon be used to tile the plane? What about a hexagon, or a polygon with even more sides?

Let's try to answer a more specific question. Which *regular* polygons can be used to tile the plane? Recall that a polygon is regular if all its sides are congruent and all its angles are congruent. The equilateral triangle and the square are familiar examples. A tiling based upon a regular polygon is called a *regular* tiling. In Activity 9, you are asked to think about elementary tilings with regular polygons. Can you fit equilateral triangles together around a vertex without overlapping? What about regular pentagons?

To answer these questions, it is helpful to know the measure of the congruent angles of a regular n-gon. It is easy to derive a formula for this. Pick any point P in the interior of the n-gon and construct segments from P to the vertices. This creates n triangles, each with the angle sum of 180°. The total angle sum for the n triangles would be $180° \cdot n$. However, one angle of each triangle is interior to the polygon; these angles surround the point P. The angle sum of these interior angles should not be included in the total for the n-gon, so we need to subtract 360°. Thus, the angle sum for a regular n-gon is $(n-2)180°$. To find the size of each angle, divide by n.

$$\text{The measure of one angle of a regular } n\text{-gon} = \frac{(n-2)180°}{n}.$$

Now think about putting k of regular n-gons together around a vertex of a tiling. If they are to fit without overlapping, we must have

$$k\frac{(n-2)180°}{n} = 360°.$$

Solving for k gives

$$k = \frac{2n}{n-2}.$$

The value k must be a natural number and cannot be less than 3. (Do you see why not?) By trying some values, this leaves only $n = 3, 4, 6$ as solutions. Therefore, the only regular tilings are those using equilateral triangles, squares, and regular hexagons.

Some fascinating patterns can be created using two or more regular polygons for the tiling. If every vertex in a tiling like this is identical, it is called a *semiregular* tiling. Figure 10.12 shows an example with octagons and squares. There is a well-developed theory of semiregular tilings; we encourage you to read further on this topic.

FIGURE 10.12
A Semiregular Tiling

The *Penrose tiles* are a curious phenomenon. They are named for the physicist Roger Penrose, who discovered them. A pair of tiles is constructed from a rhombus by dividing it into two quadrilaterals called a "kite" and a "dart," as shown in Figure 10.13. In this figure, ϕ represents the *golden ratio* $\frac{1}{2}(1 + \sqrt{5})$. With these shapes, the plane can be tiled in a nonperiodic way. In other words, a Penrose tiling does not have translational symmetry. This is quite different from regular and semiregular tilings, which have lots of translations as symmetries. (See Figures 10.13 and 10.14.)

FIGURE 10.13
The Penrose Tiles
[Data from Wells, David. *The Penguin Dictionary of Curious and Interesting Geometry.* Penguin Books, London. 1991.]

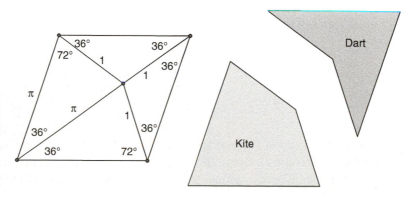

FIGURE 10.14
Examples of Penrose Tilings
[Data from Wells, David. *The Penguin Dictionary of Curious and Interesting Geometry.* Penguin Books, London. 1991.]

10.3 EXERCISES

Give clear and complete answers to the following problems and questions. Write your explanations clearly using complete sentences. Include diagrams whenever appropriate.

1. For each of the sets of letters you found in Activity 4, tell what the symmetry group is.

2. Label the vertices of a square as 1, 2, 3, and 4, going counterclockwise from the upper-right corner. Listed below are some cycles. Decide which of these are legitimate symmetries for your square. For the cycles that are symmetries, tell specifically what each is.

$$(1\ 3)\ (2\ 4)$$

$$(1\ 2\ 3)\ (4)$$

$$(1\ 3)\ (2)\ (4)$$

$$(1\ 4\ 3\ 2)$$

$$(1\ 2)\ (3)\ (4)$$

3. Here are some compositions of symmetries for a square (labeled as in Exercise 2). Compute these compositions. Then identify each symmetry in the composition, and the symmetry of the result.

$$(1\ 4)\ (2\ 3) \circ (1\ 2\ 3\ 4)$$

$$(1\ 2)\ (3\ 4) \circ (1\ 3)\ (2\ 4)$$

$$(1)\ (2\ 4)\ (3) \circ (1\ 4\ 3\ 2)$$

4. Describe in detail all symmetries of a regular n-gon for $n = 3, 4, 5,$ or 6. Then generalize, describing the symmetries of a regular n-gon.

5. What are the symmetries of a circle? Of a line? Give an example of a symmetry that a circle has that a line does not, and vice versa.

6. Look in the Yellow Pages or online for company logos. Find examples of at least eight different symmetry groups and label each example with its symmetry group.

7. Identify the symmetries of each of the friezes in Figure 10.8.

8. Find examples of each of the seven types of friezes. (Try to find examples that are more interesting than the letter patterns in the text. If you have difficulty finding these, you may create your own in GeoGebra.) Mark the basic pattern used to generate each frieze. Tell what symmetries each of your examples has.

9. Create a figure that has the symmetry group C_5. Do the same for C_6, D_5, and D_6. Label your figures with their symmetry group.

10. The groups C_2 and D_1 each contain two isometries. From the perspective of group theory, the two groups are identical (isomorphic). However, they are different geometrically. Show this by finding a figure that has C_2 but not D_1 as its symmetry group, and another figure that has D_1 but not C_2 as its symmetry group.

11. There are two different groups of order 4, shown in the tables below. Create a geometric figure whose symmetry group is isomorphic to the group represented by each table. (Two groups are *isomorphic* if their group tables are identical except for the symbols used.) Explain how you create these figures to match the tables.

*1	a	b	c	d
a	a	b	c	d
b	b	c	d	a
c	c	d	a	b
d	d	a	b	c

*2	w	x	y	z
w	w	x	y	z
x	x	w	z	y
y	y	z	w	x
z	z	y	x	w

12. A group you are familiar with is the "clock arithmetic" group, which uses the integers from 1 to 12. In this group, $6 + 9 = 3$, since 9 hours after 6 o'clock is 3 o'clock. Create a geometric figure whose symmetry group is isomorphic to the clock arithmetic group. (*Hint*: Think about commutativity.)

13. Suppose that S is the finite set of symmetries for a planar figure. Using composition as the operation, verify that the four group axioms hold for S.

14. In the operation table of a finite group, prove that any column contains all of the elements of the group.

15. The property given in Exercise 14 is also true for infinite groups. Find a proof for the infinite case.

16. Consider the cyclic group C_3, and the dihedral group D_3.
    a. Create the table for C_3. Verify that the four group axioms hold.
    b. Repeat part (a) for D_3.
    c. Show that all the elements of C_3 are contained in the group D_3, thus confirming that C_3 is a *subgroup* of D_3.

17. Consider the cyclic group C_n, and the dihedral group D_n.
    a. Prove that C_n is a group.
    b. Prove that D_n is a group.
    c. Show that all the elements of C_n are contained in the group D_n, thus confirming that C_n is a *subgroup* of D_n.

18. Prove that the rotations of D_n account for half of its symmetries. Thus D_n has twice the number of elements as C_n.

19. Using GeoGebra, construct the regular tilings for $n = 3$, for $n = 4$, and for $n = 6$.

20. Construct an arbitrary triangle. Use this triangle to create a tiling of the plane.

21. Create an example of a semiregular tiling different from Figure 10.12. A suggestion: There are at least two that can be made with hexagons and triangles.

22. Make a set of Penrose tiles, and explore ways to tile the plane with them. Construct at least one Penrose tiling that does not have translational symmetry. Prove that your tiling does not have translational symmetry.

Exercises 23 and 24 are especially for future teachers.

23. The National Council of Teachers of Mathematics (NCTM) recommends in the *Principles and Standards for School Mathematics* that "Instructional programs from prekindergarten through grade 12 should enable all students to . . . apply transformations and use symmetry to analyze mathematical situations" [NCTM 2000, 41]. What does this mean for you and your future students?
    a. Study the Geometry Standard for one grade band (i.e., pre-K–2, 3–5, 6–8, or 9–12). What are the recommendations of the NCTM

regarding transformations such as slides, flips, turns, and combinations of these motions?

b. Find copies of school mathematics textbooks for these same grade levels. How are the NCTM standards reflected in those textbooks? Cite specific examples.

c. Write a report in which you present and critique what you learn. Your report should include your responses to parts (a) and (b).

24. Design several classroom activities involving symmetries and combinations of symmetries that would be appropriate for students in your future classroom. Write a paragraph or two explaining how the activities you design reflect both what you have learned in studying this chapter, and the recommendations of the NCTM.

Reflect on what you have learned in this chapter.

25. Review the main ideas of this chapter. Describe, in your own words, the concepts you have studied and what you have learned about them. What are the important ideas? How do they fit together? Which concepts were easy for you? Which were hard?

26. Reflect on the learning environment for this course.

a. Describe aspects of the learning environment that helped you understand the main ideas in this chapter. Which activities did you like? Dislike? Why?

b. How will you use what you are learning about your own experiences learning geometry in this course in your future career as a teacher?

10.4 CHAPTER OVERVIEW

In this chapter, we have explored the various ways in which a geometric figure can be congruent to itself. These are the *symmetries* of the figure. We discussed in greater depth the mathematical structure known as a *group*.

A *group* is a set G together with a binary operation $\circ$ such that

- For any two elements x, y of G, $x \circ y$ is in G (the *closure* property).
- For any elements x, y, z of G, $x \circ (y \circ z) = (x \circ y) \circ z$ (the *associative* property).
- There is an element i of G so that $i \circ x = x \circ i = x$ (the *identity* property).
- For any element x of G, there is an element x^{-1} also in G so that $x \circ x^{-1} = x^{-1} \circ x = i$ (the *inverse* property).

Sets of symmetries with the operation of composition are classic examples of groups. Cycle notation for symmetries gives a convenient way to calculate compositions of symmetries.

We saw a variety of examples of figures with finite symmetry groups. Such figures must be bounded. The finite symmetry groups can be *cyclic*, made up solely of rotations, or they can be *dihedral*, containing both rotations and reflections. A major theorem, credited to Leonardo da Vinci, says that any finite symmetry group for a planar figure must be one of these two types.

Leonardo's Theorem A finite symmetry group for a figure in the plane must be either the cyclic group C_n or the dihedral group D_n.

Symmetry groups that contain translations must belong to unbounded figures. If all translations in the group are parallel to each other, the figure is called a *frieze*. There are seven possible types of friezes; we proved this and gave simple examples. On the other hand, the translations might use more than one direction. This gives rise to the seventeen *wallpaper patterns*. The *Crystallographic Restriction* says that only certain angles can be rotational symmetries for a wallpaper pattern.

The Crystallographic Restriction   The minimal angle of rotation for a wallpaper symmetry is 60°, 90°, 120°, 180°, or 360°. All other rotation angles for a symmetry must be multiples of the minimal angle for that pattern.

An idea related to wallpaper symmetry is *tiling* the plane, filling the plane with congruent copies of a polygon. We saw that any quadrilateral and any triangle can be used to tile the plane. Triangles, squares, and regular hexagons can be used to tile the plane; when such a tiling uses just one kind of regular polygon, it is called a *regular tiling*. *Semiregular* tilings use two regular polygonal shapes. The surprising Penrose tiles can be used to produce tilings that fill the plane without any translational symmetry.

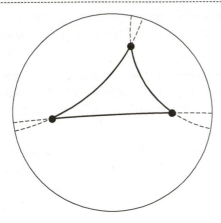

CHAPTER ELEVEN

Hyperbolic Geometry

How important are axioms or postulates in a mathematical system? Recall that in Chapter 2 we presented Euclid's postulates (see page 26), which form the foundation for Euclidean geometry. Euclid's Fifth Postulate, the one about parallel lines, is a more complicated statement than the other four postulates. For many centuries, mathematicians tried to show that the Fifth Postulate could be proved from the other postulates. It was only in the nineteenth century that mathematicians understood that the Fifth Postulate could not be proved because there are legitimate geometries in which the Fifth Postulate is false. One of these geometries, hyperbolic geometry, is the topic of this chapter.

In Chapter 3 we introduced the universal and existential quantifiers, $\forall x$ and $\exists x$, and discussed how to negate quantified statements. You might want to review this discussion, which begins on page 58. Playfair's statement of Euclid's Fifth Postulate reads: *Given a line ℓ and any point P not on ℓ, there is exactly one line through P that is parallel to ℓ*. If you read Playfair's statement carefully, you will see that it has been triply quantified; that is, contains a nested trio of quantifications. "Given a line ℓ and any point P not on ℓ" means "$\forall$ lines ℓ and $\forall$ points P not on ℓ"; and "there is exactly one line through P" means

"∃ exactly one line through P." This is a complicated statement involving three layers of quantification. Let us look at the structure of the statement

$$\forall \ell \ (\forall P \ (\exists m \ (\text{something about } \ell, P, \text{ and } m))).$$

To negate a complicated statement of this form, begin at the outermost layer and work toward the center layer by layer. Thus,

$$\neg(\forall \ell \ (\forall P \ (\exists m \ (\text{something about } \ell, P, \text{ and } m))))$$

is equivalent to

$$\exists \ell \ \neg(\forall P \ (\exists m \ (\text{something about } \ell, P, \text{ and } m))),$$

which is equivalent to

$$\exists \ell \ (\exists P \ \neg(\exists m \ (\text{something about } \ell, P, \text{ and } m))).$$

This in turn is equivalent to

$$\exists \ell \ (\exists P \ (\forall m \ \neg(\text{something about } \ell, P, \text{ and } m))),$$

and then we get the equivalent statement

$$\exists \ell \ (\exists P \ (\forall m \ (\text{negation of something about } \ell, P, \text{ and } m))).$$

Finally, we have to decide how to negate the statement "there is exactly one …(whatever)." There are two possibilities to consider. Either "there are none" or "there is more than one." So one way to negate Playfair's Postulate would be to say:

> There is a line ℓ, and there is a point P not on ℓ, such that either no lines through P are parallel to ℓ, or two or more (distinct) lines through P are parallel to ℓ.

You might express this more clearly as:

> There is a line ℓ, and there is a point P not on ℓ, such that either every line through P intersects ℓ, or at least two distinct lines through P are parallel to ℓ.

What would happen if we used one of these two possible negations of Playfair's Postulate in place of the usual Euclidean Parallel Postulate? How much difference could negating one of Euclid's postulates really make? In this chapter we will investigate the geometry that we get when we use one of these two possible negations—the one that says that "There is a line ℓ, and there is a point P not on ℓ, such that at least two distinct lines through P are parallel to ℓ." We will see just how profound an impact this seemingly minor change makes!

It is difficult to investigate the hyperbolic plane directly. For one thing, we are so accustomed to the Euclidean worldview that any differences are hard to detect—or even to imagine! To guide our intuition into new directions, we need a *model* of the hyperbolic plane in which to work. The Poincaré disk is just such a model. It is a geometric situation that satisfies all of the axioms for the hyperbolic plane. This includes a changed version of Euclid's Fifth Postulate, the hyperbolic parallel postulate. We invite you to explore the not-so-small ramifications of this change.

This chapter has a slightly different format from the previous chapters. We have divided the activities and the discussion for this chapter into two sections. In Part I, we invite you to do some preliminary explorations in the Poincaré disk. You are invited to explore what lines, triangles, and circles look like in this universe, and observe how they behave. Then, in Part II, we take a deeper look at the Parallel Postulate, and begin to explain what is going on in this strange new universe. Your investigations of the Hyperbolic Parallel Axiom—one of the two possible negations of Euclid's Parallel Postulate—will lead to being able to explain why the things you observe in the Poincaré disk are happening.

PART I: EXPLORING A NEW UNIVERSE

11.1 ACTIVITIES: PART I

To do the activities in this chapter, you will need the hyperbolic geometry tools. There is a special GeoGebra file for these tools. Under the File menu, select **Open from GeoGebra Tube**. Search for **Hyperbolic Geometry in the Poincaré Disk**. There are several files by this name; the one from *soundmanbrad* is a good choice. (Your instructor may also have posted this file in your Learning Management System.) The tools for hyperbolic constructions are located on the buttons marked with a wrench.

Do the following activities, writing your explanations clearly in complete sentences. Include diagrams whenever appropriate. Save your work for each activity, as later work sometimes builds on earlier work. You will find it helpful to read ahead into the chapter as you work on these activities.

1. Open the Poincaré Disk model.
   a. Adjust the GeoGebra pane so that you can see most of the white disk in the document. We will refer to the boundary of this white disk as the *fundamental circle* of the hyperbolic plane.
   b. Choose the **Hyperbolic Segment** tool. Draw several hyperbolic segments within the space of the white disk. How are these segments similar to ordinary Euclidean segments? How are these hyperbolic segments different from ordinary Euclidean segments?
   c. After you have several hyperbolic segments in the Poincaré disk, construct some Euclidean segments with the same endpoints. Construct at least one example showing Euclidean and hyperbolic segments that appear to coincide. Construct at least one example showing Euclidean and hyperbolic segments sharing the same endpoints that clearly do not coincide.
   d. Choose the **Hyperbolic Line** tool and construct several hyperbolic lines. Construct some hyperbolic lines that contain some of the

hyperbolic segments you have already constructed. What do you notice about the way the hyperbolic lines meet the fundamental circle? How could you test your conjecture about what you observe?

e. What happens to a hyperbolic segment (or a hyperbolic line) if you drag one of its points outside the fundamental circle? Does the same thing happen when you drag the endpoints of a Euclidean segment across the fundamental circle?

GEOGEBRA WARNING The Poincaré model of hyperbolic geometry uses only the points in the interior of the fundamental circle. The GeoGebra tools in this file allow you to move points across this boundary, but those exterior points are not legitimate parts of the model. Another issue is that moving objects across the center of the fundamental circle may cause difficulties with the GeoGebra constructions.

2. Open the Poincaré Disk model.

a. Use one of the hyperbolic circle tools to construct a hyperbolic circle, c_1, in the Poincaré disk. Once you've constructed this circle, you can select the object and choose Object Properties. This will open a window that will allow you to easily rename the circle.

GEOGEBRA TIP Using the **Hyperbolic Circle** tool is similar to using the ordinary Euclidean *Circle by Center through Point* tool. For the **Hyperbolic Circle w Given Radius** tool, first create a hyperbolic segment to indicate the desired radius and use **Hyperbolic Distance** to measure the segment's length. Then select the desired center point of the circle and specify the measurement value from the Algebra pane.

b. Construct a point, P, on c_1, and measure the hyperbolic distance from the center of the circle to the point P. (You must use the appropriate hyperbolic tool to do this measurement.) Move P around the circle. What do you observe about the hyperbolic distance from P to the center of the circle?

c. Move c_1 around the Poincaré disk, changing both its center and radius. Are your observations consistent with what you already know about circles? Can you explain what is going on?

d. Now use the usual Circle tool to create a Euclidean circle in the interior of the Poincaré disk. Construct a point, Q, on this circle and measure the *hyperbolic distance* from the center of the circle to this point Q. Move Q around the circle. What do you observe about the hyperbolic distance from Q to the center of the Euclidean circle?

e. How are hyperbolic circles similar to Euclidean circles? How are they different?

3. Open the Poincaré Disk model. Construct a hyperbolic line AB. Then create a new point, C, not on the line AB and construct hyperbolic segments AC and BC. This creates a triangle. Use the **Hyperbolic Angle** tool to measure

the exterior angle at B and the two opposite interior angles of $\triangle ABC$. Vary points A, B, C to examine other triangles. Does the Exterior Angle Theorem still hold in the Poincaré disk?

GEOGEBRA TIP When you measure an angle, GeoGebra displays the value as a number in the Algebra pane. You can right click on that number and select Object Properties to see what the number represents. You will find it helpful as you are learning to use these new hyperbolic tools to compare the measures of $\angle ABC$ and $\angle CBA$. Can you explain what is going on?

4. Open the Poincaré Disk model.
   a. Construct a hyperbolic triangle.
   b. Measure the hyperbolic angles of this triangle. Calculate the angle sum for this triangle.
   c. Drag one of the vertices of this triangle, and observe how the angle sum changes. (If the value jumps drastically, look again at the angles and make sure the measurements of the interior angles for the triangle are still being done clockwise.) Is there a maximum and/or a minimum value for this sum? If so, what are these maximum or minimum values?
   d. Describe the size, shape, and position of a hyperbolic triangle whose angle sum seems to be as large as possible. What factors seem to contribute to making the angle sum larger? Describe the size, shape, and position of a hyperbolic triangle whose angle sum seems to be as small as you can make it. What factors seem to contribute to making the angle sum smaller?

5. In the Poincaré disk, construct a triangle with one of its vertices on the fundamental circle. (Since the vertex on the fundamental circle is not considered part of the Poincaré disk, this is a limiting case in which two sides of the triangle are asymptotic to each other.) With the Hyperbolic Angle tool, measure its angles and one of its exterior angles. Does the Exterior Angle Theorem hold for this special kind of triangle? Vary the ordinary vertices of the triangle and check again. Is your answer the same if two of the triangle's vertices are on the fundamental circle?

6. Open the Poincaré Disk model.
   a. Construct a hyperbolic triangle. Use the **Hyperbolic Perpendicular Bisector** tool to construct the hyperbolic perpendicular bisector of each side of the triangle. Construct the intersection of two of these perpendicular bisectors, and label this point O. In Chapter 3, we saw that the point of concurrence of the three perpendicular bisectors of a triangle in Euclidean space is the circumcenter of the triangle (see page 70).

   GEOGEBRA TIP To use the Hyperbolic Perpendicular Bisector tool, first select the tool, then click on the endpoints of the line segment for which you want the perpendicular bisector.

   b. For a Euclidean triangle, the three perpendicular bisectors of the sides are concurrent. Is this true for a hyperbolic triangle? Always true? Sometimes true? Drag one of the vertices of your hyperbolic triangle. What do you observe?

c. If the three perpendicular bisectors are concurrent at point O, is O the center of a circumcircle of $\triangle ABC$? Is this circumcircle—when it exists—unique? What would you need to know in order to prove your conjecture?

d. In earlier chapters (for instance, see page 74), we have assumed that if two lines, ℓ and m, are perpendicular to two different sides of $\triangle ABC$, then ℓ and m must intersect each other. What is going on here?

7. Open the Poincaré Disk model.

a. Construct a hyperbolic triangle $\triangle ABC$. Use the **Hyperbolic Angle Bisector** tool to construct the hyperbolic angle bisector of each angle of the triangle. Construct the point of intersection of two of these angle bisectors, and label this point I.

b. Are the three angle bisectors concurrent? Always? Sometimes? Can you make a conjecture?

c. If the three angle bisectors are concurrent at I, is I the incenter of an incircle of $\triangle ABC$? Is the incircle of $\triangle ABC$—if it exists—unique? What would you need to know in order to prove your conjecture?

GEOGEBRA TIP As you investigate this situation, you may wish to use the **Hyperbolic Drop Perpendicular** tool. To use the Hyperbolic Drop Perpendicular tool, click on any two distinct points of the line ℓ, then click on the point P. This will give you the unique perpendicular from P to ℓ.

11.2 DISCUSSION: PART I

Many of the attempts to prove Euclid's Fifth Postulate began by assuming the negation of the postulate and seeking a contradiction. The Italian mathematician Saccheri took this approach and established many basic properties. Because his results were so foreign to his conception of geometry, he felt that he had encountered a contradiction. However, later mathematicians realized that a different interpretation of the basic concepts of point and line would allow these strange results to make sense. Klein, Beltrami, and especially Poincaré created *models* of the new axioms, that is, geometric systems in which the altered axioms were satisfied. These new models let them explore the new possibilities. In this chapter, we will focus on the Poincaré disk model.

HYPERBOLIC LINES AND SEGMENTS

As you worked on the activities that introduced this chapter, you observed that hyperbolic lines are somewhat different from Euclidean lines. In the Poincaré disk model of the hyperbolic plane, a line is a circular arc that meets the fundamental circle orthogonally. Two circles are *orthogonal* if the tangents constructed at their points of intersection are perpendicular. Consider the fundamental circle and a hyperbolic line, ℓ, in the Poincaré disk. Let X be a point where ℓ meets the fundamental circle. If t_1 is the tangent at X to the fundamental circle and t_2 is the tangent at X to the circular arc that represents ℓ, then t_1 is perpendicular to t_2.

As you worked on Activity 1, you probably observed that some hyperbolic lines appear to be less curved than other lines. You may have noticed that those hyperbolic lines that pass through the center point of the fundamental circle appear to coincide exactly with Euclidean lines and that the further the hyperbolic line is from the center of the fundamental circle, the more curved it appears. This apparent curvature is due to the distortion caused by our attempt to represent the infinite hyperbolic plane in a bounded disk on a flat surface. In the world of the hyperbolic plane, all hyperbolic lines look the same.

Any diameter of a Poincaré disk should also be included as a hyperbolic line. We can think of a diameter of the fundamental circle as an arc of a circle of infinite radius. Since a diameter is perpendicular to the tangent lines constructed at its endpoints, any diameter of the fundamental circle is a hyperbolic line in the Poincaré disk model.

THE POINCARÉ DISK MODEL OF THE HYPERBOLIC PLANE

The Poincaré disk is a model of a geometric world in which a different set of rules apply. In Chapter 2 we introduced Euclid's postulates, and since then we have been exploring geometric structures of Euclidean space using the model of a flat plane as represented in a GeoGebra diagram. Working with the Poincaré disk model will help us to become familiar with geometric structures that are possible in the hyperbolic plane.

Whenever we set up a model of a geometric world, we must identify what we are using to represent *points* and *lines* in the model. Then we must verify that the axioms we are using are accurately represented in that model. In the Poincaré disk model, the *points* of the hyperbolic plane are the points interior to the fundamental circle. The points that lie on or exterior to the fundamental circle are not points in the hyperbolic plane. The points that lie *on* the fundamental circle play an important role even though they do not lie in the hyperbolic plane. (The points exterior to the fundamental circle are of no concern to us in this model.) *Lines* in the Poincaré disk are the circular arcs that are orthogonal to the fundamental circle, including diameters (which are circles of infinite radius).

Hyperbolic lines, like their Euclidean counterparts, extend as far as possible in the plane. We could say that any line "extends to infinity." This idea of points at infinity requires a special name.

DEFINITION 11.1 The points where a hyperbolic line meets the fundamental circle are *ideal points*. These points are said to lie "at infinity for the hyperbolic plane." We denote these points at infinity with the Greek letter Ω (read as "omega"). These points are sometimes called "Omega points," though properly speaking they are not part of the hyperbolic plane.

Euclid's first four postulates should hold in this model, since the only axiom we are changing is the Parallel Postulate. Let's see how this works in the Poincaré disk model.

1. *Given two distinct points A and B in the hyperbolic plane, there is a unique line through A and B.*

When you are working with the Poincaré disk, you can draw or construct points anywhere inside the fundamental circle. Using the special hyperbolic tools, you can construct hyperbolic lines and hyperbolic segments through any pair of these points. These hyperbolic lines and segments are the portions of circular arcs that lie inside the fundamental circle and are orthogonal to it.

The construction we are describing is a Euclidean construction. Given two points A and B, we can always treat these as the endpoints of a chord of an ordinary (Euclidean) circle. In Chapter 4, we learned that we can construct infinitely many (Euclidean) circles with the chord AB (see page 96). So the question arises here: For any two points in the hyperbolic plane, is *at least one* of these circles orthogonal to the fundamental circle? Is *exactly one* circle through the points A and B orthogonal to the fundamental circle? From your investigations in the activities, you may suspect that the answers to these questions are "yes," and "yes." But these need to be proved.

2. *Any line segment can be extended indefinitely.*

   The points of the hyperbolic plane are the points interior to the fundamental circle, and do not include the points of the fundamental circle itself. In a certain sense, the fundamental circle is the boundary of the hyperbolic plane—but the hyperbolic plane does not include the points on its boundary. Thus, a hyperbolic line does not have endpoints.

   A hyperbolic *segment*, like a Euclidean segment, does have endpoints. We say that a segment is *closed* because it includes its endpoints. A hyperbolic *line*, like its Euclidean counterpart, does not include its endpoints, and so is said to be *open*. A hyperbolic line is open, even though it is bounded by the fundamental circle. So you can always extend a hyperbolic line segment—even if only a little bit. When you are using a GeoGebra worksheet with the Poincaré disk model, you may be limited by the pixels on the computer screen in actually carrying this out—but there is always room in the hyperbolic plane to extend a line segment even if we cannot draw this using GeoGebra. (This may be more believable after our discussion of distance and measurement a little later.)

3. *Given two distinct points A and B, a circle centered at A with radius AB can be drawn.*

   The Poincaré disk model does have tools for constructing hyperbolic circles—either by center and point or by center and radius. As you worked on Activity 2, you constructed several examples of hyperbolic circles, and you probably observed that these hyperbolic circles look a lot like Euclidean circles, except that the center of the hyperbolic circle may have seemed to be a bit off center.

   When you measured the hyperbolic distance from the center to a point on a hyperbolic circle, you should have observed that this distance is constant, as it should be. But it probably didn't appear to your eye to be constant—at least not for all your examples of hyperbolic circles. Remember that we are trying to represent an infinite unbounded plane in a small space, so things are bound to be distorted to our eyes. This has to do with the way that distance is measured in the hyperbolic plane. We will discuss the hyperbolic metric—the distance measure—a little later. For the moment, we can say that yes, this postulate, too, is satisfied in the hyperbolic plane.

4. *Any two right angles are congruent.*

The Poincaré disk model has a tool for constructing the hyperbolic perpendicular to any line. The underlying construction—a circular arc that is orthogonal to the given hyperbolic line—is a Euclidean construction. For the hyperbolic lines to be perpendicular, the Euclidean circular arcs representing those lines must be orthogonal. Arcs are orthogonal if their tangent lines at the intersection point are perpendicular. So the question about orthogonal hyperbolic lines is actually a question about perpendicular Euclidean lines. Thus, hyperbolic lines are perpendicular if the corresponding Euclidean tangent lines are perpendicular. Because of this, just as all right angles are congruent in Euclidean space, all hyperbolic right angles are congruent in the Poincaré disk.

So Euclid's first four postulates do hold in the Poincaré disk. These four postulates are also postulates or axioms for the hyperbolic plane. In Part II of this chapter, we will investigate the hyperbolic parallel postulate. Once we have verified that all five hyperbolic axioms hold in the Poincaré disk, we will be able to say that the Poincaré disk is a model of the hyperbolic plane.

The Poincaré disk is just one model of the hyperbolic plane. There are other models. One of them is the upper-half-plane model, which we will explore in the exercises.

MEASURING DISTANCE IN THE POINCARÉ DISK MODEL

Measuring the length of a segment in the Poincaré disk is a bit tricky. The idea is that the hyperbolic plane, like the Euclidean plane, is infinite. Axiom 2 requires that any line segment can be extended indefinitely. This means that our method for measuring distance must give lines of infinite length even though they are bounded by the fundamental circle.

A rule for measuring distance is called a *metric*. You are familiar with the usual distance formula for measuring distance in the Euclidean plane, which is based on the Pythagorean Theorem. If the point A has coordinates (a_1, a_2) and the point B has coordinates (b_1, b_2), the Euclidean distance between A and B, denoted $d(A, B)$, is given by the formula

$$d(A, B) = \sqrt{(a_1 - b_1)^2 + (a_2 - b_2)^2}.$$

Chapter 6 introduced a different metric for the Euclidean plane, the *taxicab metric*, based on horizontal and vertical distances. Both the taxicab metric and the Pythagorean metric satisfied three basic axioms, and a metric for the Poincaré disk must also satisfy these same three axioms. Let us restate briefly these axioms:

Suppose A and B are points in the space. The distance from A to B must satisfy the following requirements:

1. If A and B are points, then $d(A, B) \geq 0$; and $d(A, B) = 0$ if and only if $A = B$.
2. If A and B are points, then $d(A, B) = d(B, A)$.
3. The *triangle inequality*: If A, B, and C are points, then $d(A, B) + d(B, C) \geq d(A, C)$.

The formula for measuring the distance between points in the Poincaré disk must meet these three requirements as well as allow the length of a line to be infinite even though the hyperbolic plane is bounded by the fundamental circle. (We said that this was going to be a bit tricky!) Poincaré developed the following formula for the distance between two points:

$$d(A, B) = \left| \ln \left(\frac{\left(\frac{AM}{AN} \right)}{\left(\frac{BM}{BN} \right)} \right) \right| = \left| \ln \left(\frac{AM \cdot BN}{AN \cdot BM} \right) \right|.$$

To use this formula, you must imagine the Poincaré line segment AB extended until it reaches the boundary of the hyperbolic plane (i.e., until it reaches the fundamental circle). The two points where it meets the boundary are M and N. (It does not matter which is which.) Then the calculation uses four Euclidean distances: AM, AN, BM, and BN.

Let us examine the three metric axioms and what they mean for this distance formula.

- The first axiom requires that $d(A, B) \geq 0$, and the absolute value takes care of this for us. But what about the requirement that $d(A, B) = 0$ if and only if $A = B$? What value does the natural logarithm, $\ln(x)$, produce if A and B are the same point? On the other hand, if the natural logarithm equals 0, what does this imply about the quantity inside it? Must A equal B in this situation?

- The second axiom requires that $d(A, B) = d(B, A)$. In other words, we must show that

$$\left| \ln \left(\frac{AM \cdot BN}{AN \cdot BM} \right) \right| = \left| \ln \left(\frac{BM \cdot AN}{BN \cdot AM} \right) \right|.$$

The expressions $\left(\frac{AM \cdot BN}{AN \cdot BM} \right)$ and $\left(\frac{BM \cdot AN}{BN \cdot AM} \right)$ are reciprocals of each other. What is going on in the hyperbolic distance formula that allows $d(A, B)$ to be the same as $d(B, A)$?

- The third axiom, the triangle inequality, can be proved by integration in the complex plane. This requires mathematical ideas that go well beyond the scope of this course.

In the exercises, you will have an opportunity to prove that the formula developed by Poincaré does indeed satisfy the first two axioms for a metric in the hyperbolic plane.

Axiom 2 requires that any hyperbolic segment can be extended indefinitely. Does the Poincaré distance formula set a maximum length for line segments in the hyperbolic plane? Suppose that the segment AB lies on the line ℓ in the Poincaré disk. In order for the length of the segment AB to increase, the points A and B must each move closer to the edge of the hyperbolic plane. One way that this could happen would be for A to move closer to N and B closer to M. Thus, the Euclidean lengths of AN and BM would both decrease, and would even approach 0. Meanwhile, the Euclidean lengths of AM and BN would be getting longer (possibly, up to the maximum diameter of the Poincaré disk). In other words,

$$\left| \ln \left(\frac{AM \cdot BN}{AN \cdot BM} \right) \right| \rightarrow \left| \ln \left(\frac{MN \cdot MN}{0 \cdot 0} \right) \right|.$$

Thus, even though hyperbolic lines are bounded by the Poincaré disk, they may be infinitely long. (There is another case to consider: The case where A moves closer to M and B closer to N. You will have an opportunity to complete this proof in the exercises.)

HYPERBOLIC CIRCLES

A *circle* is a set of points that are equidistant from a fixed center point. The *radius* of a circle is the distance from the center to a point on the circle. As you saw from your work on Activity 2, there are circles in the hyperbolic plane. Hyperbolic circles do look like Euclidean circles. They appear to be round, just as ordinary Euclidean circles are, but the center appears to be a bit off-center. However, the distance from the center of the circle to any point on the circle is, in fact, constant, just as in Euclidean space.

In the Euclidean plane, as the radius, r, of a circle increases toward infinity, the curvature of the circle decreases. That is, the arc of the circle gets straighter and straighter. Eventually, in the limit as $r \rightarrow \infty$, the circle converges to a straight line. It is sometimes useful to think of a line as a circle with infinite radius and its center infinitely far away. Working with the Poincaré disk, we find that we are not allowed to construct hyperbolic circles *on* or *outside of* the fundamental circle. We can, however, imagine the limiting situation where the hyperbolic circle has its center on the fundamental circle. Using the hyperbolic distance formula, this circle would have infinite radius. Such an object is called a *horocycle* [Baragar 2001; Coxeter 1969; Greenberg 1980].

HYPERBOLIC TRIANGLES

As you worked on Activity 4, what did you observe as the angle sum of a hyperbolic triangle? Recall that when we proved that the angles of a triangle add up to two right angles (in Chapter 3; see page 64), we used Euclid's Fifth Postulate. So in a geometric world where Euclisd's Fifth Postulate does not hold, the angle sum of a triangle might not be 180°.

You were most likely able to construct a triangle in the Poincaré disk whose angle sum was almost 180°. What did this triangle look like? Compare the size of the triangle to the size of the Poincaré disk. It also matters whether the triangle is close to the center or to the boundary of the Poincaré disk. There is a visual distortion in the Poincaré disk that is less apparent near the center of the disk. This distortion is greater near the edge of the disk. Relatively large triangles and triangles close to the boundary of the Poincaré disk will appear more distorted than relatively small triangles close to the center of the Poincaré disk. This distortion is due to the way that distance is measured in this model.

The idea that the angle sum of a hyperbolic triangle is less than 180° is so startling that we define the difference between 180° (the expected angle sum of a triangle) and the actual angle sum of a hyperbolic triangle as the *defect of the triangle*.

DEFINITION 11.2   The *defect of triangle* $\triangle ABC$ is the difference between 180° and the angle sum of that triangle: defect($\triangle ABC$) = 180° − ($m\angle(A) + m\angle(B) + m\angle(C)$).

In the hyperbolic plane, every triangle has a positive defect. (We will prove this later in this chapter.)

In Activity 3, you were asked to compare an exterior angle of a hyperbolic triangle to the opposite interior angles of that triangle. What did you observe? In Euclidean geometry, the sum of the two interior angles equals the measure of the exterior angle. That is not the case for hyperbolic triangles. This tells us that the Parallel Postulate is involved somehow in this equality. However, the exterior angle will be greater than either of the opposite interior angles. This is the *Exterior Angle Theorem*, which we first saw in Chapter 2. This property of an exterior angle for a triangle does not depend on Euclid's Fifth Postulate, so it is valid for both Euclidean triangles and for hyperbolic triangles. Later in this chapter we will see a proof of this important theorem.

Points lying on the fundamental circle—the Ω-points—are not considered to be points in the hyperbolic plane. If two lines share a common Ω-point, we say that these lines "do not intersect." That is, if the lines do not intersect in the world inside the Poincaré disk model, they do not intersect in the hyperbolic plane.

DEFINITION 11.3   Lines that do not intersect are said to be *parallel lines*.

Nevertheless, we can use Ω-points to create geometric figures. For instance, consider a triangle with one vertex on the fundamental circle and two vertices inside the Poincaré disk. This triangle has two sides that do not properly intersect, that is, two sides that are parallel. We can describe this geometric figure as two parallel rays whose endpoints are connected by a segment. How could you describe a triangle with two of its vertices on the fundamental circle? How about a triangle with all three vertices on the fundamental circle?

A geometric figure with three vertices, some of which lie on the fundamental circle, is called an *asymptotic triangle*. An asymptotic triangle has one, two, or perhaps all three of its vertices at infinity. Of course, these vertices are not really in the hyperbolic plane. In some sense, these vertices lie just beyond the edge of hyperbolic space. In an asymptotic triangle, sides that meet at infinity do not intersect; that is, some (or all) of the sides of an asymptotic triangle are parallel.

An asymptotic angle, an angle $\angle PQR$ with its vertex Q actually on the fundamental circle, would have an (hyperbolic) angle measure of 0° at Q. Can you prove this? Think about the hyperbolic lines $\overleftrightarrow{PQ}$ and $\overleftrightarrow{QR}$, and how these lines meet the fundamental circle. If $\overleftrightarrow{PQ}$ and $\overleftrightarrow{QR}$ are both orthogonal to the fundamental circle at Q, what can you conclude about the measure of $\angle PQR$?

Since the sides of an asymptotic triangle cannot be extended outside the fundamental circle, it makes no sense to talk about an exterior angle at an Ω-point. However, at a "normal" vertex inside the Poincaré disk, there can be an exterior angle and it can be compared to the opposite interior angles. According to your observations in Activity 5, does the Exterior Angle Theorem still hold for asymptotic triangles?

It is possible to create an asymptotic triangle with all three vertices on the fundamental circle. This sort of triangle is triply asymptotic, meaning that the three sides are all parallel to each other. What is the defect of a triply asymptotic triangle? Can you justify your conjecture?

To find the angle sum of a quadrilateral, a pentagon, or any n-gon, an effective strategy is *to triangulate the figure.* That is, construct diagonals to break up the figure into triangles. In the Euclidean plane, for example, we can divide any quadrilateral into two triangles by drawing one diagonal. So the angle sum of a quadrilateral is equal to the angle sum of two triangles—which is 360° for *Euclidean* quadrilaterals.

We can do the same thing in the hyperbolic plane. We can triangulate a hyperbolic polygon by constructing an appropriate number of diagonals. The fact that hyperbolic triangles have angle sum less than 180° has a profound impact on the angle sum for quadrilaterals and other polygons in the hyperbolic plane.

CIRCUMCIRCLES AND INCIRCLES OF HYPERBOLIC TRIANGLES

In Chapter 3 we saw that the perpendicular bisectors of the three sides of Euclidean $\triangle ABC$ are concurrent. The point where these lines intersect, which we have been calling O, is equidistant from the three vertices of the triangle. Because the distances OA, OB, and OC are equal, the point O is the center of a circle through the three vertices A, B, and C. This circle surrounds $\triangle ABC$, and so it is called the circumcircle of $\triangle ABC$.

Euclidean Theorem   The three perpendicular bisectors of the sides of a triangle are concurrent. The point where they intersect, called the *circumcenter,* is often denoted as O. (See Theorem 3.10, page 70.)

What is the situation in the hyperbolic plane? As you worked on Activity 6, you probably observed that when the three perpendicular bisectors of the sides of the triangle did intersect, they were concurrent (i.e., they intersected in the same point). In this case, the point of concurrency appears to be the center of the circumcircle of the triangle. (This needs to be proved.) However, there is the disturbing fact that sometimes the three perpendicular bisectors of the sides of the triangle did not intersect! Somehow these lines, which were constructed perpendicular to the three sides of a triangle, turned out to be parallel. Instead of the definite statement we were able to make in the Euclidean theorem, here the best statement is a conditional one:

Conjecture 1   If the three perpendicular bisectors of the sides of a triangle in the Poincaré disk are concurrent at a point O, then the circle with center O and radius OA also contains the points B and C.

Your proof for this conjecture will be similar to your proof of the corresponding Euclidean theorem, but you must now account for the bewildering case where the three perpendicular bisectors do not intersect. Our explorations of the Parallel Postulate in Part II of this chapter will give you the tools you need to explain what is happening.

Another of the concurrence properties for Euclidean triangles, which we explored in Chapter 3, stated that the angle bisectors of a triangle are concurrent.

Euclidean Theorem   The three angle bisectors of a triangle are concurrent. The point where they intersect, called the *incenter,* is often denoted as I and is the center of the circle inscribed in the triangle. (See Theorem 3.4, page 66.)

As you worked on Activity 7, it does appear that the three angle bisectors are concurrent, and a proof of this concurrence will be similar to the proof given in Chapter 3 for Theorem 3.4.

Conjecture 2   The three angle bisectors of a triangle in the Poincaré disk are concurrent. The point where they intersect, called the *incenter,* is often denoted as I and is the center of the circle inscribed in the triangle.

One way to prove this conjecture is to drop perpendiculars from I to each of the sides of the triangle; call the feet of these perpendiculars W, X, and Y. As you work through the details of this proof, you should be able to prove that $IW \cong IX \cong IY$ so that the point I is the center of a circle through the points W, X, and Y. Is this circle an incircle of the hyperbolic $\triangle ABC$? And if so, is this incircle unique? Of course, your answers to these questions will require proofs.

To answer these and other questions about what is going on in the hyperbolic plane, we need to develop a deeper understanding of the Parallel Postulate as it pertains to the hyperbolic plane. This will be the focus of Part II of this chapter.

CONGRUENCE OF TRIANGLES IN THE HYPERBOLIC PLANE

Your proofs of the previous two conjectures will require you to determine whether two triangles in the hyperbolic plane are congruent. Since distances are visually distorted in the Poincaré disk, we cannot rely on visual inspection; we must approach the question of congruence of triangles by using the axioms and theorems of the hyperbolic plane. Since Euclid's first four postulates hold in the hyperbolic plane, any theorems that we proved using only these first four postulates will also hold in the hyperbolic plane.

In Chapter 3 (see page 65), we agreed to accept the SAS criterion for congruence of triangles as an axiom. Using SAS with Euclid's first four postulates, we were able to prove the ASA, SSS, AAS, and Right Angle–Hypotenuse–Leg criteria for triangle congruence *without using Euclid's Fifth Postulate*. (See page 65 and Exercises 16–19, Chapter 3.) Because the Fifth Postulate was not involved in any of these proofs, we can continue to use these criteria to prove congruence of triangles in the hyperbolic plane.

An important difference between the Euclidean plane and the hyperbolic plane is the AAA criterion. In the Euclidean plane, two triangles that have three pairs of congruent angles will be similar but not necessarily congruent. In the hyperbolic plane, however, two triangles with three pairs of congruent angles must be congruent. After learning some facts about quadrilaterals in the hyperbolic plane, you will be asked to prove this in the exercises.

How can we determine whether two asymptotic triangles are congruent? For asymptotic triangles, we can think of the angle at the Ω-point as having a measure of zero. This angle is the same in any two asymptotic triangles. To establish congruence, we need to check only two other items: the finite sides and another pair of angles.

THEOREM 11.1 Two asymptotic triangles are congruent if and only if the finite sides are congruent and one pair of corresponding angles are congruent.

Proof Suppose that $\triangle AB\Omega_1$ and $\triangle DE\Omega_2$ are two asymptotic triangles, with Ω_1 and Ω_2 being the vertices at infinity. In other words, the rays $A\Omega_1$ and $B\Omega_1$ are parallel, as are the rays $D\Omega_2$ and $E\Omega_2$. Further suppose that the segments AB and DE are congruent, and that $\angle AB\Omega_1 \cong \angle DE\Omega_2$. It is necessary to prove that the other corresponding angles are congruent as well.

Assume that $\angle BA\Omega_1$ is greater than $\angle ED\Omega_2$. Construct a ray AP so that $\angle BAP$ is congruent to $\angle EF\Omega_2$. The new ray will intersect $B\Omega_1$ at a point C. Then construct a segment EF on the side $E\Omega_2$ so that $EF \cong BC$. This creates $\triangle DEF$, which is congruent to $\triangle ABC$ by Side–Angle–Side. However, this implies that $\angle ED\Omega_2 \cong \angle BAC \cong \angle EDF < \angle ED\Omega_2$. This contradiction says that $\angle BA\Omega_1$ cannot be greater than $\angle ED\Omega_2$. Using the same argument, we also can prove that $\angle BA\Omega_1$ cannot be less than $\angle ED\Omega_2$. Therefore, these angles must be congruent [Smart 1988, 308].

There is an assumption hidden in this proof, namely that an angle interior to $\angle BA\Omega_1$ will have to intersect the side $B\Omega_1$. In the Euclidean situation, this follows from the Fifth Postulate, but what about in the hyperbolic situation? How can we be sure that the new ray interior to the parallel sides is not also parallel to $B\Omega_1$? This point needs some careful thought. For now, we ask that you accept this intersection, and we will try to clarify the reasons in the next portion of this chapter.

PART II: THE PARALLEL POSTULATE IN HYPERBOLIC GEOMETRY

Playfair's Postulate, which in the presence of the first four of Euclid's postulates is equivalent to the Fifth Postulate, says:

Given any line ℓ and any point P not on ℓ, there is exactly one line on P that is parallel to ℓ.

In the Euclidean plane, two lines either intersect or they are parallel. In fact, we can use this postulate to define what we mean when we say that two lines are parallel.

DEFINITION 11.4   Two lines, ℓ and m, are *parallel* if they do not intersect.

We will continue to use this definition for parallel lines in the hyperbolic plane. If two hyperbolic lines do not intersect, they are parallel. However, in the Poincaré disk, there are two different situations that give nonintersecting hyperbolic lines: there are hyperbolic lines that intersect (or appear to intersect) on the fundamental circle, and there are hyperbolic lines that do not intersect at all. We will investigate both of these kinds of hyperbolic lines.

11.3   ACTIVITIES: PART II

Do the following activities, writing your explanations clearly in complete sentences. Include diagrams whenever appropriate. Save your work for each activity, as later work sometimes builds on earlier work. You will find it helpful to read ahead into the chapter as you work on these activities.

8. Open the Poincaré Disk model.
   a. Construct a hyperbolic line, ℓ, in the Poincaré disk. Label the points where ℓ meets the fundamental circle as O_1 and O_2. (To get subscripts in GeoGebra, you can type the labels as **O_1** and **O_2**.) The points O_1 and O_2 represent the Ω-points of ℓ. In effect, O_1 and O_2 are points at infinity on this line.
   b. Construct points P and T not on ℓ. Construct a hyperbolic line through these points and call this line m. As you move point T, what do you observe about lines ℓ and m?
   c. Construct lines PO_1 and PO_2. The two rays PO_1 and PO_2 on these lines are said to be the *limiting parallel rays* from P to the line ℓ. (To clarify your diagram, make the segments dashed or a different color.) How is the line m related to the two limiting parallel rays if m does not intersect ℓ? How is m related to the two rays if m intersects ℓ?

9. Open the Poincaré Disk model.
   a. Construct a hyperbolic line, ℓ, in the Poincaré disk.

b. Construct a point P that is not on ℓ. Using the Hyperbolic Drop Perpendicular tool, construct a perpendicular from P to ℓ. Label the foot of the perpendicular from P to ℓ as Q.

c. Construct the limiting parallel rays $\overrightarrow{PO_1}$ and $\overrightarrow{PO_2}$ as you did in Activity 8c. Measure the hyperbolic angles $\angle QPO_1$ and $\angle QPO_2$, remembering that this tool measures clockwise. What do you observe?

d. Move the point P. Does your observation about the measures of angles $\angle QPO_1$ and $\angle QPO_2$ continue to hold? Can you make a conjecture?

10. A quadrilateral $ABCD$ with right angles at A and B and congruent sides AD and BC is called a *Saccheri quadrilateral*.

a. Open the Poincaré Disk model. Carefully construct an example of a Saccheri quadrilateral. Be sure that vertices A and B have right angles and that the sides AD and BC are constructed to be congruent. *Hint:* The tools for hyperbolic circles may be useful for this construction. Measure the hyperbolic distance on one side and use this value as the radius for a circle to construct the other side. Label the vertices.

b. Measure the angles at the vertices C and D. What do you observe?

c. Use the Hyperbolic Perpendicular Bisector tool to construct the perpendicular bisector of the *base AB*. Then use this tool to construct the perpendicular bisector of the *summit CD*. What do you observe? What does this suggest about the segment joining the midpoints of the base and summit of the Saccheri quadrilateral? Measure the length of this segment, using the appropriate distance tool. Also measure the lengths of the sides AD and BC. What do you observe?

11. A quadrilateral with three right angles is called a *Lambert quadrilateral*. In the Poincaré disk model, construct a quadrilateral with three right angles. (The **Hyperbolic Perpendicular at Point** tool can be helpful for this.) What do you observe about the fourth angle of this quadrilateral? Is it possible to construct a quadrilateral with four right angles in the Poincaré disk?

12. In the Poincaré disk model, construct a hyperbolic triangle ABC.

a. Use the Hyperbolic Perpendicular Bisector tool to locate the midpoint D of the hyperbolic segment AB. Also locate the midpoint E of the hyperbolic segment AC. Construct the hyperbolic line DE. (Once the midpoints are located, the perpendicular bisectors can be hidden.)

b. Use Hyperbolic Drop Perpendicular to construct segments AX, BY, and CZ that are perpendicular to the line DE, with the points X, Y, Z on this line.

c. Find the hyperbolic length of the segments BY and CZ. What does this tell you about the quadrilateral $YZCB$?

d. Find all pairs of congruent triangles in your diagram. Do these triangles stay congruent as you vary the vertex A?

13. The *defect* of a hyperbolic triangle is the amount by which its angle sum differs from $180°$. In the Poincaré disk model, construct a hyperbolic triangle ABC. Measure the sum of its angles and calculate the defect. Then construct another hyperbolic triangle DEF entirely interior to $\triangle ABC$,

measure its angles, and calculate its defect. How are the two defects related? Does this stay true if you increase the size of $\triangle ABC$? How large and how small can the defect be?

So far in this chapter you have seen several ways in which the hyperbolic plane is different from the Euclidean plane. The issue of parallel lines is the critical difference, of course, and this leads to some dramatic contrasts between the two geometric systems. However, there are some important similarities as well. Anything that can be proved without using the concept of parallelism, that is, using only Euclid's first four postulates, will be true in both geometries. For example, the fact that base angles of an isosceles triangle are congruent is true in both systems. So is the SSS criterion for congruent triangles. An example we have emphasized is the Exterior Angle Theorem for triangles. This property, true in both Euclidean and hyperbolic geometry, is an important tool for many proofs.

The study of the consequences of the first four postulates is called *absolute geometry*, or sometimes *neutral geometry*. Because Euclid's four axioms are common to both Euclidean and hyperbolic geometry, anything valid in absolute geometry is also valid in both the Euclidean and hyperbolic planes. (You can think of absolute geometry as the intersection of the two systems.) It is worthwhile to look carefully at a proof to see whether parallelism is used, for if it is not, then the theorem will hold in both geometries.

THE HYPERBOLIC AND ELLIPTIC PARALLEL POSTULATES

At the beginning of this chapter, we discussed how to develop the negation of Playfair's Postulate. We found that the negation of Playfair's Postulate is as follows:

> There is a line ℓ and there is a point P not on ℓ such that either there are no lines through P parallel to ℓ or there is more than one line through P parallel to ℓ.

This negation of Playfair's Postulate says that either one thing happens (that there are no lines through P parallel to ℓ) or another thing happens (that there is more than one line through P parallel to ℓ). Let us make two separate statements from this negation of Playfair's Postulate. By doing so, we will get two different non-Euclidean postulates—one for elliptic space and another for hyperbolic space.

The Elliptic Parallel Postulate

If we take the first part of the negation of Playfair's Postulate, we get the statement that there is a line ℓ and there is a point P not on ℓ, such that there are no lines through P parallel to ℓ. Since lines are either parallel or intersecting, we can state this a little more simply as follows:

Elliptic Parallel Postulate There is a line ℓ and there is a point P not on ℓ, such that every line through P intersects ℓ.

Spherical geometry is one possible model of an *elliptic space*. Consider the geometry of our planet Earth, as an airplane pilot must: A straight line from any city to another must follow some kind of curve (or the airplane would be on a trajectory into outer space!). The straightest line, or *geodesic,* on a sphere is a great circle. A *great circle* on a sphere is a circle whose center and radius coincide with the center and radius of the sphere itself. Thus, the diameter of a great circle is the same as the diameter of the sphere. The great circles that we are most familiar with on the Earth are the longitude lines and the equator. Of course, there are many other great circles. If you look at the routes traveled by airlines from one city to another, you will see that many of these routes follow the path of a great circle—although you might have to look at the cities on a globe rather than on a flat map to see this. Any flat map of our world necessarily has some distortion. Our world is not flat, and to represent it on a flat piece of paper requires that we stretch it or tear it in some way to fit it to the paper. Mapmakers have grappled with this issue for centuries, and there is some interesting mathematics for the problem of representing a sphere on a plane.

The elliptic parallel postulate as stated above is an existential statement, claiming that there is at least one situation in which this property of points and lines is true. (Playfair's Postulate is a universal statement, which states that its property holds in every situation. The negation of a universal statement is always an existential statement. See page 59 to review the process of negating a quantified statement.) In elliptic space, it is possible to prove that a slightly stronger statement follows from the elliptic parallel postulate. Since this is not the focus of our study in this chapter, we will simply state this theorem here.

THEOREM 11.2 **Elliptic Parallel Theorem** Suppose we assume the Elliptic Parallel Postulate. Then given any line ℓ and any point P not on ℓ, every line through P intersects ℓ.

For an example of this, consider the Earth (assuming it has a perfect spherical shape) as a model of elliptic geometry. The *points* in this model are the points on the surface of the Earth, and the *lines* are the great circles. Thus, the equator and all the longitude lines are considered lines in this model. Consider the equator as the line ℓ and pick any point P not on the equator. There is a longitude line through P that intersects the equator twice. In fact, there are many lines (great circles) through P besides that longitude line, and every line (every great circle) through P will intersect the equator twice—at diametrically opposite points. (Unfortunately, the spherical model has some difficulty with Euclid's First Postulate, for a pair of diametrically opposite points has more than one line connecting them. A sphere is not a perfect model of elliptic geometry.)

The Hyperbolic Parallel Postulate

In this chapter, we are focusing on the hyperbolic parallel postulate. We want to investigate the consequences of accepting this postulate in place of the Euclidean Parallel Postulate. In Activity 8, you began to investigate a world in which it is possible to have a line ℓ and a point P not on ℓ with more than one line through P that does not intersect ℓ. In the Poincaré disk model, we have a world in which the hyperbolic parallel postulate holds.

Hyperbolic Parallel Postulate   There is a line ℓ and there is a point P not on ℓ, such that more than one line through P is parallel to ℓ.

The Poincaré disk is one possible model of the *hyperbolic plane*. As with an elliptic plane, any attempt to represent the hyperbolic plane on a flat surface—such as a sketch on paper or an interactive diagram on a computer screen—introduces some distortion. Nevertheless, we can learn a lot about the hyperbolic plane by studying images in the Poincaré disk model.

In Activity 8, there was nothing special about the line ℓ and the point P you selected. Different choices for ℓ and for P would produce the same result: a multitude of lines m that pass through P and remain parallel to ℓ. This is a stronger statement than the hyperbolic parallel postulate. The mathematicians Saccheri and Legendre, decades apart, proved that this stronger statement results from the hyperbolic parallel postulate.

THEOREM 11.3   **Hyperbolic Parallel Theorem**   Given any line m and any point P not on m, there are at least two lines through P that do not intersect m.

The full proof of this theorem is somewhat involved and will not be given here (see [Greenberg 1980, 152] for a detailed presentation). Instead, we will investigate some of the surprising consequences of this theorem.

THE ANGLE OF PARALLELISM

In the sense we are accustomed to, two lines are *parallel* if they do not intersect. As you saw when you were working on Activity 8, in the Poincaré disk there are different ways in which lines do not intersect. Two lines might seem to intersect at a point on the fundamental circle; however, this point is not actually in the hyperbolic plane. These lines are certainly parallel since they fail to intersect—but just barely. Such lines might be said to *intersect at a point at infinity*. We call such lines *limiting parallels*.

If you start with a hyperbolic line, ℓ, and a point P not on ℓ, as you did in Activity 8, you can construct two limiting parallel rays through P. Assume the Ω-points are labeled so that $\overrightarrow{PO_1}$ and $\overrightarrow{PO_2}$ are the limiting parallel rays to ℓ. These limiting parallel rays divide the family of all possible rays through P into three sets. One set contains the rays interior to $\angle O_1 P O_2$; these rays intersect line ℓ. The second set contains the rays exterior to $\angle O_1 P O_2$; these rays do not intersect line ℓ. The third set consists of just the rays $\overrightarrow{PO_1}$ and $\overrightarrow{PO_2}$. These rays $\overrightarrow{PO_1}$ and

$\overrightarrow{PO_2}$ are the boundary between the rays that intersect ℓ and the rays that do not. (You might find it helpful to interact with your GeoGebra diagram for Activity 8 as you reread this paragraph.)

All the lines through P that lie outside the angle formed by the two limiting parallel rays—there are infinitely many of them—are also parallel to ℓ. Various authors refer to lines that are parallel in this way as *hyperparallel*, *ultraparallel*, or *superparallel* lines [Baragar 2001; Coxeter 1969; Greenberg 1980].

This distinction between limiting parallel lines—or more simply, parallel lines—and hyperparallel lines lets us properly understand Theorem 11.1 on the congruence of asymptotic triangles. In the proof of that theorem, a new line AC was constructed in the interior of $\Delta BA\Omega_1$ and we asserted that AC intersected the opposite side $B\Omega_1$. If $A\Omega_1$ is hyperparallel to $B\Omega_1$, this is not necessarily true. However, if $A\Omega_1$ is parallel to $B\Omega_1$ in the sense of a limiting parallel, then the intersection will occur and the proof is valid. Therefore, an asymptotic triangle must include two limiting parallel sides.

As you worked on Activity 9, you started with a line ℓ and a point P not on ℓ. You constructed the point Q, which is the foot of the perpendicular from P to ℓ. Then you constructed the limiting parallel rays $\overrightarrow{PO_1}$ and $\overrightarrow{PO_2}$. You might have observed that $\overrightarrow{PQ}$ bisects $\angle O_1PO_2$, or that the angles $\angle QPO_1$ and $\angle QPO_2$ are congruent. The angle between PQ and either one of the limiting parallel rays $\overrightarrow{PO_1}$ or $\overrightarrow{PO_2}$ is called the *angle of parallelism*.

THEOREM 11.4   For a given line ℓ and a point P not on ℓ, the two angles of parallelism are congruent.

Proof   Use the notation of the previous paragraph and of Activity 9. Notice that PQO_1 and PQO_2 are asymptotic triangles with right angles at Q and the finite segment PQ congruent to itself. By Theorem 11.1, the two triangles are congruent. Hence, the corresponding angles QPO_1 and QPO_2 are congruent.

This theorem is perhaps not surprising, for it is true in the Euclidean plane as well. In the Euclidean situation, the angle of parallelism is $90°$, and this is the same value in both directions. The distinction for the hyperbolic plane is that the angle of parallelism must be less than $90°$.

THEOREM 11.5   For a given line ℓ and a point P not on ℓ, the two angles of parallelism are acute.

Proof   This proof consists of eliminating the two other possibilities, that is, we show that the angle α of parallelism cannot be a right angle and cannot be an obtuse angle. As before, let the segment PQ be perpendicular to line ℓ.

First assume that $\alpha = 90°$ and let m be the line on P perpendicular to PQ. Any other line n on P will make an angle β with PQ. If $\beta < 90°$, then n intersects ℓ. If $\beta > 90°$ then, on the other side of PQ, we have $180° - \beta < 90°$, again implying that n intersects ℓ. Thus, the line m must be the unique parallel line for this P and ℓ, which contradicts the hyperbolic parallel theorem. So α cannot be $90°$.

Now assume that $\alpha > 90°$. Pick any angle β so that $180° - \alpha < \beta < \alpha$ and create a line m on a point P that makes angle β with PQ on one side of PQ. Because $\beta < \alpha$, the line m will intersect ℓ on that side of PQ. However, because $180° - \beta < \alpha$, line m will also intersect ℓ on the other side of PQ. Since m and ℓ cannot intersect twice, this is another contradiction.

We have eliminated the possibilities that α could be a right angle or an obtuse angle. Therefore, α must be an acute angle.

Pause for a moment to look at this proof carefully. The first portion, that the angle of parallelism cannot equal 90°, relied upon the hyperbolic parallel theorem. So this portion is true in hyperbolic geometry, but it is not true in Euclidean geometry. (In fact, in Euclidean geometry, the angle of parallelism is exactly 90°.) The second portion of the proof, however, relied on Euclid's First Postulate and made no use of parallelism. Therefore, this proof works in absolute geometry, meaning that α cannot be obtuse in hyperbolic geometry or in Euclidean geometry.

THE EXTERIOR ANGLE THEOREM

Earlier in this chapter, we observed that the Exterior Angle Theorem appears to hold in hyperbolic geometry as well as in Euclidean geometry. This was the point of Activity 3. In Euclidean geometry, this theorem is quite easy to prove: for $\triangle ABC$ with exterior angle at A, the exterior angle equals $180° - \angle A = 180° - (180° - \angle B - \angle C) = \angle B + \angle C$, which will be greater than either $\angle B$ or $\angle C$. This proof uses the "fact" that the sum of the three interior angles is 180°. However, in hyperbolic geometry, this proof does not work because this "fact" is not true in hyperbolic geometry! (We will prove this later.) Nevertheless, the Exterior Angle Theorem is still true. In fact, it can be proved without making use of any assumptions about parallels, so that the theorem is valid for both Euclidean triangles and for hyperbolic triangles.

THEOREM 11.6   If ABC is a triangle in the hyperbolic plane and $\angle BCD$ is exterior for this triangle, then $\angle BCD$ is larger than either $\angle CAB$ or $\angle ABC$.

Proof   Let M be the midpoint of the side BC. Construct a segment AE for which M is also the midpoint. Then construct segment EC. (See Figure 11.1.)

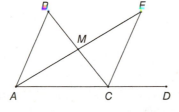

FIGURE 11.1
Proof of the Exterior
Angle Theorem

The vertical angles $\angle AMB$ and $\angle EMC$ are congruent, as are the segments BM and CM, and also the segments MA and ME. By SAS, therefore, the triangles ABM and ECM are congruent. So $\angle ABC = \angle ABM \cong \angle ECM$, and $\angle ECM$ is interior to $\angle DCM$.

To prove that ∠DCB is greater than ∠BAC, extend the side BC to form an angle vertical to ∠DCB. Locate the midpoint of the side AC and do the same argument as before.

Nowhere in this proof do parallel lines occur. Only the basic properties of segments, angles, and the SAS criterion are used. So the Exterior Angle Theorem is part of absolute geometry, and therefore is valid in hyperbolic geometry as well as Euclidean geometry.

Activity 5 asked you to investigate the Exterior Angle property in the situation of an asymptotic triangle. We could create an asymptotic triangle in the Euclidean plane with a line segment and two parallel rays. In Euclidean geometry, however, the exterior angle at one vertex would equal the interior angle at the other vertex because these would be corresponding angles on a transversal of the two parallels. For asymptotic triangles in the hyperbolic plane, however, a slight variation of the Exterior Angle Theorem still holds.

THEOREM 11.7   If ABΩ is an asymptotic triangle in the hyperbolic plane and ∠CBΩ is exterior for this triangle, then ∠CBΩ is greater than ∠BAΩ.

Proof   To prove this, we can eliminate the other two possibilities. First assume that ∠CBΩ is less than ∠BAΩ. Construct an angle BAD congruent to CBΩ. The ray AD must intersect BΩ, so let us put D on BΩ. However, this creates an ordinary triangle ABD with an exterior angle equal to an opposite interior angle, contradicting the last theorem.

Now assume that ∠CBΩ equals ∠BAΩ. Locate the midpoint M of AB and construct the segment MD perpendicular to the line AΩ. There are two possible situations: either point D lies between A and Ω, as shown on the right in Figure 11.2, or A is between D and Ω. For the situation shown in the figure, extend the ray BΩ in the opposite direction to the point E, with BE ≅ AD. Then ∠MBE ≅ ∠CBΩ, making ∠MBE ≅ ∠MAD. Then by SAS, ΔMAD ≅ ΔMBE. This implies that ∠BEM is a right angle, that ∠BME ≅ ∠AMD, and, therefore, that E, M, and D are collinear. This, however, is a situation with a line AD and point E for which the angle of parallelism is 90°—a contradiction. In the second situation, when A is between D and Ω (not shown), locate the point E on the ray BΩ so that BE ≅ AD. Again, ΔMAD ≅ ΔMBE by SAS. This shows that ∠BEM is a right angle, that ∠BME ≅ ∠AMD, and that the points E, M, and D are collinear. Just as before, the line AD and the point E have the angle of parallelism equal to 90°, a contradiction.

FIGURE 11.2
Proof of the Exterior Angle
Theorem for Asymptotic
Triangles

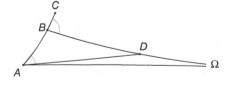

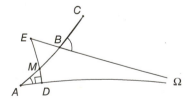

(Actually, there is a third possibility that point D coincides with the point A. In other words, $\angle BA\Omega = 90°$ and $\angle CB\Omega = 90°$. Using the point B and the line $A\Omega$, this is an immediate contradiction.)

Since $\angle CB\Omega$ cannot be less than $\angle BA\Omega$ and cannot equal $\angle BA\Omega$, $\angle CB\Omega$ must be greater than $\angle BA\Omega$ [Smart 1988, 307].

QUADRILATERALS IN THE HYPERBOLIC PLANE

Activities 10 and 11 invited you to investigate properties of quadrilaterals in the hyperbolic plane. The quadrilateral you constructed in Activity 10 has much in common with a standard Euclidean rectangle: two adjacent angles were right angles and two opposite sides were congruent. There are some additional similarities to rectangles, but this quadrilateral has some striking differences as well.

DEFINITION 11.5   A quadrilateral with a pair of congruent sides that are both perpendicular to a third side is called a *Saccheri quadrilateral.*

In Activity 10 you constructed a Saccheri quadrilateral $ABCD$ with right angles at A and B and congruent sides AD and BC. The two right angles, $\angle A$ and $\angle B$, are called the *base angles* and the side AB, which lies between the base angles, is called the *base* of the Saccheri quadrilateral. The angles above the base angles, $\angle C$ and $\angle D$, are the *summit angles*, and the side CD is the *summit* of the Saccheri quadrilateral. As you worked on Activity 10, you probably observed that the summit angles are congruent. The key to proving this is Figure 11.3. By finding congruent triangles, it is not difficult to show that the summit angles, C and D, are congruent. You will be asked to develop this proof in the exercises.

FIGURE 11.3
Proving That Summit Angles Are Congruent

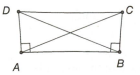

A more difficult issue is the size of these angles. We are accustomed to Euclidean rectangles, in which the summit angles are right angles. That is not the case in the hyperbolic plane.

THEOREM 11.8   The summit angles of a Saccheri quadrilateral are acute.

Proof   This is another situation in which we can eliminate the other two possibilities. Let $ABCD$ be a Saccheri quadrilateral, with right angles at A and at B, and with sides AD and BC congruent. Extend the base AB and the summit DC. Also, create rays at D and C that are parallel to the base. Because AD is congruent to BC and the segments DA and CB are perpendicular to the line AB, the angle of parallelism α is the same for both rays. See Figure 11.4.

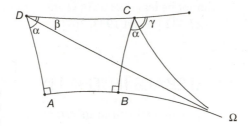

FIGURE 11.4
Proving That Summit Angles Are
Acute

First assume that the summit angles at C and D are right angles. This would make $\beta = \gamma$. However, γ is an exterior angle for the asymptotic triangle $DC\Omega$, so $\gamma > \beta$. Thus, the summit angles cannot be right angles.

Now assume the summit angles are obtuse. This would make $\alpha + \beta > 90°$ and also $\alpha + \gamma < 90°$. This implies that $\gamma < 90° - \alpha < \beta$. Once again, however, γ is an exterior angle of $\Delta DC\Omega$, so $\gamma > \beta$. Thus, the summit angles cannot be obtuse angles. This leaves acute angles as the only possibility for the summit angles [Smart 1988, 310].

This theorem shows yet another dramatic difference between the Euclidean and hyperbolic planes. There is more to come; this theorem about Saccheri quadrilaterals will lead us to a surprising fact about triangles in the next section. Before leaving quadrilaterals, however, here is one more result about Saccheri quadrilaterals, something you investigated in part (c) of Activity 10.

THEOREM 11.9   The segment joining the midpoints of the base and summit of a Saccheri quadrilateral is perpendicular to both the base and the summit.

Proof   Suppose that E is the midpoint of the base AB and that F is the midpoint of the summit DC. The triangles DAE and CBE are congruent by Side-Angle-Side, so the segments DE and CE are congruent. Then the triangles DFE and CFE are congruent by Side-Side-Side. The corresponding angles $\angle DFE$ and $\angle CFE$ are congruent, and each is half of $180°$.

A similar argument works for the angles at the base. Triangles ADF and BCF are congruent by Side-Angle-Side, so the segments AF and BF are congruent. Then $\Delta AEF \cong \Delta BEF$ by Side-Side-Side. So AEF is congruent to BEF, and each is half of $180°$.

(You should draw figures to make sure you understand this proof.)

A Saccheri quadrilateral is not quite a rectangle, for it has two right angles and two acute angles. Activity 11 introduced another quadrilateral that is not quite a rectangle.

DEFINITION 11.6   A quadrilateral with three right angles is called a *Lambert quadrilateral*.

The fourth angle is the challenge. It is not difficult to create a sequence of three right angles, but it may take some maneuvering to make these lines connect to create a fourth angle. Once you have the Lambert quadrilateral, what did you observe about the fourth angle? After seeing that Saccheri quadrilaterals contain acute angles, it may not have been surprising that a Lambert quadrilateral also has an acute angle.

The notions of Lambert quadrilateral and Saccheri quadrilateral are strongly related. Suppose *ABCD* is a Lambert quadrilateral with right angles at *A*, *B*, and *C*. Reflect *ABCD* across the line *AB* to get another Lambert quadrilateral *ABC'D'*. This creates a Saccheri quadrilateral *CC'D'D*, with right angles at *C* and *C'*. (The segment *AB* connects the midpoints of the base and summit, as in the last theorem.) The ∠*D* is the summit angle of a Saccheri quadrilateral and therefore is acute.

ANOTHER LOOK AT TRIANGLES IN THE HYPERBOLIC PLANE

One of the astonishing observations about triangles in the hyperbolic plane is that the angles do not sum to 180°. The sum of the three angles consistently yields a value less than 180°, and earlier we defined the *defect* of a triangle as the gap between the sum of its angles and the upper bound of 180°. With our understanding of Saccheri quadrilaterals, we are now ready to prove that this sum is less than 180°, so that the defect is always positive.

The key to this proof is the figure you constructed in Activity 12. In this figure, there are congruent triangles, and these are needed for the proof. Moving the vertex *A* created several possible figures, and these will need to be examined separately in the proof.

THEOREM 11.10   In the hyperbolic plane, the sum of the angles in any triangle is less than 180°.

Proof   Suppose that *ABC* is a triangle in the hyperbolic plane. Let *D* be the midpoint of the segment *AB* and let *E* be the midpoint of the segment *AC*. Construct segments *AX*, *BY*, and *CZ* that are perpendicular to the line *DE*, with the points *X*, *Y*, *Z* lying on the line *DE*.

There are three possibilities for this construction, depending upon the location of the vertex *A*. Figure 11.5 shows two of these three cases. The third case is when *AC* is perpendicular to *BC*, which makes *E = X = Z*.

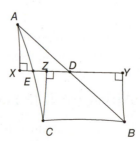

FIGURE 11.5
Two Cases for Proving
Theorem 11.10

Case 1, when the point X is between the points Y and Z: By Angle-Angle-Side, $\triangle CEZ \cong \triangle AEX$. So $CZ \cong AX$. Also by Angle-Angle-Side, $\triangle BDY \cong \triangle ADX$. So $BY \cong AX$. Consequently, $CZ \cong BY$, which makes $ZYBC$ a Saccheri quadrilateral. Now notice the congruent angles from these congruent pairs of triangles: $\angle ECZ \cong \angle EAX$ and $\angle YBD \cong \angle XAD$. Also notice that $\angle CAB = \angle EAX + \angle XAD$. Therefore,

$$\angle A + \angle B + \angle C = \angle CAB + \angle ABC + \angle BCA$$
$$= \angle EAX + \angle XAD + \angle DBC + \angle BCE$$
$$= \angle ECZ + \angle YBD + \angle DBC + \angle BCE$$
$$= \angle BCZ + \angle YBC$$
$$= 2 \cdot \angle BCZ.$$

Since $\angle BCZ$ is an acute angle in the Saccheri quadrilateral, this implies that $\angle A + \angle B + \angle C < 180°$.

Case 2, when the point X is exterior to the segment YZ: The second image in Figure 11.5 shows A to the left of YZ. If A is to the right, the argument is similar. As before, find congruent triangles and verify that $ZYBC$ is a Saccheri quadrilateral. Then

$$\angle A + \angle B + \angle C = \angle CAB + \angle ABC + \angle BCA$$
$$= \angle XAD - \angle EAX + \angle DBC + \angle BCZ + \angle ZCE$$
$$= \angle YBD + \angle DBC + \angle BCZ$$
$$= \angle YBC + \angle BCZ$$
$$= 2 \cdot \angle BCZ.$$

Once again, $\angle BCZ$ is an acute angle in the Saccheri quadrilateral and $\angle A + \angle B + \angle C < 180°$. (We have omitted some details here, which you should verify for yourself.)

Case 3, when point X equals point Z (and thus also equals point E): This is the simplest of the cases, and we leave it as an exercise.

An immediate corollary of this theorem is that the sum of the angles in a quadrilateral is less than 360°. To see this, construct a diagonal that cuts the quadrilateral into two triangles. It is not just the special situations of Saccheri and Lambert quadrilaterals that are deficient in their angles; in the hyperbolic plane, this is a property for quadrilaterals in general. So in the hyperbolic universe, rectangles and squares really do not exist!

AREA IN THE HYPERBOLIC PLANE

It is very inconvenient that squares do not exist in the hyperbolic plane, for squares are the basic tool used to define area in the Euclidean plane. The usual way to explain area is that a unit square measuring 1×1 has an area of 1 by definition; that an $m \times n$ rectangle has an area of mn because this area can be filled by that many unit squares; that a parallelogram can be cut into two pieces that reassemble as a rectangle; and that a triangle can be doubled to form a parallelogram. The areas of other polygons can be calculated by cutting them into triangular pieces and finding the sum of these triangular areas. Finding the area of regions with curved boundaries is a much more complicated question, and the integral calculus was developed in part to answer that question.

Activity 13 asked you to investigate area in a general way. It is difficult to judge area in the Poincaré disk. Remember that distance is not a simple calculation in the Poincaré model of hyperbolic geometry. Points near each other in the neighborhood of the fundamental circle can have a large distance value, while points near the center that appear to be farther apart can have a small distance value. However, we can say that whenever one triangle is entirely interior to another, the interior triangle will have the smaller area.

As you increased the size of $\triangle ABC$ in Activity 13, the defect should have increased. The largest possible triangle will be triply asymptotic; that is, the vertices will appear to lie on the fundamental circle of the Poincaré model. For this sort of triangle, the defect will have its largest possible value. Since the angle sum of a triply asymptotic triangle is 0°, its defect is 180°. A triangle with a smaller area will have a smaller defect, though we know that the defect is always positive.

In the early nineteenth century, Carl Gauss showed that the area of a triangle in the hyperbolic plane is directly proportional to the defect of the triangle. In a formula, this says that $Area = k \cdot (180 - \sum angles)$, where k is the same constant in every situation. The proof is somewhat intricate, and we will not present it here. See [Coxeter 1969] for a detailed presentation. This formula applies to asymptotic triangles also, with the understanding that the angle at the Ω vertex is 0°.

Since the sum of angles is a value between 0° and 180°—and thus the defect lies between 0 and 180 as well—the area of a triangle is between 0 and $k \cdot 180$. This has the peculiar consequence that there is a maximum size for the area of a triangle. In the Euclidean plane, of course, we can increase the area of a triangle without limit. However, that is not the case in the hyperbolic plane.

11.5 EXERCISES

Give clear and complete answers to the following problems and questions. Write your explanations clearly using complete sentences. Include diagrams whenever appropriate.

1. Prove, by using the underlying Euclidean concepts, that any two right angles in the Poincaré disk model are congruent.

2. Consider a circle C in the Euclidean plane.

   a. Prove that for any two points P and Q that lie interior to C, there is exactly one circular arc through P and Q that is orthogonal to C.

   b. Explain how this construction verifies that Euclid's first postulate holds in the Poincaré disk model of the hyperbolic plane.

3. Prove that the first two metric axioms hold for any two points in the Poincaré disk.

4. Construct an example in the Poincaré disk that illustrates the third metric axiom.

5. Complete the proof that the maximum length of a line in the Poincaré disk is ∞ (see page 258).

6. Let A be any point in the Poincaré disk. Prove that the distance from A to the fundamental circle is infinite.

7. Suppose that R and T are two points in the Poincaré model of the hyperbolic plane, and that S is an Ω point. Prove that the measure of $\angle RST$ is $0°$.

8. Suppose that $AB\Omega$ is an asymptotic triangle and that $\angle A \cong B$. If M is the midpoint of the finite side AB, prove that the line $M\Omega$ is perpendicular to AB.

9. Suppose that $A_1B_1\Omega_1$ and $A_2B_2\Omega_2$ are asymptotic triangles with $\angle A_1 \cong \angle A_2$ and $\angle B_1 \cong \angle B_2$. Prove that the two triangles are congruent, that is, prove that $A_1B_1 \cong A_2B_2$.

10. Will an asymptotic triangle have a circumcircle? Will an asymptotic triangle have an incircle? Either construct an example of each in the Poincaré disk or explain why it is impossible to do so.

11. Under what conditions will the perpendicular bisectors of the sides of a triangle be concurrent? Under what conditions will they be parallel?

12. Prove that if the three perpendicular bisectors of the sides of $\triangle ABC$ in the hyperbolic plane are concurrent at a point O, then the circle with center O and radius OA also contains the points B and C. Prove that this circumcircle is unique.

13. Consider $\triangle ABC$ in the hyperbolic plane.
    a. Prove that the bisectors of $\angle A$, $\angle B$, and $\angle C$ are concurrent. Denote the point of concurrency as I.
    b. Prove that I is the center of the *unique* incircle.

14. Does the Pythagorean Theorem hold in the hyperbolic plane? Develop an appropriate example in the Poincaré disk to investigate this question. How would you prove your conjecture?

15. What is the angle of parallelism for a line ℓ and a point P in the Euclidean plane? Explain why.

16. Given a line ℓ and a point P not on ℓ in the hyperbolic plane, construct a segment PQ perpendicular to ℓ. Prove that if a line m through P does not lie between the limiting parallels for ℓ, then m will not intersect ℓ.

17. For a given line ℓ, suppose that P_1 and P_2 are two points not on ℓ. If P_2 is farther from ℓ than P_1, prove that the angle of parallelism for P_2 is smaller than the angle of parallelism for P_1.

18. Any pair of lines in the hyperbolic plane must intersect, be limiting parallels, or be hyperparallel. If the base and summit of a Saccheri quadrilateral are extended to lines, which is true for these lines? Justify your answer from the properties of the hyperbolic plane, not from the Poincaré model.

19. Use Figure 11.3 to develop a proof that the summit angles of a Saccheri quadrilateral are congruent.

20. Let PQ be a common perpendicular to lines ℓ and m in the hyperbolic plane. Prove that PQ is the only common perpendicular.

21. Suppose $ABCD$ is a Lambert quadrilateral with right angles at A, B, and C. Prove that AD is longer than BC. (*Hint:* Look for contradictions for the other two possibilities.)

22. Let PQ be a common perpendicular to lines ℓ and m in the hyperbolic plane.
    a. Use the result of Exercise 21 to prove that any hyperbolic segment joining a point of ℓ to a point of m will be longer than PQ.
    b. What does part (a) imply about a Saccheri quadrilateral?

23. Refer to the proof of Theorem 11.10 on pages 273–274.
    a. Write a detailed version of the proof for Case 2.
    b. Prove Case 3.

24. Suppose ABC is a triangle in the hyperbolic plane and D is a point on the segment BC. The segment AD divides $\triangle ABC$ into two new triangles. How are the defects of $\triangle ABD$ and $\triangle ACD$ related to the defect of $\triangle ABC$?

25. Prove that the angle sum of a quadrilateral in the hyperbolic plane is always less than $360°$.

26. Suppose that a quadrilateral in the hyperbolic plane has four congruent angles. Prove that the four angles must be acute. Construct an example in the Poincaré disk.

27. Can you construct a pentagon with only right angles? Can you construct a hexagon with only right angles? A heptagon? An octagon? Either give an example of each in the Poincaré model or explain why it cannot be done.

28. Let $P_1 P_2 \ldots P_n$ be an n-sided polygon in the hyperbolic plane. Find upper and lower bounds for the angle sum of this polygon. Justify your answers.

29. In the hyperbolic plane, prove that AAA is a congruence criterion for ordinary triangles (i.e., not asymptotic triangles). In other words, if two ordinary triangles are similar, they are also congruent.

30. What is the angle sum of a triply asymptotic triangle? Explain.

31. Draw a sequence of diagrams showing how area is calculated in the Euclidean plane. Show how to justify this calculation for rectangles, parallelograms, triangles, and more general polygons.

32. Derive and prove a formula for the area of a quadrilateral in the hyperbolic plane.

33. If we assume Euclid's first four postulates, prove that Playfair's Postulate is equivalent to Euclid's Fifth Postulate.

The Upper-Half-Plane Model

The Poincaré disk is one model of the hyperbolic plane. Another interesting model to investigate is the upper-half-plane model. In this model, the points of the hyperbolic plane are represented by the points in the Euclidean plane that lie *above* the x-axis. (This is why it is called the *upper*-half-plane model.) The points which lie *on* the x-axis are the Ω points. The lines of this model are of two types:

- *Type 1 lines:* vertical rays emanating from the x-axis;

- *Type 2 lines:* semicircular arcs whose centers lie on the x-axis.

For two lines, ℓ and m, to intersect in this model, at least one of them must be a *Type 2 line*. To measure an angle between any two lines in this model, consider the angle between the tangents to the semicircular arcs at the point of intersection, or consider the angle between the ray and the tangent to the semicircular arc at the point of intersection. Exercises 34–39 are to be done in the upper-half-plane model of the hyperbolic plane.

34. Given any two points A and B in the upper half-plane, prove that there is a *unique* line through A and B. (*Note:* There are two cases to consider.)

35. Verify that Euclid's first four postulates hold in the upper-half-plane model.

36. Verify that the hyperbolic parallel theorem holds in the upper-half-plane model.

37. Create a rectangular coordinate system in a GeoGebra worksheet.
    a. Construct examples of hyperbolic triangles in the upper-half-plane model. Calculate the angle sum of these triangles.
    b. If triangles are classified as different types depending on the number of sides which are represented by Type 1 lines, how many different types of triangles are there? Explain.
    c. Construct examples of right triangles in this model. Prove or disprove the Pythagorean Theorem in this model.
    d. Construct an example of a triangle in the upper-half-plane model that has a positive defect.
    e. Construct an example of a Saccheri quadrilateral in the upper-half-plane model.
    f. Construct an example of a Lambert quadrilateral in the upper-half-plane model.

38. Prove that it is impossible to construct a rectangle in the upper-half-plane model.

39. Prove that every triangle in the upper-half-plane model has a positive defect.

Exercises 40–42 are especially for future teachers.

40. In the *Principles and Standards for School Mathematics*, the National Council of Teachers of Mathematics (NCTM) observes that "Being able to reason is essential to understanding mathematics. By developing ideas, exploring phenomena, justifying results, and using mathematical conjectures in all content areas and—with different levels of sophistication—at all grade levels, students should see and expect that mathematics makes sense." Further, "Reasoning and proof cannot simply be taught in a single unit on logic, for example, by 'doing proofs' in geometry. . . . Reasoning and proof should be a consistent part of students' mathematical experience in prekindergarten through grade 12" [NCTM 2000, 56]. What does this mean for you and your future students?

    a. Read the discussion on Reasoning and Proof in the *Principles and Standards for School Mathematics* [NCTM 2000, 56–59]. Then study the Geometry Standard for at least two grade bands (i.e., pre-K–2, 3–5, 6–8, and/or 9–12). What are the recommendations of the NCTM regarding the development of logical reasoning and mathematical proof? How is this focus on logical reasoning developed across several grade levels? Cite specific examples.

    b. Find copies of school mathematics textbooks for the same grade levels as you studied in part (a). How are the NCTM standards for reasoning and proof implemented in those textbooks? Again, cite specific examples.

    c. Write a report in which you present and critique what you learn. Your report should include your responses to parts (a) and (b).

41. Beginning in the earliest grades and developing through high school, students need to learn increasingly sophisticated ways of thinking, reasoning, and proving. Design several classroom activities involving logical reasoning and mathematical proof that would be appropriate for students in your future classroom. Write a short report explaining how the activities you design

reflect both what you have learned in studying this chapter and the NCTM recommendations.

42. Find the Common Core State Standards for Mathematics online: http://www.corestandards.org.

    a. Which of the eight Standards for Mathematical Practice have to do with reasoning and proof?

    b. "During high school, students begin to formalize their geometry experiences from elementary and middle school, using more precise definitions and developing careful proofs. Later in college some students develop Euclidean and other geometries carefully from a small set of axioms" (*Common Core State Standards for Mathematics*, 74). Study the Common Core State Standards for Mathematics: High School—Geometry.

        i. What kinds of proofs are high school students expected to be able to develop? At what times in the high school curriculum do students develop these proof-writing skills?

        ii. How has your study of the geometry of the hyperbolic plane helped to strengthen your own understanding of Euclidean geometry? Give several specific examples.

Reflect on what you have learned in this chapter.

43. Review the main ideas of this chapter. Describe, in your own words, the concepts you have studied and what you have learned about them. What are the important ideas? How do they fit together? Which concepts were easy for you? Which were hard?

44. Reflect on the learning environment for this course.

    a. Describe aspects of the learning environment that helped you understand the main ideas in this chapter. Which activities did you like? Which challenged you to reason and problem solve at a higher level of sophistication? Why?

    b. "Reasoning and proof cannot simply be taught in a single unit on logic, for example, by 'doing proofs' in geometry. . . . Reasoning and proof should be a consistent part of students' mathematical experience in prekindergarten through grade 12" [NCTM 2000, 56]. How will you use what you are learning about reasoning and proof in your own future classroom?

11.6 CHAPTER OVERVIEW

In this chapter, you have had an opportunity to explore a strange new universe. The hyperbolic plane has a lot in common with the Euclidean plane. Euclid's first four postulates still hold. Yet, everything looks quite strange!

The hyperbolic parallel postulate is one of two possible negations of Euclid's Parallel Postulate:

Hyperbolic Parallel Postulate   There is a line ℓ and there is a point P not on ℓ, such that more than one line through P is parallel to ℓ.

Using the hyperbolic parallel postulate as an axiom, it is possible to prove a stronger statement:

Hyperbolic Parallel Theorem   Given any line ℓ and any point P not on ℓ, there will be more than one line through P that is parallel to ℓ.

To guide our understanding, we have focused in this chapter on the Poincaré disk model of the hyperbolic plane. In this model, the *points* of the hyperbolic plane are represented by the points interior to the fundamental circle. The *lines* of the hyperbolic plane are represented by circular arcs that lie interior to the fundamental circle and are orthogonal to it. Distance in the Poincaré disk is measured very differently from the usual Euclidean metric; however, the Poincaré metric satisfies the same three metric properties.

1. If A and B are points, then $d(A, B) \geq 0$; and $d(A, B) = 0$ if and only if $A = B$.
2. If A and B are points, then $d(A, B) = d(B, A)$.
3. If A, B, and C are points, then $d(A, B) + d(B, C) \geq d(A, C)$.

This different way of measuring distances causes circles to look different, for the center of a circle in the Poincaré disk is not in the expected location.

This new way of interpreting lines gives rise to new sorts of triangles. We still have the usual sort of triangle, with three vertices and three sides. (One of the exercises asks you to prove that, in the hyperbolic plane, AAA is a criterion for congruence of the usual sort of triangles.) In addition, however, there is now the concept of an *asymptotic triangle* for which one, two, or even all three vertices are points at infinity. Even for asymptotic triangles, it still makes sense to talk of congruence, and we proved one criterion for checking this congruence.

Many things about triangles are true in both Euclidean geometry and hyperbolic geometry. Consider two of the concurrence theorems from Chapter 3. One of these holds in the hyperbolic plane:

Theorem The three angle bisectors of a triangle are concurrent.

A proof of this theorem in the hyperbolic plane can follow the same steps as the proof we gave for the Euclidean plane. The same proof works because the proof is based on results that follow solely from Euclid's first four postulates. However, a second theorem must be modified to make sense in the hyperbolic plane.

Theorem If the three perpendicular bisectors of the sides of a triangle in the hyperbolic plane are concurrent at a point O, then the circle with center O and radius OA also contains the points B and C.

The condition is necessary because the three perpendicular bisectors may be parallel to each other. Thus, while an incircle with center I can be constructed for any hyperbolic triangle, a circumcircle can only be constructed for those hyperbolic triangles for which the point O exists.

The second portion of this chapter investigated the properties of the hyperbolic plane more deeply. The hyperbolic parallel theorem asserts that given any point P and any line ℓ, there will be more than one line through P that is parallel to ℓ. In fact, there will be an infinite collection of lines parallel to ℓ, and these lines are divided into the *limiting parallels* and the *hyperparallels*. The angle formed by one of the limiting parallels and the perpendicular from P to ℓ is the *angle of parallelism*. For a given point P and a given line ℓ, the two angles of parallelism are congruent and acute.

The Exterior Angle Theorem remains true in the hyperbolic plane as well as in the Euclidean plane. It is a theorem of *absolute geometry*, that portion of geometry that can be proved from just the first four of Euclid's axioms. In essence, the Exterior Angle Theorem is neutral with regard to parallelism; it holds with or without a Parallel Postulate. However, we were able to prove that the Exterior Angle Theorem works for asymptotic triangles also.

A *Saccheri quadrilateral* has a base, two congruent sides that form right angles with the base, and a fourth side called the summit. We proved that the angles at the summit are congruent and, furthermore, that in the hyperbolic plane they are acute. This is a dramatic contrast to Euclidean geometry, in which this figure would be a rectangle. The properties of the Saccheri quadrilateral show that rectangles do not exist in hyperbolic geometry. The *Lambert quadrilateral* is another way to show this.

The culmination of this chapter was the theorem that the sum of the angles of a triangle will be less than 180°. The proof used facts about Saccheri quadrilaterals. The difference between 180° and the sum of the angles is called the *defect* of the triangle. The defect is the key to measuring area in hyperbolic geometry, for the area of a triangle is proportional to its defect.

Although we illustrated these ideas using examples in the Poincaré disk model, we proved them using the axioms and theorems of the hyperbolic plane. These phenomena are theorems and will hold in any model of the hyperbolic plane.

In the exercises, we introduced a second model of the hyperbolic plane. All of the examples that we explored in the Poincaré disk model can also be developed in the upper-half-plane model. The two models of the hyperbolic plane, the Poincaré disk model and the upper-half-plane model, are *isomorphic*. That is, in a deep geometric sense, they are the same. (A proof of this fact is beyond the scope of this course.)

In this chapter, we have only touched the surface of hyperbolic geometry. Indeed, an entire course could focus on the properties of the hyperbolic plane. We hope that, by studying this chapter you have begun to develop an appreciation for the impact that a choice of axioms has on the nature of the objects in a geometric space.

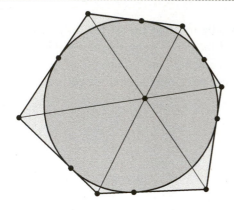

Projective Geometry

Projective geometry is a well-developed subject within geometry. Its mathematical roots go back to Pappus in the fourth-century C.E. and even earlier to the ancient Greek mathematicians. It also has roots in art, through the theory of perspective drawing. The idea of a horizon line and the notion that parallel lines converge at the horizon brought a new realism to Renaissance painting, and many special techniques were invented for portraying objects in perspective. However, this shifted the focus of the underlying geometry, for objects that were the same size in reality could no longer be drawn the same size in a picture. Instead, the objects should appear to shrink as they recede in the picture. The theory of perspective and projective geometry thus place more emphasis on incidence properties than on measurement.

We will present three approaches to studying projective geometry. First, we will examine an axiom system for a projective plane and prove some basic theorems. There are several interesting models for this axiom system, both finite models and some infinite models. The notion of duality provides a powerful proof technique and leads to some important theorems. Second, we will take an analytic approach by applying coordinate systems to these models. Third, we will introduce projective transformations and give some of their properties, leading to the Fundamental Theorem of Projective Geometry.

Give clear and complete answers to the following problems and questions. Write your explanations clearly using complete sentences, and including diagrams whenever appropriate. Save your work for each activity, as sometimes later work builds on earlier work. It will be helpful to read ahead into the chapter as you work on these activities.

1. Create a coordinate system and construct the horizontal line $y = 1$.
   a. Construct a point P on this line, and construct the line ℓ through P and the origin. Measure the abscissa (the x-coordinate) of P and measure the slope of ℓ. Drag or animate P and observe these values. How are these values related? Does every point P have a slope value? Does every slope value have a point P?
   b. Does every such point P on the line $y = 1$ have a corresponding line from the origin? Does every line from the origin have a corresponding point P? Explain why or why not.
   c. Now add to your diagram a unit circle centered at the origin. Construct the points where ℓ intersects this circle. Think of this situation as a function that maps a point on the circle to a corresponding point on the line. What is the domain of this function? Is it a one-to-one function? Is it onto? Does this function have an inverse function?

2. Create a line ℓ and construct a segment AB on this line. (You should be able to drag the segment without disturbing the line.) Label the endpoints of this segment.

   Now create another line m and also a point P not on either ℓ or m. Construct the points $C = \overleftrightarrow{PA} \cap m$ and $D = \overleftrightarrow{PB} \cap m$. Then construct the segment CD. (Using several colors and thicknesses will make your diagram easier to follow.) Drag the segment AB along its line ℓ and observe what happens to the segment CD. What changes? What stays the same?

   Now move the point P to another location. Again drag AB and observe what happens. Try several locations for P. Do your observations still hold? Does anything change if the line m is moved?

3. Create three lines that are concurrent at a common point P. Construct points A_1, A_2 on one of these lines, points B_1, B_2 on a second line, and C_1, C_2 on the third line. Label these points.

   Construct segments to form the triangles $\Delta A_1 B_1 C_1$ and $\Delta A_2 B_2 C_2$, and construct the interiors of the triangles. (Using different colors will make your diagram easier to follow.) These triangles are said to be *perspective* from point P.

   Now extend the side $A_1 B_1$ to a line. Then extend $A_2 B_2$ to a line as well and construct the intersection point of these two new lines. Repeat this for the sides $B_1 C_1$ and $B_2 C_2$, and also for $C_1 A_1$ and $C_2 A_2$.

   You should now have three intersection points of corresponding sides of the triangles. How are these three points related to each other? Vary the points A_1, A_2, B_1, B_2, and C_1, C_2. Does your observation still hold? Does your observation hold if the two triangles are on the same side of P? Does it hold if the triangles are on opposite sides of P? Does it hold if P is interior to both triangles?

4. a. Create two lines ℓ_1 and ℓ_2. Construct three points A_1, B_1, C_1 on ℓ_1 and three points A_2, B_2, C_2 on ℓ_2. Then construct the *cross joins* $X = \overleftrightarrow{A_1 B_2} \cap \overleftrightarrow{A_2 B_1}$, $Y = \overleftrightarrow{B_1 C_2} \cap \overleftrightarrow{B_2 C_1}$, and $Z = \overleftrightarrow{C_1 A_2} \cap \overleftrightarrow{C_2 A_1}$. (Using different colors will help you understand this diagram.) What do you observe about the points X, Y, Z? Drag some lines and points; is your observation still valid?

    b. Now create a circle. Construct three points A_1, B_1, C_1 on one "side" of the circle and three points A_2, B_2, C_2 on the "other side." As before, construct the cross joins X, Y, Z. What do you observe about these points?

    In a general sense, the six points A_1, B_2, C_1, A_2, B_1, C_2 and the constructed lines form a hexagon inscribed in this circle. Select these six points, *in this order*, and construct the interior of the hexagon. Then drag vertices so that this is a convex hexagon. Does your observation still hold?

5. a. Find at least five more points that lie on the line containing the origin O and the point $P = (5, 2)$. How are the coordinates of these points related to each other?

    b. Find at least five points X for which the line OX does not intersect the line $y = 1$. What do your answers have in common?

    c. Repeat these questions in $\mathbb{R}^3$ using $P = (5, 2, 1)$ and the plane $z = 1$.

6. a. Create two lines ℓ_1, ℓ_2 and a point P_1 not on either line. Construct a point X on ℓ_1 and construct the point $Y = \overleftrightarrow{P_1 X} \cap \ell_2$.

    This creates a function $f(X) = Y$ with the points of ℓ_1 as its source and the points of ℓ_2 as the target. A function of this sort is called a *perspectivity* between the two lines. Does every input X produce an output $f(X)$? That is, does every point X of ℓ_1 have a corresponding point Y on ℓ_2? Is every point of ℓ_2 an output for some point from ℓ_1? Vary P_1 and the two lines to see if this affects your answers.

    b. Now add to your diagram a third line ℓ_3 and another point P_2 not on any of the three lines. Construct the point $Z = \overleftrightarrow{P_2 Y} \cap \ell_3$. This is a composition of two perspectivity functions, which creates a new function $g(X) = Z$, with ℓ_1 as its source and ℓ_3 as its target. The new function g is a *projectivity* between ℓ_1 and ℓ_3. Does every point of ℓ_1 produce an output point on ℓ_3? Does every point on ℓ_3 have a corresponding point on ℓ_1?

    c. Do your answers in part b change if $\ell_3 = \ell_1$, that is, if the source and target are the same line? In this situation, can $g(X)$ ever equal X?

7. Create two lines ℓ_1 and ℓ_2. Construct six points: A_1, B_1, C_1 on ℓ_1 and A_2, B_2, C_2 on ℓ_2. Define a function from ℓ_1 to ℓ_2 as follows: Construct the

points $P = \overleftrightarrow{A_1B_2} \cap \overleftrightarrow{A_2B_1}$ and $Q = \overleftrightarrow{A_1C_2} \cap \overleftrightarrow{A_2C_1}$. Construct the line $\overleftrightarrow{PQ}$. Also construct the line $\overleftrightarrow{A_1A_2}$ and the point $R = \overleftrightarrow{A_1A_2} \cap \overleftrightarrow{PQ}$.

Let X be a point on ℓ_1. Construct the point $T = \overleftrightarrow{A_2X} \cap \overleftrightarrow{PQ}$ and define $f(X) = \overleftrightarrow{A_1T} \cap \ell_2$. Drag X along ℓ_1 and observe the output $f(X)$.

a. Is this a well-defined function? That is, will every input give a unique output? If so, is it a one-to-one function? What is the domain of f? What is the range of f?

b. What are $f(A_1)$, $f(B_1)$, and $f(C_1)$?

c. Using the points and lines already in your diagram, find a perspectivity from ℓ_1 to the line $\overleftrightarrow{PQ}$. (See Activity 6.) What point are you using for the center?

d. Again using the points and lines in your diagram, find a perspectivity from $\overleftrightarrow{PQ}$ to ℓ_2. Where is the center of this perspectivity?

12.2 DISCUSSION

AN AXIOM SYSTEM

The axiomatic approach is an important method in mathematics. By stating a specific set of assumptions, we know exactly what properties can be used when developing proofs. Further, any theorems proved from those axioms will apply to every situation that fits the axioms. At several places in this book, we have examined axiom systems and how to reason from a set of axioms. This started with our discussion of Euclid's five axioms (postulates) for plane geometry in Chapter 2. Another example was the set of axioms for a group, which we first presented in Chapter 8. In some other chapters, we explored the consequences of altering an axiom. Chapter 6, for instance, explored the surprising effects of changing the way in which distance is measured. The axioms for hyperbolic geometry presented in Chapter 11 are the same as the axioms for Euclidean geometry, except for one major change in the Fifth Postulate. As you saw, this one change led to a radically different, and sometimes surprising, set of theorems. Parallelism is a critical issue for hyperbolic geometry, and it will be an issue for projective geometry as well.

Our first look at projective geometry was in Chapter 7, where we presented one possible set of axioms and examined finite situations that fit those axioms. All of the theorems proved from the axioms are true for each of those models. In this chapter, we return to that axiom system and look at an infinite model created by extending the familiar Euclidean plane.

Here again are the axioms we will use for a projective plane.

Axiom 1 A line lies on at least two points.

Axiom 2 Any two distinct points have exactly one line in common.

Axiom 3 Any two distinct lines have at least one point in common.

Axiom 4 There is a set of four distinct points, no three of which are collinear.

As we noted in Chapter 7, Axiom 4 says that there are points in the projective plane, and then Axiom 2 guarantees that there will be lines as well. Also notice that Axiom 3 specifically requires that any two lines in a projective plane will intersect.

Recall two of the results already proved from these axioms. These are Theorem 7.7 and Lemma 7.1, and they are proved in Chapter 7.

THEOREM 12.1   Any two distinct lines have exactly one point in common.

THEOREM 12.2   The points on one line can be put into one-to-one correspondence with the points on any other line.

Axiom 3 together with Theorem 12.1 have profound consequences. These statements mean that there are no parallel lines in projective geometry. Our experiences with perspective agree with this, for parallel lines such as railroad tracks or highway lines appear to intersect at the horizon. Of course, we can never reach those intersection points; they will always appear infinitely far away. (This idea will be important when we discuss models for projective geometry.)

In Activity 6a, you created a function between one line and another line, using one particular point to define the function. The idea from that activity can be used to prove Theorem 12.2. This function is known as a *perspectivity* between the two lines. We will work with perspectivities later in this chapter.

MODELS FOR THE PROJECTIVE PLANE

The *undefined terms* of this axiom system are *point, line, lies on*. Common notions of Euclidean geometry such as distance and angle are not the focus of projective geometry. Instead, the focus is on incidence of points and lines; points lying on lines and lines lying on points.

A *model* of an axiom system is a situation in which all of the axioms hold true. This may require a different interpretation of what a point is or what a line is. We will encounter both of these issues as we present three very different models for the axioms of a projective plane.

The Real Projective Plane

Activity 1 asked for a correspondence between the points on the line $y = 1$ and the lines through the origin. Most of the time this is pretty easy to do; a point lying on this horizontal line determines a line from the origin and a line lying on the origin intersects this horizontal line to determine a point. However, one of the lines through the origin does not intersect $y = 1$, namely the horizontal line $y = 0$. There are not enough points on $y = 1$ to account for all these lines in this way. Here is where we can borrow an idea from artistic perspective. In a perspective drawing, parallel lines that recede into the picture intersect at the horizon line, which is imagined to be infinitely far away. So the artist includes a point at infinity to mark the intersection of the parallel lines. This is mathematical nonsense—after all, parallel lines, by definition, do not intersect—but it suggests a way to extend the Euclidean plane and to make Axiom 3 work. The idea is to put in *points at infinity* where the parallels will intersect. Then the infinite point on $y = 1$ will also be the infinite point on $y = 0$ and the two horizontal lines will intersect at the infinite point.

Let us do this carefully. For any line in the Euclidean plane, there will be a collection of lines that are parallel to it. The lines in this collection are *equivalent* to each other in a very strong way, for parallelism is an *equivalence relation*. This means three things: Any line ℓ is parallel to itself (the *reflexive* property); if ℓ is parallel to m, then m is parallel to ℓ (the *symmetric* property); and if ℓ is parallel to m and m is parallel to n, then ℓ is parallel to n (the *transitive* property). In the sense of parallelism, all these lines are essentially the same; they are equivalent.

Equivalence relations are useful tools in many areas of mathematics. The most important theorem about equivalence relations says that any such relation separates its set of objects into disjoint *equivalence classes*. Each equivalence class is a set containing all the objects that are related to each other. In our situation of Euclidean lines related by parallelism, one example of an equivalence class is the set of lines with slope 2. Every line with its slope equal to 2 belongs to this particular equivalence class, and lines with different slopes do not belong. The set of all vertical lines is another example of an equivalence class. Every Euclidean line belongs to exactly one of these equivalence classes.

Each equivalence class will be called an *ideal point*. Two lines that are parallel are in the same equivalence class, so they share a common ideal point. The set of ideal points forms the *ideal line*. The set of ordinary points in the Euclidean plane together with the points of the ideal line forms the *real projective plane*. A line is now one of two types: a Euclidean line plus its ideal point or the ideal line. To verify that Axiom 3 works in this model, we must examine two cases: when the two lines are both of the first type or when one of the two lines is the ideal line. (You will get a chance to do this in the exercises.)

The real projective plane has properties beyond the axioms and the simple theorems mentioned earlier. For instance, something must be said about continuity. One approach is to add an axiom that for any line, all but one of the points can be put into one-to-one correspondence with the set of real numbers. Then the continuity of the real line $\mathbb{R}^1$ will produce continuity in the real projective plane. (The classic reference for this model is *The Real Projective Plane* by Coxeter [1949].)

Notice that the projective axioms say nothing about the ideal line. It is merely one line among many lines. This can be a great advantage when proving theorems. A proof that is based solely on the projective axioms avoids having to worry about special cases that involve parallel lines. For instance, here is a proof of the theorem from Activity 4a. This proof uses Menelaus' Theorem from Chapter 3, working on a triangle created by some of the lines in the theorem [Coxeter & Greitzer 1967, 67–69].

THEOREM 12.3 **Pappus' Theorem** Suppose that A_1, B_1, C_1 are distinct points on one line ℓ_1 and that A_2, B_2, C_2 are distinct points on a second line ℓ_2. Form the cross joins

$X = \overleftrightarrow{A_1B_2} \cap \overleftrightarrow{A_2B_1}$, $Y = \overleftrightarrow{B_1C_2} \cap \overleftrightarrow{B_2C_1}$, and $Z = \overleftrightarrow{C_1A_2} \cap \overleftrightarrow{C_2A_1}$. Then the three points X, Y, Z are collinear.

Proof See Figure 12.1. Suppose that the lines $\overleftrightarrow{A_1B_2}$ and $\overleftrightarrow{B_1C_2}$ intersect at a point D, that $\overleftrightarrow{B_1C_2}$ and $\overleftrightarrow{C_1A_2}$ intersect at E, and that $\overleftrightarrow{C_1A_2}$ and $\overleftrightarrow{A_1B_2}$ intersect at F. This uses three of the eight lines given in the hypothesis, and the other five lines are transversals of the triangle $\triangle DEF$. From Menelaus' Theorem, each transversal creates a product.

From A_1ZC_2 we get

$$\frac{DC_2}{C_2E} \cdot \frac{EZ}{ZF} \cdot \frac{FA_1}{A_1D} = -1$$

From B_1XA_2 we get

$$\frac{DB_1}{B_1E} \cdot \frac{EA_2}{A_2F} \cdot \frac{FX}{XD} = -1$$

From C_1YB_2 we get

$$\frac{DY}{YE} \cdot \frac{EC_1}{C_1F} \cdot \frac{EB_2}{B_2D} = -1$$

From $A_1B_1C_1$ we get

$$\frac{DB_1}{B_1E} \cdot \frac{EC_1}{C_1F} \cdot \frac{FA_1}{A_1D} = -1$$

From $A_2B_2C_2$ we get

$$\frac{DC_2}{C_2E} \cdot \frac{EA_2}{A_2F} \cdot \frac{FB_2}{B_2D} = -1$$

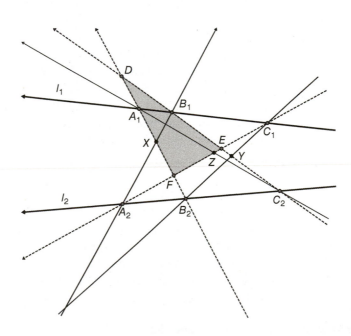

FIGURE 12.1
Proof of Pappus' Theorem

Now divide the product of the first three expressions by the product of the last two. After much cancelation, this produces

$$\frac{DY}{YE} \cdot \frac{EZ}{ZF} \cdot \frac{FX}{XD} = -1$$

Therefore, the points X, Y, Z are collinear.

Pappus' Theorem has a very projective flavor to it, for it talks only about incidence of lines and points. The proof given here, of course, uses measurement concepts. Later we will see a proof based on projective transformations that avoids both measurement and parallelism, thus combining all possible cases into one short proof.

A Finite Model: The Fano Plane

Chapter 7 included several important theorems about finite projective planes and showed two of the smaller finite models. The smallest finite projective plane is the *Fano plane*. This structure has seven points and seven lines. It can be done in a very abstract way as follows:

- The points are the numbers 1, 2, 3, 4, 5, 6, 7.
- The lines are the

$$\left\{\begin{array}{c}1\\2\\5\end{array}\right\}, \left\{\begin{array}{c}3\\4\\5\end{array}\right\}, \left\{\begin{array}{c}1\\3\\6\end{array}\right\}, \left\{\begin{array}{c}2\\4\\6\end{array}\right\}, \left\{\begin{array}{c}1\\4\\7\end{array}\right\}, \left\{\begin{array}{c}2\\3\\7\end{array}\right\}, \left\{\begin{array}{c}5\\6\\7\end{array}\right\}.$$

It takes only a few moments to check that all four axioms are satisfied by this structure. A more difficult challenge is to create a picture of the Fano plane. Starting with the points 1, 2, 3, 4, no three of which can be collinear, we can construct six lines. These six lines intersect in pairs to produce three additional points. The seventh line can only be drawn by bending it. The GeoGebra command **Circle Through 3 Points** may be helpful if you wish to try this yourself. Figure 12.2 shows a drawing of the Fano plane that is different from the two drawings in Chapter 7.

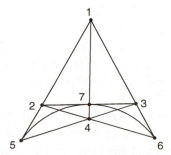

FIGURE 12.2
The Fano Plane

A Model on the Sphere

In Activity 1c, you looked for a correspondence between lines through the origin and points on the unit circle. Of course, each such line intersects the circle twice, so this is really a correspondence between a line and a pair of points, not just individual points. These diametrically opposed points are called *antipodes*. Lines through the origin also intersect the horizontal tangent line $y = 1$, so we can use these lines to create a correspondence between points on the horizontal tangent and pairs of antipodes on the unit circle. Each point on $y = 1$ corresponds to an antipodal pair on the circle, and each antipodal pair corresponds to a point on the tangent line.

There is, of course, one exception: the line along the horizontal axis does not intersect $y = 1$. In this case, the pair $(1, 0)$ and $(-1, 0)$ on the unit circle corresponds to the ideal point of the tangent line. So if we consider each pair of antipodes as only one point, the unit circle acts as a projective line, including its ideal point.

Let's extend this idea to one higher dimension. In Chapter 11 we briefly examined the sphere as a model of elliptic geometry. The lines in this model were the *great circles* on the sphere. It may be helpful to visualize a great circle as the intersection of the sphere with a plane that passes through the center of the sphere. A great circle uses the center of the sphere as its own center. A great circle has the largest possible radius for a circle on the surface of the sphere. The Earth's equator is perhaps the most familiar example of a great circle. If two great circles are drawn on the sphere, they will intersect twice, and these intersection points are diametrically opposed points—antipodes.

To use the sphere as a model of a projective plane, consider each antipodal pair of points to be a single point [Coxeter 1969, 93–94]. The lines will be the great circles. It is not difficult to see that the four axioms of a projective plane are satisfied in this model. A great circle has at least two points, that is, two antipodal pairs. Any two points lie on exactly one great circle. (This takes a little care. For instance, there are many great circles that contain both the "North Pole" and the "South Pole," which seems to violate Axiom 2. However, these are antipodes, so in this model they are considered to be the same point.) Any two great circles intersect in a single antipodal pair. Finally, there are many possible choices for four distinct points, no three of which lie on a common great circle.

The spherical model is, in fact, isomorphic to the real projective plane. Think of the sphere as sitting on a plane, so that the plane is tangent to the sphere. See Figure 12.3. Imagine lines through the center of the sphere. Each such line intersects the sphere twice and intersects the tangent plane once. Thus, a point in the plane corresponds to an antipodal pair of points on the sphere, that is, to a single projective point. The exceptions are the points on the equator, for which the line from the center does not intersect the tangent plane. A pair of antipodal points on the equator corresponds to an ideal point for the tangent plane, and the equator corresponds to the ideal line.

This relationship between the sphere and the tangent plane is called *central projection*. A pair of points on the sphere is projected from its center to a point on the tangent plane, and any point on the tangent plane is the result of one of

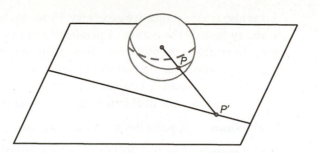

FIGURE 12.3
Central Projection

these projections. A great circle on the sphere is centrally projected to a line in the tangent plane. Do you see why? Imagine an arbitrary plane through the center of the sphere. This plane intersects the sphere to create a great circle and intersects the tangent plane to create a line. Of course, if this plane through the sphere's center is parallel to the tangent plane, it will intersect the sphere at the equator. This corresponds to the ideal line of the tangent plane.

With the spherical model we encounter a disturbing fact about the real projective plane: It is a *nonorientable* surface. In the Euclidean plane, clockwise and counterclockwise are familiar concepts, and a clockwise rotation looks the same anywhere in the plane. This is not so in the real projective plane. Think of a small circle drawn in the upper half of a sphere, with arrows going clockwise around it. This corresponds to its antipodal circle in the lower half of the sphere. However, if you look at the antipodal circle from below the sphere, the arrows are going counterclockwise! Since these two circles are considered the same circle in the projective model, a clockwise/counterclockwise orientation is not possible.

DUALITY

In the set of axioms for a projective plane, Axioms 2 and 3 are very similar. There is also a strong similarity between Axiom 2 and Theorem 12.1. Axiom 2 says "Any two distinct points have exactly one line in common" and the theorem says "Any two distinct lines have exactly one point in common." The only difference between the statements is that the words *point* and *line* have been interchanged. This is the idea of *duality*; if two major concepts are interchanged in a statement, the new statement also could be true. For projective geometry, the two major concepts are *point* and *line*. Switching these terms in the projective axioms creates four new statements. All of these new statements are also true, and it is straightforward to verify this. We will also examine two dual concepts of perspective and the surprising fact that they are equivalent.

So projective geometry has the duality property. Any of the axioms can be restated into its dual axiom. We can take this further: Any proof can be restated into its dual proof, and, therefore, any theorem can be restated into its dual theorem. Since the dual axioms will be true in a projective plane, any dual proof is valid and any dual theorem is also true. Duality is a very strong property.

Euclidean geometry does not have the duality property, nor does hyperbolic geometry. In both of those axiom systems, two distinct points determine a line.

This is also true in projective geometry. However, both Euclidean and hyperbolic geometry include the notion of parallelism. So two distinct lines do not necessarily determine a point, for the lines might not intersect. Projective geometry includes an axiom stating that two distinct lines will intersect, which is very different from Euclidean or hyperbolic geometry.

Here again are the dual statements for the axioms of a projective plane.

Dual Axiom 1   A point lies on at least two lines.

Dual Axiom 2   Any two distinct lines have exactly one point in common.

Dual Axiom 3   Any two distinct points have at least one line in common.

Dual Axiom 4   There is a set of four distinct lines, no three of which are concurrent.

Recall that *concurrent* means lying on a common point, whereas *collinear* means lying on a common line. So *concurrent* and *collinear* are dual concepts.

Are these dual statements true in a projective plane? Dual Axiom 2 is Theorem 12.1 and Dual Axiom 3 is a weaker form of Axiom 2, so they are both true statements. As for Dual Axiom 1, suppose we begin with a point P. By Axiom 4, there are at least three more points A, B, C such that no three of P, A, B, C are collinear. Pair P with each of these points and apply Axiom 2 to get at least two lines on the point P. Dual Axiom 4 also can be proven by applying Axiom 4, then Axiom 2.

This shows that the projective plane has the *duality* property. If the terms *point* and *line* are interchanged in any true statement about a projective plane, we get another true statement. Of course, this interchange must occur for any term that is derived from the concepts of point and line, such as switching *concurrent* for *collinear*. Duality works for the axioms, as we have just shown, but it also works for any theorem of the projective plane. Suppose we have a proof of some theorem, a proof based on the four projective axioms. By writing the dual statements for every line of the proof, we get a proof of the dual theorem that is based on the dual axioms. Since we know that these dual axioms are true in a projective plane, we know that this dual proof is valid as well. So anything derived from the dual axioms also will be true in a projective plane.

Here is an example of a dual theorem:

A Dual Theorem   The lines on one point can be put into one-to-one correspondence with the lines on any other point.

Notice the similarity to Theorem 12.2. As in the original theorem, the proof consists of defining a mapping (function) and verifying that it is one-to-one and onto. In the exercises, you will be asked to prove the original theorem and then to write the dual proof. For the original theorem, a point P can be used to create the mapping; for the dual proof, a line p can be used. The set of lines lying on a single point is called a *pencil* of lines. The mapping created for the proof of this theorem is a *perspectivity* between the two pencils.

Duality can also be used when making definitions. For example, a *triangle* is defined as a set of three noncollinear points and the lines connecting them. (Remember that projective geometry deals only with incidence. Since betweenness is not available, we cannot discuss line segments.) The dual definition is the *trilateral*, a set of three nonconcurrent lines and the points connecting them, that is, the points where lines intersect. But this is the same thing! The triangle is a *self-dual* concept.

What happens with more vertices? In Euclidean geometry, you have seen many objects created from four vertices and line segments of differing lengths. Projective geometry does not deal with length, only incidence, so there is not this variety. Here is the definition: A *quadrangle* is a set of four points, no three collinear, and the lines connecting them. There are six lines generated by these four points and these lines intersect at three additional points, which create the *diagonal triangle* of the quadrangle. In the Fano plane, the diagonal triangle will be degenerate, that is, the vertices will lie on a single line. In the real projective plane, this will be a more normal triangle.

Now for the dual definition: A *quadrilateral* is a set of four lines, no three concurrent, and the points connecting them. This is sometimes called a *complete quadrilateral*. Try drawing this general quadrilateral; how many intersection points will there be from the four lines? Notice that a quadrilateral is not the same thing as a quadrangle. The numbers of points and of lines are different, for instance. There are six points on the four lines of a quadrilateral. (Compare to the quadrangle to see the duality in these numbers!) The six intersection points of the lines in a complete quadrilateral can be connected to make three additional lines. These lines form a diagonal triangle (trilateral) here as well.

We have already discussed two simple mappings, perspectivity between two lines and perspectivity between two pencils. These are dual concepts. Suppose we focus on these concepts more precisely.

DEFINITION 12.1   Two triangles $\Delta A_1 B_1 C_1$ and $\Delta A_2 B_2 C_2$ are *perspective from a point P* if the lines $\overleftrightarrow{A_1 A_2}$, $\overleftrightarrow{B_1 B_2}$, and $\overleftrightarrow{C_1 C_2}$ are concurrent at P.

In the dual definition, we will use the notation $a_1 a_2$ to represent the point of intersection for the lines a_1 and a_2.

DEFINITION 12.2   Two trilaterals $\Delta a_1 b_1 c_1$ and $\Delta a_2 b_2 c_2$ are *perspective from a line p* if the points $a_1 a_2$, $b_1 b_2$, and $c_1 c_2$ are collinear on p.

It may help you understand the first definition if you imagine yourself looking through a window with your eye located at the perspective point. Choose an object outside the window and trace the image of this object onto the window, so that the outline on the glass matches the object outside. Buildings can be good choices for this, for most buildings have linear contours. The image and the object are in perspective from your eye's location. (Figure 12.4 shows a famous etching by Albrecht Dürer in which an artist is looking through a grid at his subject and thus using perspectivity to locate precisely where to draw his image.)

In Activity 3 you constructed two triangles that were perspective from a point. As long as their corresponding vertices are collinear with the perspective point P, the triangles will be in perspective. This holds no matter where the corresponding

FIGURE 12.4
An Application of Perspectivity
(Darling Archive/Alamy
Stock Photo)

vertices are with respect to P. So the mathematical definition is a more general meaning of perspective than the artist's meaning.

Perspectivity from a line is a bit more difficult to visualize. Corresponding sides of two triangles will intersect, for every pair of lines intersects in the projective plane. With three corresponding pairs of sides, there are three intersection points. If these three points are collinear, the triangles are perspective from that line.

A remarkable fact is that in the real projective plane, these dual concepts of perspective are equivalent. This theorem holds in many other projective planes as well, though there are some situations where it is not true.

THEOREM 12.4 **Desargues' Theorem**   In the real projective plane, if two triangles are perspective from a point, then they are perspective from a line.

In the Euclidean plane, when corresponding sides of the triangles are not parallel, Theorem 12.4 can be proven using Menelaus' Theorem. It is also possible to prove this in the real projective plane as a consequence of Pappus' Theorem. In fact, many axiomatic treatments of the real projective plane use the Pappus Theorem as an axiom, and then prove Desargues' Theorem and its converse. We give a proof that is interesting and unusual because it uses a three-dimensional result to prove the two-dimensional one [Graustein 1930, 23–25].

Proof   Suppose that the triangles $\Delta A_1B_1C_1$ and $\Delta A_2B_2C_2$ are perspective from the point P. First assume that these triangles are in different planes π_1 and π_2, respectively. These planes intersect in a line ℓ. The points P, A_1, A_2, B_1, B_2 are on two lines, so they lie in a common plane. Thus, the lines $\overleftrightarrow{A_1B_1}$ and $\overleftrightarrow{A_2B_2}$ intersect at a point D. This point will lie in both planes π_1 and π_2, so D is on line ℓ. Now we can do the same argument for the lines $\overleftrightarrow{B_1C_1}$ and $\overleftrightarrow{B_2C_2}$ intersecting at E, and again for the lines $\overleftrightarrow{A_1C_1}$ and $\overleftrightarrow{A_2C_2}$ intersecting at F. All three points where corresponding sides intersect, D, E, and F, lie on the line ℓ. (It would be a good idea for you to create a drawing of this situation, to make sure you understand where all these points and lines lie!)

Now suppose that the two triangles are in the same plane. The approach is to create a new triangle perspective to both but not in the same plane, and then show that the points D, E, F lie on the intersection of the two planes.

Let R_1 and R_2 be points collinear with P but not in the plane of the two triangles. Construct the lines connecting R_1 to the vertices of $\Delta A_1B_1C_1$ and the lines connecting R_2 to the vertices of $\Delta A_2 B_2 C_2$. The points R_1, R_2, A_1, A_2 lie in a common plane, so the lines $\overleftrightarrow{R_1 A_1}$ and $\overrightarrow{R_2 A_2}$ intersect at a point A_3. Similarly, the lines $\overleftrightarrow{R_1 B_1}$ and $\overleftrightarrow{R_1 B_2}$ intersect at B_3 and $\overleftrightarrow{R_1 C_1}$ and $\overleftrightarrow{R_1 C_2}$ intersect at C_3. This creates a triangle $\Delta A_3 B_3 C_3$ in a different plane from the original two triangles. (Examine Figure 12.5 carefully to identify the three triangles and the perspectivities.)

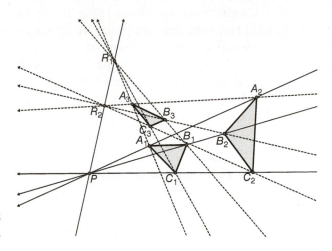

FIGURE 12.5
Proof of Desargues' Theorem

We now have the triangles $\Delta A_1 B_1 C_1$ and $\Delta A_3 B_3 C_3$ perspective from R_1, and also the triangles $\Delta A_2 B_2 C_2$ and $\Delta A_3 B_3 C_3$ perspective from R_2. Using the result from the three-dimensional case, this implies that $\Delta A_1 B_1 C_1$ and $\Delta A_3 B_3 C_3$ are perspective from the line ℓ where the two planes intersect. Furthermore, $\Delta A_2 B_2 C_2$ and $A_3 B_3 C_3$ also are perspective from ℓ. So the lines $\overleftrightarrow{A_1 B_1}$ and $\overrightarrow{A_3 B_3}$ are concurrent with ℓ, and also $\overleftrightarrow{A_2 B_2}$ and $\overrightarrow{A_3 B_3}$ are concurrent with ℓ. This must happen at a single point on ℓ, where $\overleftrightarrow{A_1 B_1}$ and $\overleftrightarrow{A_2 B_2}$ intersect ℓ. Similar arguments show that the other corresponding sides also intersect on ℓ, making ℓ the line of perspectivity.

For the two forms of perspectivity to be equivalent, we must also have the reverse implication. To verify this reverse implication, we will use Desargues' Theorem in the proof.

The Dual (and Converse) of Desargues' Theorem In the real projective plane, if two triangles are perspective from a line, then they are perspective from a point.

Proof Suppose triangles $\Delta A_1 B_1 C_1$ and $\Delta A_2 B_2 C_2$ are perspective from the line ℓ. Let $D = \overleftrightarrow{A_1 B_1} \cap \overleftrightarrow{A_2 B_2}$, $E = \overleftrightarrow{B_1 C_1} \cap \overleftrightarrow{B_2 C_2}$, $F = \overleftrightarrow{C_1 A_1} \cap \overleftrightarrow{C_2 A_2}$, and let $P = \overleftrightarrow{A_1 A_2} \cap \overleftrightarrow{B_1 B_2}$. The point P will be the point of perspectivity; all we need to verify is that P is collinear with C_1 and C_2.

Think about the triangles $\Delta F A_1 A_2$ and $\Delta E B_1 B_2$. These are perspective from point D. Hence, according to Desargues' Theorem, the triangles are perspective from a line. This line contains the points $\overleftrightarrow{FA_1} \cap \overleftrightarrow{EB_1} = C_1$, $\overleftrightarrow{A_1A_2} \cap \overleftrightarrow{B_1B_2} = P$, and $\overleftrightarrow{FA_2} \cap \overleftrightarrow{EB_2} = C_2$.

Desargues' Theorem and its converse hold in the Euclidean plane, though special treatment is needed when parallel lines are involved. The theorem and its converse are also true in the Fano plane, but it can be difficult to find two triangles that satisfy the hypothesis. (*Hint*: The six vertices do not have to be distinct points.) However, there are projective planes that do not have this property. An example will appear in the Exercises.

In Activity 4a you saw Pappus' Theorem. What did you observe in part b? The situation in part b is very similar to Pappus' Theorem and, in a sense we will discuss later, this is a more general version of Pappus' result. The theorem that goes with Activity 4b was first proved by Pascal in 1640, when he was sixteen years old! Pascal's original proof has been lost, though many other proofs have been given since then.

Pascal's Theorem (for Circles)   If a hexagon is inscribed in a circle, the three points of intersection from pairs of opposite sides will be collinear.

This statement may need some clarification. A *hexagon* is a set of six points, no three of them collinear, and the lines connecting them cyclically. (In the Euclidean plane, we would use line segments; in the projective plane we use lines.) In more precise language, a hexagon is six points A_1, ..., A_6 and the lines A_1A_2, A_2A_3, ..., A_6A_1. Inscribing the hexagon in a circle means that all six vertices lie on a common circle. The hexagon does not have to be convex, and the sides could cross each other. In the real projective plane opposite sides like $\overleftrightarrow{A_1A_2}$ and $\overleftrightarrow{A_4A_5}$ will intersect; in the Euclidean plane they could be parallel.

Pascal's Theorem in the Euclidean plane can be proven by Menelaus' Theorem or by Desargues' Theorem. It is necessary in the Euclidean case to assume that the intersections are ordinary points, not ideal points. It turns out that a much stronger version of Pascal's Theorem holds: The six points can be inscribed on any conic curve—a circle, an ellipse, a parabola, or a hyperbola—and the cross joins will be collinear. Even the degenerate conic consisting of two lines will work, which means that Pappus' Theorem is actually a special case of Pascal's Theorem.

A century and a half after Pascal's result, the dual version was proved.

Brianchon's Theorem (for Circles)   If a hexagon is circumscribed around a circle, the three lines connecting pairs of opposite vertices are concurrent.

This too can be strengthened to apply to any conic curve.

COORDINATES FOR PROJECTIVE GEOMETRY

Coordinates for a Projective Line

The idea of coordinates on a line is a familiar one; the set of real numbers matches up with the points of the line in a one-to-one correspondence. However, the real numbers are not enough for the projective line, for there is nothing to use for the ideal point. Something stronger is needed.

Consider the point $x = \frac{5}{2}$ on a number line. This coordinate can be written in many ways.

$$x = \frac{5}{2} = \frac{10}{4} = \frac{15}{6} = \frac{-20}{-8} = \cdots$$

Any of these pairs of numbers represents the same point.

How are these fractions related to Activity 5a? A line through the origin has many possible direction vectors. The line through (0, 0) and (5, 2) has (5, 2), (10, 4), and (−20, −8) as some of its direction vectors, as well as $\left(\frac{5}{2}, 1\right)$. All of these vectors represent the same direction, so they represent the same line through the origin. If we think of the horizontal line $y = 1$ as our desired number line, all of these vectors represent the same point on the number line.

This is the idea of *homogeneous coordinates*. A point on the line is represented by an ordered pair of numbers (x_1, x_2) with the understanding that any nonzero multiple of this, (ax_1, ax_2), represents the same point. Thus, (10, 4) represents the same point as (5, 2) because each coordinate is multiplied by the same constant. Notice that the pair (0, 0) does not fit this system, for if we allowed the multiples by 0, every point would be the same! So (0, 0) is excluded from homogeneous coordinates. It is easy to convert homogeneous coordinates to Euclidean coordinates by using $x = \frac{x_1}{x_2}$.

Where does the point (1, 0) lie on this number line? If we think of it as a direction vector in a plane, (1, 0) is the horizontal direction. In Activity 5b, you may have listed this as one of your points on the horizontal line $y = 0$. This line is parallel to $y = 1$ so the pair (1, 0) represents the ideal point on the projective line.

On the projective line, we now have (0, 1) for the origin, (1, 1) for the unit point, and (1, 0) for the ideal point. Converting these into Euclidean coordinates gives precisely the values we want for the origin and for the unit point, namely, $x = 0$ and $x = 1$. The ideal point cannot be converted into a real number. This is not a problem, of course, because the ideal point does not belong in the Euclidean line.

Coordinates for the Real Projective Plane

Homogeneous coordinates also work for a plane, but for one additional dimension we need one additional coordinate [Smart 1988, 244–249]. A point now is represented by an ordered triple of numbers (x_1, x_2, x_3) with the understandings that the triple (ax_1, ax_2, ax_3) is the same point as (x_1, x_2, x_3) and that (0, 0, 0) is excluded. To convert between Euclidean and homogeneous coordinates, use the substitutions

$$x = \frac{x_1}{x_3}, \quad y = \frac{x_2}{x_3}.$$

As we did with the projective line, we can interpret this as a Euclidean system of one higher dimension. Think of our projective plane as being the plane $z = 1$ in $\mathbb{R}^3$. Most lines through the origin will intersect $z = 1$, and a direction vector for such a line gives homogeneous coordinates for the intersection point of the line and the plane. The vector (10, 4, 2), for instance, gives the direction of a line that intersects $z = 1$ at the point (5, 2, 1), so (10, 4, 2) is one way to describe this point. Lines that do not intersect $z = 1$ have direction vectors ending in 0, like

(1, 2, 0), and these correspond to ideal points for the projective plane. The set of ideal points makes up the ideal line.

In the real projective plane, there are three lines of special importance:

$$x_1 = 0, \qquad \text{the } y\text{-axis}$$

$$x_2 = 0, \qquad \text{the } x\text{-axis}$$

$$x_3 = 0, \qquad \text{the ideal line}$$

Do these equations make sense when you convert into Euclidean coordinates? In two cases, you should get a familiar equation; what happens in the third case? Together these three lines create the *fundamental triangle* in the real projective plane; see Figure 12.6. Each region created by these lines has a distinctive pattern of positive and negative entries for its homogeneous coordinates. When we cross one of these lines, the sign of one coordinate will change. Notice, however, that there are only four regions, despite the eight possible patterns of plus or minus. The homogeneity causes the pattern $(+, -, +)$ to be the same as $(-, +, -)$ since it is a multiple by -1. The other patterns each have a match as well.

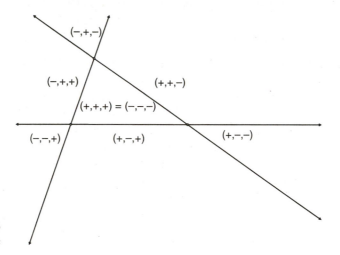

FIGURE 12.6
The Fundamental Triangle

In the Euclidean plane, the equation of a line can always be written in the form $ax + by + c = 0$ with a, b, c not all zero. If we use the substitutions to convert this into homogeneous coordinates, this equation becomes

$$a\left(\frac{x_1}{x_3}\right) + b\left(\frac{x_2}{x_3}\right) + c = 0$$

which simplifies to

$$ax_1 + bx_2 + cx_3 = 0.$$

Since every variable in this equation is raised to the same power and there is one variable in each term, the degree in each term is 1. This is a *homogeneous equation* of degree 1.

For example, the equation $2x_1 - 5x_2 + x_3 = 0$ describes a line. So does the equation $4x_1 - 3x_3 = 0$. Where do these lines intersect? Try this yourself before reading further. . . . There is a difficulty in that there are three variables but only two equations. So there is not a unique solution. We can solve this in homogeneous coordinates, however. An immediate observation is that

$$x_1 = \frac{3}{4}x_3.$$

Eliminating x_1 from the two given equations gives us

$$x_2 = \frac{1}{2}x_3.$$

From these relationships, we get the coordinates $\left(\frac{3}{4}x_3, \frac{1}{2}x_3, x_3\right)$. This is indeed the solution; pick any nonzero value for x_3 and it produces a representation of the point. Another way to see this is to rewrite the coordinates as $x_3 \cdot \left(\frac{3}{4}, \frac{1}{2}, 1\right)$. In this form, we can see easily that the solution is one point, represented by all its multiples.

Let's look at this situation more closely. For convenience, choose $x_3 = 4$ to represent this point with integer values as $(3, 2, 4)$. This point lies on the line $2x_1 - 5x_2 + x_3 = 0$, so substituting the coordinates of the point will produce a valid equation:

$$2 \times 3 - 5 \times 2 + 4 = 0.$$

This equation can be written nicely as a dot product of two vectors.

$$[2, -2, 1] \cdot (3, 2, 4) = 0.$$

In general, the homogeneous linear equation $ax_1 + bx_2 + cx_3 = 0$ can be written as

$$[a, b, c] \cdot (x_1, x_2,\ x_3) = 0.$$

The triple (x_1, x_2, x_3) is, of course, the homogeneous coordinates of a point lying on this line. What role does the triple $[a,\ b,\ c]$ play in this equation? Think of duality. These are the *homogeneous coordinates of the line*! Just as points have coordinates in the real projective plane, lines too have coordinates.

Here is an example of line coordinates: Consider the Euclidean line $x = y$. In homogeneous coordinates, this becomes $x_1 = x_2$. Now write this in the form used above: $x_1 - x_2 + 0x_3 = 0$. Therefore, the coordinates of this line are $[1, -1, 0]$. The origin lies on this line, and a quick calculation confirms it: $[1, -1, 0] \cdot (0, 0, 1) = 0$. This calculation still works if other representations are used, such as $[-2, 2, 0] \cdot (0, 0, 15)$. We can also ask for the coordinates of the ideal point on this line. To find these coordinates, set $x_3 = 0$ and solve the equation $[1, -1, 0] \cdot (x_1, x_2, 0) = 0$.

Pappus' Theorem, Pascal's Theorem, and Desargues' Theorem all are concerned with three points being collinear. With homogeneous coordinates, there is a calculation that checks for collinearity.

THEOREM 12.5   Three projective points (x_1, x_2, x_3), (y_1, y_2, y_3), and (z_1, z_2, z_3) are collinear if and only if

$$det \begin{bmatrix} x_1 & x_2 & x_3 \\ y_1 & y_2 & y_3 \\ z_1 & z_2 & z_3 \end{bmatrix} = 0$$

(This computation is the determinant of the 3×3 matrix.)

Proof Using the linear homogeneous equation $ax_1 + bx_2 + cx_3 = 0$ this is routine but a bit messy to prove with basic algebra. Here is a more sophisticated proof using linear algebra.

The three points are collinear if and only if the linear system

$$\begin{cases} ax_1 + bx_2 + cx_3 = 0 \\ ay_1 + by_2 + cy_3 = 0 \\ az_1 + bz_2 + cz_3 = 0 \end{cases}$$

has a nontrivial solution for $[a, b, c]$. This solution exists if and only if the column vectors

$$\begin{bmatrix} x_1 \\ y_1 \\ z_1 \end{bmatrix}, \quad \begin{bmatrix} x_2 \\ y_2 \\ z_2 \end{bmatrix}, \quad \begin{bmatrix} x_3 \\ y_3 \\ z_3 \end{bmatrix}$$

are linearly dependent. This dependence occurs if and only if the given determinant is 0.

What is the dual version of this theorem? You will get a chance to state and prove this in the exercises.

The linear algebra approach in this proof gives us another useful fact. Since the determinant equals 0 if and only if the row vectors are dependent as well, we can say that three points are collinear if and only if any one of them can be written as a linear combination of the others. For example, consider the line $x_2 = 2x_1$ (or $y = 2x$) in the real projective plane. This line contains the points $(0, 0, 1)$, which is the origin, and also contains $(1, 2, 1)$. The ideal point $(1, 2, 0) = -1 \cdot (0, 0, 1) + 1 \cdot (1, 2, 1)$ thus belongs on this line.

Homogeneous Coordinates for the Fano Plane

The Fano plane is the smallest projective plane, having merely seven points and seven lines. Since it is a finite system, we must have a finite list of possible coordinates. Unfortunately, using real numbers creates an infinite set of possible coordinates. So we must restrict ourselves to a finite number system.

If you have studied abstract algebra, you would have encountered modular arithmetic. The most familiar example of modular arithmetic is clock arithmetic with the numbers $1, \ldots, 12$. If it is presently 5 o'clock and we add 10 hours, the answer is 3 o'clock. This is written as $5 + 10 \equiv 3 \pmod{12}$. Similarly, 8 o'clock plus 12 hours is 8 o'clock, so $8 + 12 \equiv 8 \pmod{12}$. This demonstrates that 12 is an identity for addition in this system. We also know that 6 o'clock plus 6 hours is 12 o'clock, so 6 is its own inverse for addition. However, it is more common in mathematics to say $6 + 6 \equiv 0 \pmod{12}$. It is written this way because we are accustomed to using 0 to represent the additive identity. Mathematicians would say we are using the modular numbers $0, \ldots, 11$.

For the coordinates of the Fano plane, we will use the modular number system with only two values, 0 and 1. This system is denoted by $\mathbb{Z}_2$. Here are the addition and multiplication tables for $\mathbb{Z}_2$:

+	0	1
0	0	1
1	1	0

×	0	1
0	0	0
1	0	1

This is an example of a *finite field*. It has (almost) all of the properties of the real numbers: closure, commutativity, associativity, distributivity, identities, and inverses. One major difference, however, is that the real numbers are *ordered* because we can clearly separate positive from negative. This cannot be done in $\mathbb{Z}_2$, for $-1 + 1 = 0 = 1 + 1$, which would make $-1 = 1$.

To set up homogeneous coordinates for the Fano plane, we must have three components for the coordinates: one for each dimension and one to distinguish the ideal points. Suppose we start with the "origin" $A = (0, 0, 1)$ and one of the ideal points $B = (1, 0, 0)$. These points lie on a common line and that line has a third point $C = (z_1, z_2, z_3)$. According to the preceding theorem,

$$
det \begin{bmatrix} 0 & 0 & 1 \\ 1 & 0 & 0 \\ z_1 & z_2 & z_3 \end{bmatrix} = 0.
$$

Expanding this determinant gives $z_2 = 0$. C is not an ideal point so $z_3 \neq 0$. Further, $C \neq A$ so the first coordinate cannot be 0. So the coordinates of the third point must be $C = (1, 0, 1)$.

Actually, this is easier to do by linear combinations. In $\mathbb{Z}_2$ we have only two coefficients to try, namely, 0 and 1. So there are very few linear combinations of A and B, and the only new point generated is $1 \cdot A + 1 \cdot B = 1 \cdot (0, 0, 1) + 1 \cdot (1, 0, 0) = (1, 0, 1)$.

Now pick any point D not on this line ABC. For instance, we could pick $D = (1, 1, 1)$. The determinant test shows that D is not collinear with A, B. Another way to check this is to find the coordinates of the line $\overleftrightarrow{AB}$, that are $[0, 1, 0]$. (You should verify this.) Then $[0, 1, 0] \cdot (1, 1, 1) \neq 0$ so D is not on this line. Now use D to form the lines $\overleftrightarrow{AD}$, $\overleftrightarrow{BD}$, and $\overleftrightarrow{CD}$. Each of these will have a third point, and it is not hard to find the coordinates of these new points. For instance, the third point on AD is $1 \cdot A + 1 \cdot D = 1 \cdot (0, 0, 1) + 1 \cdot (1, 1, 1) = (1, 1, 0)$.

Figure 12.7 shows the Fano plane with its points labeled by their homogeneous coordinates—at least, one possible way to label these points. Notice that the triple $(0, 0, 0)$ does not appear in this diagram. Where is the ideal line in this figure?

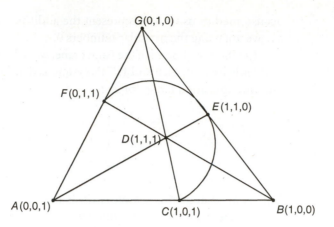

FIGURE 12.7
Coordinates in the Fano Plane

PROJECTIVE TRANSFORMATIONS

In Activity 2 you looked at a relationship between two lines. Any point on the line ℓ is related to a corresponding point on the line m. How could you describe this correspondence?

DEFINITION 12.3   For two lines ℓ and m in a projective plane and a point P not on either of these lines, a *perspectivity* is a mapping between the sets of points on these lines defined by $f(X) = \overleftrightarrow{PX} \cap m$ for a point X on ℓ. The point P is the *center* of the perspectivity. The fact that these lines correspond in this way is denoted $\ell \overline{\wedge} m$.

In Activity 2 you experimented with a perspectivity. Notice that the length of the initial segment AB did not match the length of its image; in fact, if the lines ℓ and m are not parallel, the two segments are not even proportional. The order of the points could reverse, depending on where P is located. In the Euclidean plane, on the other hand, betweenness is preserved. If the point X is between A and B on the line ℓ, then $f(X)$ will be between $f(A)$ and $f(B)$ on the line m. Betweenness is an *invariant* of the mapping. Based on your observations, what are some other invariants for this perspectivity? Suppose you created a perspectivity in three-dimensional space between two planes. What properties do you think would be invariants in that situation?

The mapping in Activity 6a is also a perspectivity. This function is almost a one-to-one correspondence between the sets of points on the two lines, but there is a difficulty. It is possible to position the point X so that P_1X is parallel to ℓ_2. In this situation, we need the ideal point of ℓ_2 to act as the point Y. The ideal point of ℓ_1 is needed also, otherwise there will be a point on ℓ_2 that cannot be an output for this mapping. (Think about P_1Y when it is parallel to ℓ_1.) With the addition of these ideal points, this function f becomes truly a one-to-one correspondence between the two projective lines.

This one-to-one correspondence was the important fact for proving that two lines in a finite projective plane have the same number of points (see page 169). Notice that the inverse of a perspectivity uses the same center, just reversing the domain and range sets. In addition, any line is perspective to itself. To see this, pick any point P not on the line ℓ to use as the center. The mapping in this situation will be the identity function.

In projective space, we can define a perspectivity between two planes in a similar fashion, using a center point not on either plane. Lines in one plane will be perspective to lines in the other plane. Incidence of points and lines is preserved by this perspectivity, so collinear points in one plane are perspective to collinear points in the other and concurrent lines are perspective to concurrent lines. The image of a circle, however, might not be a circle; it could be an ellipse or some other curve.

A classic example of this is the cross sections of a cone. Figure 12.8 shows a cone sliced by a plane in various ways. There are a variety of curves along the intersections: circles, ellipses, parabolas, and hyperbolas—or even a pair of intersecting lines. These curves are the *conic sections,* and they have many interesting properties. One of these properties is that any two conic section curves are perspective from the point at the apex of the cone.

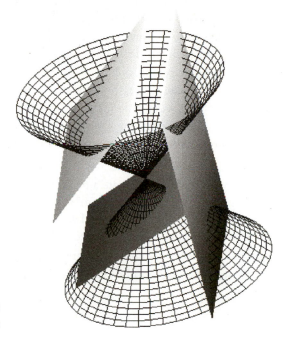

FIGURE 12.8
Sections of a Cone

This perspectivity property allows us to extend Pascal's Theorem. The theorem was originally stated for a hexagon inscribed in a circle but it is in fact true for any conic curve. The conic curve is created by a plane intersecting the cone. A hexagon inscribed on the conic curve is a set of lines in this plane. Now imagine a second plane intersecting the cone to form a circle. The hexagon lines of the conic curve are perspective to other lines in the second plane, lines that form a hexagon on the circle. Incidence of lines is invariant, so the collinear cross joins for the hexagon in the circle correspond to collinear cross joins for the hexagon on the conic curve. Furthermore, the line common to the cross joins for the circle corresponds to a line common to the cross joins for the curve. (This is not really a proof, but it gives some idea why the more general theorem works.)

Because perspectivities are functions, they can be composed. This creates a new sort of mapping.

DEFINITION 12.4 For two lines ℓ_1 and ℓ_2, a *projectivity* is a mapping between the sets of points on the two lines creating by composing a sequence of perspectivities. The fact that these lines correspond in this way is denoted $\ell_1 \barwedge \ell_2$.

In Activity 6b, you created a projectivity by composing two perspectivities. Euclidean betweenness is invariant for a projectivity, just as it is for the individual perspectivities. It is also possible for a line to be projective to itself. Because perspectivities have inverses, projectivities will have inverses as well. So the next theorem should not be a surprise.

THEOREM 12.6 The set of projectivities in a projective plane forms a group.

Proof This theorem is routine to prove. Closure is easy: A composition of one sequence of perspectivities followed by another such sequence forms a single, longer sequence of perspectivities, that is, a projectivity. Composition of functions is always associative. The function $f(X) = X$, a projectivity from any line to itself, serves as the identity for the group. Inverses are the major issue. Look first at a single perspectivity $f(X) = \overleftrightarrow{PX} \cap \ell_2$ for points X on a line ℓ_1. If we switch the domain and range, the same center will produce the inverse perspectivity $f^{-1}(Y) = \overleftrightarrow{PY} \cap \ell_1$ for points Y on ℓ_2. Because a projectivity is a sequence of perspectivities, the inverses of these perspectivities, composed in the reverse order, will be the inverse of the projectivity.

Activity 7 asked you to create a projectivity, in a somewhat roundabout way. (Did you recognize Pappus' Theorem?) This mapping was deliberately designed to make $f(A_1) = A_2$, $f(B_1) = B_2$, and $f(C_1) = C_2$. This projectivity can actually be done as a sequence of two perspectivities. The first uses A_2 as the center of perspectivity between ℓ_1 and $\overleftrightarrow{PQ}$, while the second uses A_1 as the center for a perspectivity between $\overleftrightarrow{PQ}$ and ℓ_2. This procedure will always work, so we can state a theorem.

THEOREM 12.7 Three distinct points on one line can be projectively related to three distinct points on another line by a sequence of exactly two perspectivities.

Proof Follow the construction of Activity 7. An example is shown in Figure 12.9. With A_2 as the center of perspectivity, we have $A_1B_1C_1 \barwedge RPQ$. With A_1 as the center we have $RPQ \barwedge A_2B_2C_2$. Therefore, $A_1B_1C_1 \barwedge A_2B_2C_2$ in exactly two steps.

A detail to consider: What if $A_1B_1C_1$ is directly perspective to $A_2B_2C_2$? In this case, use the identity as the first perspectivity and use the given perspectivity to complete the sequence.

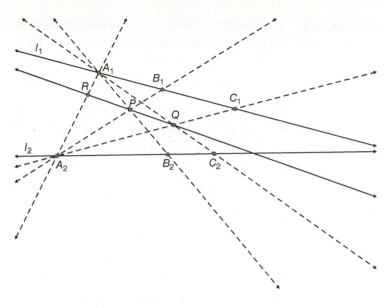

FIGURE 12.9
The Axis of Projectivity

Notice the important role played by the line RPQ in this proof. This line is called the *axis of projectivity* for this particular mapping. Once constructed, it can be used to perform the projectivity, instead of using a pair of perspective centers. For any point X on ℓ_1, find $X_0 = \overleftrightarrow{A_2X} \cap \overleftrightarrow{PQ}$ and then find $f(X) = \overleftrightarrow{A_1X_0} \cap \ell_2$.

Theorem 12.7 does assume that the domain and range are different lines. As was noted earlier, however, a line can be projective to itself. This requires only one additional step.

COROLLARY 12.1   Any three distinct collinear points are projective to any other three distinct collinear points by means of at most three perspectivities.

Proof   If the domain and range are different lines, Theorem 12.7 says that only two perspectivity steps are needed. If the domain and range are the same line ℓ_1, create any second line ℓ_2 and a point P not on these two lines. Perform the perspectivity centered at P from ℓ_1 to ℓ_2. This is one step. Then it takes only two more steps to complete the projectivity from ℓ_2 to the original range ℓ_1.

These results say that any three collinear points can be projectively related to any other three collinear points, and that only a few perspectivity steps are needed to do so. However, a projectivity between lines usually has more than three points in its domain, except in the Fano plane. What happens to these other points? Can there be different projectivities that agree for three particular points but disagree elsewhere? The answer is no; knowing what happens to three points completely determines the projectivity. This is the *Fundamental Theorem of Projective Geometry*.

The proof of the Fundamental Theorem builds on the preceding results but is somewhat long. We will state, but not prove, one final portion.

LEMMA 12.1   If a projectivity from a line ℓ to itself leaves three distinct points fixed, that projectivity must be the identity.

Now we are ready to prove the main result.

Fundamental Theorem of Projective Geometry   Given three distinct collinear points A_1, B_1, C_1 and three corresponding distinct collinear points A_2, B_2, C_2, there is exactly one projectivity for which

$$A_1 B_1 C_1 \barwedge A_2 B_2 C_2.$$

Proof   We already know that at least one projectivity can be found. Consider any other point D_1 on the line ℓ_1. If there are two different projectivities, then

$$A_1 B_1 C_1 D_1 \barwedge A_2 B_2 C_2 D_2 \quad \text{and} \quad A_1 B_1 C_1 D_1 \barwedge A_2 B_2 C_2 D_3$$

for points D_2 and D_3 on the line ℓ_2. Our task is to show that $D_2 = D_3$. Use the inverse of the first projectivity to get

$$A_2 B_2 C_2 D_2 \barwedge A_1 B_1 C_1 D_1 \barwedge A_2 B_2 C_2 D_3$$

and hence

$$A_2 B_2 C_2 D_2 \barwedge A_2 B_2 C_2 D_3.$$

This composition is a projectivity from ℓ_2 to itself that leaves three points fixed. Therefore, it is the identity projectivity and $D_2 = D_3$.

We have discussed two types of projective transformations, the perspectivities and the projectivities. Projectivities are defined as compositions of perspectivities, so they are more complicated functions. The following corollary gives an easy way to tell if a projectivity is actually the simpler mapping, a perspectivity.

This corollary is an "if and only if" statement. That means it is actually two statements together, an implication and its converse. So there are two things to prove, and our proof will be in two parts.

COROLLARY 12.2   A projectivity between two distinct lines is a perspectivity if and only if the intersection of the lines is a fixed point of the projectivity.

Proof (*only if*)   If the projectivity consists of a single perspectivity, the center P will not be on either line. So the intersection point $A = \ell_1 \cap \ell_2$ will not be transformed because $PA \cap \ell_2 = A$.

(*if*) Let $A = \ell_1 \cap \ell_2$. Pick two more points B_1, C_1 on ℓ_1 and find their images B_2, C_2 on ℓ_2. Thus, we have

$$AB_1 C_1 \barwedge AB_2 C_2.$$

Let $P = \overleftrightarrow{B_1 B_2} \cap \overleftrightarrow{C_1 C_2}$. This point P will be the center of a perspectivity that makes

$$AB_1 C_1 \doublebarwedge AB_2 C_2$$

and therefore the projectivity equals the perspectivity from P.

This corollary is an interesting result, but its real value is that it allows us to give a more general proof of Pappus' Theorem. Because this proof uses only projective ideas, the theorem holds even when ideal points or the ideal line are involved.

Pappus' Theorem Suppose that A_1, B_1, C_1 are three distinct points on one line and A_2, B_2, C_2 are three distinct points on another line. Form the cross joins $X = \overleftrightarrow{A_1B_2} \cap \overleftrightarrow{A_2B_1}$, $Y = \overleftrightarrow{B_1C_2} \cap \overleftrightarrow{B_2C_1}$, and $Z = \overleftrightarrow{C_1A_2} \cap \overleftrightarrow{C_2A_1}$. Then the points X, Y, Z are collinear.

Proof (It will be helpful if you create a diagram of this proof.) We need a few more points. Let $P = \overleftrightarrow{A_1B_1} \cap \overleftrightarrow{A_2B_2}$, $Q = \overleftrightarrow{A_1C_2} \cap \overleftrightarrow{A_2B_1}$, and $R = \overleftrightarrow{B_1C_2} \cap \overleftrightarrow{A_2C_1}$. This gives

$$A_2XQB_1 \; \overline{\barwedge} \; A_2B_2C_2P \; \overline{\barwedge} \; RYC_2B_1,$$

where A_1 is the center of the first perspectivity and C_1 is the center of the second. The composition of these two perspectivities forms a projectivity between the lines $\overleftrightarrow{A_2B_1}$ and $\overleftrightarrow{B_1C_2}$ that has B_1 as a fixed point. By the corollary, this projectivity can be done as a single perspectivity. The center of this perspectivity is

$$\overleftrightarrow{A_2R} \cap \overleftrightarrow{QC_2} = \overleftrightarrow{A_2C_1} \cap \overleftrightarrow{A_1C_2} = Z.$$

X is perspective to Y under this perspectivity, so X, Y, Z are collinear.

It is worth noting that duality can be applied to the theorems and corollaries in this section to produce a new set of theorems.

This chapter has been only an introduction to projective geometry. Pappus' Theorem, Desargues' Theorem, and the Fundamental Theorem are interrelated in intricate ways that are worth studying. When using coordinates, Pappus' Theorem also has a deep connection to the commutativity of the number system. (This was proved by David Hilbert. See [Robinson 1946, 92–94].) There are many other interesting topics, such as the cross ratio—a calculation involving distances that is invariant under a projectivity. The theory of conics is another major topic within projective geometry. Furthermore, matrix equations can be used to represent projectivities, similar to what was done in Chapter 9. Thus, algebraic tools can be used to study projective geometry. In recent years, these matrix tools have found important applications in computer graphics.

12.3 EXERCISES

Give clear and complete answers to the following problems and questions. Write your explanations clearly using complete sentences. Include diagrams whenever appropriate.

1. From the axioms, prove that two distinct lines have exactly one point in common.

2. a. Prove that the points on one line can be put in a one-to-one correspondence with the points on any other line.

   b. State the dual of part a. Then write the dual proof and check that this proves the dual statement.

3. In the Euclidean plane, prove that parallelism is an equivalence relation for lines.

4. Verify that the real projective plane satisfies the axioms for a projective plane. Include both cases for Axiom 3.

5. For the spherical model, give a careful proof that Axiom 2 holds.

6. Prove Dual Axiom 4, using the axioms of the projective plane.

7. Construct examples of a quadrangle and a quadrilateral. Identify the diagonal triangle in each of your examples.

8. Write the dual of Pappus' Theorem and construct an example.

9. Construct an example of Brianchon's Theorem.

10. Consider Desargues' Theorem in the Euclidean plane. Use Menelaus' Theorem to prove the special case in which none of the lines in the configuration is parallel.

11. Find an example of Desargues' Theorem in the Fano plane.

12. Convert the homogeneous equations $x_1 = 0$, $x_2 = 0$, and $x_3 = 0$ to Euclidean form. Do your answers make sense? Explain why or why not.

13. a. Find the homogeneous coordinates of the point where the lines $x_1 - 2x_2 + 3x_3 = 0$ and $5x_1 + 2x_2 - x_3 = 0$ intersect.
    b. Find the homogeneous coordinates of the line connecting the points $\left(\frac{1}{2}, -3, 0\right)$ and $(4, 4, 7)$.

14. In the real projective plane, list all possible $+/-$ patterns for three coordinates. Then match these triples to the regions of the Fundamental Triangle. Also, locate the usual four Euclidean quadrants in the Fundamental Triangle.

15. Consider the real projective plane. What is $[1, 0, 0]$? What is $(1, 0, 0)$? What is $[0, 1, 0]$? What is $(0, 1, 0)$? What is $[0, 0, 1]$? What is $(0, 0, 1)$?

16. Can the point (a, b, c) ever lie on the line $[a, b, c]$? Either give an example in some model or explain why not.

17. See Figure 12.7. Find the coordinates of every line in this labeling of the Fano plane. Which one is the ideal line?

18. Identify the type of curve for each of the following Euclidean equations. Convert each to homogeneous coordinates. Then find any ideal points that lie on each curve.

$$y = px^2, \quad \frac{x^2}{a^2} + \frac{y^2}{b^2} = 1, \quad \frac{x^2}{a^2} - \frac{y^2}{b^2} = 1.$$

19. Here are homogeneous coordinates for six points.

$$A_1 = (1, 0, 1)$$
$$B_1 = (2, 0, 1)$$
$$C_1 = (5, 0, 1)$$
on the line $[0, 1, 0]$
$$A_2 = (1, -2, 0)$$
$$B_2 = (1, -2, 1)$$
$$C_2 = (-1, 2, 1)$$
on the line $[2, 1, 0]$

(Notice that A_2 is an ideal point.) Refer to the statement of Pappus' Theorem on page 307. Find the coordinates of the cross joins X, Y, and Z, and find the coordinates of their common line.

20. a. See Theorem 12.5 on collinear points on page 299. State the dual of this theorem.
    b. Prove this dual theorem.

21. Write the dual definitions for perspectivity and projectivity, and construct examples.

The following problems are more advanced.

22. *Moulton's Geometry*: [Robinson 1946, 126–128] Start with a Euclidean plane having a rectangular coordinate system. The lines to use are the following: If the Euclidean line is vertical, has negative slope, or is horizontal, include this as a Moulton line. If, however, the Euclidean line $y = m(x - a)$ has positive slope, replace it by

$$y = \begin{cases} m(x - a) & \text{for } x < a \\ \frac{m}{2}(x - a) & \text{for } x \geq a \end{cases}$$

(Think of a beam of light refracting as it crosses a boundary.) To this collection of points and Moulton lines, add ideal points as before.

    a. Verify that Moulton's Geometry satisfies the axioms for a projective plane.

    b. Draw some triangles, including some that cross the horizontal axis.

    c. Find a pair of triangles for which Desargues' Theorem holds.

    d. Find a pair of triangles for which Desargues' Theorem does not hold.

23. In GeoGebra, create five points A_1, A_2, B_1, B_2, and C_1 in general position (meaning that no three are collinear). Construct the point $P = \overleftrightarrow{A_1 B_2} \cap \overleftrightarrow{A_2 B_1}$ and create a line ℓ through P. Now construct the point

$$X = A_1(\ell \cap \overleftrightarrow{A_2 C_1}) \cap B_1(\ell \cap \overleftrightarrow{B_2 C_1}).$$

(Be careful with this statement. Is it clear when to form lines and when to form points?) Trace the location of X as ℓ varies. What curve is produced? Try this for different arrangements of the original five points.

    How is this problem related to Pascal's Theorem?

24.   a. Suppose you wish to create a perspective drawing of a floor that is tiled in a checkerboard pattern. If one edge of the floor is directly in front of you and parallel to the horizon, the lines moving away from it will appear to intersect at the horizon, at a *vanishing point*. This is *one-point perspective*. The lines parallel to the horizon are called *transversals* and the lines moving away are called *orthogonals*. The challenge to constructing this picture is that corresponding diagonals of the checkerboard must appear parallel, so these diagonals too must intersect at the horizon. Construct this picture.

    b. (For the ambitious:) If only one corner of the checkerboard is directly in front of you, not an entire edge, there will be two vanishing points: one for the parallel lines going left and another for the parallel lines going right. This is *two-point perspective*. As before, the diagonals should appear parallel, so they must intersect on the horizon as well. Construct this picture. Once you are satisfied with your construction, draw the diagonals in the other direction and see if they also intersect on the horizon.

    (There is also a technique called *three-point perspective*. It is used for objects seen from an unusual angle, such as a bird's-eye view of a tower.)

Exercises 25 and 26 are especially for future teachers.

25. In the *Principles and Standards for School Mathematics*, the National Council of Teachers of Mathematics (NCTM) observes that "Geometry has long been regarded as the place in the school mathematics curriculum where students learn to reason and to see the axiomatic structure of mathematics." Further, "Through the middle grades and into high school, . . . students should learn to use deductive reasoning and more formal proof techniques to solve problems and prove conjectures. At all levels, students should learn to formulate convincing explanations for their conjectures and solutions . . . They should also be able to understand the role of definitions, axioms, and theorems and be able to construct their own proofs" [NCTM 2000, 41–42]. What does this mean for you and your future students?

    a. Read the discussion on Geometry in the *Principles and Standards for School Mathematics* [NCTM 2000, 41–43]. Then study the Reasoning and Proof Standard for at least two grade bands (i.e., two of pre-K–2, 3–5, 6–8, or 9–12). What are the NCTM recommendations regarding the teacher's role in helping students recognize reasoning and proof as fundamental aspects of mathematics? How is this focus on reasoning and proof developed across several grade bands? Cite specific examples.

    b. Find copies of school mathematics textbooks for the same grade levels as you studied for part a. How are the NCTM standards for reasoning and proof implemented in those textbooks? Again, cite specific examples.

c. Write a report in which you present and critique what you learn. Your report should include your answers to parts a and b.

26. In the *Principles and Standards for School Mathematics*, the National Council of Teachers of Mathematics (NCTM) recommends that "Instructional programs from prekindergarten through grade 12 should enable all students to . . . develop and evaluate mathematical arguments and proofs" [NCTM 2000, 56]. Throughout this course, you have investigated several different kinds of axiom systems. For example, you worked with Euclid's Postulates, the axioms of metric geometry, the axioms of the hyperbolic plane, and the axioms of the projective plane.

    a. Design several classroom activities involving logical reasoning and mathematical proof that would be appropriate for students in your future classroom.

    b. Write a short report explaining how the activities you design reflect both what you have learned as you have worked with various axiom systems and the NCTM recommendations.

Reflect on what you have learned in this chapter.

27. Review the main ideas of this chapter. Describe, in your own words, the concepts you have studied and what you have learned about them. What are the important ideas? How do they fit together? Which concepts were easy for you? Which were hard?

28. Reflect on the learning environment for this course. Describe aspects of the learning environment that helped you understand the main ideas in this chapter. Which activities did you like? Dislike? Why?

12.4 CHAPTER OVERVIEW

In Chapters 11 and 12, we have presented two systems of geometry that are very different from Euclidean geometry. In both cases, parallelism is the key difference. Hyperbolic geometry allows the existence of many parallels to a given line, while in projective geometry there are no parallel lines at all! The axiom system for a projective plane given in this chapter is very short and simple, but it leads to surprisingly strong results. After a discussion of these axioms, a few basic theorems about points and lines were presented.

For these axioms and theorems to be meaningful, of course, there must be mathematical situations (models) to which they apply. Three models were shown. The first was the real projective plane, which begins with the Euclidean plane and adds an ideal point—a point at infinity—to each line. A major theorem of the real projective plane is Pappus' Theorem. The second model was a finite one, the Fano plane. This is the finite projective plane of smallest possible order. The third model shown was the spherical model, which is related to the real projective plane by central projection. To create a projective plane from the sphere, it is necessary to identify antipodal points, those points that lie diametrically across from each other.

A remarkable property of the projective plane is duality. The notions of point and line are interchangeable in the axioms, and hence are interchangeable in any theorem proven from those axioms. Of particular interest were the ideas of perspective from a point or from a line. These led to Desargues' famous Theorem and its converse, which together state that the two notions of perspective are equivalent. We also saw Pascal's Theorem about a hexagon inscribed in a circle and its dual, Brianchon's Theorem about a hexagon circumscribed around a circle.

The introduction of homogeneous coordinates brought algebraic tools to the study of projective geometry. We saw that instead of four quadrants, the real projective plane has the fundamental triangle and its four regions. Because of duality, we can have coordinates for a line as well as for a point.

The final topic of the chapter was transformations in the projective plane. These come in two types: the *perspectivity*, a mapping between two lines that uses one center point; and the *projectivity*, which is a composition of perspectivities. Just as the Euclidean isometries did, the projectivities form a group. Several basic theorems about how these projectivities are constructed led to the Fundamental Theorem of Projective Geometry. The Fundamental Theorem states that knowing the correspondence between two sets of three points is enough information to completely determine how the projectivity functions. This led to a projective proof of Pappus' Theorem. In the Euclidean plane, the cases of Pappus' Theorem involving parallel lines would each require special treatment. The projective approach covers all the cases in one proof that is both more general and more powerful.

Desargues' Theorem   In the real projective plane, if two triangles are perspective from a point, then they are perspective from a line.

The Dual (and Converse) of Desargues' Theorem   In the real projective plane, if two triangles are perspective from a line, then they are perspective from a point.

Pascal's Theorem for Circles   If a hexagon is inscribed in a circle, the three points of intersection from pairs of opposite sides will be collinear.

Brianchon's Theorem for Circles   If a hexagon is circumscribed around a circle, the three lines connecting pairs of opposite vertices are concurrent.

Fundamental Theorem of Projective Geometry   Given three distinct collinear points A_1, B_1, C_1 and three corresponding distinct collinear points A_2, B_2, C_2, there is exactly one projectivity for which

$$A_1 B_1 C_1 \ \overline{\wedge} \ A_2 B_2 C_2.$$

Pappus' Theorem   Suppose that A_1, B_1, C_1 are three distinct points on one line and A_2, B_2, C_2 are three distinct points on another line. Form the cross joins $X = \overleftrightarrow{A_1 B_2} \cap \overleftrightarrow{A_2 B_1}$, $Y = \overleftrightarrow{B_1 C_2} \cap \overleftrightarrow{B_2 A_1}$, and $Z = \overleftrightarrow{C_1 A_2} \cap \overleftrightarrow{C_2 A_1}$. Then the points X, Y, Z are collinear.

W e assume that you have studied trigonometry before. This appendix is not intended to be a thorough, detailed presentation of the subject. Rather, it will be another look at triangles and at the six trigonometric functions. We will provide different ways of developing some trigonometry facts, ways that emphasize their ties to geometry. (Many of the ideas in this appendix are based on the presentation in *Trigonometric Delights*, by Eli Maor, Princeton University Press, 1998.)

A.1 ACTIVITIES

Do the following activities, writing your explanations clearly in complete sentences. Include diagrams whenever appropriate. Save your work for each activity, as later work sometimes builds on earlier work. You will find it helpful to read ahead into this appendix as you work on these activities.

1. Figure A.1 shows a square and an equilateral triangle. Use these diagrams to calculate the exact values of $\sin(\frac{\pi}{6})$, $\cos(\frac{\pi}{6})$, $\tan(\frac{\pi}{6})$, $\sin(\frac{\pi}{4})$, $\cos(\frac{\pi}{4})$, $\tan(\frac{\pi}{4})$, $\sin(\frac{\pi}{3})$, $\cos(\frac{\pi}{3})$, and $\tan(\frac{\pi}{3})$.

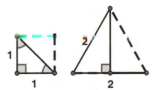

FIGURE A.1
Two Standard Triangles

2. Figure A.2 shows a triangle $\triangle ABC$ and its three altitudes. We can see that $\frac{AE}{AB} = \cos(\angle A)$, which makes $AE = AB \cdot \cos(\angle A)$. Write similar expressions for AF, FB, BD, DC, and CE, using only the sides and angles of $\triangle ABC$ in your answers.

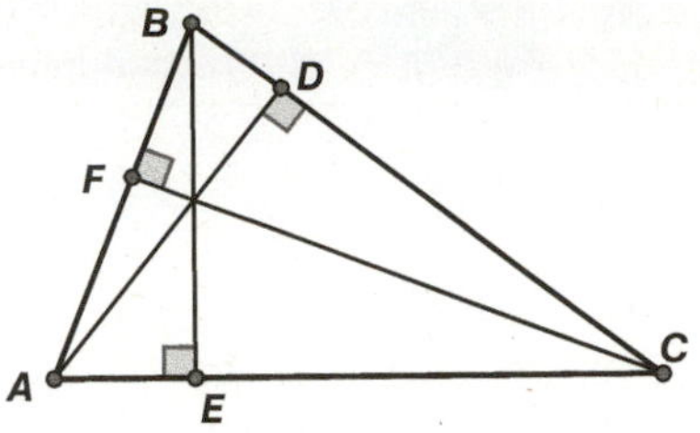

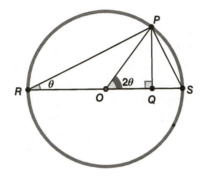

FIGURE A.2
Looking for Cosines

3. Figure A.3 shows a unit circle centered at point O. $\angle PRQ$ has measure θ, and $\angle POQ$ has measure 2θ. (Recall that a unit circle has a radius of 1.)

FIGURE A.3
Double-Angle Formulas

    a. In $\triangle RPQ$, find expressions for $\sin(\theta)$ and $\cos(\theta)$.
    b. In $\triangle OPQ$, find expressions for $\sin(2\theta)$ and $\cos(2\theta)$.
    c. In $\triangle RPS$, find an expression for $\cos(\theta)$.
    d. Use the results from parts a, b, and c to prove the double-angle formulas:

$$\sin(2\theta) = 2\sin(\theta)\cos(\theta)$$

$$\cos(2\theta) = 2\cos^2(\theta) - 1$$

4. In Figure A.4, a unit circle is drawn on a coordinate system with the origin at A. The lines through C and E are tangents to the circle and parallel to the y- and x-axes, respectively. D is a point on the circle, and $\angle CAD = \theta$. Line $\overleftrightarrow{AD}$ intersects the line $y = 1$ at F, and the line $x = 1$ at H.
    a. With D in the first quadrant (as shown in Figure A.4), find segments equal to $\sin(\theta)$, $\cos(\theta)$, $\tan(\theta)$, $\sec(\theta)$, $\csc(\theta)$, and $\cot(\theta)$.
    b. Repeat part a for the situation when D has been moved to the second quadrant.

5. In Figure A.4, the three triangles $\triangle ADB$, $\triangle AHC$, and $\triangle FAE$ are similar to each other.
    a. Draw each triangle separately and label the sides of each with the appropriate trigonometric function of θ.
    b. Use the similarity among these triangles to write $\tan(\theta)$ in terms of $\sin(\theta)$ and $\cos(\theta)$.
    c. Repeat part b for $\sec(\theta)$, $\csc(\theta)$, and $\cot(\theta)$.

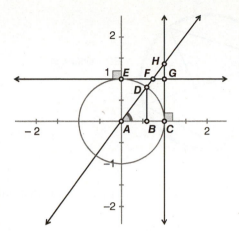

FIGURE A.4
Finding Trigonometric
Functions

6. Each of the following equations has several solutions in the interval $0 \le t < 2\pi$. Find these solutions for each equation.

$$\sin(t)\tan(t) = \sin(t)$$

$$4\sin(t)\cos(t) + 2\sin(t) - 2\cos(t) = 1$$

7. Figure A.5 shows an angle α inscribed in a circle, its corresponding central angle and its corresponding chord a, and a segment perpendicular to that chord. Find the value of $\frac{\sin(\alpha)}{a}$.

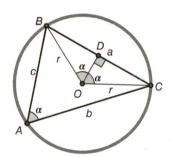

FIGURE A.5
Ratio of Sine to Side

Draw similar diagrams and find the values of $\frac{\sin(\beta)}{b}$ and $\frac{\sin(\gamma)}{c}$, where $\beta = \angle ABC$ and $\gamma = \angle BCA$. What do you observe?

8. Draw a circle and use it to construct a cyclic quadrilateral $ABCD$. Construct the diagonals AC and BD of this quadrilateral. Measure the lengths of these six segments and calculate the products

$$AB \cdot CD, \quad BC \cdot DA, \quad \text{and} \quad AC \cdot BD.$$

What relationship do you observe among these three products? Make a conjecture.

9. Figure A.6 shows a cyclic quadrilateral for which the diagonal AC is a diameter of the circle. Suppose that the length of this diameter is 1.

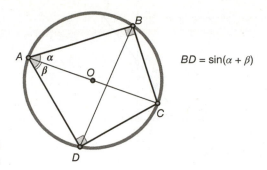

$$BD = \sin(\alpha + \beta)$$

FIGURE A.6
Angle Sum

a. Use the result of Activity 7 to show that the segment BD has length $\sin(\alpha + \beta)$.
b. Label the four sides of the quadrilateral as $\sin(\alpha)$, $\cos(\alpha)$, $\sin(\beta)$, or $\cos(\beta)$.
c. Now use your observation from Activity 8 to write a formula for $\sin(\alpha + \beta)$.

A.2 DISCUSSION

You might be used to thinking about angles as measured in degrees. But this unit of measure is arbitrary. Euclid avoided measuring angles in degrees. In the early part of *The Elements*, he spoke of straight angles and right angles, obtuse angles and acute angles without measuring them. In this appendix, we focus our discussion on the use of radians rather than degrees to measure angles. One radian is the size of an angle whose arc is equal to its radius. Thus, the measure of an angle in radians is the length of the circular arc divided by the length of the radius. As a quantity that is given as a length divided by a length, a radian is considered a "unitless" measure. A measure of the arc of a complete circle would be $\frac{2\pi r}{r} = 2\pi$ radians, so 2π corresponds to $360°$; π corresponds to $180°$, that is, a half circle or "straight angle." Thus, you can easily convert from degrees to radians by multiplying by $\frac{\pi}{180°}$, and from radians to degrees by multiplying by $\frac{180°}{\pi}$; either way, you are simply multiplying by one.

RIGHT TRIANGLE TRIGONOMETRY

From the three sides of a right triangle, there are six possible ways to form a ratio. The values of these ratios are affected by the size of the other angles in this triangle; change any one of the angles and you change the six ratios. These ratios are the six trigonometric functions:

$$\sin(\theta) = \frac{\text{opposite side}}{\text{hypotenuse}} \qquad \tan(\theta) = \frac{\text{opposite side}}{\text{adjacent side}} \qquad \sec(\theta) = \frac{\text{hypotenuse}}{\text{adjacent side}}$$

$$\cos(\theta) = \frac{\text{adjacent side}}{\text{hypotenuse}} \qquad \cot(\theta) = \frac{\text{adjacent side}}{\text{opposite side}} \qquad \csc(\theta) = \frac{\text{hypotenuse}}{\text{opposite side}}$$

$$(A.1)$$

For example, consider the $\frac{\pi}{3}$-angle of the $\frac{\pi}{6}$-$\frac{\pi}{3}$-$\frac{\pi}{2}$ triangle shown in Figure A.1. This shows a triangle with a hypotenuse of 2 and a side of 1 adjacent to the $\frac{\pi}{3}$-angle. By the Pythagorean Theorem, the side opposite the $\frac{\pi}{3}$-angle is $\sqrt{3}$. With these three numbers, all six functions can be computed. For example, $\sin(\frac{\pi}{3}) = \frac{\sqrt{3}}{2}$.

How do we know that these functions are well defined? That is, will a different right triangle with the same angles produce the same ratios? Consider a $\frac{\pi}{6}$-$\frac{\pi}{3}$-$\frac{\pi}{2}$ triangle with a hypotenuse of 10. Because the angles are the same, this larger triangle is similar to our example triangle. Thus, the side adjacent to the $\frac{\pi}{3}$-angle has length 5, and the opposite side is $5\sqrt{3}$. In this larger triangle, $\sin(\frac{\pi}{3}) = \frac{5\sqrt{3}}{10}$, which reduces to $\frac{\sqrt{3}}{2}$. For similar triangles, ratios between corresponding sides will always be equal.

Activity 2 presents a triangle with its three altitudes. Each altitude creates two new triangles. In the triangle $\triangle ABE$, AE is the side adjacent to $\angle A$ and AB is the hypotenuse. Thus $\cos(\angle A) = \frac{AE}{AB}$ and $AE = AB \cdot \cos(\angle A)$. In the triangle $\triangle CBE$, CE is adjacent to $\angle C$ and BC is the hypotenuse. Thus $CE = BC \cdot \cos(\angle C)$. Each of the six segments listed in this activity can be expressed as one of the sides of $\triangle ABC$ times the cosine of one of its angles.

Suppose we wanted to calculate the area of the $\triangle ABC$ from Activity 2. The usual formula for the area of a triangle is

$$Area = \frac{1}{2} \cdot base \cdot altitude.$$

This could be calculated using $\frac{1}{2} \cdot AC \cdot BE$. Notice, however, that BE is the side opposite $\angle A$ in the triangle $\triangle ABE$. Thus $BE = AB \cdot \sin(\angle A)$, so that the area of this triangle can also be calculated using

$$Area\ of\ \triangle ABC = \frac{1}{2} \cdot AC \cdot AB \cdot \sin(\angle A).$$

In the six definitions of the trigonometric functions, only three lengths were used. Consequently, there are many interconnections between these six functions. For instance, $\sec(\theta) = \frac{1}{\cos(\theta)}$. (There are two other reciprocal pairs; do you see them?) Another useful fact is

$$\tan(\theta) = \frac{opposite}{adjacent} = \frac{\left(\frac{opposite}{hypotenuse}\right)}{\left(\frac{adjacent}{hypotenuse}\right)} = \frac{\sin(\theta)}{\cos(\theta)}.$$

UNIT CIRCLE TRIGONOMETRY

The definitions given earlier for the various trigonometric functions work well for acute angles. But what about right angles or obtuse angles? These do not fit into a right triangle, so these definitions cannot apply. It gets even worse: We can measure angles greater than π or less than 0; how do we compute trigonometric functions for these angles? We need stronger, more general definitions.

The solution to this difficulty is to think of the desired angle on a coordinate system. Put the vertex at the origin and measure counterclockwise from the positive x-axis. (Clockwise angles are considered negative.) This allows angles of any size to be drawn.

To define the trigonometric functions, imagine a circle of radius 1 centered at the origin. This is the *standard unit circle*. The terminal side of an angle is a ray that will intersect the circle at a point (x, y). The six functions are now defined as follows:

$$\sin(\theta) = \frac{y}{1} \quad \tan(\theta) = \frac{y}{x} \quad \sec(\theta) = \frac{1}{x}$$

$$\cos(\theta) = \frac{x}{1} \quad \cot(\theta) = \frac{x}{y} \quad \csc(\theta) = \frac{1}{y}$$

(A.2)

If the angle, θ, is acute, these definitions are equivalent to the definitions given in A-1, page A-4. Figure A.4 illustrates this. Point D gives the x and y values for the definitions. In $\triangle ADB$, the opposite side $DB = y$, the adjacent side $AB = x$, and the hypotenuse $AD = 1$. So the definitions agree.

When D moves into the second quadrant, angle θ is between $\frac{\pi}{2}$ and π. Then the *reference triangle* for θ, $\triangle ADB$, lies in the second quadrant, with the side AB along the negative x-axis. The x-coordinate of D is negative in this situation (the directed segment AB is going in the negative direction), while the y-coordinate is positive. Thus, the (x, y)-coordinates of D still provide the necessary values to compute the six trigonometric functions. The cosine, tangent, secant, and cotangent are negative for second-quadrant angles, while the sine and cosecant are positive.

Because $x^2 + y^2 = 1$ on the unit circle, whether x and y are positive, negative, or zero, we have one of the *Pythagorean identities*:

$$\sin^2(\theta) + \cos^2(\theta) = 1.$$

With a little algebra, it is easy to prove the other Pythagorean identities.

$$\tan^2(\theta) + 1 = \sec^2(\theta)$$

$$1 + \cot^2(\theta) = \csc^2(\theta)$$

In Activity 4 you should have seen that $\tan(\theta) = CH$. Triangle AHC is similar to $\triangle ADB$ and the side AC has length 1. In Activity 4b, the directed segment CH is going downward, in the negative direction. This gives another way to see that $\tan(\theta) < 0$ for this particular angle.

It is interesting to consider this segment CH as the angle θ changes. (Notice that CH is on a vertical line tangent to the unit circle. Might this be the source of the name "tangent"?) As θ approaches $(\frac{\pi}{2})$, point H becomes arbitrarily high on its vertical line. At $\frac{\pi}{2}$, the line AD is parallel to this vertical line, making $\tan(\frac{\pi}{2})$ undefined. Once θ turns into the second quadrant, $\tan(\theta)$ has negative values and approaches 0 as θ nears π. Turning into the third quadrant, the segment CH

is again positive and increasing. Then $\tan(\frac{3\pi}{2})$ is undefined for the same reason that $\tan(\frac{\pi}{2})$ is undefined. Fourth-quadrant angles have $\tan(\theta) < 0$. Think about the graph of the function $\tan(\theta)$ and how its behavior is demonstrated by the length of the segment *CH*.

SOLVING TRIGONOMETRIC EQUATIONS

When solving trigonometric equations, many of the steps are the same as when solving algebraic equations. For instance, the first step in solving the equation

$$4\sin(t)\cos(t) + 2\sin(t) - 2\cos(t) = 1$$

is to move all terms to one side, so as to have an expression equal to 0.

$$4\sin(t)\cos(t) + 2\sin(t) - 2\cos(t) - 1 = 0$$

Now break this into factors. You might find it helpful to use abbreviations; visually it may be easier to factor $4SC + 2S - 2C - 1 = 0$.

$$(2\sin(t) - 1)(2\cos(t) + 1) = 0$$

Just as in algebra, a product equals 0 only when one or more of its factors equals 0. Thus, we have two smaller equations to solve:

$$2\sin(t) - 1 = 0 \quad \text{and} \quad 2\cos(t) + 1 = 0$$

Let us consider these equations one at a time. $2\sin(t) - 1 = 0$ implies $\sin(t) = \frac{1}{2}$. Here is where trigonometry comes in. In Activity 1, you saw that $\frac{\pi}{6}$ satisfies this equation. But $\frac{\pi}{6}$ is not the only possibility. The sine function is positive in the second quadrant also, so there is a second-quadrant angle that works. On the unit circle, this angle also will have a y-coordinate of $\frac{1}{2}$. Using a reference triangle of $\frac{\pi}{6}$-$\frac{\pi}{3}$-$\frac{\pi}{2}$, we can see that $\frac{5\pi}{6}$ is another solution.

For $2\cos(t) + 1 = 0$ we simplify to $\cos(t) = \frac{-1}{2}$. The $\frac{1}{2}$ should look familiar, for it is the cosine of $\frac{\pi}{3}$. The challenge now is to place a reference triangle in the unit circle so as to produce a negative value for the cosine. The x-coordinate that represents the cosine is negative in the second and third quadrants, so that is where our reference triangle must go. Drawing the adjacent side along the horizontal axis and putting the hypotenuse at $\frac{\pi}{3}$ to the horizontal gives angles of $\frac{2\pi}{3}$ and $\frac{4\pi}{3}$.

DOUBLE-ANGLE FORMULAS

Activity 3 shows a unit circle (radius $= 1$) but without the coordinate system. The figure shows an inscribed angle and its corresponding central angle, which is twice its size. Since the segment *RS* is a diameter, $\angle RPS$ is a right angle. Thus we can say that $\cos(\theta) = \frac{RP}{RS} = \frac{RP}{2}$.

Other right triangles in this diagram lead to similar statements. By substituting, you should be able to prove the *double-angle formulas*:

$$\sin(2\theta) = 2\sin(\theta)\cos(\theta)$$

$$\cos(2\theta) = 2\cos^2(\theta) - 1$$

Using the Pythagorean identity, we can write two other forms of the double-angle formula for cosines:

$$\cos(2\theta) = \cos^2(\theta) - \sin^2(\theta) = 1 - 2\sin^2(\theta).$$

ANGLE SUM FORMULAS

Activity 8 introduces a theorem that is not well known but is surprisingly useful.

THEOREM A.1   **(Ptolemy's Theorem)**   In a cyclic quadrilateral, the product of the diagonals is equal to the sum of the products of the opposite sides.

In the notation of Activity 8, $AC \cdot BD = AB \cdot CD + BC \cdot DA$. The proof involves finding congruent angles and similar triangles. You will be asked to develop this proof in the exercises.

How can this theorem be useful? First of all, suppose the cyclic quadrilateral is a rectangle. Then every vertex is a right angle, $AB = CD$, $BC = DA$, and $AC = BD$. Ptolemy's Theorem gives us

$$(AC)^2 = (AB)^2 + (BC)^2,$$

which is the Pythagorean Theorem.

Now let $\angle BAC = \alpha$. Then $AB = AC \cdot \cos(\alpha)$ and $BC = AC \cdot \sin(\alpha)$. The Pythagorean Theorem then becomes

$$(AC)^2 = (AC \cdot \cos(\alpha))^2 + (AC \cdot \sin(\alpha))^2$$

which simplifies to a familiar identity:

$$1 = \cos^2(\alpha) + \sin^2(\alpha).$$

Figure A.7 shows a special case of Ptolemy's Theorem, in which the diagonal AC is a diameter of the circle. In this diagram, the radius of the circle is $\frac{1}{2}$. From the result of Activity 7 we can say that $BD = \sin(\alpha + \beta)$. The labels on the sides AB, BC, CD, and DA come from basic right triangle trigonometry. Now when we apply Ptolemy's Theorem we get

$$1 \cdot \sin(\alpha + \beta) = \sin(\alpha) \cdot \cos(\beta) + \sin(\beta) \cdot \cos(\alpha).$$

This is the *angle sum formula* for sine.

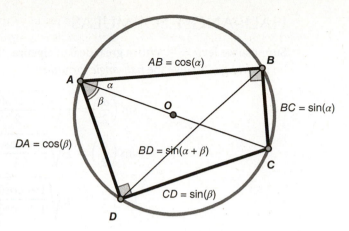

FIGURE A.7
A Special Case of
Ptolemy's Theorem

We will not derive the angle sum formulas for cosine and tangent, merely state them:

$$\cos(\alpha + \beta) = \cos(\alpha) \cdot \cos(\beta) - \sin(\alpha) \cdot \sin(\beta)$$

$$\tan(\alpha + \beta) = \frac{\tan(\alpha) + \tan(\beta)}{1 - \tan(\alpha) \cdot \tan(\beta)}$$

Notice that these formulas can be used for the difference of two angles, as long as we adjust for even versus odd functions:

$$\sin(\alpha - \beta) = \sin(\alpha + (-\beta))$$

$$= \sin(\alpha) \cdot \cos(-\beta) + \sin(-\beta) \cdot \cos(\alpha)$$

$$= \sin(\alpha) \cdot \cos(\beta) - \sin(\beta) \cdot \cos(\alpha).$$

Similarly,

$$\cos(\alpha - \beta) = \cos(\alpha) \cdot \cos(\beta) + \sin(\alpha) \cdot \sin(\beta),$$

and

$$\tan(\alpha - \beta) = \frac{\tan(\alpha) - \tan(\beta)}{1 + \tan(\alpha) \cdot \tan(\beta)}.$$

We can use the angle sum formulas to confirm the double-angle formulas given earlier:

$$\sin(2\theta) = \sin(\theta + \theta) = \sin(\theta) \cdot \cos(\theta) + \sin(\theta) \cdot \cos(\theta) = 2\sin(\theta)\cos(\theta)$$

$$\cos(2\theta) = \cos(\theta + \theta) = \cos(\theta) \cdot \cos(\theta) - \sin(\theta) \cdot \sin(\theta)$$

$$= \cos^2(\theta) - \sin^2(\theta)$$

From these, we can get one more double-angle formula:

$$\tan(2\theta) = \frac{\sin(2\theta)}{\cos(2\theta)} = \frac{2\tan(\theta)}{1 - \tan^2(\theta)}.$$

HALF-ANGLE FORMULAS

Suppose we let $\theta = \frac{\alpha}{2}$. With a great deal of algebra, the double-angle formulas can be rearranged to give the *half-angle formulas*:

$$\sin\left(\frac{\alpha}{2}\right) = \pm\sqrt{\frac{1 - \cos(\alpha)}{2}}$$

$$\cos\left(\frac{\alpha}{2}\right) = \pm\sqrt{\frac{1 + \cos(\alpha)}{2}}$$

$$\tan\left(\frac{\alpha}{2}\right) = \pm\sqrt{\frac{1 - \cos(\alpha)}{1 + \cos(\alpha)}}$$

A more useful form of the last formula is

$$\tan\left(\frac{\alpha}{2}\right) = \frac{1 - \cos(\alpha)}{\sin(\alpha)}.$$

THE LAW OF SINES AND THE LAW OF COSINES

In Activity 7, you are comparing the sine of an inscribed angle α to the chord it subtends (the chord joining the endpoints of the angle). You can do this indirectly by looking at the corresponding central angle. Since the central angle is twice the inscribed angle, this central angle is 2α. Because $\triangle OBC$ is isosceles, the perpendicular to the chord bisects the central angle. Thus, we can find $\sin(\alpha)$ by examining $\triangle OBD$.

The answer to the question of this activity is $\frac{\sin(\alpha)}{a} = \frac{1}{2r}$. The value of this ratio is determined solely by the radius of the circle. Furthermore, the diagram for $\beta = \angle ABC$ will show that $\frac{\sin(\beta)}{b}$ also equals $\frac{1}{2r}$. In fact,

$$\frac{\sin(\alpha)}{a} = \frac{\sin(\beta)}{b} = \frac{\sin(\gamma)}{c} = \frac{1}{2r}.$$

This is the *Law of Sines*.

The *Law of Cosines* is a generalization of the Pythagorean Theorem. It states that

$$c^2 = a^2 + b^2 - 2ab\cos(\gamma),$$

where γ is the angle between sides a and b. In a right triangle, $\gamma = \frac{\pi}{2}$ and the cosine term is 0, so that the Law of Cosines reduces to the Pythagorean Theorem.

The Law of Sines and the Law of Cosines are useful for solving triangles. This means that if you have enough information about sides and angles of a certain triangle, it is possible to calculate the other sides and angles using these formulas.

This appendix has been a very condensed presentation of trigonometry, and it is by no means complete. There are many more interesting, important facts and applications. Our intent is to refresh your memory and give you helpful tools for the study of geometry.

Give clear and complete answers to the following problems and questions. Write your explanations clearly using complete sentences. Include diagrams whenever appropriate.

1. We saw that the area of triangle $\triangle ABC$ can be calculated by $\frac{1}{2} \cdot AB \cdot AC \cdot \sin(\angle A)$. Write corresponding formulas for the area of $\triangle ABC$, which use $\angle B$ and $\angle C$.

2. Convert each of the following angle measures to radians.
   a. $15°$
   b. $75°$
   c. $150°$
   d. $210°$
   e. $415°$

3. Convert each of the following angle measures to degrees.
   a. $\frac{\pi}{6}$
   b. $\frac{2\pi}{3}$
   c. $\frac{3\pi}{4}$
   d. $\frac{4\pi}{5}$
   e. $\frac{5\pi}{6}$

4. Use the sum or difference formulas and facts about the two standard triangles to calculate the following.
   a. $\cos(15°)$ Do this two ways.
   b. $\sin(75°)$
   c. $\tan(105°)$
   d. $\cos(135°)$
   e. $\sin(150°)$ Do this two ways.
   f. $\cos(210°)$
   g. $\tan(225°)$

5. For which angles is $\sec(\theta) < 0$? Explain.

6. Use the standard unit circle to determine which of the trigonometric functions are negative for fourth-quadrant angles. Explain your reasoning.

7. Use the standard unit circle to determine the sign of each of the trigonometric functions for θ if
$$\frac{13\pi}{2} \le \theta \le 7\pi.$$
Explain your reasoning.

8. Use the angle sum formulas for sine and cosine to derive the angle sum formula for tangent.

9. Derive the Pythagorean identities:
   a. $\tan^2(x) + 1 = \sec^2(x)$
   b. $1 + \cot^2(x) = \csc^2(x)$

10. If $0 < \theta < \frac{\pi}{2}$ and $\tan(\theta) = \frac{4}{5}$, what is the value of $\cos(\theta)$?
    a. Use a trigonometric version of the Pythagorean Theorem to find a solution to this problem.
    b. Solve this problem again using a right triangle whose legs measure 4 units and 5 units, respectively.
    (This problem has been adapted from an example given on page 39 of the *Praxis Study Guide for the Mathematics Tests*, ETS, 2003.)

11. Suppose that $a = 5$, $b = 10$, and $\angle C = 135°$ in triangle $\triangle ABC$. Find the third side c.

12. a. The base of an isosceles triangle measures 4 inches, and the base angles are $52°$. Find the altitude of this triangle.
    b. The base of an isosceles triangle measures b units, and the base angles are θ. Find an expression for the altitude of this triangle.

13. a. Find the area of an equilateral triangle whose sides measure 5 cm.
    b. Find the area of an equilateral triangle whose sides measure a units.

14. Use the given information to find (if possible) the remaining sides and angles of $\triangle ABC$. If two solutions exist, find both. If no solution exists, explain how you know this.
    a. $A = \frac{\pi}{6}$, $B = \frac{\pi}{4}$, $a = 10$ units
    b. $A = \frac{\pi}{3}$, $B = \frac{\pi}{18}$, $b = 4.5$ cm

c. $A = \frac{5\pi}{6}, C = \frac{\pi}{9}, a = 200$ units

d. $A = 100°, a = 125$ cm, $b = 10$ cm

e. $C = \frac{2\pi}{3}, a = 4$ inches, $b = 6$ inches

f. $A = 58°, a = 4.5$ cm, $b = 12.8$ cm

g. $A = 58°, a = 4.5$ ft, $b = 5$ ft

h. $A = 110°, a = 125$ cm, $b = 200$ cm

15. Find the area of $\triangle ABC$ if $C = \frac{2\pi}{3}$, $a = 4$ inches, $b = 6$ inches.

16. Find the area of $\triangle ABC$ if $B = 130°$, $a = 62$ feet, $c = 20$ feet.

17. Suppose that the $\triangle ABC$ has $\angle A = \frac{\pi}{6}$ with the opposite side $a = 12$. Find the radius of the circumcircle of $\triangle ABC$.

18. Suppose that α, β, γ are the angles of a triangle. Prove that $\tan(\alpha) + \tan(\beta) + \tan(\gamma) = \tan(\alpha) \cdot \tan(\beta) \cdot \tan(\gamma)$.

19. Solve the following trigonometric equations. Give all solutions in the interval $0 \le x < 2\pi$.

a. $\sin(x) \cdot \tan(x) + 1 = \sin(x) + \tan(x)$

b. $2 \sin(x) = \sqrt{3} \tan(x)$

c. $\sin^2(x) + \frac{1}{2} \sin(x) = \frac{1}{2}$

d. $2 \cos^2(x) - 2\sqrt{2} \cos(x) + 1 = 0$

20. Explain why $\cos(\theta) = \sin(\frac{\pi}{2} - \theta)$.

21. Explain why $\sin(\theta) = \cos(90° - \theta)$.

22. Write out a careful detailed proof of the Law of Sines.

23. Prove the Law of Cosines.

24. Prove the double-angle formulas:

a. $\sin(2\theta) = 2 \sin(\theta)\cos(\theta)$

b. $\cos(2\theta) = 2 \cos^2(\theta) - 1$

c. $\cos(2\theta) = \cos^2(\theta) - \sin^2(\theta)$

d. $\cos(2\theta) = 1 - 2 \sin^2(\theta)$

25. Prove the angle sum formulas for cosine and tangent:

a. $\cos(\alpha + \beta) = \cos(\alpha) \cos(\beta) - \sin(\alpha) \sin(\beta)$

b. $\tan(\alpha + \beta) = \dfrac{\tan(\alpha) + \tan(\beta)}{1 - \tan(\alpha) \cdot \tan(\beta)}$

26. Prove the half-angle formulas:

a. $\sin\left(\dfrac{\alpha}{2}\right) = \pm \sqrt{\dfrac{1 - \cos(\alpha)}{2}}$

b. $\cos\left(\dfrac{\alpha}{2}\right) = \pm \sqrt{\dfrac{1 + \cos(\alpha)}{2}}$

c. $\tan\left(\dfrac{\alpha}{2}\right) = \dfrac{1 - \cos(\alpha)}{\sin(\alpha)}$

27. Prove that $\tan(2\theta) = \dfrac{2 \tan(\theta)}{1 - \tan^2(\theta)}$.

28. Prove Ptolemy's Theorem. (*Hint*: Construct a point E on the diagonal AC so that $\angle ABE$ is congruent to $\angle DBC$. Then look for pairs of similar triangles. Remember that $AC = AE + EC$.)

29. Use Ptolemy's Theorem to derive an angle sum formula for the cosine.

V ectors and matrices are the fundamental objects of a course in linear algebra. There are many important and interesting facts about matrices, and many important applications as well. For the purposes of this book, however, we need only a few basic ideas: how to calculate linear combinations of vectors, how to calculate the dot product of two vectors, how to multiply matrices, what the inverse of a matrix means, and some facts about the determinant.

The activities of this appendix do not require GeoGebra. The emphasis here is strictly on computation, so that you have the tools needed for Chapters 9 and 12.

B.1 ACTIVITIES

Give clear and complete answers to the following problems and questions. Write your explanations clearly, using complete sentences. Include diagrams whenever appropriate.

1. Fill in the missing values in the following statements.

   a. $\begin{bmatrix} ? \\ 2 \end{bmatrix} + 4 \begin{bmatrix} 4 \\ ? \end{bmatrix} = \begin{bmatrix} 21 \\ 26 \end{bmatrix}$

   b. $? \begin{bmatrix} 1 \\ -2 \end{bmatrix} + 5 \begin{bmatrix} -4 \\ 1 \end{bmatrix} = \begin{bmatrix} -16 \\ ? \end{bmatrix}$

   c. $10 \begin{bmatrix} 8 \\ 2 \end{bmatrix} + 3 \begin{bmatrix} ? \\ ? \end{bmatrix} = \begin{bmatrix} 50 \\ 50 \end{bmatrix}$

   d. $? \begin{bmatrix} 3 \\ 2 \end{bmatrix} + ? \begin{bmatrix} 5 \\ 6 \end{bmatrix} = \begin{bmatrix} 1 \\ ? \end{bmatrix}$

2. Fill in the missing values in the following statements.

   a. $(5, 6) \cdot (x, ?) = 5x + 6y$

   b. $(?, ?) \cdot (a, b) = 12a - 2b$

   c. $(1, 2, 4) \cdot (x, y, x) = ?$

   d. $(-2, 3) \cdot (6, 4) = ?$

   e. $(2x, -1, x) \cdot (x, x, 3) = ?$

3. Fill in the missing values in the following statements.

a. $\begin{bmatrix} 3 & 1 \\ ? & ? \end{bmatrix} \begin{bmatrix} x \\ 2 \end{bmatrix} = \begin{bmatrix} 3x+2 \\ 5x-4 \end{bmatrix}$

b. $\begin{bmatrix} 6 & 0 \\ -2 & 1 \end{bmatrix} \begin{bmatrix} ? \\ 2 \end{bmatrix} = \begin{bmatrix} ? \\ 0 \end{bmatrix}$

c. $\begin{bmatrix} 0 & 7 \\ 1 & -2 \end{bmatrix} \begin{bmatrix} x \\ y \end{bmatrix} = \begin{bmatrix} ? \\ ? \end{bmatrix}$

4. Multiplying matrices is similar to what you did in Activity 3. For example,

$$\begin{bmatrix} 1 & 2 \\ 3 & 4 \end{bmatrix} \begin{bmatrix} \cos(\theta) & -\sin(\theta) \\ \sin(\theta) & \cos(\theta) \end{bmatrix} = \begin{bmatrix} \cos(\theta) + 2\sin(\theta) & -\sin(\theta) + 2\cos(\theta) \\ 3\cos(\theta) + 4\sin(\theta) & -3\sin(\theta) + 4\cos(\theta) \end{bmatrix}$$

Calculate the following products. Simplify your answers.

a. $\begin{bmatrix} \cos(\theta) & -\sin(\theta) \\ \sin(\theta) & \cos(\theta) \end{bmatrix} \begin{bmatrix} 1 & 2 \\ 3 & 4 \end{bmatrix}$

b. $\begin{bmatrix} 1 & 0 \\ 0 & 1 \end{bmatrix} \begin{bmatrix} x & 4 \\ -1 & y \end{bmatrix}$

c. $\begin{bmatrix} 1 & 2 \\ 3 & 4 \end{bmatrix} \begin{bmatrix} -1 & 2 \\ 3 & -4 \end{bmatrix}$

d. $\begin{bmatrix} \cos(\theta) & -\sin(\theta) \\ \sin(\theta) & \cos(\theta) \end{bmatrix} \begin{bmatrix} \cos(\theta) & -\sin(\theta) \\ \sin(\theta) & \cos(\theta) \end{bmatrix}$

(After you study rotations in Chapter 9, the last of these products will have a special meaning.)

5. Fill in the missing values in the following statement.

$$\begin{bmatrix} -\dfrac{1}{2} & \dfrac{3}{2} \\ 1 & -2 \end{bmatrix} \begin{bmatrix} 4 & ? \\ ? & ? \end{bmatrix} = \begin{bmatrix} 1 & 0 \\ 0 & 1 \end{bmatrix}$$

6. Any square matrix has a value called its *determinant*. Here are two examples of determinants for 2×2 matrices.

$$det \begin{bmatrix} x & 1 \\ y & 2 \end{bmatrix} = 2x - y$$

$$det \begin{bmatrix} 7 & z \\ -4 & 3 \end{bmatrix} = 21 + 4z$$

Explain how these determinants were computed. Then find the following determinants.

a. $det \begin{bmatrix} 1 & 3 \\ 2 & 6 \end{bmatrix}$

b. $det \begin{bmatrix} \dfrac{3}{5} & \dfrac{-4}{5} \\ \dfrac{4}{5} & \dfrac{3}{5} \end{bmatrix}$

7. a. Here are two matrices.

$$A = \begin{bmatrix} 4 & 3 \\ 5 & 4 \end{bmatrix} \qquad B = \begin{bmatrix} 8 & 6 \\ 10 & 8 \end{bmatrix}$$

How is B related to A? How is $det(B)$ related to $det(A)$?

b. Compare the following matrices to A. Then predict $det(C)$ and $det(D)$. Check your answers.

$$C = \begin{bmatrix} 1 & 0.75 \\ 1.25 & 1 \end{bmatrix} \qquad D = \begin{bmatrix} -20 & -15 \\ -25 & -20 \end{bmatrix}$$

B.2 DISCUSSION

LINEAR COMBINATIONS OF VECTORS

Conceptually, a vector is a joining of two ideas: direction and distance. This makes vectors a convenient method for describing motion. As you will see in Chapter 9, translations can be described very nicely in vector notation.

In Activity 1, we have written the vectors as columns, such as $\begin{bmatrix} 1 \\ -2 \end{bmatrix}$. It is also possible to write vectors as rows, such as $(1, -2)$. Row vectors are more convenient for typing, but we will see that the difference can be important. This particular vector says to move 1 unit to the right and 2 units down. The starting point for the vector can be anywhere, as long as the ending point is 1 unit to the right and 2 units down from it.

If we put a coefficient with this vector, such as $4 \begin{bmatrix} 1 \\ -2 \end{bmatrix}$, each entry of the vector will be multiplied by 4 to give $\begin{bmatrix} 4 \\ -8 \end{bmatrix}$. The coefficient 4 is called a *scalar* and this process is called *scalar multiplication*.

Multiplying a vector by 4 means what you probably expect that it means, namely, the vector is added to itself four times. Is it clear how to add vectors? The entries correspond in the natural way, and that is how we add; corresponding entries are added together. For instance, the first sum in Activity 1 can be separated into two computations:

$$? + 4 \cdot 4 = 21$$
$$2 + 4 \cdot ? = 26$$

These computations include both addition and scalar multiplication of vectors, as do the other sums in Activity 1. Such sums are called *linear combinations* of the vectors. Notice that only two operations are used, addition and multiplication by a constant, which are exactly the operations used to create linear equations.

DOT PRODUCT OF VECTORS

Activity 2 shows examples of the *dot product* of two vectors. To perform a dot product, each vector must have the same number of components. The corresponding components are multiplied together, then these values are added. So a dot product produces a single real number as its result.

We were somewhat casual about the notation in Activity 2. The correct representation of the first product is

$$(5, 6) \cdot \begin{bmatrix} x \\ ? \end{bmatrix} = 5x + 6y$$

so that we are multiplying a row vector times a column vector. However, it is often convenient to write the dot product with two row vectors, such as $(1, 2, 4) \cdot (x, y, x)$. Some authors use brackets instead of parentheses, such as [5, 6], and usually the different notation does not matter. However, in Chapter 12 the two notations will mean different things. Vectors with parentheses, such as (3, 2, 4), will represent points in a projective plane, while vectors with brackets, such as [2, −1, 1], will represent lines. In projective geometry, a point lies on a line if and only if the dot product of the two vectors equals zero.

MULTIPLYING A MATRIX TIMES A VECTOR

Activity 3 presents a different form of multiplication, a matrix times a column vector. For this multiplication to make sense, the sizes of the matrix and the vector must match properly. Consider the first product. The matrix is 2×2, meaning that it has two rows and two columns. The vector is 2×1, with two rows and only one column. So the product looks like $(2 \times 2) \cdot (2 \times 1)$. The innermost values match—both are 2—so the product can be done. The outermost values tell the size of the result, namely 2×1. In this problem, the sizes match properly and the product can be calculated. In the other calculations of Activity 3, the matrices and vectors are the same size as this. So these products make sense as well.

To do these products, it is best to work with one row of the matrix at a time. For instance, in the calculation:

$$\begin{bmatrix} 3 & 1 \\ ? & ? \end{bmatrix} \begin{bmatrix} x \\ 2 \end{bmatrix} = \begin{bmatrix} 3x + 2 \\ 5x - 4 \end{bmatrix}$$

we can begin with the first row times the column vector. Written as a separate problem, this looks like:

$$\begin{bmatrix} 3 & 1 \end{bmatrix} \begin{bmatrix} x \\ 2 \end{bmatrix}$$

Notice that this is a dot product! The answer is $3x + 2$, which is $3 \cdot x + 1 \cdot 2$.

The second entry in this product is another dot product.

$$\begin{bmatrix} ? & ? \end{bmatrix} \begin{bmatrix} x \\ 2 \end{bmatrix} = [5x - 4]$$

Do you see what values belong in the second row of the matrix? The multiplication follows the same pattern as before.

MULTIPLYING TWO MATRICES

Activity 4 presents several problems involving the product of two matrices. The example in this activity is

$$\begin{bmatrix} 1 & 2 \\ 3 & 4 \end{bmatrix} \begin{bmatrix} \cos(\theta) & -\sin(\theta) \\ \sin(\theta) & \cos(\theta) \end{bmatrix} = \begin{bmatrix} \cos(\theta) + 2\sin(\theta) & -\sin(\theta) + 2\cos(\theta) \\ 3\cos(\theta) + 4\sin(\theta) & -3\sin(\theta) + 4\cos(\theta) \end{bmatrix}$$

One way to think of this multiplication is as the left matrix times the first column of the second matrix, together with the left matrix times the second column. So we have the following two products:

$$\begin{bmatrix} 1 & 2 \\ 3 & 4 \end{bmatrix} \begin{bmatrix} \cos(\theta) \\ \sin(\theta) \end{bmatrix} = \begin{bmatrix} \cos(\theta) + 2\sin(\theta) \\ 3\cos(\theta) + 4\sin(\theta) \end{bmatrix}$$

$$\begin{bmatrix} 1 & 2 \\ 3 & 4 \end{bmatrix} \begin{bmatrix} -\sin(\theta) \\ \cos(\theta) \end{bmatrix} = \begin{bmatrix} -\sin(\theta) + 2\cos(\theta) \\ -3\sin(\theta) + 4\cos(\theta) \end{bmatrix}$$

(Notice that each of these calculations uses two dot products.) These two products are put together to make the 2×2 matrix that is the answer.

It is not necessary to take the matrices apart to do this multiplication. We can use the following general pattern:

$$AB = \begin{bmatrix} \text{first row of } A \text{ times} & \text{first row of } A \text{ times} \\ \text{first column of } B & \text{second column of } B \\ \text{second row of } A \text{ times} & \text{second row of } A \text{ times} \\ \text{first column of } B & \text{second column of } B \end{bmatrix}$$

As this shows, each entry of the matrix product is calculated by doing the product of a row and a column.

Multiplication of matrices is associative, as long as the sizes match correctly. (It is somewhat tedious to prove this, even in the 2×2 case.) However, multiplication of matrices is *not* commutative. You may have noticed this in Activity 4. The reverse of the example gave a very different product.

The matrix $I = \begin{bmatrix} 1 & 0 \\ 0 & 1 \end{bmatrix}$ is called the *identity matrix*. As you saw in Activity 4, $IX = X$ for any matrix X. This is also true in the reverse order; $XI = X$. Any matrix X does not change when multiplied by the identity I. (The multiplication must make sense, of course, meaning that the sizes of the matrices must match properly. We have shown you only the 2×2 identity matrix. However, there is an identity matrix for any square size.)

The identity serves the same role that the number 1 does in normal multiplication. Just as in normal multiplication, we have the question of inverses. A reminder: Two numbers x, y are *inverses* for multiplication if $xy = 1$ and $yx = 1$. In the same way, two matrices X, Y are *inverses* if $XY = I$ and $YX = I$.

In Activity 5 you are asked to complete the entries of the matrix that is the inverse

of $\begin{bmatrix} -\dfrac{1}{2} & \dfrac{3}{2} \\ 1 & -2 \end{bmatrix}$. You must find the values that make the matrix product equal the identity.

A warning: Not every matrix will have an inverse. This is one major difference between multiplying numbers and multiplying matrices. For instance, $\begin{bmatrix} 1 & 3 \\ 2 & 6 \end{bmatrix}$ does not have an inverse. In the next section, you will see a quick way to determine whether a particular matrix has an inverse.

THE DETERMINANT OF A MATRIX

A matrix has many numbers associated with it. This includes its entries, of course, but also various values that can be calculated from these entries. Many interesting theorems have been proven about these numerical descriptions of a matrix. One of the most useful is the *determinant*. This number combines all the entries of the matrix into a single value.

There are several ways to define the determinant, and there are also several ways to compute it. For the case of the small 2 × 2 matrices, the determinant is fairly simple.

$$det \begin{bmatrix} a & b \\ c & d \end{bmatrix} = ad - bc$$

Does this agree with what you did in Activity 6?

It occasionally will be necessary in Chapter 12 to calculate the determinant of a 3 × 3 matrix, a square matrix with nine entries. There are several ways to proceed; here is one fairly direct way.

$$det \begin{bmatrix} a_{11} & a_{12} & a_{13} \\ a_{21} & a_{22} & a_{23} \\ a_{31} & a_{32} & a_{33} \end{bmatrix} = a_{11} \cdot det \begin{bmatrix} a_{22} & a_{23} \\ a_{32} & a_{33} \end{bmatrix} - a_{12} \cdot det \begin{bmatrix} a_{21} & a_{23} \\ a_{31} & a_{33} \end{bmatrix}$$

$$+ a_{13} \cdot det \begin{bmatrix} a_{21} & a_{22} \\ a_{31} & a_{32} \end{bmatrix}$$

For example,

$$det \begin{bmatrix} 1 & 2 & 3 \\ 4 & 5 & 6 \\ 7 & 8 & 9 \end{bmatrix} = 1 \cdot det \begin{bmatrix} 5 & 6 \\ 8 & 9 \end{bmatrix} - 2 \cdot det \begin{bmatrix} 4 & 6 \\ 7 & 9 \end{bmatrix} + 3 \cdot det \begin{bmatrix} 4 & 5 \\ 7 & 8 \end{bmatrix}$$

$$= 1 \cdot (-3) - 2 \cdot (-6) + 3 \cdot (-3) = 0$$

This is only one of many ways to calculate a determinant for a 3 × 3 matrix. Larger matrices require more complicated methods, but we will not need those in this course.

Using this pattern, it is quick to calculate the determinants in Activity 6. Notice that the determinant of $\begin{bmatrix} 1 & 3 \\ 2 & 6 \end{bmatrix}$ equals 0, even though none of the entries is 0. This will prove to be important.

Here are some basic facts about determinants.

THEOREM B.1 $det(AB) = det(A) \cdot det(B)$.

For 2×2 matrices, straightforward algebra will verify this. For larger matrices, more advanced methods of proof are required. Consult any linear algebra text.

THEOREM B.2 The square matrix A has an inverse if and only if $det(A) \neq 0$.

Partial Proof Suppose B is the inverse of A. Then $AB = I$. Since $det(I) = 1$, this gives us $det(B) = \dfrac{1}{det(A)}$. Thus $det(A)$ cannot be 0.

THEOREM B.3 The inverse of the matrix $A = \begin{bmatrix} a & b \\ c & d \end{bmatrix}$ is the matrix $A^{-1} = \dfrac{1}{ad - bc}\begin{bmatrix} d & -b \\ -c & a \end{bmatrix}$, provided that this matrix exists.

THEOREM B.4 For a 2×2 matrix A and a scalar s, $det(sA) = s^2\, det(A)$.

This final theorem is the key to Activity 7. The matrices C and D are multiples of matrix A, and $det(A) = 1$. Once you decide what scalar is involved, it is an easy calculation to determine the determinants of C and D.

B.3 EXERCISES

Give clear and complete answers to the following problems and questions. Remember to write in correct English. Include diagrams whenever appropriate.

1. Let $(m \times n)$ denote a matrix of size m by n. Which matrix products are not defined? Explain why or why not for each situation.
   a. $(2 \times 2) \cdot (1 \times 2)$
   b. $(4 \times 2) \cdot (2 \times 1)$
   c. $(2 \times 3) \cdot (2 \times 1)$
   d. $(3 \times 2) \cdot (2 \times 2)$

2. For the vectors $\vec{a} = \begin{bmatrix} -3 \\ 1 \end{bmatrix}$ and $\vec{b} = \begin{bmatrix} 0 \\ 2 \end{bmatrix}$ compute the following:

   a. $-4\vec{a}$
   b. $2\vec{a} + \vec{b}$
   c. $5\vec{a} + 5\vec{b}$

3. a. Find scalars a, b so that

   $$a\begin{bmatrix} 2 \\ -5 \end{bmatrix} + b\begin{bmatrix} -6 \\ 15 \end{bmatrix} = \begin{bmatrix} 0 \\ 0 \end{bmatrix}.$$

   b. Find scalars c, d so that

   $$c\begin{bmatrix} 4 \\ 7 \end{bmatrix} + d\begin{bmatrix} 2 \\ -3 \end{bmatrix} = \begin{bmatrix} 0 \\ 0 \end{bmatrix}.$$

   c. How are these problems different? Explain the difference.

4. Calculate the following dot products.
   a. $[8, 3] \cdot [2, 5]$

   b. $(7, -1, 4) \cdot (0, 4, 2)$

   c. $(-1, 0, 1) \cdot \begin{bmatrix} 2 \\ 1 \\ 2 \end{bmatrix}$

   d. $[1, -2, 3, 4, 5] \cdot [10, 9, 8, -7, 6]$

5. Find at least three vectors (a, b, c) so that

$$(4, -1, -4) \cdot (a, b, c) = 0.$$

6. Compute the following products.

   a. $\begin{bmatrix} 7 & \frac{1}{2} \\ 4 & 2 \end{bmatrix} \begin{bmatrix} 1 & -1 \\ -1 & 4 \end{bmatrix}$

   b. $\begin{bmatrix} 6 & 2 \\ 3 & -3 \end{bmatrix} \begin{bmatrix} 1 & 0 \\ 0 & 1 \end{bmatrix}$

   c. $\begin{bmatrix} 1 & -1 \\ -1 & 4 \end{bmatrix} \begin{bmatrix} 7 & \frac{1}{2} \\ 4 & 2 \end{bmatrix}$

   d. $\begin{bmatrix} 4 & 2 \\ -1 & \frac{-1}{2} \end{bmatrix} \begin{bmatrix} 1 & \frac{1}{2} \\ -2 & -1 \end{bmatrix}$

7. For the products in Exercise 6, calculate the determinant of each factor and the determinant of the product. Compare your answers to the theorem $det(AB) = det(A) \cdot det(B)$.

8. Which of the following matrices has an inverse? For each invertible matrix, find its inverse.

   a. $\begin{bmatrix} 2 & 3 \\ 3 & 4 \end{bmatrix}$

   b. $\begin{bmatrix} 7 & -6 \\ 3 & -3 \end{bmatrix}$

   c. $\begin{bmatrix} 2 & -3 \\ -8 & 12 \end{bmatrix}$

9. Calculate the determinant of $\begin{bmatrix} 1 & -1 & 4 \\ 3 & 2 & -2 \\ 4 & 0 & 2 \end{bmatrix}$.

10. A square matrix is called *unimodular* if its determinant is 1 or −1. The matrix is *totally unimodular* if every square submatrix has a determinant equal to 1, 0, or −1. For a 3×3 matrix M, this means that the determinant of M is 1 or −1; that the determinant of every 2×2 submatrix is 1, 0, or −1; and that the determinant of every 1×1 submatrix is 1, 0, or −1. Therefore every entry must be 1, 0, or −1. Find at least four examples of a totally unimodular 3×3 matrix.

Baragar, Arthur. *A Survey of Classical and Modern Geometries*. Prentice Hall, Upper Saddle River, NJ. 2001.

Batten, Lynn Margaret. *Combinatorics of Finite Geometries*. Cambridge University Press, Cambridge, Great Britain. 1986.

Bix, Robert. *Topics in Geometry*. Academic Press, Inc., San Diego, CA. 1994.

Common Core State Standards Initiative. *Common Core State Standards for Mathematics*. http://www.corestandards.org (accessed November 22, 2020).

"Court aids Bambi Bar bid for liquor permit," *The Courier-Journal*, Louisville, KY. 12 December 2006.

Court, Nathan. *College Geometry, 2nd edition*. Barnes & Noble, Inc., New York, NY. 1952.

Coxeter, H. S. M. *The Real Projective Plane*. McGraw-Hill, New York, NY. 1949.

Coxeter, H. S. M. *Introduction to Geometry*. John Wiley & Sons, Inc., New York, NY. 1961.

Coxeter, H. S. M. *Introduction to Geometry*, 2nd ed. John Wiley & Sons, Inc., New York, NY. 1969.

Coxeter, H. S. M. and S. L. Greitzer. *Geometry Revisited*. The Mathematical Association of America, New Mathematical Library, Washington, D.C. 1967.

de Villiers, Michael D. *Rethinking Proof with The Geometer's Sketchpad*. Key Curriculum Press, Emeryville, CA. 2003.

Educational Testing Service (ETS). *Praxis Study Guide for the Mathematics Tests*. Princeton, NJ. 2003.

Eves, Howard. *An Introduction to the History of Mathematics, 4th edition*. Holt, Rinehardt and Winston, New York, NY. 1976.

Fenton, William E. and Ed Dubinsky. *Introduction to Discrete Mathematics with ISETL*. Springer, New York. 1996.

Graustein, William C. *Introduction to Higher Geometry*. The Macmillan Company, New York, NY. 1930.

Greenberg, Marvin Jay. *Euclidean and Non-Euclidean Geometries*. W. H. Freeman and Company, New York, NY. 1980.

Hartshorne, Robin C. *Geometry: Euclid and Beyond*. Springer-Verlag, New York. 2000.

Heath, Sir Thomas (translator). *The Thirteen Books of Euclid's Elements*. Dover Publications, New York, NY. 1956.

Jacobson, Nathan. *Basic Algebra I*. W. H. Freeman and Company, San Francisco, CA. 1974.

Joyce, D. E. *Euclid's Elements*. https://mathcs.clarku.edu/~djoyce/java/elements/elements.html (accessed September 26, 2020).

Kay, David C. *College Geometry: A Discovery Approach*. Harper Collins College Publishers, New York, NY. 1994.

Kimberling, Clark. *Geometry in Action*. Key College Publishing, Emeryville, CA. 2003.

Knight, Robert. *Using Laguerre Geometry to Discover Euclidean Theorems*. Unpublished dissertation, University of California–San Diego, 2000.

Krause, Eugene F. *Taxicab Geometry*. Addison Wesley Publishing Co., Menlo Park, CA. 1975.

Lam, C. W. H. "The Search for a Finite Projective Plane of Order 10." *The American Mathematical Monthly 98*, no. 4 (April 1991): 305–318.

Lay, David C. *Linear Algebra and Its Applications, 2nd edition*. Addison-Wesley Longman, Reading, MA. 1997.

Maher, Richard J. "Step by Step Proofs and Small Group Work in Courses in Algebra and Analysis." *PRIMUS 4*, no. 3 (September 1994).

Maor, Eli. *Trigonometric Delights*. Princeton University Press, Princeton, NJ. 1998.

National Council of Teachers of Mathematics (NCTM). *Principles and Standards for School Mathematics*. Reston, VA: The National Council of Teachers of Mathematics, 2000.

Nelsen, Roger. "Proofs Without Words," *Mathematics Magazine*, April 2002.

Ogilvy, C. Stanley. *Excursions in Geometry*. Dover Publications, Inc., New York, NY. 1990.

Reynolds, Barbara E. *Taxicab Geometry: An Example of Minkowski Space*. Unpublished dissertation, Saint Louis University, St. Louis, MO. 1979.

Reynolds, Barbara E. "Taxicab Geometry," *Pi Mu Epsilon Journal*, Spring 1980.

Robinson, Gilbert de B. *The Foundations of Geometry*. The University of Toronto Press, Toronto, Canada. 1946.

Rogers, Elizabeth C., Barbara E. Reynolds, Neil A. Davidson, and Anthony D. Thomas (Editors), *Cooperative Learning in Undergraduate Mathematics: Issues That Matter & Strategies That Work*. MAA Notes Series #55, The Mathematical Association of America, Washington, D.C. 2001.

Shorlin, Kelly A., John R. de Bruyn, Malcolm Graham, and Stephen W. Morris. "Development and Geometry of Isotropic and Directional Shrinkage Patterns," *Physical Review E 61*, no. 6 (June 2000): 6950–6957, http://arxiv.org/pdf/patt-sol/9911003 (accessed September 26, 2020).

Sibley, Thomas Q. *The Geometric Viewpoint: A Survey of Geometries*. Addison-Wesley Longman, Inc., Reading, MA. 1998.

Smart, James R. *Modern Geometries, 3rd edition*. Brooks/Cole Publishing Company, Pacific Grove, CA. 1988.

Smith, Douglas, Maurice Eggen, and Richard St. Andre. *A Transition to Advanced Mathematics*. Brooks Cole, Pacific Grove, CA. 2001.

Sved, Marta. *Journey to Geometries*. Spectrum Series, The Mathematical Association of America, Washington, D.C. 1991.

Thomas, David. *Modern Geometry*. Brooks Cole, Pacific Grove, CA. 2002.

Wallace, Edward C. and Stephen F. West. *Roads to Geometry*. Prentice-Hall, Inc., Englewood Cliffs, NJ. 1992.

Wells, David. *The Penguin Dictionary of Curious and Interesting Geometry*. Penguin Books, London. 1991.

Yaglom, I. M. *Geometric Transformations*. The New Mathematical Library. The L. W. Singer Company (Random House), New York, NY. 1962.

Note: GeoGebra commands are shown in **boldface** in this index.

Polygon, 4–5
  Regular Polygon, 8
  Rigid Polygon, 8
Polygons, 10–11
  tiling with, 239–244
Power of a point, 99–100
Predicate, 57, 58
Print Preview, 8
Projection, 192
Projective geometry, 282–311
  axiom system, 285–286
  Brianchon's Theorem, 296
  central projection, 290–291
  coordinates for, 296–302
    Fano plane, 300–302
    homogeneous coordinates, 297
    projective line, 296–297
    for real projective plane, 297–300
  Desargues' Theorem, 294–296
  duality, 291–296
  Fano plane, 168, 170, 177, 179–180, 289, 300–302
  Fundamental Theorem of Projective Geometry, 305–306
  ideal line and ideal points, 174, 175, 287
  model on the sphere, 290–291
  models for projective plane, 286–291
    real projective plane, 286–289
  order, 169
  Pascal's Theorem, 296
  perspectivity, 286
Projective transformations, 302–307
Projectivity, 304
  axis of projectivity, 305
  defined, 304
  as a group, 304
Proofs, 35–36. *See also* Step-by-step proofs
  constructing a proof by contradiction, 92
  coordinates use in, 125–127
    concurrence of altitudes, proving, 126–127
  counterexamples as disproof, 62
  direct proof, 60–62
  indirect proof, constructing, 91–92
  isometries in, 198–199
  mathematical arguments, 90–91
  matrices, use in, 217–219
  statement of form P ↔ Q, proving, 92–93
  using robust constructions in, 35–36
Proposition, 57
Ptolemy's Theorem, 104, A-8–A-9
Pythagorean identities, A-6
Pythagorean Theorem, 29–30, 61–62
  Converse of Pythagorean Theorem, 30

Quadrangle, 173, 293
Quadrilaterals, 11–15, 93–95, 173, 293
  complete quadrilateral, 173, 293
  convex, 12
  cyclic quadrilateral, 8, 38, 93–95
  defined, 11
  dual to quadrangle, 173, 293
  in hyperbolic plane, 271–273
    base angles, 271
    base of Saccheri quadrilateral, 271
    Lambert quadrilateral, 273
    rectangles don't exist, 274
    Saccheri quadrilateral, 271, 273
    summit angles, 271
    summit of Saccheri quadrilateral, 271
  midpoint quadrilateral, 4, 11
  square, 13
  tiling with, 241–242
  types of quadrilaterals, 13–15
Quantified statements
  negating a, 59–60

Radian, 36
Radical axis, 100–102, 127
Radius, 15, 89
Ray, 32
Real projective plane, 176, 286–289
  coordinates for, 297–300
  duality, 291–296
  equivalence classes, 287
  ideal line, 287
  ideal point, 287
  Pappus' Theorem, 287–289
  points at infinity, 287
Rectangle, 7, 58
Reference triangle, A-6
Reflect about Line, 185, 225
Reflections, 185, 188, 199, 203
  fixed points and, 189
  frieze patterns and, 236–238
  inverse, 197
  matrices to represent, 211–213
  in a point, 200
Reflexive property, 175
Regular polygon, 11
Regular Polygon, 8
Regular tiling, 242
Remote interior angles, 25
Rhombus, 17
Right Angle-Hypotenuse-Leg (RHL)
    criterion for triangle congruence, 77, 262
Right angles, 36
Right triangle, 38
Right triangle trigonometry, A-4–A-5